DEVELOPMENTAL
THERAPY

DEVELOPMENTAL THERAPY

A Textbook
for Teachers as Therapists
for Emotionally Disturbed
Young Children

Edited by

Mary M. Wood

Associate Professor of Special Education
University of Georgia;

Director, Rutland Center Early
Childhood Project

University Park Press

Baltimore ● London ● Tokyo

UNIVERSITY PARK PRESS
International Publishers in Science and Medicine
Chamber of Commerce Building
Baltimore, Maryland 21202

Typeset by The Composing Room of Michigan, Inc.
Printed in the United States of America by Bay Printing, Inc.
Second printing, November 1976

Library of Congress Cataloging in Publication Data
Main entry under title:

Developmental therapy.

Includes index.
1. Child psychotherapy. 2. Mentally ill children—
Education. I. Wood, Mary M. [DNLM: 1. Child behavior
disorders—Therapy. WS350 D489]
RJ504.D46   371.9'4   75-9777
ISBN 0-8391-0761-7

Contents

Contributors

Anthony Beardsley, M.Ed. Coordinator of Training, The National Technical Assistance Office, 698 N. Pope Street, Athens, Georgia 30601

Livija R. Bolster, M.Ed. Educational Therapist, The Gateway School, West Paces Ferry Road, Atlanta, Georgia 30305

Carolyn Combs, M.Ed. Instructor in Special Education, University of Georgia, Athens, Georgia 30602

Cynthia Cook, M.S. Educational Therapist, Rutland Center, 698 N. Pope Street, Athens, Georgia 30601

Marylyn Galewski, M.S.W. Social Worker/Monitor; on leave from the Rutland Center, 698 N. Pope Street, Athens, Georgia 30601

Barbara Geter, M.S.W. Social Worker/Monitor, Rutland Center, 698 N. Pope Street Athens, Georgia 30601

Ola Jennings, M.S.W. Social Worker/Monitor, Rutland Center, 698 N. Pope Street, Athens, Georgia 30601

Andrea Lomax, M.Ed. Educational Therapist, Rutland Center, 698 N. Pope Street, Athens, Georgia 30601

Bonnie Lee Mailey, Ed.S. Director, Comprehensive Community Mental Health Program for Pre-School Emotionally Disturbed Children, Jesse Mae Jones Elementary School, Atlanta, Georgia

William W. Swan, Ed.D. Director, The National Technical Assistance Office, and Coordinator of Evaluation, Rutland Center, 698 N. Pope Street, Athens, Georgia 30601

Diane Weller, M.Ed. Coordinator of Psychoeducational Services, Rutland Center, 698 N. Pope Street, Athens, Georgia 30601

Ann Reed Williams, M.Ed. Educational Therapist, Rutland Center, 698 N. Pope Street, Athens, Georgia 30601

Mary Margaret Wood, Ed.D. Associate Professor of Special Education, University of Georgia, Athens, Georgia 30601; Director, Technical Assistance Office to the Georgia Psychoeducational Center Network, 698 N. Pope Street, Athens, Georgia 30601

Acknowledgments

The material for this text has evolved over a period of six years. During that time, many people have contributed to planning, implementing, evaluating, and modifying the various components of Developmental Therapy. To the families of these many individuals, the authors extend their deepest appreciation for providing a climate where each personal contribution had enthusiastic backing and understanding.

The project has had four consultants who have maintained long, loyal relationships to the effort: James Flanagan, M.D., in child psychiatry; Carl J. Huberty, Ph.D., in research design and evaluation; Arthur E. Alper, Ph.D., in clinical psychology; and David R. Levine, Ph.D., in social work. Their contributions have influenced every aspect of Developmental Therapy.

The advice, expertise, and assistance of a number of outside consultants have also influenced the philosophy and practices of Developmental Therapy as it emerged at the Rutland Center. The time and interest of these consultants is gratefully acknowledged: Norbert Enzer, M.D., and Sam Rubin, M.D., in psychiatry; William Frankenberg, M.D., and William Bonner, M.D., in pediatrics; Robert Lange, Ph.D., and Herbert Quay, Ph.D., in research design and evaluation; Frank Wilderson, Ph.D., Ida Wilderson, Ph.D., and Dorothy Campbell, Ph.D., in special education; Laura Fortson, Ph.D., and Glenna Bullis, for infant and preschool education; Richard Graham, Ph.D., in music therapy; Milton Blue, Ph.D., and William Ambrose, Ph.D., in language development and hearing.

Perhaps the most significant contributions to the early formulation of what was to become Developmental Therapy can be attributed to Stanley Ainsworth, Ph.D., Kathryn Blake, Ph.D., and Frances Scott, Ph.D., at the University of Georgia, and to Nicholas Long, Ph.D., at American University, Hillcrest Children's Center and the Rose School in Washington, D.C.

The Technical Assistance Development System (TADS) at the Frank Porter Graham Child Development Center, University of North Carolina, has helped put the entire effort into perspective over a three-year period. In particular, David Lillie, Ph.D., Donald Stedman, Ph.D., Dan Davis, Ph.D., Patrick Trohanis, Ph.D., and Richard Surles, Ph.D., have worked closely with the Rutland Center staff as the model emerged.

Finally, Developmental Therapy, as a transportable model, was tested from 1971 to the present in other centers treating seriously disturbed children. Participating in this effort were several highly effective treatment centers in other locations in Georgia, notably: Carrollton, Georgia, Dr. Peggy Pettit, director; Savannah, Georgia, Mrs. Mignon Lawton, director; Brunswick, Georgia, Dr. Virginia Boyle, director; also, Senora Ana Alegria in Trujillo, Peru, has translated Developmental Therapy in a Spanish-speaking culture. The contributions of these directors and their staffs have been enormous. Each location has demonstrated that Developmental Therapy can be effective in a variety of locations and can provide a common language among professionals trained in vastly different approaches.

In addition to her contributions as an evaluator to the project, Dr. Faye Swindle provided editorial review of this manuscript. Mrs. Eileen Patrick typed and retyped the many drafts. For their careful work and cheerful encouragement, all of the authors are deeply indebted.

The list of acknowledgments would be incomplete without recognition of the immense talent and effort contributed by every member of the Rutland Center staff during the years of development. The authors recognize that Developmental Therapy is a product of the contributions of each:

James Bachrach
Mary Beussee
Nancy Bonney
William Butler
Robert Clarke
Carmie T. Cochrane
Janis Conlin
John Cook
Allan Crimm
Nancy Cudmore
William Cudmore
Allen Curry
John Davis
Steve Davis
Kathleen Deeney
Leroy Dowdy
Amy Fendley
Daisy Fleming
Ruby Ann Free
Joyce Garrett
Clementine Gigliotti
Barbara Goldberg
Harry Goodwin
Belita Griffith
Angela Hiley
John Humphreys
Linda Javitch
Laura Levine
Tucker McClellen
Karen McDonough
Sarah McGinley

Patricia McGinnis
Ann McPherson
David Mendenhall
Marilyn Mendoza
Nora Mitchell
Walter Moore
Ada Mosley
Margaret Obremski
Diane Perno
Jennie Purvis
John Quirk
Kathleen Quirk
Steve Reese
JoAnne Rizza
Dixie Lou Rush
Shelley Samet
Ann Seward
Linda Shackleford
Jacqueline Smith
Peggy Smith
Allan Sproles
Patricia Stovall
Carol Stuart
Faye Swindle
Judi Trebony
Sally Westerfield
Lesley Whitson
Geraldine Williams
Patricia Willis
Nedra Zisa

Introduction

Traditionally, the word *therapy* has been sacrosanct. At the turn of the century, under the aegis of the medical profession, the term was extended to include paramedical practices such as physical therapy. Subsequently, the concept of therapy was broadened to embrace music, art, recreation, occupational, and psychological therapies. With Developmental Therapy the term is extended further, to include the rehabilitation of emotionally disturbed children by educators. This may be unsettling to some educators, who define their responsibilities strictly in relation to cognitive process and academic accomplishment. To other educators, who have seen that social and emotional maturation can be a significant product of the educational process, it may seem quite natural, for these educators recognize the healing potential of the maturation process itself.

Special education for emotionally and behaviorally disturbed children gained significant momentum during the early 1960's. Great effort went into identifying and defining the characteristics of such children, and many programs resulted from attention to questions like: How many children need this service? How many children should be enrolled in one class? What support services should be offered? What will it cost?

Only a few professionals spoke out with concern about the need to consider the nature of the processes occurring within these therapeutic classes. Individuals such as William Morse, Carl Fenichel, William Rhodes, Nicholas Long, Norris Haring, and Frank Hewett recognized the potential for effective, new forms of child therapy. Although formulating approaches that were significantly different, they held to the common premise that special education could become an effective vehicle for therapy. Two approaches predominated: one with psychodynamic foundations, the other with principles from theories of learning. From the enormous contributions of both approaches, came many elaborations and improvements in special education for disturbed children.

This book might be viewed as a product of both approaches. On the one hand, Developmental Therapy accepts a number of psychodynamic constructs such as feelings, individuation and identity, guilt, conflict, attitudes, values, and self concept. On the other hand, Developmental Therapy also accepts principles of learning such as drives, motivation, reinforcement, task analysis, operant behavior, sequencing, successive approximations, pairing, intermittent contingencies, success, and failure.

An enormous amount of research and clinical writing exists on all of these subjects, yet there has been a major ingredient missing—how it can be translated into classroom procedures for disturbed children of many different ages and problems.

It is difficult for the educator to travel through the maze of psychopathology, contingency schedules, and the like. Today, the field has many approaches, each viewing the disturbed child through the glasses of a particular theoretical position or different professional background, and each with its unique vocabulary. The teacher of disturbed children may still ask, "That all sounds impressive and probably true, but what does it mean to me in the classroom?"

Developmental Therapy has tried to respond to the teacher's dilemma by translating many theoretical constructs into educational practice. Yet it also makes its own contribution by refocusing therapy around the normal developmental milestones all children face. By doing this, Developmental Therapy stands as a "growth model" instead of a "deficit model." It emphasizes the normal processes in every child and works systematically to strengthen these aspects as a means to enhance social and emotional growth. It is a framework that provides for change as soon as it occurs during treatment. A child's behavior, personality, and intellectual system evolve through the sum of small, daily experiences. The therapeutic process that utilizes these experiences will expedite the emergence of normal growth patterns, because new maturational skills will be emerging even as old, maladaptive responses linger.

Another treatment concept is that there are elements of a sequential, relatively slow changing or unchanging nature even within a dynamic, change-oriented therapy approach. The teacher and parent must recognize within a child elements of substance that can be utilized as a strength, helping the child to continue to grow in these areas. This concept also suggests that gains made early in therapy must be continued and built upon systematically during subsequent therapy.

As a psychoeducational approach to child treatment, Developmental Therapy uses a therapeutic curriculum with developmental objectives as the guidelines for the treatment process and for the evaluation of treatment progress. It is conducted in a therapeutic classroom setting by an educational therapist or other professional or paraprofessional trained in this approach.

This text offers Developmental Therapy on several levels simultaneously. If you have had theoretical, academic preparation in child psychopathology, child development, special education, or in the learning theories, you should be able to find pedogogical translations of many familiar constructs. After you explore the basis of Developmental Therapy, you will undoubtedly see a number of ways you can expand upon it from your own experience and style of teaching.

If you are new to the field of emotionally disturbed children, you may find the vignettes and word pictures vivid enough that such children and their problems take on real meaning for you. The descriptions of what their teachers say and do, and the marginal comments explaining why, can be used as models to begin learning interaction skills and the basic processes of Developmental Therapy.

For all readers, the book intends to convey a way of looking at children of many ages and conditions through the focus of normal social and emotional development.

The first three chapters describe therapy for emotionally disturbed children from the developmental point of view. Included are an introduction to Developmental Therapy, directions for using the Developmental Therapy curriculum objectives, and a description of a group of children who received Developmental Therapy. The next three chapters describe activities, materials, and teacher management techniques. Particularly emphasized are the changes at each stage of Developmental Therapy. Chapter 6 explores methods whereby teachers can develop the skills for using Developmental Therapy.

Chapters 7 through 10 are devoted to the first four stages of Developmental Therapy and contain actual case studies of Developmental Therapy classes. The last two chapters discuss Developmental Therapy center activities, describing center-sponsored programs for the parents and school personnel of center children. Finally, the Appendix contains the entire list of 144 Developmental Therapy curriculum objectives, with examples.

Throughout the book names are fictitious but the situations are real.

chapter 1

DEVELOPMENTAL THERAPY

Mary Margaret Wood

Trust

Comfort

Growth

Pleasure

Skills

Cooperation

Mastery

Exploration

Security

Pride

Confidence

Reality

Success

INTRODUCTION

Developmental Therapy[1] is a psychoeducational approach to therapeutic intervention with young children who have serious emotional and behavioral disorders. The approach has particular reference to children between the ages of three and eight years and is applicable to children of varying ethnic and socioeconomic groups. These procedures also have been used successfully with disturbed children to age 14 and preschool children with other handicapping conditions.

Developmental Therapy is designed for special education teachers, mental health workers, preschool teachers, parents, and paraprofessionals using the therapeutic classroom setting with five to eight children in a group. It is a treatment process which (a) does not isolate the disturbed child from the mainstream of normal experiences; (b) uses normal changes in development as a means to guide and expedite the therapeutic process; and (c) has an evaluation system as an integral part of the curriculum.

By using the goals established for each area of the Developmental Therapy curriculum and by following the treatment sequences outlined by the developmental objectives, a teacher can facilitate the social and emotional growth of a child. When a child learns successful, pleasure-producing responses, pathological and nonconstructive behaviors will no longer be necessary. With Developmental Therapy the teacher assists the child in assimilating experiences designed to encourage mastery of developmental milestones. Interpersonal techniques and educational activities are used as the vehicles for this process.

---

[1] This treatment method was developed in part through special project grants from the Georgia Department of Education and the U.S. Office of Education, Bureau of Education for the Handicapped, Handicapped Children's Early Education Assistance Act, P. L. 91-230, Part C (1970–1973).

The model is described in Wood (1972).

WHAT DO YOU BELIEVE ABOUT DISTURBED CHILDREN?

Most teachers are familiar with a number of major writings, theory and research, in the fields of child development, child psychopathology, developmental psychology, special education, and learning theories. Such studies have provided a broad base for understanding how children develop. If you are preparing to work with emotionally disturbed children, you will have encountered many of these same ideas and formulated certain conclusions of your own regarding how to help such children. What you believe about emotional disturbance in children should have direct influence on the type of therapy you conduct.

Developmental Therapy was formulated by drawing upon the vast knowledge available about children and their development. It makes certain assumptions which are essential to its successful implementation. These assumptions, with implications for therapy, are outlined below.

If these assumptions fit with your approach, you should be comfortable with Developmental Therapy.[2] If not, perhaps the material in the following chapters can convince you that a developmental approach has certain merit because it recognizes the sequential, maturational process as a powerful force in therapy.

Assumption 1: *Emotional and behavioral disturbances in a young child are interwoven with normal functioning and often are difficult to differentiate. The healthy, normal aspects of a disturbed*

---

[2] A full review of the theoretical basis for Developmental Therapy may be found in Wood (1975).

3

child are often overlooked or misinterpreted as atypical. (See Lapouse and Monk, 1958; Shepherd, Oppenheim, and Mitchell, 1966.)

Implication for Therapy: Because of this interweaving of normal and disturbed functions, a plan of therapeutic intervention must include both the normal and disturbed elements within a child. If this is not done, therapy tends to emphasize deficits and problems, neglecting healthy, growing forces. When these are used in therapy they seem to stimulate rapid progress.

Assumption 2:   *Normal processes of physical and psychological development follow in a hierarchy of stages and sequences well documented in the literature.* These sequences produce natural, striking changes during the growth process and occur spontaneously in normal and disturbed children alike. Often such growth introduces an entirely new array of behaviors and skills in relatively short periods of time. (See Anthony, 1970; Bobroff, 1960; Erikson, 1959; Gesell and Amatruda, 1941; Hebb, 1949; Hewett, 1968; Parten, 1932; Piaget, 1967.)

Implication for Therapy: Utilizing change and new behavior is the key to successful therapeutic intervention. Constructive change occurs when nonconstructive, maladaptive behavior is disrupted and not permitted to continue, and when developmentally appropriate behavior is substituted.

Assumption 3:   *The normal process of change is uniquely individual, yet predictable, and occurs in relation to environmental conditions, experiences, biological constituents and to the foundation laid in prior experience.* (See Baumrind, 1967; Lewis, 1970; MacFarlane, 1943.)

Implication for Therapy: The therapeutic process for growth

and change should be planned in relation to two standards: (a) the general sequence of normal development for all children; and (b) the individual child's patterns of development, his strengths and weaknesses revealed through the presence or absence of developmental milestones.

Assumption 4:   *The young child's knowledge of himself, his confidence in himself, his willingness to risk himself in new situations, grows out of significant, pleasurable experiences.* (See Hill and Sarason, 1966; Keister, 1938.)

Implication for Therapy: Therapy must provide a way for the child to have a toehold of success, and the teacher must be able to mirror this success for him to see. If therapy experiences tend to be pleasurable, a child will assimilate the learning. If the experiences are frightening, confusing, complicated, meaningless, or failure producing, he may tend to avoid further involvement, or negative learning may occur.

Assumption 5:   *The young child learns and grows by experiences.* What he does is often more significant than what he hears. What he experiences will have impact on what he learns. Meaning comes through experience. (See Montessori, 1912; NAEYC, 1970; Rhodes, 1963.)

Implication for Therapy: Therapy for children implies an essentially experiential emphasis, learning through experiences rather than through words. Child therapy must have relevance to the child's world beyond the treatment program. He must associate particular responses, learned in treatment, with satisfying results transferred to real-life experiences.

Developmental Therapy is a psychoeducational treatment paradigm built upon these assumptions. The process is seen as a developmental progression in which the elimination of pathological behavior and the stimulation of developmentally appropriate behavior closely follow normal sequences of maturation. By systematically utilizing developmentally suitable experiences in the therapy program, the occurrence of constructive behaviors is stimulated. Each small, sequential experience represents a step toward normal maturation and development. Concurrently, nonconstructive behaviors are redirected, outgrown, or extinguished as a child learns more rewarding and satisfying adaptations to his world.

A THERAPEUTIC CURRICULUM

Curriculum is understood to be a course of study, and as such the Developmental Therapy curriculum represents areas of learning and sequences of skills to be learned within these areas. The desired result of this course of study for a young child is greater social and emotional growth. The purpose, therefore, of this therapeutic curriculum is to provide a broad outline to guide the teacher/therapist in planning appropriate sequences of experiences for the young, disturbed child.

Reflecting the assumptions presented previously, several standards were used in constructing the Developmental Therapy curriculum.

1. The curriculum should be broad enough to cover any serious emotional or behavioral problems seen in the young disturbed child.
2. The curriculum should provide for sequences of experiences which stimulate growth and utilize new skills as they spontaneously emerge in the child.
3. The curriculum should be adaptable to individual differences but effective and applicable in a group setting.
4. The curriculum should be broad enough to allow for clinical inference and for parent and teacher judgments, yet specific enough to provide objective evaluation.
5. The curriculum should include several essential processes.

    a. A process for meaningful experiences, not dependent upon verbal ability.
    b. A process for constructive learning.
    c. A process appropriate to a child's individual sequence of maturation.
    d. A process appropriate to the sequence of normal maturation for all children.

Utilizing these standards, the current version of the Developmental Therapy curriculum emerged. This course of study contains four basic curriculum areas: *behavior, communication, socialization,* and *(pre)academics.* These areas have proved adequate for planning treatment programs to encompass the wide variety of problems of seriously disturbed young children.

Behavior

Behavior has reference to the physical, adaptive responses which a child makes toward his environment. At its most basic point, behavior refers to a child being aware of where he is. With awareness, other processes can begin to grow: attending to a stimulus, simple motor responses, body control, recognizing essentials and nonessentials, and participating in routine activities. More advanced behavior processes include impulse control, organizing responses according to expectations of others, and involvement with rules as one basis for functioning in a group. These behavior processes are essential before more complex communication and socialization special skills can develop fully.

Communication

Communication implies interpersonal processes. For this reason, the area of communication includes all forms of verbal and nonverbal efforts to interact with another child or adult. Included in this area are gestures, watching and imitating others, producing speech sounds and verbal approximations, and using sequences of words. As communication skills increase, a child learns to listen, describe feelings and characteristics of himself and others, convey information, and express his feelings through words. A child must have some of these basic communication processes functioning in order to progress in socialization and academic areas. For this reason, program emphasis on basic communication skills must precede emphasis in the other areas of the curriculum.

Socialization

Socialization involves processes which lead a child into group experiences. These processes begin with awareness of adults and peers and soon develop into parallel and cooperative play. Socialization takes on a definitive form when a child has the interpersonal skills for successful interactions with a number of different people. To do this he must have a sense of self, self confidence, and an interest in others. Processes at work then include taking turns, suggesting activities, sharing, participating in what others suggest, recognizing characteristics of others, developing preferences for friends, supporting others, and eventually participating as an invested member of a group.

(Pre)academics

(Pre)academics, as an area of Developmental Therapy, includes processes used for cognitive functions which will contribute to mastery of academic content. Such processes include eye-hand and perceptual skills, body coordination, memory, discriminating similarities and differences in all sensory modalities, classifying, concept building, receptive language, use of objects, recognizing details in pictures, and concepts of number and conservation. These basic processes lead to more complex ones such as expressive language and recognizing signs and symbols, and are used to serve oneself and to communicate with others. Eventually, these processes are formalized for academic activities, personal enrichment, and creative problem solving.

STAGES OF DEVELOPMENTAL THERAPY

As the four areas of the therapeutic curriculum were applied successfully to small groups of young disturbed children, it became apparent that within each area there were key milestones which followed in developmental sequence. These sequences suggested five rather distinct stages of therapy. Progress through these five stages, in each area of the curriculum, results in an increasingly well adjusted child. A summary of these Developmental Therapy stages is presented in Table 1. The general therapeutic goals for each area of the curriculum, at each stage of therapy, are presented in Table 2. Specific objectives which sequence the steps toward each goal are contained in the Appendix.

The stages of Developmental Therapy represent an integration of developmental aspects of cognitive, psychosocial, affective, and sensory motor systems. The developmental sequences

While it is clear that certain areas of the curriculum must receive intensive effort before other areas, this should not be taken to mean that a child's program focuses on only one area at a time. Quite to the contrary, the interaction of these areas makes them inseparable.

It is important to emphasize that the academic objectives in Developmental Therapy are concerned with processes which assist a child in all areas of functioning. Developmental Therapy should not be considered remedial education.

are applicable across wide ranges of age, problems, and cultural and socioeconomic conditions. Each stage is translated into all four areas of curriculum, and an individual child may be in different stages in each of the four curriculum areas. Within each stage and area there is a sequence of specific objectives, representing developmental milestones. Children progress at varying rates through this developmental hierarchy within each curriculum area. The teacher's role, the

Each stage of Developmental Therapy requires a different emphasis, different techniques, and different materials and experiences.

Table 1. Summary of Developmental Therapy Stages[a]

STAGE I: Responding to the environment with pleasure

General Description:	*Responding and trusting*
TEACHER'S ROLE:	Arouser and satisfier of basic needs
TECHNIQUES:	Body language, controlled vocabulary, routine, stimulating activities
INTERVENTION:	Constant physical contact; caring, arousing
ENVIRONMENT AND EXPERIENCES:	Routine constant, luring rather than demanding; stimulating, arousing activities (sensory)

STAGE II: Responding to the environment with success

General Description:	*Learning individual skills*
TEACHER'S ROLE:	Verbal reflector of success; redirector of old coping behaviors to successful outcomes
TECHNIQUES:	Routine, consistency, holding limits, redirection
INTERVENTION:	Frequent, both physical and verbal
ENVIRONMENT AND EXPERIENCES:	Activities leading to self confidence, communication, exploration, and success

STAGE III: Learning skills for successful group participation

General Description:	*Applying individual skills to group procedures*
TEACHER'S ROLE:	Reflector of feelings and progress; encourager; holder of limits
TECHNIQUES:	Reflector of feelings; predictability; frequent verbal intervention, consistency
INTERVENTION:	Frequent, group focus, mostly verbal
ENVIRONMENT AND EXPERIENCES:	Focus on rules; focus on group; focus on consequences of behavior; approximate real life as much as group can tolerate; sharing

STAGE IV: Investing in group processes

General Description:	*Valuing one's group*
TEACHER'S ROLE:	Reflector of reality and success; counselor, group leader
TECHNIQUES:	Reality reflection, individual Life Space Interview, group discussions aimed at problem solving, group planning
INTERVENTION:	Intermittent, approximating real life
ENVIRONMENT AND EXPERIENCES:	Approximates real life with normal expectations; emphasis on learning experiences, unsimulated normal expectations, role play, field trips, plans developed by children

References to chronological age have been deliberately omitted in order to emphasize that the sequence of development is important rather than a comparison to a norm.

(Continued)

Table 1.. *continued*

STAGE V: Applying individual and group skills in new situations

General Description:	*Generalizing and valuing*
TEACHER'S ROLE:	Counselor, teacher
TECHNIQUES:	Normal expectations; relationships between feelings, behaviors, and consequences; nonclinical
INTERVENTION:	Infrequent
ENVIRONMENT AND EXPERIENCES:	Normal childhood settings; conversations about real-life experiences; support in solving problem situations; independent skill building

---

[a]From Wood (1972, p. 70).

amount of intervention required, the types of activities and materials, the experiences needed, and the type of participation change with each stage. The following sections provide a general description of each stage of therapy.

Stage One: Responding to the Environment with Pleasure

Not all children enter the program at Stage One. Entry stage is determined by development as reflected by the Developmental Therapy Objectives Rating Form described in Chapter 2.

The Stage One child does not trust his surroundings or himself. He may be immobilized from constructive activity, retreating into helpless, regressive behavior, or acting out in rage. Often Stage One children have no speech or do not use it if they have it. They may not be in touch with their surroundings. Their concepts are fragmentary, unrelated bits and pieces. If they have a preference they may not know how to communicate it. A few Stage One children have imaginary worlds which dominate them to the point that nothing else is real. Others seem to exist with no world at all, either imaginary or real. Distorted fears and extreme disorganization characterize most Stage One children. There is a pervasive feeling of floundering and helplessness.

During this first stage of therapy the quality of the child's response is not a concern, but responses and participation are required.

This first stage of therapy must arouse and mobilize a child to respond to the environment, to trust the teacher,

and to trust himself enough to venture forth. Stage One focuses upon these processes until the child has mastered each with proficiency. Children will move through this stage at widely varying rates: one week to one year.

The teacher's role at Stage One is defined as the "arouser," the adult who will provide satisfactions and pleasures under certain conditions, communicated through acceptance, nurturance, and body language.

Activities selected for children at this stage emphasize sensory experiences: smelling, tasting, touching, hearing. Activities are planned to move the child from diffused to selective responding. Expected responses include listening, talking, eating, remembering, smiling, running, climbing, coloring, and cutting and pasting. Experiences need to be predictable, simple, and familiar. Repetition of experience is essential. Every aspect of the classroom organization is carefully planned. Every happening is a product of the teacher's effort. Yet for all of this, the activities appear to be less formal than at other stages.

A minimum requirement for participation at this stage of therapy is two hours each day, five days a week. Concomitant enrollment in a regular school or preschool at this stage may not be recom-

Table 2. Developmental Therapy Goals for Each Curriculum
Area at Each Stage of Therapy[a]

Stage	Behavior	Communication	Socialization	Academic skills
I	To trust own body and skills	To use words to gain needs	To trust an adult sufficiently to respond to him	To respond to the environment with processes of classification, discrimination, basic receptive language concepts, and body coordination
II	To successfully participate in routines and activities	To use words to affect others in constructive ways	To participate in activities with others	To participate in classroom routines with language concepts of similarities and differences, labels, use, color; numerical processes of ordering and classifying; and body coordination
III	To apply individual skills in group processes	To use words to express oneself in the group	To find satisfaction in group activities	To participate in the group with basic expressive language concepts; symbolic representation of experiences and concepts; functional semiconcrete concepts of conservation; and body coordination
IV	To contribute individual effort to group success	To use words to express awareness of relationship between feelings and behavior in self and others	To participate spontaneously and successfully as a group member	To successfully use signs and symbols in formalized school work and in group experiences
V	To respond to critical life experiences with adaptive, constructive behavior	To use words to establish and enrich relationships	To initiate and maintain effective peer group relationships independently	To successfully use signs and symbols for formalized school experiences and personal enrichment

[a]From Wood (1972, p. 71).

mended. Exposure to a variety of children, adults, materials, and expectations tends to compound the complexities of the child's world and may work against initial mobilization.

General therapeutic goals for each area of the Stage One curriculum are:

Behavior: to trust own body and skills
Communication: to use words to gain needs
Socialization: to trust an adult sufficiently to respond to him
(Pre)academics: to respond to the environment with processes of classification, discrimination, basic receptive language, and body coordination

When a child accomplishes these goals, he is ready to progress from the first stage to the next stage of therapy. In the area of behavior, spontaneous, constructive responses have been mobilized. The child can respond in an organized way to play materials. In communication, the child has begun using words to obtain needs. In socialization, the child can trust the adult sufficiently to seek him out spontaneously and to accept his touch. For preacademics the child has increased his concepts of the world immediately surrounding him and has mastered fundamental cognitive skills of discrimination and classification, expressed with increased eye-hand and general body coordination.

Mastery of this first stage of Developmental Therapy is seen as the primary step in the mobilization of the child's resources for the treatment process. The basic elements for constructive behavior are mobilized: awareness, attention, responding, remembering, and feeling good about one's self in the therapeutic setting. The child has made a significant movement in the therapeutic program by responding to the adult and to the thera-

peutic environment. The accomplishment of the general therapeutic goals of Stage One prepares a child with the rudimentary foundations for progress in Stage Two, where emerging behaviors become more organized.

Stage Two: Responding to the Environment with Success

A Stage Two child has at least basic receptive and expressive language skills. He can direct his physical movements to obtain what he wants. He is generally highly mobile, restless, and fairly disorganized in his activity. He begins Stage Two with little self confidence and self esteem, a limited awareness of cause and effect, ineffective responses to peers, and only the most primitive beginnings of an organized value system.

Children beginning Stage Two generally are ineffective in communication. This necessitates a systematic, simplified sequencing of communication activities which increase in complexity as a child shows he is able to handle the less complex situations comfortably. Too much language with too little specificity, lacking concreteness, will slow down the therapeutic process. A Stage Two child may not be able to assimilate new meanings from such experiences.

This second stage of Developmental Therapy emphasizes learning individual skills, organizing information, participating in classroom routine, successful exploration, and testing others in order to verify newly formulated perceptions about oneself. The child explores, organizes, and masters new but uncomplicated experiences. Attention span increases and play materials are used more appropriately than at Stage One. Responses learned at Stage One are channelled into individual successes and skills at Stage Two. For some children this stage of treatment may represent discomfort, conflict, and insecurity as inappropriate behaviors are redirected and new responses are taught. Periodically, Stage Two children revert to old coping behaviors. At such times it is important that the teacher remobilize the child to appropriate behavior, reducing inappropriate responses to a minimum.

The Stage Two teacher has a significant, demanding role. She is the predictable point of reference, expecting appropriate responses and reflecting success, and holding limits while encouraging exploration. Considerable physical intervention on the teacher's part is generally necessary. Through the relationship with the teacher, a Stage Two child learns about himself in relation to others.

For this second stage of Developmental Therapy, general treatment goals for each area of the curriculum are:

Behavior: to participate successfully in routines and activities
Communication: to use words to affect others in constructive ways
Socialization: to participate in activities with others
Preacademics: to participate in classroom routine with language concepts of similarities and differences, labels, use, color; numerical processes of ordering and classifying; and body coordination

Although Stage Two children are not yet able to see themselves as members of a group, simple group experiences are essential to accomplish individual objectives. Within the group, the child's receptivity for change must be sensitively directed into new, successful experiences. It is important that the teachers reduce to a minimum opportunities for regressive or other inappropriate behavior.

This stage is a critical one for learning new, appropriate responses and organizing these responses into functioning systems.

Stage Two can be viewed as an organizing effort requiring elements of *structure, consistency, routine,* and *predictability,* with many experiences for exploring and testing new skills. The teacher must carefully sequence these new experiences and each new confrontation so that the child sees himself as an individual with some basic capacity to accomplish and master the situation. Such an end result implies successful participation. Because most Stage Two children are in the beginning phases of skill development, their successes must be defined in individual terms.

The therapeutic classroom simulates experiences which help the child to grow in individual skills that will eventually generalize into new, broader competencies. Critical issues are often explored from the safety of make-believe. Individualized instruction is planned for teaching preacademic skills but is conducted in a group setting. Frequently programmed instruction is used at this stage in contrast to Stage Three, where it is used less often, or to Stage One, where it is not used at all.

During this stage of therapy it is essential that the therapeutic class be conducted at least four days a week, for two-hour sessions each day. Concomitant enrollment in a regular school, preschool, or kindergarten program generally should be started. Children who have not had ongoing, normal group experiences during Stage Two of therapy subsequently seem to move more slowly through Stage Three. However, a child should not be placed in a regular program if the developmental discrepancies are so great that further stress is created.

Stage Two has been described as the "testing" stage. These children must have new experiences in order to try out their newly learned skills. But keep in mind that Stage Two is also called the "success" stage. Each venture must have a successful outcome if progress is to continue.

The essence of organization in Stage Two is to provide simple verbal links between what is happening and what a child is feeling or doing. It is too soon, however, to expect the child to do this. Later, if successfully prepared by the teacher at Stage Two, a Stage Three child can learn to recognize and express these important relationships.

Most young, preschool children leave therapy when they complete a majority of the developmental objectives for Stage Two. They are ready for the Stage Three objectives but no longer require therapeutic intervention for the normal maturational process to function.

A child is ready to leave this class for the next stage class when he has learned to direct his own behavior constructively with only intermittent intervention from the teacher; when he uses words spontaneously for interpersonal communication; when he is not afraid to participate in activities with others; and when he is confident that there are play and work activities he can do successfully.

Stage Three: Learning Skills for Successful Group Participation

Stage Three represents a turning point in the therapeutic environment, in the teacher's role, and in the type of experiences selected for a child's program. In contrast to Stage Two, where extrinsic control and structure are paramount, Stage Three begins the critical movement of assimilation within the child himself. The Stage Three child begins this stage with the basic intellectual, social, emotional, and physical skills and an emerging sense of self worth. He has functioning communication and sensorimotor systems which give him the capacity to translate preferences and feelings into constructive actions. He begins to see both the world and himself in organized ways. Awareness of cause and effect relationships is beginning. This is the period when a child learns the social expectations created by being a member of a group. He also learns to enjoy the results of group membership. If this is to happen, many Stage Three children must be taught basic group skills such as taking turns, sharing materials, participating in group planning, accepting suggestions from other children, developing reciprocal relationships, and recognizing the characteristics and needs of others.

In this stage of therapy the child is provided with situations and experiences where he can apply newly mastered skills

A few children actually begin therapy at Stage Three. These children are most often elementary school children with moderately severe behavior disorders.

and concepts, especially with the peer group. In play and team games these Stage Three processes most often emerge. Early in Stage Three there is an emphasis on make-believe and magical solutions. Increasingly, these social situations become governed by rules based in reality. This is a major Stage Three milestone. For children at this stage, developing rules and insisting that peers conform to rules are significant reference points—sources for security.

It becomes quite evident that the therapeutic classroom at this stage has a group emphasis. The members of the group have mastered essential individual skills as prerequisites for group participation. Less structure is required to elicit participation, and the group is encouraged to develop and maintain its own rules, regulations, and consequences.

The Stage Three teacher functions as a model for group participation, the adult who can uphold the rules, recognize and reflect real success, and provide direction for an individual child who may falter within the group setting. A Stage Three teacher spends considerable time helping the children understand relationships between what they do and what happens as a result. This requires sensitivity to underlying feelings and supportive responses when things go badly. Intervention on the teacher's part is intermittent, and direct physical intervention is seldom necessary.

Both group and individual experiences for this stage of therapy are selected to link closely to a child's regular school program. When experiences are planned within the therapeutic classroom setting, the activities, expectations, materials, and processes more closely simulate real life situations than at previous stages of therapy. It is essential for the teacher to resist accepting inappropriate behavior at this stage.

The group at Stage Three generally requires a program three to four times a week, and sessions usually are one and one half hours long. Concomitant enrollment in a regular preschool or school program is essential for all Stage Three children. Such an arrangement will be facilitated if a child has been enrolled in a regular program during the previous stage of therapy.

For Stage Three of Developmental Therapy, the goals for each area of the curriculum are:

Behavior: to apply individual skills in group processes

Communication: to use words to express oneself in the group

Socialization: to find satisfaction in group activities

Academics: to participate in the group with expressive language concepts; symbolic representation of experiences and concepts; functional, semiconcrete concepts of conservation; and body coordination

With the mastery of Stage Three a child has the basic skills for successful group interaction. He is able to regulate his own behavior with decreasing need for outside controls. Expression of emotion has fallen under greater self direction and in a verbal way rather than by physical acting out. The child has attached some value to the group and is willing to invest himself in appropriate group behavior. He has discovered that social cooperation and communication can be pleasurable. Facilitating all of these accomplishments is the child's ability to use symbols for representation of his personal experiences.

Stage Four: Investing in Group Processes

Children participating in Developmental Therapy at Stage Four need a less clinical, contrived environment and a more reality-oriented one. When they enter this stage, their individual skills and abilities, however modest, are held by themselves and others to be adequate, in behavior, socialization, communication, and school work. The task to be accomplished at Stage Four is one of enlarging each child's capacity to function effectively with peers and the adult world with the ordinary rules, constraints, freedoms, and consequences children experience in their environments away from the center.

The Stage Four child has a background of success as a participating member of a group, from his Stage Three experiences. He understands the necessity for yielding his will to that of the group. He is willing to abide by the rules of the group, knowing the rationale for rules and the consequences when rules are broken. He knows that his skill level is acceptable no matter how meager. He has reached a point in his development where he is not only willing to participate but values the participation.

Stage Four is often characterized by vacillation between extremes. It is typical to see a Stage Four child happy one minute and sad the next, or praising his parent for help with a decision then denouncing the parent for that very same assistance. This vacillation is but one manifestation of the struggle the Stage Four child goes through in formulating a value system. He wants to be adult-like and sophisticated but clings to the security of his own child-like behavior; he dreams great dreams of accomplishment and achievement but the limitations of his abilities defy those dreams; he may have long-fantasized notions of an ideal self but is now faced with accepting himself as he is. Family, peer, and school groups are all significant forces in this process. By sifting through his own con-

Most primary grade children a *terminated when they have ma* *tered Stage Three objectives. .* *would be inappropriate, in mo* *instances, to continue them in* *Stage Four. They no longer nee* *special therapy to continue t* *progress.*

Rarely does a seriously disturbe *child begin Developmental The* *apy at Stage Four. The lack o* *developmental skills of previou* *stages makes it impossible fo* *most entering children to begin a* *this level.*

Since group participation and acceptance are his means of appraising himself, the Stage Four child is very dependent on his interactions with others for making determinations about himself.

cerns and those of others he becomes aware of many different value systems. By learning more about others the Stage Four child learns more about himself, seeking a comfortable balance between his inner and outer life.

For children at this stage of development the opinions of a significant individual are of crucial importance. Such a person values the child and serves as an appropriate model whose behavior the child can emulate. This person also must recognize the unique value of the child and express that recognition in honest, open terms. The Stage Four teacher often becomes this significant person to each child in the group, or she may involve a particular child's significant person directly in the group's activities when that person is someone from the child's family or neighborhood.

The teacher's role at Stage Four is that of group leader and counselor, reflecting reality and guiding the group as it plans its own activities and determines its own expectations, rules, procedures, and consequences. In many instances the teacher is the bridge resolving a child's personal needs with those of the group. The teacher projects reality for the group to consider, suggests experiences, and assists the group in utilizing the abilities of each member.

The goals for each curriculum area of Stage Four are:

Behavior: to contribute individual effort to group success

Communication: to use words to express awareness of relationships between feelings and behavior, in self and others

Socialization: to participate spontaneously and successfully as a group member

Academics: to successfully use signs and symbols in formalized school work and in group experiences

For information about Life Space Interviewing, refer to Chapter 5 and to Long, Morse, and Newman (1971).

While Stage Four emphasizes normal behavioral expectations, there are a number of opportunities for the teacher to come to the aid of a particular child who is just beginning to move toward these goals. The Life Space Interview is used extensively to assist a child toward greater self direction as an outgrowth of a crisis. As a group leader, the teacher has responsibility to reflect for the group members the reality they face both at the center and away.

The center experiences planned for children at Stage Four are developed by the children themselves through group planning and discussion. The teacher helps them generalize from these experiences to school and home situations. Field trips and role playing are effective means by which the children try on new behaviors in supportive, preplanned, and real-life ways. Games and activities have elements of normal competition and game rules are not modified. Through these experiences, each child is helped to bring his own impulsivity and behavior under greater inner control. He is encouraged to support others as well as to accept support. With a greater awareness of cause and effect of behavior, in himself and others, and with acceptance of himself by his group, the child at Stage Four is able to tolerate greater stresses away from the center and is able to solve problems with greater maturity and insight.

As this emotional maturity begins to emerge, children at Stage Four often exhibit a new eagerness for assistance in academic work. Regular tutorial and remedial work is pursued with new meaning. The openness to accept actual academic difficulties and the determination to overcome them emerge as characteristic of this stage. Group learning, using ordinary school materials and texts used in a regular school, is preferred.

Often, children use the study time at the center to review class work from school or to get help with homework.

Groups at Stage Four generally meet two or three times per week for approximately an hour to an hour and one half. Often these groups can be scheduled after regular school hours. Recreation, art, music, and role playing should be available for them as they plan their time schedule and select their group activities.

As the group moves solidly into mastery of Stage Four objectives, it is essential to keep an orientation toward success in places away from the center. This stage begins the separation process, where each member of the group is seen as having more important and rewarding experiences away from the center. Often the child himself will let the teacher know of his readiness to terminate by statements that he does not think he needs to come back anymore. On such occasions, the child and teacher have a private conference to explore the realities of possible termination and to discuss a plan for intermittent support in the school, should it be indicated.

Stage Five: Applying Individual and Group Skills in New Situations

Few children are kept at the center for this final stage of therapy. Each of the stated objectives is more adequately accomplished in a normal school setting and at home. Children at this stage are classified as "provisionally terminated." It is essential, however, that parents and teachers understand the therapeutic goal in each curriculum area at this stage of therapy. Support of a child, independent of the center, depends upon the understanding of the goals on the part of the people in the child's normal environment. With a healthy school environment the child will need nothing more than a periodic visit to his home

and regular preschool or school program. Extensive consultation with his regular school and parents may be needed initially. Effective support probably can be maintained through once-a-month consultation.

The center teacher's role during this stage of therapy is primarily that of the child's friend. Clinical techniques are not used. She uses the teacher role when visiting his school and home. By functioning also as a consultant, the center teacher helps the school formulate translations of the therapeutic objectives for Stage Five into suitable practices. General goals and objectives of Developmental Therapy at this stage are used to help the school focus on individual strengths and abilities and to plan ways to continue remediation in areas of academic deficit.

The regular teacher should be advised to anticipate occasional flare-ups. She should not attempt to modify routine, nor should she provide a method of management which might isolate or set the child apart. Within the standards of behavior and participation set for the normal group, the teacher should be encouraged to hold the same expectations. If the preceding stages of therapy have been successful, the child no longer should be perceived as an emotionally or behaviorally disturbed child.

At Stage Five, general therapeutic goals for each area of the curriculum are:

Behavior: to respond to critical life experiences with adaptive, constructive behavior

Communication: to use words to establish and enrich relationships

Socialization: to initiate and maintain effective peer group relationships independently

Academics: to successfully use signs and symbols for formalized school experiences and personal enrichment

Because Stage Five does not require special interventions, it is not included in the remaining chapters of this book. This stage should be viewed as an epilogue to the treatment process for older children.

Successful adjustment to this stage of therapy will depend upon several factors: (a) the child's mastery of therapeutic goals at previous stages of therapy; (b) previous adjustment of the child to concomitant placement in a regular school program during the therapeutic process; (c) the education of the regular school staff to the Developmental Therapy goals and objectives; and (d) the implementation of Developmental Therapy practices by parents during all stages of therapy.

LITERATURE CITED

Anthony, E. 1970. The behavior disorders of childhood. *In* P. Mussen (ed.), Carmichael's Manual of Child Psychology, pp. 730–733. Vol. 2. John Wiley & Sons, New York.

Baumrind, D. 1967. Child care practices anteceding three patterns of preschool behavior. Genet. Psychol. Monogr. 75: 43–88.

Bobroff, A. 1960. The stages of maturation in socialized thinking and in the ego development of two groups of children. Child Dev. 31: 321–338.

Erikson, E. H. 1959. Identity and the life cycle. Psychol. Issues 1: 50–100.

Gesell, A. and C. Amatruda. 1941. Developmental Diagnosis. Hoeber, New York.

Hebb, D. 1949. The Organization of Behavior, pp. 235–261. John Wiley & Sons, New York.

Hewett, F. 1968. The Emotionally Disturbed Child in the Classroom, pp. 41–59. Allyn and Bacon, Boston.

Hill, K. and S. Sarason. 1966. The relation of test anxiety and defensiveness to test and school performance over the elementary school years: a further longitudinal study, pp.

1–76. Monograph of the Society for Research in Child Development. Vol. 31. University of Chicago Press, Chicago.

Keister, M. 1938. The behavior of young children in failure: an experimental attempt to discover and to modify undersirable responses of preschool children to failure. Univ. Iowa Stud. Child Welfare 14: 27–82.

Lapouse, R. and M. Monk. 1958. An epidemiologic study of behavior characteristics in children. Amer. J. Public Health. 48: 1134–1144.

Lewis, W. 1970. Child advocacy and ecological planning. Ment. Hyg. 54(4): 475–483.

Long, N. J., W. C. Morse, and R. G. Newman. 1971. Conflict in the Classroom. 2nd Ed. Wadsworth, Belmont, Cal.

MacFarlane, J. 1943. Study of personality development. *In* R. Barker, J. Kounin, and H. Wright (eds.), Child Behavior and Development. McGraw-Hill, New York.

Montessori, M. 1912. The Montessori Method (trans. by A. George). Schocken Books, New York.

NAEYC. 1970. Play in Play Grounds. National Association for the Education of Young Children, New York.

Parten, M. 1932. Social participation among preschool children. J. Abnorm. Soc. Psychol. 27: 243–269.

Piaget, J. 1967. Six Psychological Studies, pp. 3–73. Random House, New York.

Rhodes, W. 1963. Curriculum and disordered behavior. J. Excep. Child. 30: 61–66.

Shepherd, M., A. Oppenheim, and S. Mitchell. 1966. Childhood behavior disorders and the child guidance clinic: an epidemiological study. J. Child Psychol. Psychiatr. 7: 39–52.

Wood, M. M. (ed.). 1972. The Rutland Center Model for Treating Emotionally Disturbed Children. 2nd Ed. Rutland Center Technical Assistance Office, Athens, Ga.

Wood, M. M. 1975. A developmental curriculum for social and emotional growth. *In* D. L. Lillie (ed.), Early Childhood Curriculum: An Individualized Approach. Science Research Associates, Palo Alto.

chapter 2
DEVELOPMENTAL THERAPY CURRICULUM OBJECTIVES

Carolyn Combs

Attending

Responding

Remembering

Recognizing

Discriminating

Classifying

Approximating

Imitating

Organizing

Sharing

Participating

Cooperating

Labeling

Reading

Writing

Answering

Listening

Contributing

Exchanging

Telling

Suggesting

Refraining

Accepting

Caring

Describing

Expressing

INTRODUCTION

Think of your task in educating disturbed children as navigating each child to a particular destination, far away. There are many alternative routes to travel. Some routes are direct, some circuitous. If you have key landmarks you can plot the most direct course. When you seem to lose direction you can take another reading on where you are and where you need to be. The Developmental Therapy curriculum objectives can be your landmarks, major developmental milestones outlining the way to social and emotional maturity for a young child. The distances between each milestone objective will vary with the particular child and with your attributes as a navigator. You may feel that side trips apart from an objective are appropriate for a child. You may be correct. But don't lose sight of your landmark. And remember that time is a critical force in a young child's life. It would be a tragedy to take so many side trips that the child arrives too late.

DESCRIPTION

The curriculum objectives of Developmental Therapy, found in the Appendix, are 144 general statements outlining a series of sequential, developmental milestones in the four curriculum areas of *behavior, communication, socialization,* and *(pre)academics.* These statements are intended to be used as treatment objectives to guide teachers in planning appropriate sequences of experiences for young, disturbed children. Thus, they serve as the curriculum foundation and provide the framework for implementing a program for emotional growth. In addition, they function as the basis for a criterion-referenced evaluation system.

The Developmental Therapy curriculum objectives are used with the Developmental Therapy Objectives Rating Form (DTORF), which contains abbreviated statements of each of the objectives (see Sample Form 1). The DTORF is used for rating and recording the developmental objectives that a child has and has not mastered. The objectives not mastered become the major therapy emphasis for the child.

The child's treatment team (lead teacher, support teacher, and monitor/parent worker) together rate the child on the series of objectives in each of the four curriculum areas. These objectives serve to delineate the major focus of treatment for the child during each 10-week treatment period. At least one objective, and no more than four, are used in each of the curriculum areas.

The objectives are rated sequentially, with mastery of previous objectives being necessary before new objectives are initiated. This sequential progression provides direction for parents and teachers anticipating what will come next. It also is a general control against providing too much, too rapidly, for a child to assimilate. By selecting objectives sequentially within each of the four curriculum areas, uneven patterns of development will be quite evident. That is, a child may be at different Developmental Therapy stages in behavior, communication, socialization, and (pre)academics.

PURPOSES

The Developmental Therapy objectives may be utilized in three ways.

To Aid in Grouping Children for Treatment

Children are grouped in therapy classes according to the selected objectives, as indicated by the DTORF. In this way, classes are composed of children at similar developmental stages. A child's average stage of development in the four curriculum areas determines his general stage of therapy and, thus, his group placement. For example, a child may be

The content of this chapter should be mastered as the first step in understanding Developmental Therapy.

Groups, in Developmental Therapy, are composed of children who have essentially the same treatment objectives. Other factors, such as age and sex, are of secondary importance for grouping. However, they may be considered when there are enough children working on similar objectives to form more than one group at the same stage.

rated Stage Two in behavior, Stage Three in communication, and Stage Two in socialization and academics. He would be grouped with Stage Two.

Children are regrouped at the end of each 10-week treatment period on the basis of their current DTORF ratings. Current ratings also are required for a child to be changed from one group to another during a 10-week treatment period.

To Plan a Child's Treatment Program

By delineating a child's level of mastery within each curriculum area and by determining where developmental skills are not mastered, the points of intervention are established. The treatment team can then select activities and plan strategies to provide a child with experiences that are appropriate for his specific objectives in each of the four curriculum areas.

Since the developmental objectives represent major milestones, they are not necessarily inclusive of every small step that might be necessary in a treatment program. They are intended to guide the team in planning.

In addition to providing a focus for individualizing a child's program, the Developmental Therapy objectives aid in planning for a total class group. By determining which of the objectives apply to all children in the group, experiences, materials, and strategies can be selected for the benefit of the entire group.

To Document the Progress of a Child During Treatment

It can be seen by comparing growth profiles that children progress at varying rates through the Developmental Therapy curriculum. Some children progress very quickly, indicating the transient nature of their disturbance. For others, progress is very slow. Their problems encompass all areas of development and are more resistant to treatment.

The DTORF is completed for the first time after the child has participated in the program for eight class days. It is subsequently completed on each child at the middle (five weeks) and end (10 weeks) of each treatment period (See Sample Forms 2 and 3). Used in this manner, the DTORF reflects a child's developmental baseline at the time of enrollment, the most current level of functioning, and the changes that occur over time. These changes in mastery of developmental objectives are summarized in a growth profile for the five- and 10-week intervals (see Sample Form 4) and may be further summarized in a Short Summary DTORF (see Sample Form 5) which reports percentages of objectives mastered over 10-week intervals.

PROCEDURE FOR USING THE DTORF

At the time of enrollment, staff members who have had direct contact with the child, his family, and his school during the referral and intake process are asked to give a general consensus rating of the child's current stage of development in each of the Developmental Therapy curriculum areas. This staff consensus determines the stage at which the child will enter the program. To make this decision, the staff uses information obtained from individual testing, parents, and school conferences and compares it with the general goals for each stage. A list of these general goals is included as Table 2 in Chapter 1.

These initial estimates of functioning usually prove to be accurate. However, children may react quite differently in an individual testing situation and may not exhibit the problems for which they were referred. This is particularly true where the problems involve group socialization skills or withdrawn, overcontrolling children.

To establish the initial focus for treatment, the treatment team completes a DTORF baseline after a child has been in the program for a period of eight class days. Since most children feel comfortable in the classroom setting and begin to show their typical, individual responses after a few days, it is felt that such a baseline gives an accurate assessment of a child's current level of functioning.

If major discrepancies occur between the initial placement at the time of acceptance and the DTORF eighth-day baseline, it is then possible to change a child's group placement.

As previously mentioned, each child is rated on the objectives by his treatment team at the end of five weeks and again at the end of the 10-week treatment period. This 10th week rating provides the basis for determining placement for a child during the next treatment period and gives the next treatment team the major treatment objectives for the child during the subsequent five-week treatment period.

The DTORF should be done by consensus of the three members constituting a treatment team. *It is completed without consulting any previous DTORF data.* Since both subjective and observational data from home, school, and center are to be considered as the basis for ratings, each team member's opinions must be considered, and no one member should be allowed to dominate or overly influence the rating process. It is helpful, also, to include the opinions and observations of any other staff members who may work with the child in the treatment program, such as recreation, art, or music therapists.

When rating a child, the treatment team must consider every Developmental Therapy objective and decide whether or not a child (a) has achieved mastery of the objective, (b) is ready for work toward mastery of the objective, or (c) is not yet ready to work on the objective.

It is usually necessary to have one person on a treatment team designated to be responsible for making sure that a DTORF is completed for each child in a group on predetermined dates. Usually the lead teacher assumes this responsibility.

Symbols used to record information on the DTORF and their definitions are as follows:

√ indicates mastery of an objective. The child does this nine out of 10 times at the center, home, and school and will need only minimum support to retain the behavior.

X indicates a treatment objective. The child is ready to begin or needs to continue intensive work on this objective. At least one, but no more than four treatment objectives should be marked for a child in each curriculum area in any one rating period.

NR (not ready) indicates that a child is not yet ready to begin work on an objective. After four X marks have been recorded in a particular curriculum area the remaining objectives are automatically marked NR.

It is important that each objective on the DTORF be marked in one of these three ways and that no blank spaces occur. The treatment team member designated to be responsible for completion of the DTORF should check to make sure that every objective is marked so that there are no blank spaces. It is difficult to determine in retrospect reasons for blank spaces, and such omissions make evaluation data invalid.

Ordinarily, the objectives should be selected in the order in which they occur on the rating form, no more than four at a time. Those selected would then continue to be treatment objectives until mastered. Exceptions to selecting objectives in sequence will occur occasionally. When these exceptions do occur and an objective is selected out of sequence, the

The child needs to be placed in a group with children who have attained a similar level of mastered skills in order to interact effectively and to experience success in the group setting. Placement in a group with children who possess significantly lower or higher skills would produce frustration and inhibit growth.

For teachers in situations without a treatment team, the reliability of a consensus rating would not be possible, of course. However, all other procedures should be followed as closely as possible in order to keep documentation as accurate as possible.

Teachers often are concerned about rating a child X on an objective which they know he can do but won't. Because the DTORF should reflect this resistance, it is appropriate to continue to mark the objective X until the child meets the criterion for mastery.

There may be times when a child may actually be ready for the next objective beyond the four marked X's. However, such objectives should be marked NR, indicating that within the specified limit of four X objectives, a fifth X would be too many. This may seem to be an unwarranted restriction on the progress of the child in a particular area; but it is an important safeguard against moving a child too rapidly in one area while he is struggling in another area.

treatment team should write a brief explanation on the rating form.

Cross referenced objectives occur in all four of the curriculum areas. They indicate that a significant developmental milestone represented by an objective in another area should be mastered in order for the sequence of objectives to be fully accomplished. It is possible that a child may be rated *NR* on an objective in one area and be rated *X* on that same objective in another area. However, it would not be appropriate to have an objective rated   in one area and *X* or *NR* in another area. In such a case a child should be rated as having mastered the objective in both areas.

THE SUMMARY DTORF

Apparently, occasional regression may be expected with some children after an objective has been mastered, but it should not occur repeatedly. It may suggest that the objective was initially mastered too rapidly or that the child is under unusual duress outside of treatment. There also seems to be a necessary practice period, with successful outcomes, in order for responses to become assimilated completely. If the practice period is too short, and the child is moved on to the next objective, regression may occur.

The Summary DTORF contains data collected from every DTORF for a particular child and allows these data to be compiled on a single form (see Sample Form 4). It is most useful for graphically illustrating progress over a period of time. The form enables treatment personnel, parents, and teachers to see the type and rate of progress that a child has made since the time of enrollment.

To increase the visual clarity of the form, objectives that have been mastered while enrolled in the program can be marked in color. This includes only objectives that have been marked, at some time, as treatment objectives (*X*). Objectives mastered prior to the time of enrollment are not designated by the same color. Another color can be used to designate any regression that may have occurred. Regression is evident when an objective that has been marked ✓ as mastered is marked again at a later date as *X*, indicating it has become a treatment objective again.

The actual data pertaining to this case can be found on the sample forms cited in the previous section of this chapter.

CASE STUDY: JOHN

The following case study of a child with moderate behavior problems will serve to illustrate how the curriculum objectives of Developmental Therapy are used to fulfill the three purposes for which they are intended: (a) grouping for treatment, (b) planning the treatment program, and (c) documenting treatment progress.

John is an eight-year-old boy who attends a third grade class in a rural elementary school. He lives with his natural mother, a stepfather, an older sister, and a younger half brother.

John was referred to the center by his third grade teacher who cited the following problems as the reasons for referral: resistance to authority, continually disruptive classroom behavior, negative attitude toward all aspects of school, difficulty relating to peers, and poor academic performance.

When informed by the school of John's disruptive behavior and generally poor adjustment to school, his parents gave their consent to the referral and expressed their willingness to cooperate in obtaining assistance for him.

John was accepted for intake at the center and was given both a psychological and an educational assessment. Since there was no suggestion of either severe pathology or neurological impairment, a psychiatric assessment was not included.

John's parents met for an intake conference with a center social worker to provide relevant home information. They reported that John's behavior at home was often similar to the behavior noted by the classroom teacher. They stated that he had difficulty interacting with his brother and sister and that he was often defiant and disobedient in his relations with his parents. Difficulty getting John to perform chores around the house and frequent arguments over doing homework were also reported.

When John's case was presented to the staff, all who had worked with him were present: the psychologist, the educational evaluator, the center teacher who had talked with John's teacher and observed him in class, and the social worker who had met with John's parents. They all contributed to determining the type of program needed to assist John. Since John was relatively young, possessed normal intelligence, and had no apparent neurological dysfunctioning or mental illness, the degree of severity of John's problem was rated as "three" by the staff on a five-point rating scale from "mild" to "severe." His prognosis

was rated as "one" ("excellent" on a five-point rating scale). A prediction for length of treatment was made: two 10-week treatment periods.

By consensus, the intake staff determined the stages of Developmental Therapy at which John should begin his program. The general goals in each of the curriculum areas were used in making this determination, rather than the specific developmental objectives.

Area	Stage	Goal
Behavior	II	To participate successfully in routines
Communication	III	To use words to express oneself in the group
Socialization	II	To participate in activities with others
Academics	III	To participate in the group with basic expressive language concepts; symbolic representation of experiences and concepts; functional, semiconcrete concepts of conservation; and body coordination

The procedures described here illustrate how a child is initally grouped by developmental stage.

Based on this general assessment, John was slated to enter the treatment program with placement in a Stage Two class. Primary emphasis was to be on assisting John to follow the classroom routine and in learning to successfully participate with other children.

John was placed in a Stage Two group of six children (four boys and two girls). The ages of the children ranged from six to nine years. The class met for two hours a day, four days a week. During the remainder of the time, John would continue to attend his regular third grade class.

At the end of eight center class days, John's treatment team (lead teacher, support teacher, and monitor) completed a baseline DTORF on John (see Sample Form 1). It can be seen from this rating that John's initial placement in a Stage Two group, based on intake information, was correct. The only discrepancy between the consensus staff rating and the baseline DTORF was in the area of communication. John was seen by his treatment team to be functioning at

Stage Two in communication, whereas the original staffing had placed him in Stage Three.

John's areas of difficulty in the center class were basically the same as those for which he was referred by his classroom teacher. He appeared to resent adult authority and frequently attempted to disrupt or withdraw from class activities. He needed a great deal of support, both physical and verbal, in order to complete his academic work. He avoided interacting with the other children in the group, preferring to play alone, and initiated only minimal verbal exchange with the teachers or the other children. He often became angry when he was not permitted to have his own way; and he frequently reverted to cursing and aggressive, acting-out behavior to express his frustration. More and more, John was appearing to be an alienated, unhappy youngster.

Based on the objectives marked with an X on the baseline DTORF (i.e., treatment objectives), certain strategies of intervention and experiences were planned to help John learn new

The original placement is verified by the baseline DTORF.

It should be noted that program planning for mastery of objectives is an ongoing process for the treatment team. Daily planning should relate the objectives, activities, and materials for each child to the group as a whole. This discussion, concerning an individual treatment program, is intended simply to illustrate how strategies and experiences can be selected on the basis of objectives.

These activities and strategies are representative of a Stage Two class in Developmental Therapy.

The techniques teachers use in such situations are described in Chapter 5.

skills and to further his developmental growth. For example, since both verbal and physical encouragement from the teachers was necessary to assist John in completing a number of activities, John was placed next to the support teacher at the table. With this arrangement, the teacher could be more readily available to provide the attention necessary for enabling John to begin successful participation in the classroom routine (behavior objective B-10 [refer to Appendix]). Tasks were kept short and made simple enough to ensure success. It was understood that, as John evidenced more willingness to perform academic work, the tasks gradually would be made more difficult.

Since John often refused to participate in activities such as game time or play time, all activities were kept individually oriented in the beginning with very simple, structured requirements for cooperative activity (behavior objectives B-10 and B-11; socialization objectives S-17 and S-18). Games were noncompetitive with little emphasis placed on rules. Outdoor activities were highly motivating and required only a minimum of physical skill. It was understood that, as John and the other children in the group developed greater self confidence and increased their skills for group participation, other elements would be introduced into their game and play activities. However, the emphasis would remain always on successful, individual participation. The teachers had noticed that John seemed to particularly enjoy music and art. The classroom schedule contained daily activities in these areas, and the teachers gave John considerable praise and recognition for his voluntary participation (communication objective C-14).

During activities which he did not seem to enjoy, such as story time, he received a lot of encouragement to remain with the group (behavior objective B-10; academic objective A-31). The support teacher stationed herself beside John and sought, through both verbal and physical means, to maintain his interest. Whenever possible the art activity for the day was related to the story to provide a link between the two activities. Because several of the children in his group were learning to write basic words from memory (academic objective A-47), the teachers selected basic words from the story and had the children write them on the back of their art work, which pertained to the story. Basic role playing was frequently used in conjunction with the story, since drama seemed to be another area that sparked John's interest (communication objective C-13; socialization objectives S-17 and S-18). Stories were always chosen to appeal to the children's interest level, and they were given many opportunities to respond to the material. Questions were kept simple but were stated so as to elicit many verbal responses (academic objective A-44; communication objective C-12).

To further aid John in achieving the developmental objectives in socialization (socialization objectives S-15, S-16, S-17, and S-18), the teachers created situations where John could be paired with another boy in the class who possessed a higher level of social skills and who had initially made friendly overtures toward John. It was felt that through continued exposure to an appropriate model, John would begin to respond and develop more advanced social skills.

Play time was frequently structured so as to encourage social interaction (socialization objectives S-15, S-16, and S-17; communication objectives C-11 and C-13). For example, the two boys would be given dump trucks and building blocks. The teacher would then suggest that they transport the blocks to a building site and build a house.

Materials were deliberately limited so that the children would find it necessary to share (socialization objectives S-16 and S-18). When John encountered difficulty, he was encouraged by the teachers to let them know about the problem (communication objectives C-11 and C-12). The teachers would suggest an appropriate response such as, "Tell him you want to use the green paint," and follow the interaction to see that it had a successful outcome for both children.

Strategies were also determined for helping John learn to cope with his feelings of anger and frustration. When John became angry and reverted to cursing and aggressive behavior, he was taken to the corner of the room by the support teacher and helped to calm down. She attempted to make him aware of his feelings, expressed her understanding, and suggested other ways that John could behave.

Every week conferences were held with John's parents and his third grade teacher to share information about John's progress. Suggestions were offered on ways that his parents and teacher could work on the objectives at home and at school.

At the end of five weeks of treatment, the team again completed a DTORF on John (Sample Form 2). It can be seen by comparing the baseline DTORF with the fifth-week DTORF that John made progress. In the area of behavior, John was beginning to participate in various activities (work time and snack time) with less frequent physical intervention from the teacher. That objective (behavior objective B-10) was nearly mastered, and the teachers felt that only minimum work and support would be needed to help John attain mastery. However, behavior objective B-9 had become a treatment objective even though it had been rated as mastered on the baseline DTORF. Assertiveness, expressed through inability to wait his turn, frequently occurs when a child begins to develop a stronger sense of self worth than he has had before.

In the area of communication John was using words appropriately to express his needs and desires. This objective (communication C-11) was marked (✓) as mastered. In addition, John was spontaneously exchanging information with the adults and with the other children in the class. Since John was doing this consistently, these objectives (communication objective C-12, C-13) also were marked (✓) to indicate mastery. The treatment team felt that John still needed more help learning to accept praise and success appropriately (communication objective C-14). Therefore, that objective was marked (X) again. Because the next communication objective cross references with behavior objective B-13, it was marked (NR) as it was marked under behavior. However, the next communication objective C-16 (using words spontaneously to describe own activities, work, or self . . .) seemed appropriate to add to John's treatment program. The team felt that two objectives in communication would be sufficient

for the next five weeks, due to the rapid progress he had made in mastering the other Stage Two communication objectives. The team was concerned also that his progress in behavior and socialization had not been as rapid.

In the area of socialization, John was initiating movement toward other children in the group and was engaging in social interaction. Thus, the treatment team marked that objective mastered (socialization objective S-15). He had also made some progress in learning to participate in a verbally directed sharing activity and in cooperative activities (socialization objectives S-16, S-17, and S-18). However, these objectives had to be again marked X, as he required the teacher's intervention on a number of occasions.

In the area of academics, John was still having difficulty listening during story time (academic objective A-31). As a result, this objective was retained as a treatment objective and was indicated as such by an X. His difficulty at story time was the main reason that a previous objective (behavior objective B-10) was not marked as completely mastered.

He had made progress in being able to write basic words from memory and dictation (academic objective A-47), but had not met the standard of being able to write the selected words nine out of ten times without assistance. Perhaps John's most successful accomplishment during those first five weeks was his mastery of academic objective A-48. In this, John was able to use all of his potential in the highly structured group activities which centered around role playing, story telling, and cooperative art projects. This was a fairly good indicator that his progress during the next five weeks would be fairly rapid in all of the areas. With this outlook, the team added academic objective A-49 to his treatment program: writing his full name, address, and date from memory. This skill is almost essential in a regular third grade classroom if a child is to feel competent.

John's parents and his classroom teacher were shown the fifth week DTORF. It was compared with the baseline DTORF as a graphic means of demonstrating actual movement within the treatment program. Additional suggestions were offered as to ways that the

Generally, parents and teachers select only two or three objectives which they feel that they can successfully implement. The center teacher assists them with suggestions for activities and techniques. By limiting the number of objectives, parents and teachers are able to focus on a few aspects of what may appear to them to be an overwhelming problem and to succeed in implementing some constructive change in the child.

A child often displays more strength in one curriculum area than in others. For instance, a shy, withdrawn child may achieve a developmentally appropriate level of mastery in the area of behavior but show a significant lag in the areas of communication and socialization.

parents and teacher could assist John to demonstrate and solidify his new skills at home and at school.

At the end of 10 weeks, the treatment team completed the 10th week DTORF (Sample Form 3). It can be seen from this rating that John continued to make significant gains. With only a few exceptions, the majority of objectives selected for John on the 10th week DTORF are in Stage Three. As a result, John was regrouped and placed in a Stage Three class for the next 10 weeks with other children who were rated, according to the DTORF, as being developmentally similar.

The objectives marked on the 10th week DTORF provided the next treatment team with a beginning point for program planning at Stage Three, thus preserving, in an unbroken process, gains that John had made in the previous 10-week treatment period.

John continued in treatment for the next 10 weeks in a Stage Three class. At the end of that 10-week period the objectives marked were at high Stage Three and Stage Four levels, indi-

The DTORF documents progress, or its lack, for parents, staff, and teachers. Over time, definite growth trends should be evident which eventually culminate in termination from treatment.

cating that John was functioning at an appropriate developmental level for his age and ability. Progress made during that period can be seen by looking at Sample Form 4.

At this point, John's treatment team felt that John was ready to be terminated from treatment at the center. Conferences were held with John's parents and classroom teacher to obtain their perceptions of John's degree of progress and to ascertain their willingness for John to be terminated. Both John's parents and teacher agreed that he had progressed significantly and stated their approval for termination.

The lead teacher on John's treatment team arranged a conference with John and very specifically pointed out to him the things that he had learned in classes at the center. She discussed with him his feelings about terminating.

John was terminated at the end of his second treatment period, with periodic follow-up to take place in his home and at school to ensure that he continued to make a satisfactory adjustment.

Sample Form 1. Baseline DTORF

Child's Name _____John_____   Class Stage _2_ Raters: _Smith, Jones, Brown_

Date _____9/13/73_____   Type Rating (Check one)—Baseline _XX_ , 5th week _____ , 10th week _____

	Behavior	Communication	Socialization	(Pre)academics
STAGE I	✓ 1. respond by attending ✓ 2. respond by sust. attend. ✓ 3. single mot. response ✓ 4. complex mot. response ✓ 5. assist in self help ✓ 6. respond indep. play mat. ✓ 7. respond w/recall/routine	✓ 1. attend/speaker ✓ 2. resp./motor beh. ✓ 3. resp./verbal approx. ✓ 4. init./vb. approx. ✓ 5. recog. word/to adult ✓ 6. recog. word/to child ✓ 7. word sequence	✓ 1. aware/adult ✓ 2. attend/adult beh. ✓ 3. resp. to name ✓ 4. imitat. acts/adult ✓ 5. solit. play ✓ 6. resp. request/come ✓ 7. resp. single request ✓ 8. same as C-5 ✓ 9. same as C-6 ✓ 10. same as C-7 ✓ 11. exhibit emerg./self ✓ 12. seek contact/adult	✓ 1. same as B-1 ✓ 2. same as B-2 ✓ 3. same as B-3 ✓ 4. same as B-4 ✓ 5. resp. fine/motor/24 mo. ✓ 6. imitate wds./acts of adults ✓ 7. resp. by simple discrim. of obj. ✓ 8. same as C-3 ✓ 9. same as C-4 ✓ 10. short-term memory/ obj. & people ✓ 11. resp. w/classif./simil. obj. w/diff. attri. ✓ 12. short term memory/vb. express. ✓ 13. body coord./3–4 yr. lev. ✓ 14. match similar pictures ✓ 15. recog. color names ✓ 16. eye-hand coord./4-yr. lev. ✓ 17. recog. body parts
STAGE II	✓ 8. use play mat./appro. ✓ 9. wait/no interven. X 10. partic. work time/ no intervention X 11. partic. play time/ no interven. X 12. spon. partic.	✓ 8. answer/recog/word ✓ 9. recept. vocab. ✓ 10. label feel./pict. X 11. command activ./ simple wrd. seq. X 12. use words ex. min. info./adult X 13. use words ex. min. info./child	✓ 13. paral. play/spon. ✓ 14. same as B-9 ✓ 15. init. min. move./child X 16. partic./sharing X 17. coop. act/child at play X 18. coop. act./child in organ. activ.	✓ 18. recog. use of obj. ✓ 19. recog. detail in pictures ✓ 20. rote count to 10 ✓ 21. count to 5 (1 to 1) ✓ 22. name colors ✓ 23. count to 10 (1 to 1) ✓ 24. eye-hand coord./5-yr. lev. ✓ 25. recog. diff./shapes, symbols, numerals, words ✓ 26. categorize diff. items/ similar charac. ✓ 27. write recog. approx. of first name w/o asst. ✓ 28. discrim. differences (up-down, etc.) ✓ 29. body coord./5-yr. lev. ✓ 30. recog. grps. to 5 X 31. listen to story telling
STAGE III	NR 13. vb. recall rules/proc. NR 14. contrib. to grp. NR 15. vb. conseq. NR 16. vb. reasons NR 17. vb. other ways beh./ indiv. NR 18. refrain when others not NR 19. main. control & comply	X 14. accept praise NR 15. same as B-13 NR 16. spon. describe work NR 17. same as B-14 NR 18. same as B-15 NR 19. pride/words/gestures NR 20. vb./feeling/resp. NR 21. same as B-16	NR 19. turns w/o remind. NR 20. share/min. remind. NR 21. sug. to teacher NR 22. partic./act. suggest child NR 23. pref./child NR 24. des. charac. of others	✓ 32. recog. grps. to 10 ✓ 33. left-right visual orien. ✓ 34. recog. writ. names for color words ✓ 35. recog. written labels ✓ 36. recog. & write numerals for groups/1–10 ✓ 37. write first/last name/date with sample

(Continued)

Sample Form 1., *continued*

	Behavior	Communication	Socialization	(Pre)academics
STAGE III				✓ 38. eye-hand coord./6-yr. lev. ✓ 39. body-coord./6-yr. lev. ✓ 40. recog. & write numerals for grps./11–20 ✓ 41. write alpha./simple words ✓ 42. add-subtract/0–10 ✓ 43. use ordinal/concepts verbally X 44. lstn. to story & resp. appro. ✓ 45. read prim. vocab./sentences ✓ 46. add-subtract above 10 ✓ 47. write basic words/memory or dictation ✓ 48. part. group. act./write, tell, mural
STAGE IV	NR 20. resp. appro./leader choice NR 21. spon. partic./activ. prev. avoid NR 22. implem. alter. beh. NR 23. vb. express cause & ef. NR 24. resp./provocation/ control NR 25. resp. appro./ new suggest.	NR 22. vb. recog. feel/others NR 23. vb. recog. feel/self NR 24. verb. praise/others NR 25. non vb./express./ feel./art, music NR 26. spon. express. own feel./words NR 27. express others feel. NR 28. vb. express. exper./ feel./art, music NR 29. same as B-23	NR 25. suggest. act./grp. NR 26. same as B-20 NR 27. same as B-21 NR 28. diff. charac./others NR 29. phys./vb. support/ others NR 30. partic. grp. plng. & pb. solv.	NR 49. write name, ad., date/memory NR 50. read, write/sentences NR 51. read, write quant. words NR 52. contribute grp. project/ expressive skills NR 53. write indiv. exper. stories
STAGE V	NR 26. construc. suggest.	NR 30. maintain posit. rel. verb.	NR 31. init. & main./ interp. & grp. rel.	NR 54. write for commun. NR 55. read/pleas. & info. NR 56. write of feel. & attit. NR 57. read/info. feel. & beh. of others

Progress Notes

Sample Form 2. Fifth Week DTORF

Child's Name ___John_____ Class Stage _2_ Raters: _Smith, Jones, Brown___

Date _9/21/73_____ Type Rating (Check one)—Baseline _____, 5th week _XX_, 10th week _____

	Behavior	Communication	Socialization	(Pre)academics
STAGE I	✓ 1. respond by attending ✓ 2. respond by sust. attend. ✓ 3. single mot. response ✓ 4. complex mot. response ✓ 5. assist in self help ✓ 6. respond indep. play mat. ✓ 7. respond w/recall/routine	✓ 1. attend/speaker ✓ 2. resp./motor beh. ✓ 3. resp./verbal approx. ✓ 4. init./vb. approx. ✓ 5. recog. word/to adult ✓ 6. recog. word/to child ✓ 7. word sequence	✓ 1. aware/adult ✓ 2. attend/adult beh. ✓ 3. resp. to name ✓ 4. imitat. acts/adult ✓ 5. solit. play ✓ 6. resp. request/come ✓ 7. resp. single request ✓ 8. same as C-5 ✓ 9. same as C-6 ✓ 10. same as C-7 ✓ 11. exhibit emerg./self ✓ 12. seek contact/adult	✓ 1. same as B-1 ✓ 2. same as B-2 ✓ 3. same as B-3 ✓ 4. same as B-4 ✓ 5. resp. fine/motor/24 mo. ✓ 6. imitate wds./acts of adults ✓ 7. resp. by simple discrim. of obj. ✓ 8. same as C-3 ✓ 9. same as C-4 ✓ 10. short-term memory/ obj. & people ✓ 11. resp. w/classif./simil. obj. w/diff. attri. ✓ 12. short term memory/vb. express. ✓ 13. body coord./3–4 yr. lev. ✓ 14. match similar pictures ✓ 15. recog. color names ✓ 16. eye-hand coord./4-yr. lev. ✓ 17. recog. body parts
STAGE II	✓ 8. use play mat./appro. X 9. wait/no interven. X 10. partic. work time/ no intervention X 11. partic. play time/ no interven. X 12. spon. partic.	✓ 8. answer/recog/word ✓ 9. recept. vocab. ✓ 10. label feel./pict. ✓ 11. command activ./ simple wrd. seq. ✓ 12. use words ex. min. info./adult ✓ 13. use words ex. min. info./child	✓ 13. paral. play/spon. ✓ 14. same as B-9 ✓ 15. init. min. move./child X 16. partic./sharing X 17. coop. act/child at play X 18. coop. act./child in organ. activ.	✓ 18. recog. use of obj. ✓ 19. recog. detail in pictures ✓ 20. rote count to 10 ✓ 21. count to 5 (1 to 1) ✓ 22. name colors ✓ 23. count to 10 (1 to 1) ✓ 24. eye-hand coord./5-yr. lev. ✓ 25. recog. diff./shapes, symbols, numerals, words ✓ 26. categorize diff. items/ similar charac. ✓ 27. write recog. approx. of first name w/o asst. ✓ 28. discrim. differences (up-down, etc.) ✓ 29. body coord./5-yr. lev. 30. recog. grps. to 5 X 31. listen to story telling
STAGE III	NR 13. vb. recall rules/proc. NR 14. contrib. to grp. NR 15. vb. conseq. NR 16. vb. reasons NR 17. vb. other ways beh./ indiv. NR 18. refrain when others not NR 19. main. control & comply	X 14. accept praise NR 15. same as B-13 X 16. spon. describe work NR 17. same as B-14 NR 18. same as B-15 NR 19. pride/words/gestures NR 20. vb./feeling/resp. NR 21. same as B-16	X 19. turns w/o remind. NR 20. share/min. remind. NR 21. sug. to teacher NR 22. partic./act. suggest child NR 23. pref./child NR 24. des. charac. of others	✓ 32. recog. grps. to 10 ✓ 33. left-right visual orien. ✓ 34. recog. writ. names for color words ✓ 35. recog. written labels ✓ 36. recog. & write numerals for groups/1–10 ✓ 37. write first/last name/date with sample

(Continued)

Sample Form 2., *continued*

	Behavior	Communication	Socialization	(Pre)academics
STAGE III				✓ 38. eye-hand coord./6-yr. lev. ✓ 39. body-coord./6-yr. lev. ✓ 40. recog. & write numerals for grps./11–20 ✓ 41. write alpha./simple words ✓ 42. add-subtract/0–10 ✓ 43. use ordinal/concepts verbally ✗ 44. lstn. to story & resp. appro. ✓ 45. read prim. vocab./sentences ✓ 46. add-subtract above 10 ✗ 47. write basic words/memory or dictation ✓ 48. part. group. act./write, tell, mural
STAGE IV	NR 20. resp. appro./leader choice NR 21. spon. partic./activ. prev. avoid NR 22. implem. alter. beh. NR 23. vb. express cause & ef. NR 24. resp./provocation/ control NR 25. resp. appro./ new suggest.	NR 22. vb. recog. feel/others NR 23. vb. recog. feel/self NR 24. verb. praise/others NR 25. non vb./express./ feel./art, music NR 26. spon. express. own feel./words NR 27. express others feel. NR 28. vb. express. exper./ feel./art, music NR 29. same as B-23	NR 25. suggest. act./grp. NR 26. same as B-20 NR 27. same as B-21 NR 28. diff. charac./others NR 29. phys./vb. support/ others NR 30. partic. grp. plng. & pb. solv.	✗ 49. write name, ad., date/memory NR 50. read, write/sentences NR 51. read, write quant. words NR 52. contribute grp. project/ expressive skills NR 53. write indiv. exper. stories
STAGE V	NR 26. construc. suggest.	NR 30. maintain posit. rel. verb.	NR 31. init. & main./ interp. & grp. rel.	NR 54. write for commun. NR 55. read/pleas. & info. NR 56. write of feel. & attit. NR 57. read/info. feel. & beh. of others

Progress Notes

Sample Form 3. Tenth Week DTORF

Child's Name _John_ Class Stage _2_ Raters: _Smith, Jones, Brown_

Date _10/12/73_ Type Rating (Check one)—Baseline _____, 5th week _____, 10th week _XX_

	Behavior	Communication	Socialization	(Pre)academics
STAGE I	✓ 1. respond by attending ✓ 2. respond by sust. attend. ✓ 3. single mot. response ✓ 4. complex mot. response ✓ 5. assist in self help ✓ 6. respond indep. play mat. ✓ 7. respond w/recall/routine	✓ 1. attend/speaker ✓ 2. resp./motor beh. ✓ 3. resp./verbal approx. ✓ 4. init./vb. approx. ✓ 5. recog. word/to adult ✓ 6. recog. word/to child ✓ 7. word sequence	✓ 1. aware/adult ✓ 2. attend/adult beh. ✓ 3. resp. to name ✓ 4. imitat. acts/adult ✓ 5. solit. play ✓ 6. resp. request/come ✓ 7. resp. single request ✓ 8. same as C-5 ✓ 9. same as C-6 ✓ 10. same as C-7 ✓ 11. exhibit emerg./self ✓ 12. seek contact/adult	✓ 1. same as B-1 ✓ 2. same as B-2 ✓ 3. same as B-3 ✓ 4. same as B-4 ✓ 5. resp. fine/motor/24 mo. ✓ 6. imitate wds./acts of adults ✓ 7. resp. by simple discrim. of obj. ✓ 8. same as C-3 ✓ 9. same as C-4 ✓ 10. short-term memory/ obj. & people ✓ 11. resp. w/classif./simil. obj. w/diff. attri. ✓ 12. short term memory/vb. express. ✓ 13. body coord./3–4 yr. lev. ✓ 14. match similar pictures ✓ 15. recog. color names ✓ 16. eye-hand coord./4-yr. lev. ✓ 17. recog. body parts
STAGE II	✓ 8. use play mat./appro. ✓ 9. wait/no interven. ✓ 10. partic. work time/ no intervention ✓ 11. partic. play time/ no interven. X 12. spon. partic.	✓ 8. answer/recog word ✓ 9. recept. vocab. ✓ 10. label feel./pict. ✓ 11. command activ./ simple wrd. seq. ✓ 12. use words ex. min. info./adult ✓ 13. use words ex. min. info./child	✓ 13. paral. play/spon. ✓ 14. same as B-9 ✓ 15. init. min. move./child ✓ 16. partic./sharing X 17. coop. act/child at play ✓ 18. coop. act./child in organ. activ.	✓ 18. recog. use of obj. ✓ 19. recog. detail in pictures ✓ 20. rote count to 10 ✓ 21. count to 5 (1 to 1) ✓ 22. name colors ✓ 23. count to 10 (1 to 1) ✓ 24. eye-hand coord./5-yr. lev. ✓ 25. recog. diff./shapes, symbols, numerals, words ✓ 26. categorize diff. items/ similar charac. ✓ 27. write recog. approx. of first name w/o asst. ✓ 28. discrim. differences (up-down, etc.) ✓ 29. body coord./5-yr. lev. ✓ 30. recog. grps. to 5 31. listen to story telling
STAGE III	X 13. vb. recall rules/proc. X 14. contrib. to grp. X 15. vb. conseq. NR 16. vb. reasons NR 17. vb. other ways beh./ indiv. NR 18. refrain when others not NR 19. main. control & comply	✓ 14. accept praise X 15. same as B-13 ✓ 16. spon. describe work X 17. same as B-14 X 18. same as B-15 X 19. pride/words/gestures NR 20. vb./feeling/resp. NR 21. same as B-16	X 19. turns w/o remind. X 20. share/min. remind. X 21. sug. to teacher NR 22. partic./act. suggest child NR 23. pref./child NR 24. des. charac. of others	✓ 32. recog. grps. to 10 ✓ 33. left-right visual orien. ✓ 34. recog. writ. names for color words ✓ 35. recog. written labels ✓ 36. recog. & write numerals for groups/1–10 ✓ 37. write first/last name/date with sample

(Continued)

Sample Form 3., *continued*

	Behavior	Communication	Socialization	(Pre)academics
STAGE III				✓ 38. eye-hand coord./6-yr. lev. ✓ 39. body-coord./6-yr. lev. ✓ 40. recog. & write numerals for grps./11–20 ✓ 41. write alpha./simple words ✓ 42. add-subtract/0–10 ✓ 43. use ordinal/concepts verbally ✓ 44. lstn. to story & resp. appro. ✓ 45. read prim. vocab./sentences ✓ 46. add-subtract above 10 ✓ 47. write basic words/memory or dictation ✓ 48. part. group. act./write, tell, mural
STAGE IV	*NR* 20. resp. appro./leader choice *NR* 21. spon. partic./activ. prev. avoid *NR* 22. implem. alter. beh. *NR* 23. vb. express cause & ef. *NR* 24. resp./provocation/ control *NR* 25. resp. appro./ new suggest.	*NR* 22. vb. recog. feel/others *NR* 23. vb. recog. feel/self *NR* 24. verb. praise/others *NR* 25. non vb./express./ feel./art, music *NR* 26. spon. express. own feel./words 27. express others feel. *NR* 28. vb. express. exper./ feel./art, music *NR* 29. same as B-23	*NR* 25. suggest. act./grp. *NR* 26. same as B-20 *NR* 27. same as B-21 *NR* 28. diff. charac./others *NR* 29. phys./vb. support/ others *NR* 30. partic. grp. plng. & pb. solv.	✗ 49. write name, ad., date/memory ✗ 50. read, write/sentences ✗ 51. read, write quant. words ✗ 52. contribute grp. project/ expressive skills *NR* 53. write indiv. exper. stories
STAGE V	*NR* 26. construc. suggest.	*NR* 30. maintain posit. rel. verb.	*NR* 31. init. & main./ interp. & grp. rel.	*NR* 54. write for commun. *NR* 55. read/pleas. & info. *NR* 56. write of feel. & attit. *NR* 57. read/info. feel. & beh. of others

Progress Notes

Sample Form 4. Summary DTORF[a]

Name: _John_

Enrolled: 9/24/73
Terminated: 3/8/74

Behavior

Date	Stage I					Stage II				Stage III								Stage IV					Stage V
10th wk. ( )																							
5th wk. ( )																							
10th wk. ( )																							
5th wk. ( )																							
10th wk. ( )																							
5th wk. ( )																							
10th wk. ( )																							
5th wk. ( )																							
10th wk. (9-9-74)	•	•	•	•	•	•	•	•	•	•	•	•	•	×	×	×	×	×					
5th wk. (2-9-74)	•	•	•	•	•	•	•	•	•	•	×	×	×	×									
10th wk. (12-1-73)	•	•	•	•	•	×	×	×	×	×													
5th wk. (10-5-75)	•	•	•	×	×	×																	
Baseline (9-24-73)	•	•	•																				
Objectives	1	2	3	4	5	6	7	8	9	10	11	12	13	14	15	16	17	18	19	20	21	22	23	24	25	26

Communication

Date	Stage I					Stage II				Stage III								Stage IV					Stage V
10th wk. ( )																							
5th wk. ( )																							
10th wk. ( )																							
5th wk. ( )																							
10th wk. ( )																							
5th wk. ( )																							
10th wk. ( )																							
5th wk. ( )																							
10th wk. (3-8-74)	•	•	•	•	•	•	•	•	•	•	•	•	•	•	•	×	×						
5th wk. (2-8-74)	•	•	•	•	•	•	•	•	•	•	•	•	×	×	×	×	×						
10th wk. (12-1-73)	•	•	•	•	•	•	•	•	•	×	×	×	×										
5th wk. (10-5-73)	•	•	•	•	•	•	×	×	×														
Baseline (9-24-73)	•	•	×																				
Objectives	1	2	3	4	5	6	7	8	9	10	11	12	13	14	15	16	17	18	19	20	21	22	23	24	25	26	27	28	29	30

(Continued)

Sample Form 4., *continued*

Socialization

	Stage I							Stage II						Stage III				Stage IV				Stage V								
Date																															
10th wk. ( )																															
5th wk. ( )																															
10th wk. ( )																															
5th wk. ( )																															
10th wk. ( )																															
5th wk. ( )																															
10th wk. ( )																															
5th wk. ( )																															
10th wk. (3-8-74)			•	•	•	•	•	•	•	•	•	•	•	•	•	•	X	X												
5th wk. (2-8-74)			•	•	•	•	•	•	•	•	X	X	X	X	X	X	X	X												
10th wk. (12-1-73)			•	•	•	•	•	•	X	X	X	X	X	X	X															
5th wk. (10-5-73)			•	•	•	•	•	X	X	X	X																			
Baseline (9-24-73)			•	•	•	•	X	X	X																						
Objectives	1	2	3	4	5	6	7	8	9	10	11	12	13	14	15	16	17	18	19	20	21	22	23	24	25	26	27	28	29	30	31

(Pre)Academics

	Stage I							Stage II																							
Date																															
10th wk. ( )																																
5th wk. ( )																																
10th wk. ( )																																
5th wk. ( )																																
10th wk. ( )																																
5th wk. ( )																																
10th wk. ( )																																
5th wk. ( )																																
10th wk. (3-8-74)			•	•	•	•	•	•	•	•	•	•	•	•	•	•	•	•	•	•											
5th wk. (2-8-74)			•	•	•	•	•	•	•	•	•	•	•	•	•	•	•	•	•												
10th wk. (12-1-73)			•	•	•	•	•	•	•	•	•	•	•	•	•	•	•	•													
5th wk. (10-5-73)			•	•	•	•	•	•	•	•	•	•	•	•	•	•	•	•													
Baseline (9-24-73)			•	•	•	•	•	•	•	•	•	•	•	•	•	•	•	•													
Objectives	1	2	3	4	5	6	7	8	9	10	11	12	13	14	15	16	17	18	19	20	21	22	23	24	25	26	27	28	29	30	31

(Pre)Academics *(continued)*

	Stage III							Stage IV							Stage V											
Date																										
10th wk. ( )																											
5th wk. ( )																											
10th wk. ( )																											
5th wk. ( )																											
10th wk. ( )																											
5th wk. ( )																											
10th wk. ( )																											
5th wk. ( )																											
10th wk. (3-8-74)			•	•	•	•	•	•	•	•	•	X	X													
5th wk. (2-8-74)			•	•	•	•	•	•	X	X	X	X														
10th wk. (12-1-73)			•	•	•	•	•	X	X	X																
5th wk. (10-5-73)			•	•	•	X	X	•	X																	
Baseline (9-24-73)			•	•	X	X	•	X	X																	
Objectives	32	33	34	35	36	37	38	39	40	41	42	43	44	45	46	47	48	49	50	51	52	53	54	55	56	57

[a] •, mastery; X, treatment objective; unmarked blocks are "not ready" (NR).

Sample Form 5. Short Summary DTORF

Name _John_ _____ Code number_____

Summer ___ Spring ___ Winter 3/74 Fall 12/73 Baseline 9/73

Curriculum Area	Percent of objectives mastered					
	Stage I	Stage II	Stage III	Stage IV	Stage V	
Behavior	7/7= 100	2/5= 40	/7=	/6=	/1=	
Communication	7/7= 100	3/6= 50	/8=	/8=	/1=	
Socialization	12/12=100	2/6= 33	/6=	/6=	/1=	
Academics	17/17= 100	13/14= 93	14/17= 82	/5=	/4=	
Behavior	7/7= 100	4/5= 80	/7=	/6=	/1=	
Communication	7/7= 100	6/6= 100	2/8= 25	/8=	/1=	
Socialization	12/12=100	5/6= 83	/6=	/6=	/1=	
Academics	17/17=100	14/14= 100	17/17= 100	/5=	/4=	
Behavior	7/7= 100	5/5= 100	5/7= 71	/6=	/1=	
Communication	7/7= 100	6/6= 100	7/8= 87	/8=	/1=	
Socialization	12/12=100	6/6= 100	4/6= 67	/6=	/1=	
Academics	17/17= 100	14/14=100	17/17= 100	3/5=60	/4=	
Behavior	/7=	/5=	/7=	/6=	/1=	
Communication	/7=	/6=	/8=	/8=	/1=	
Socialization	/12=	/6=	/6=	/6=	/1=	
Academics	/17=	/14=	/17=	/5=	/4=	
Behavior	/7=	/5=	/7=	/6=	/1=	
Communication	/7=	/6=	/8=	/8=	/1=	
Socialization	/12=	/6=	/6=	/6=	/1=	
Academics	/17=	/14=	/17=	/5=	/4=	

chapter 3
MAKING DECISIONS ABOUT TREATMENT EFFECTIVENESS

William W. Swan and **Mary Margaret Wood**

Effectiveness

Efficiency

Goals

Objectives

Progress

Procedures

Results

Assumptions

Judgments

Decisions

INTRODUCTION

Your decisions regarding the effectiveness of each child's program must rest solidly on your confidence in the procedures you are using. You may ask, "How do I know if Developmental Therapy really does provide a curriculum that emotionally disturbed children need?" Or you might ask, "How do I know I can depend on this approach?" These are both ways of asking, "Will Developmental Therapy work?"

The answers may be approached in several ways. One way is to identify a number of theoretical statements which you believe to be authentic. From these statements certain constructs emerge along with specific assumptions. Testing a curriculum's authenticity can proceed from this point by judging how logically the procedures follow the constructs and how nearly the assumptions hold true in actual practice.

Another way is to ask other people who have experience and knowledge to evaluate the curriculum by using it. The more it is used by competent people and the greater the number of children they use it with, the more likely it is that you can depend upon the outcome.

DOCUMENTING EFFECTIVE TREATMENT

When selecting a curriculum, or when planning a treatment program, a question which must always be asked is, "Will this program be effective?" To answer the question, you must define the goal of the program and select ways to record and report information which will help you document that the goal has been reached. Many people have found that this process becomes most efficient when the program goal can be refined into subgoals which in turn are further specified as objectives. If the objectives can then be translated into defined procedures with results which can be described, you have a highly effective method for evaluating your efforts. Such an approach is called a "criterion-referenced system." Figure 1 shows this in schematic form as it is applied to Developmental Therapy.

As you can see in the figure, the overall goal of Developmental Therapy is to assist children in social-emotional growth. This is further defined as mastery of selected stages of development by the accomplishment of specified developmental objectives in the four areas of the curriculum. From this point of reference, when you can show that a child has mastered a selected progression of the developmental objectives, you have shown that your general goal has been accomplished.

Of course, such a report does not tell you if the child accomplished the goal with the greatest possible speed; nor does it tell you if, by mastery of a greater number of developmental milestones, he might have accomplished the overall goal to a greater extent; and it could not tell you how the child might have progressed in another program. These are research questions. Study of such issues would involve a myriad of complex interacting variables for which there are, at present, limited measurement procedures. Therefore, recognizing that a great number of the attributes assumed to be relevant to emotional disturbance in children are not quantifiable, criterion-referenced evaluation is an efficient way to document treatment effectiveness. In fact, it may be the only way presently available.

Developmental Therapy uses criterion-referenced evaluation, with treatment team consensus, for documentation of a child's progress in mastering developmental objectives.[1] Such documentation

The results one gets from a "criterion-referenced system" can be used without translation or processing.

---

[1] Procedures for documenting a child's progress by team consensus, using the Developmental Therapy Objectives Rating Form, are described in Chapter 2.

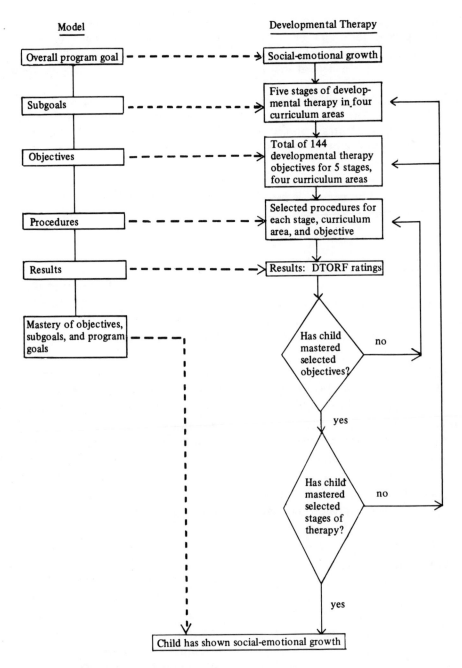

Figure 1. A model for determining treatment effectiveness, using a criterion-referenced system applied to Developmental Therapy.

does not attempt to imply that one emotionally disturbed child will progress exactly like another, nor that from one group you can predict how another group of similar children might progress. The important thing Developmental Therapy can do is document the progress an individual child makes. It can also document regression or periods of no progress. It will answer the question, "Is that child progressing toward his program goal?" This question can be answered at anytime during his participation in Developmental Therapy. Therefore, treatment effectiveness can be monitored on a continuing basis and is not limited to the point of termination.

This leads to the important question of how you determine when a child is ready to be terminated from Developmental Therapy. The decision to terminate is not based solely on the number of objectives mastered nor the number of stages accomplished. Termination is defined as a consensus decision by center staff, parents, and school personnel that a child has made the necessary progress and no longer needs the specialized services offered by the center in order to continue to progress in social-emotional growth. The information needed to make such a decision cannot be put into quantifiable terms. You might speculate that the number of objectives mastered or the number of stages accomplished would indicate when to terminate. This information would be of major importance, of course, but not sufficient. There are many other complex factors, such as:

Expectations of the child's family
Expectations of his school
Chronological age as related to developmental stage
Age at time of entry
Age at time of onset of problems(s)
Type and severity of problem(s)
Prior experiences
Prior developmental maturation
Intellectual potential
Current intellectual functioning
Neuromuscular functioning
Self confidence
Family capabilities
School (teacher's) capabilities
Availability of community support services

Not all of these factors are of equal importance in a termination decision. They will vary in significance with each child. Consider a four-year-old schizophrenic child with neurological damage and no speech (a Stage One child). With a responsive, willing family this child might have a short stay in Developmental Therapy. On the other hand, another Stage One four-year-old with less serious impairments but a disintegrating family situation may spend a longer time because his family cannot provide for his continuing social-emotional growth independent of center services. In the process, however, such a child might be expected to master a greater number of objectives in Stages One and Two than the first child. Consider also an eight-year-old autistic child in this same Stage One group. His progress in mastering each of the Stage One objectives might be so slow that he would spend twice as long on each objective. He might not have progressed far into Stage Two objectives when he reaches a point where he can participate in a community day training program. Termination is appropriate if he will continue to progress when he leaves Developmental Therapy for the day program.

The important point in these illustrations is that each child has a unique combination of skills, deficits, potential, family conditions, and community and school resources. The decision that he no longer needs highly specialized service in order to continue to mature is indeed complex. It does not imply that a child is perfectly normal at termination. Nor does it imply that his family can forget his special needs. The decision to terminate does mean that a child has mastered a sufficient number of developmental objectives to provide him with the personal resources to meet the demands of his home and school. It is clear that his

Termination is not viewed as a point of "recovery" but the point at which progress can be continued elsewhere without the center's intervention.

The effectiveness of the termination process depends upon the consistent consideration of all key factors in arriving at a particular decision.

family and school will play the significant role in the success of his post-termination experiences. For this reason, they must be included in the decision-making process and be willing to assume responsibility for the child's continuing progress.

The Developmental Therapy objectives are the basis of the criterion-referenced system.

As you review this approach to verifying treatment effectiveness, you see that the major documentation of a child's treatment progress comes from the Developmental Therapy objectives (see Appendix). For this reason considerable time and effort was expended on their construction. These procedures are described in the following section.

CONSTRUCTING THE DEVELOPMENTAL THERAPY CURRICULUM OBJECTIVES

During the period from 1964 until 1970, a structure was derived for Developmental Therapy based on the four curriculum areas of behavior, communication, socialization, and (pre)academics. Four stages within each of the curriculum areas were also derived, thus forming the basic curriculum schema. This early model was based on developmental research data, constructs about the nature of emotional disturbance and maturation process, and five years of clinical implementation with emotionally disturbed children. A general goal and subgoal statement were established for each of the stages within each of the curriculum areas. These subgoals were significant as a starting point, but they did not provide the specificity needed for guiding teachers in planning individual programs, nor were they detailed enough for determining treatment effectiveness.

These criteria were determined by an interdisciplinary team representing all program components.

The multiprofessional team at Rutland Center recognized that further specification of the model was necessary and that considerable effort should be put into identifying a sequence of measurable objectives for each stage within each curriculum area. There were no limits placed on the number of objectives to be provided, but certain criteria were established as guidelines.

1. The objectives must be broad enough to incorporate a variety of needs, yet specific enough to document accomplishment, recognizing that an objective cannot be constructed for every problem which might occur and that all behavior relevant to therapy cannot be anticipated.

2. The wording of the objectives must be in terms of desired outcomes, reflecting the mastery of normal developmental milestones rather than the elimination of deficits.

3. The content of the objectives must be inclusive for the population to be served; that is, they must be adequate for the program needs of any emotionally disturbed child between the ages of three and 14 years.

4. There must be a logical consistency among objectives, subgoals, and goals so that each is related, in a network of developmental constructs.

5. There must be a consistency in terminology among objectives, goals, and procedures so that these relationships can be easily grasped by persons with many different professional backgrounds.

6. The objectives must offer a system of priorities, to assist treatment teams in determining the order in which objectives should be selected.

7. The objectives must clearly lead to procedures which can be implemented by treatment teams.

8. The objectives must be related to a system for documenting a child's developmental stage at entry point and at

regular intervals of time during the treatment process.

9. The objectives must permit flexibility for implementing each child's program in ways uniquely suited to his own needs.

10. The objectives should permit the expression of individual skills of those responsible for implementing the program.

Thus, the objectives were to be a reasonable compromise between highly detailed behavioral objectives and the general goals already defined. The first version of the objectives was completed in December 1970, and was implemented on a trial basis during the winter of 1971. This first draft included 116 measurably stated objectives sequenced within the four areas of the curriculum. The objectives were designed to represent a sequence of significant developmental milestones, thereby allowing for assessment of progress at key points during the therapeutic process. They were specific enough to allow for evaluation, but were not so specific as to reduce the flexibility of the teachers in planning and implementing programs for individual children. In fact, the objectives actually seemed to facilitate the program planning aspect of therapy.

These initial objectives were used for six months, and each staff member was requested to make note of objectives which seemed to be sequentially out of order, were not clearly worded, or did not seem to be developmentally significant. They were asked also to note any problems they had in using the objectives. The staff included educational therapists (special educators), social workers, psychologists, psychiatrists, paraprofessionals, and volunteers. Extensive comments were encouraged, inasmuch as the objectives were designed to

be used eventually by treatment personnel from a variety of professional backgrounds.

Based upon use and review by these staff members, the objectives were revised extensively in June 1971. This revised version seemed to be the best that could be produced at that point in time; and it was agreed the staff would use them for one year, again noticing objectives which caused difficulties in understanding or application. An added dimension to the testing of these revised objectives was their trial use at two other treatment centers located in Brunswick and Savannah, Georgia. Staff members at these centers agreed to participate in recording difficulties they encountered in using the objectives during the year.

The staff at Brunswick and Savannah were trained in the model. Its use in different locales provided a broad base for testing the effectiveness of the model under different conditions.

One year later, July 1972, the objectives were reconsidered along with the comments from the staff at the three centers. The objectives were revised once again in terms of order, clarity, need, and significance as milestones of development. If a staff person felt that an objective was out of sequence or had some element which lacked clarity, it would be discussed at a general staff meeting. Often a particular objective would be reworked until the wording and implications brought consensus from the group. One significant comment suggested the need for specific examples of achievement of each objective. This was critical, the staff felt, to the utilization of the objectives in locations other than at Rutland Center, where most of the staff had been trained. The results of this revision were also significant. Some objectives were deleted, some added, some modified, and some reordered. The result was 144 objectives. The revisions were primarily within particular stages and areas; thus, the major sequences of stages in the original model remained

The teachers indicated that the objectives facilitated their program planning efforts, giving direction to their planning and freeing them to concentrate on methods of implementing the objectives.

unchanged. However, this revision did establish a fifth stage, as the original Stage Three was divided into Stages Three and Four and the original Stage Four became Stage Five.

During the following year, staff at the Rutland, Brunswick and Savannah centers and at a fourth center in Carrollton, Georgia, were asked to use the revised set of objectives and record actual examples of mastery of each objective. In addition, they were asked to continue their criticism of the objectives for order, clarity, and appropriateness. Additionally, a statistical analysis of the hierarchy of the objectives was conducted during the year. The results indicated only a few objectives out of sequence, and this information corroborated staff comments concerning the same objectives.

Adding the staff of a fourth center further increased the base for pilot testing.

There were several internal checks on this validation process. All developmental ratings were reviewed and verified by the senior person at each center. The objectives were used and reviewed by clinically competent staff from child psychiatry, psychology, social work and special education. And finally, there was an open forum for communication among those using the objectives at all four centers so that the final product represented a consensus.

Again, in the summer of 1973, modifications of the objectives were considered. However, there were few changes this time. On the basis of both professional judgment and the statistical analysis, the content was judged to represent significant developmental milestones. The sequential nature of the objectives was basically consistent, and the objectives were clear. The emphasis for this final revision was on the addition of appropriate examples illustrating the achievement of each objective.

Thus, the validation process for the objectives is at a basic point of completion. More than 50 staff members with various professional backgrounds, at four treatment centers in different geographic locations, have used the objectives with more than 625 emotionally disturbed children between the ages of three and 14 years. As a result of this work, the content of the developmental objectives, their order, clarity, appropriateness, and examples are judged to be highly relevant to rehabilitation of emotionally disturbed children.

DEVELOPING THE METHODS AND MATERIALS

During the three years of development (1970 to 1973) all center staff were given continual, intensive training in the theory and therapeutic methods of Developmental Therapy (Wood, 1971). It was of utmost importance that accurate translations were made between Developmental Therapy theory, objectives, and classroom practices. In order to keep classroom practices closely tuned to the theoretical model, an observation and information feedback system was used, in which treatment teams developed classroom procedures which observers recorded. These observations were reviewed in light of the theoretical aspects of Developmental Therapy and were disseminated to all staff for further field trial, with modifications when indicated. Eventually, the procedures were either incorporated into a growing reservoir of effective methods or were discarded.

Three separate field validation studies were conducted to verify these practices and procedures for Developmental Therapy. The first study was conducted during 10 weeks in the winter of 1971; the second study, during the spring, 1971; and the third was conducted a year later, in the spring of 1972. The processes used to gather curriculum information for all three studies were the same.

During the first study, four preschool classes were used (one class of Stages One and Two children and two classes of Stage Three children). In the second study, 11 classes were used, including school age children of all developmental stages and ages. In the final study there were 11 classes again: one Stage One class, two Stage Two classes, seven Stage Three classes, and one Stage Four class.

Two persons were assigned as observers. They were both skilled in Developmental Therapy, and one was also responsible for a large part of staff training. In their observations they were to note, in detail, specific aspects of each class: the use of the objectives, teachers' roles, techniques, materials, and activities. It was recognized that, although a number of children in each stage might be working on the same objectives, different techniques might be needed. It was also assumed that techniques and materials would be modified for the unique need of each developmental stage.

The questions to be answered by the studies were these:

1. Were treatment teams using the specific Developmental Therapy objectives prescribed for each child as the basis for selecting activities, materials, and techniques?
2. Were treatment teams using activities, materials, and techniques which reflected the general goal and needs of children as described in the model at each stage of Developmental Therapy?
3. What was the range and pattern of Developmental Therapy objectives found in classrooms designated for particular stages of therapy?

4. What activities, materials, and techniques were used at all stages of Developmental Therapy?
5. What activities, materials, and techniques were unique to specific stages of Developmental Therapy?

The final purpose of the studies was to compile, for each of the objectives, a representative sample of successful activities, materials, and techniques which could be used by others to implement the Developmental Therapy treatment model.

An information sheet was prepared for making classroom observations and recording teacher comments. A sample is included as Figure 2. After the information was obtained by an observer through a one-way mirror, the treatment team and the observer met to discuss the criteria used in selection, the general goal for the activity, each child's needs, and specific Developmental Therapy objectives for meeting these needs. The final step was to verify that the observed activities were appropriate for the children in the group according to each child's Developmental Therapy Objectives Rating Form (DTORF). To do this, all of the individual DTORF's were grouped by class and were charted by curriculum area. These summaries were compared with the observation sheets, and where discrepancies in practice occurred, adjustments were made. With each of the three studies, these procedures were used for each activity in every class, twice a week for a 10-week period.

The results of the three studies verified that the objectives were being used as the basis for program planning and for the selection of materials, methods, and activities. It was evident also that selected materials and activities reflected the needs of children at each stage. Several generalizations from the studies have be-

The accuracy of the studies t verify procedures used in Deve opmental Therapy depende upon:

1. The skill of the observers viewing classroom procedures light of the objectives.
2. The feedback between teac ers and observers to refine pra tices.
3. Continued staff training to r late practice and theory.

come a significant part of the Developmental Therapy curriculum:

1. Many different objectives can be used in each activity.
2. Individual objectives can be used in the group setting.
3. There are certain materials, activities, and methods which can be used at all stages. However, the way in which they are used must be modified for the developmental needs of each stage.
4. There are materials, activities and methods which should be used only at a particular stage. If used with children at the preceding or the following stages the procedures seem to be ineffective or detrimental.
5. The objectives are used on a continuum in each class with an overlap between stages. For example, in Stage One, objectives for Stages One and Two are used. Children in a Stage Two class will be working on a few objectives in Stage One and a few objectives in Stage Three; however, the bulk of the objectives will be at Stage Two. In beginning Stage Three classes both Stage Two and Three

Figure 2. Sample observation sheet.

Scheduled activity	Special equipment and materials	Teacher techniques	Developmental Therapy objectives used as criteria for selection of activity and techniques
Stage I Play time	Combination slide and jungle gym	The teacher moves the child's body into position and uses touch to encourage child to try.	B-3, B-4, B-6; A-13; S-4
	Books with texture	Teacher moves child's hand across book for sensory stimulation.	B-1, B-2; C-2
	Snap blocks to jump into	Teacher performs first, as model, then encourages activity with emphasis on verbalization (about activity).	B-3, B-4, B-11; S-4; A-6
	Trucks, dolls, animal blocks	There is encouragement to name object as pupil puts animals and dolls in truck.	C-5, C-7, C-9, C-11; B-6, B-8, B-11
	Hammer and peg set	A variety of techniques are used here: 1. Child is led to perform a simple skill which requires both attention and coordination.	B-1, B-2, B-6; S-5; A-5, A-13
		2. Child is asked to name colors of pegs.	A-15; C-3
		3. Toy was attractive to two pupils, so they are encouraged in awareness of each other by teacher's modeling of interactive play and controlled vocabulary.	S-4; C-2
	Open-top dollhouse (with ethnic dolls)	Teacher establishes the play situation simulating real, everyday experiences and activities at home;	B-6, B-8; S-4, S-5
		teacher verbalizes pretend activities encouraging pupil to name the experience and recreate the order of the day.	A-10, A-12; B-7, B-11

(Continued)

Figure 2., *continued*

Scheduled activity	Special equipment and materials	Teacher techniques	Developmental Therapy objectives used as criteria for selection of activity and techniques
Stage II			
Work time	Individual work folders (teacher-made work sheets) for visual-motor skills: eye-hand coordination writing first name matching shapes matching colors	1. Children given folders and proceed to do each sheet or task at individual pace.	B-10, B-12; S-13
		2. Individual instruction is provided from teachers as needed.	S-14; C-11, C-12
		3. Feedback sessions from teachers are given as needed.	C-14, C-19
	Magnet and metal cubes	1. Each child is given a set of cubes (5 or 10) and a magnet to use independently, after work folder is complete.	A-23, A-30, A-32, A-42
		2. Teacher asks, "How many do you have? Get —— more. How many do you have now?"	B-10, B-12; C-12, C-16
		3. When teacher gets two children using magnets together, more objectives are used.	S-13, S-15, S-19; C-12, C-13, C-16

objectives are used; Stage Three classes which have been ongoing will be working chiefly on objectives in Stage Three with an occasional Stage Four objective. Stage Four classes include high Stage Three objectives as well as those for Stage Four.

The idea of a gradual developmental progression through the stages is illustrated in Figures 3 through 6. These graphs summarize the developmental stages of 135 children at the time they entered Developmental Therapy. Fairly consistent patterns emerge by considering the proportion of objectives which, in each of the four curriculum areas, each group had mastered at the entry stage and at the stages immediately above and below the entry stage. For example, in Figure 3, between 45 to 75 percent of the objectives of the entry stage seem to be mastered at time of entry. At the stage immediately below entry stage, between 90 and 100 percent of the objectives have been mastered. While at the stage immediately above entry stage, from 2 to 25 percent of the objectives have been mastered. These findings apply to all of the groups, Stages One, Two, Three, and Four, in all four curriculum areas, Behavior, Communication, Socialization, and (Pre)-Academics.

The final results of the studies, a compilation of methods, are contained as Chapters 4 and 5 of this text. In these chapters specific activities, materials, and teacher techniques are described with particular reference to their application from one stage to another.

The data are grouped by stage at entry and reveal distinctly different proportions of objectives mastered, among the four stages

Proportion of objectives =

$$\frac{\textit{Number of objectives mastered at Stage X in area}}{\textit{Number of objectives of Stage X in area}}$$

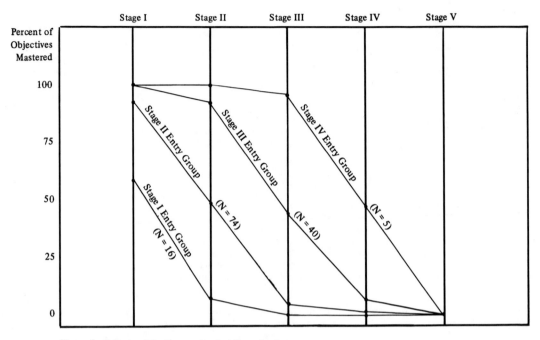

Figures 3. Behavior objectives mastered at time of entry.

DESCRIPTION OF CHILDREN RECEIVING DEVELOPMENTAL THERAPY

The previous review is basic to the confidence and understanding you have in using Developmental Therapy. But you also need to know about the children with whom these procedures were developed. This information may help you to judge whether or not Developmental Therapy has applications to the children you teach. Developmental Therapy was

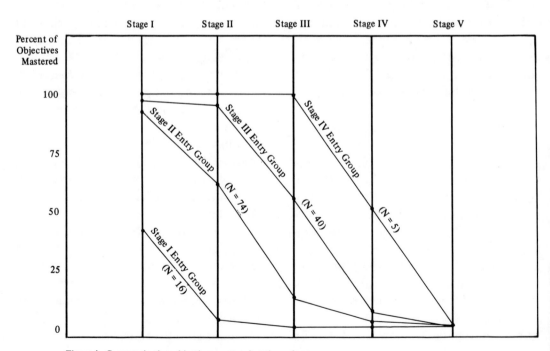

Figure 4. Communication objectives mastered at time of entry.

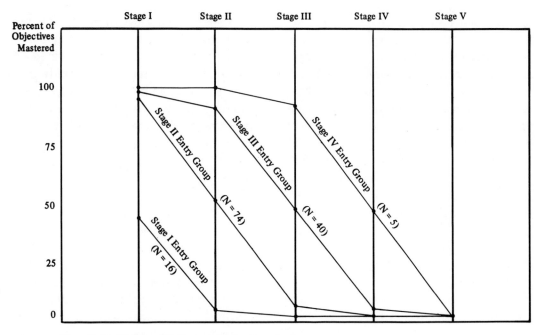

Figure 5. Socialization objectives mastered at time of entry.

formulated at the Rutland Center in Athens, Georgia. The center serves a southern, urban/rural population area of 50,000 people with approximately 15,000 preschool and school age children to age 14. Children between the ages of two and 14 years are eligible for services. Information about the center's program is disseminated in the community by newspaper articles, radio talks, and staff visits to private and public schools, day care centers, nursery

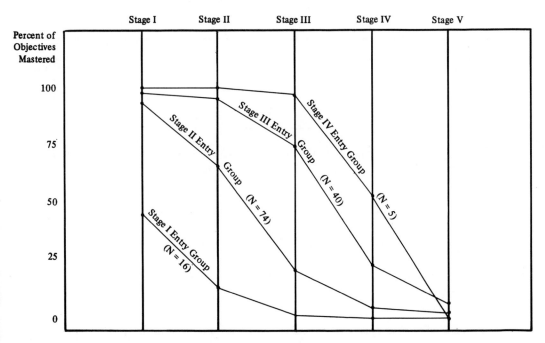

Figure 6. (Pre)academic objectives mastered at time of entry.

schools, and kindergartens. Communications with other professionals including psychologists, psychiatrists, social workers, child care workers, and teachers are actively pursued. According to the center's brochure, the program serves children with severe emotional or behavioral problems. The brochure also reports that the program cannot serve the retarded, blind, crippled, or chronically ill child. Two other restrictions used to limit referrals are: (a) availability of an alternative resource better suited to the child's needs; and (b) minor problems which can be corrected through home or school consultation.

Restrictions on types of problems accepted applied only if there was no evidence of emotional disturbance.

Because of the several major revisions in the objectives, it is not possible to provide consistent descriptions of children receiving Developmental Therapy before 1972. However, since the autumn of that year the objectives have not been substantially modified. At the time of this writing, 75 children, beginning treatment since that time, have completed their Developmental Therapy programs and have been terminated according to the procedures described earlier in this chapter. These children are used to illustrate how the Developmental Therapy process works and how they progressed with the objectives from the time they entered until they terminated.

Testing Process

Upon entry, the children received individual psychological and educational testing, and a parent interview was obtained (Figure 7). In addition, some children were seen by the child psychiatrist at the request of the psychologist, educational diagnostician, social worker, or parent. Ordinarily, such a request was made when the possibility of neurological impairment or psychosis was suspected, or when there was indication of extreme restlessness, inattentiveness, or hyperactivity.

Information from parents and (pre)-

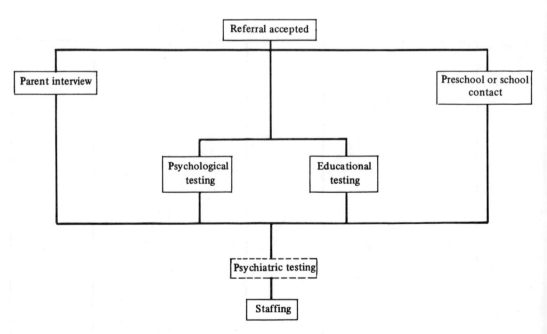

Figure 7.   The testing process.

school teacher, and observations of the child in his regular school setting also were obtained. A composite description of the child's problems and resources was established in each of the four major areas of Developmental Therapy: behavior, communication, socialization, and (pre)academics. The Referral Form Checklist (RFCL)[2] was completed independently by parent, teacher, and center staff. Psychological, psychiatric, and educational assessments; the RFCL summaries; and the parent interview report were used to arrive at the composite picture.

Not all children were given the same tests. However, a battery was prepared from which specific tests were drawn when appropriate for a particular child. The educational battery included the following:

Peabody Picture Vocabulary Test
Gesell Developmental Schedule
Ilg and Ames School Readiness Tests
Petersen School Readiness
Goodenough Draw-A-Person
Durell Analysis of Reading Difficulty (oral, silent, listening, word recognition subtests)
Ross Arithmetic Inventory of Key Math Diagnostic Arithmetic Test
Informal tests for dominance, gross and fine motor skills, eye-hand coordination and visual perceptual skills

The psychological test battery included:

Bender Gestalt Test
Stanford-Binet Intelligence Scale
Wechsler Intelligence Scale for Children (WISC)
Wechsler Preschool and Primary Scale of Intelligence (WPPSI)
Draw-a-Person
Draw-a-Family
Sentence Completion (oral)
Thematic Apperception Test (TAT)
Children's Apperception Test (CAT)
Rorschach Tests

In general, the test results were not adequate. Often a child could not concentrate, sit still, or attend. Many could not, or would not, respond verbally or nonverbally. They appeared disorganized and exhibited a wide range of severe problem behaviors. Furthermore, individual testing sessions revealed little of a child's socialization and communication skills needed for group participation. The psychological reports generally concluded that derived intelligence test scores were "depressed by emotional disturbance." A number of the children could not be tested in any standardized way. However, estimates of current developmental functioning were obtained, either through formal or informal assessment, for all of the children.

When reviewing testing results and family interview information, the center staff asked two major questions: (a) what is needed to assist this child in mastery of developmental skills needed for more successful coping in his home and school environments?, and (b) how can this assistance best be obtained?

Specifically, the staff arrived at a series of recommendations for each child, which included the following:

1. General recommendations for long term goals particularly related to developmental expectations and probable stage of Developmental Therapy necessary for termination.
2. Placement according to current stage of Developmental Therapy in each of the

Severely emotionally disturbed children represent approximately 0.5 percent of the total child population. This is the group which is generally the most difficult to assess.

---

[2] The Referral Form Checklist has a five-point rating procedure for identifying high to low priority problems (Wood, 1972, pp. A-14ff.)

four areas of behavior, communication, socialization, and (pre)academics.

3. Specific recommendations regarding current skills and problems and points of entry for therapeutic intervention.

4. Specific recommendations regarding methods, materials, and experiences needed.

5. Recommendations for type and amount of parent involvement.

6. Recommendations for type and amount of (pre)school involvement.

Following this staff review, a parent planning conference was held to report testing results and recommendations and to plan with parents ways to implement recommendations at home, school, and center.

Characteristics of the Children

These 75 children were enrolled during the period from 1972 to 1974. There were 47 boys and 28 girls; 48 were white and 27 black. The average age of the children at entry was 8.7 years, ranging from 4.9 to 12.7 years. Their average length of treatment was 23.9 weeks with a range from 10 to 60 weeks.

While these descriptions convey a picture of how the children could be described as a group, there were also great individual differences. This group contained boys and girls of many ages, both black and white, with a variety of high priority problems and prior educational experiences. They were referred by a variety of people or agencies, and they were both with and without previous treatment. Their families were both intact and split; some parents were highly educated, and some were not educated at all.

Fifty-two percent of the children were referred by teachers and 20% by parents, although referrals were received

No autistic children were in this group of terminated children. However, two autistic children received Developmental Therapy and were terminated before 1972. Five others are currently enrolled.

from a number of other sources. All of the children attended some type of educational program including nurseries, day care centers, preschools, grades 1 through 8, or special education classes. Seventy-five percent of the children had received no previous service.

In general, the children were members of intact families (57%), and 71% of the parents had at least one year of high school. Fifty-three percent of the parents had a combined annual income of $5,000 or more. There were close to three children per family, with the referred child's position among his siblings usually second of the three.

Clinical Diagnosis

Although clinical, diagnostic categories were not used by the staff in program planning, an attempt was made to establish a tentative primary diagnosis. Any number of secondary diagnoses could be included for purposes of description and communication with other professionals. No one standard nomenclature system was viewed as adequate because the staff had different professional backgrounds. A combination of several classification systems was finally compiled. The procedures required agreement among the participating staff concerning the primary and secondary problems of each child from the clinical viewpoint.

Table 1 shows the number and type of primary and secondary diagnoses for these children. In this table a child has only one primary classification but any number of secondary characteristics. The diagnostic summary suggests that clinical diagnosis and classification of young children usually involves a number of problem areas. In fact, as a group these children could be considered multihandicapped.

Table 1. Frequency of Primary and Secondary Diagnosis For 75 Children at Time of Entry[a]

Diagnosis	Primary	Secondary (confirmed or presumptive)
Reactive disorder		
Undifferentiated	28	7
Aggressive/hostile	10	5
Separation anxiety	0	1
Delayed emotional development	8	6
Neurological impairment	7	10
Severe socioeconomic deprivation	7	13
Childhood schizophrenia	4	0
Mental retardation	3	4
Obsessive-compulsive	2	1
Learning disability	2	12
Inadequate personality	2	1
Internalized neurotic	1	0
Hearing loss	1	0
Visual impairment	0	1
Aphasia	0	3
Character disorder	0	1

[a]Each child has only one primary diagnosis but may have any number of secondary diagnoses. Twenty-two children had no secondary diagnoses.

An additional rating, by agreement of the staff, was used to record overall severity of the child's problem on a rating scale from one to five (mild to severe). A majority of these children received overall ratings of moderately to severely disturbed.

Specific Referral Problems

Problems of these children as seen by their parents and classroom teachers at the time of referral revealed a wide range of specific, urgent problems. Using the Referral Form Checklist, parents and teachers independently rated each child. Of 54 possible referral problems, all problems were identified as a high priority problem at least once. Eleven of these problems were rated as high priority problems by at least 50% of the raters, indicating that some problems occurred consistently with more than half of the children. However, parents and teachers often identified different problems as high priority. Table 2 lists these problems.

A majority of parents were concerned with six problems:

Short attention span
Distractible
Restless
Easily frustrated
Demands excessive attention
Resistant to discipline

As a group the parents did not identify any problems of socialization, communi-

Although the children were considered multihandicapped, their primary problems were emotional.

Table 2. Percentage of Problems Identified in at Least Half of the Children at Time of Referral

Referral Form Checklist (54 Possible Items)	Parent (n = 73)	Teacher (n = 68)
Short attention span	51	62
Distractable	53	74
Restless, overactive	58	59
Easily frustrated	59	–
Demands excessive attention	55	59
Resistant to discipline	55	54
Apathetic	–	56
Does not follow directions	–	57
Does not complete task	–	66
Immature	–	53
Difficulty expressing feelings	–	51

cation, or academics as high priority in 50% or more of their ratings.

Using the same instrument, classroom teachers identified 10 problems to be of greatest concern to them in 50% or more of their ratings:

Immature
Short attention span
Distractible
Does not complete task
Restless
Demands excessive attention
Apathetic
Does not follow directions
Difficulty expressing feelings
Resistant to discipline

In short, the composite picture of high priority problems of these children as perceived by parents and teachers included problems for which there was agreement and problems which would not have been identified if only parents or teachers rated the children.

The Therapeutic Program

At the time of enrollment in the program, each child was placed in a therapeutic classroom with other children of corresponding developmental stage. Secondary criteria used for placement were: age, sex, race, type of problem, amount of physical intervention required, and socioeconomic background. Class groups were kept to a maximum of seven children, and all children were served only in groups.

Of these 75 children, eight began the program in a Stage One class; 33 began in Stage Two classes; 30, in Stage Three classes; and four in Stage Four classes.

Each therapeutic class met the number of days per week and hours per day suggested by the Developmental Therapy model (see Chapter 1). Each class had a lead teacher with a master's degree in Education of Emotionally Disturbed Children, and a support teacher who was a high school graduate, volunteer, or graduate student in training. The third member of each treatment team, the monitor, was a professionally trained parent worker, usually a social worker. The treatment teams received preservice and weekly inservice training in Developmental Therapy throughout the year.

All parents (or parent substitute) participated in some type of program with the treatment teams. These programs ranged from a minimum of two meetings with the parents of one child (the initial intake conference and the final termination conference) to a maximum of 71 contacts with the parents of another child (see also Wood, 1972, chap. 7).

THE PROGRESS OF THE CHILDREN

The DTORF was used, according to procedures contained in Chapter 2, to record the progress of each child in mastering selected developmental objectives. Because these 75 children had varying entry points, termination times, and length of treatment, their progress cannot be reported as a group over standard time intervals. However, review of each child's DTORF indicated that each had mastered Developmental Therapy objectives to the point that termination was judged to be appropriate.

Since 75 individual DTORF's would be difficult to append to this text in their entirety, they have been summarized to show percentages of gains made for each stage of therapy from entry to termination. Tables 3 through 6 contain these summarized results, grouped according to the children's entry stages. Developmental stage at entry seems to

be an important factor in the number of objectives mastered and stages accomplished by the time of termination. In general, the children achieved the greatest portion of objectives in the stage at which they entered and in the stage directly following entry stage. For example, children entering at Stage One made their greatest gains in Stages One and Two, while children entering at Stage Two gained predominantly in Stages Two and Three. About 80% of the entry stage objectives and between 10 and 50 percent of the objectives in the next stage were mastered by the time of termination. More than 95 percent of the objectives for the stages below entry stages were mastered and little regression was noted. The developmental progression of the stages and objectives is re-

The DTORF data for these 75 terminated children are reported from entry to termination, thus providing a pre–post measure of gain or loss.

Table 3. Progress of Stage I Children (N = 8) From Entry to Termination[a]

Area of Developmental Therapy	Percentage of Stage I objectives mastered	Percentage of Stage II objectives mastered	Percentage of Stage III objectives mastered	Percentage of Stage IV objectives mastered
Behavior				
Pre	73.3	15.0		
Post	89.3	47.5		
Net gain or loss	+16.00	+32.5		
Communication				
Pre	39.3			
Post	75.0	28.3		
Net gain or loss	+35.7	+28.3		
Socialization				
Pre	52.8	3.1		
Post	78.4	43.3	2.1	
Net gain or loss	+25.6	+40.2	+2.1	
(Pre)Academics				
Pre	55.5	7.1		
Post	83.0	46.5	1.5	
Net gain or loss	+27.5	+39.4	+1.5	

[a] Average treatment time, 22.5 weeks; range, 10–30 weeks.

Table 4. Progress of Stage II Children (N = 33) From Entry to Termination[a]

Area of Developmental Therapy	Percentage of Stage I objectives mastered	Percentage of Stage II objectives mastered	Percentage of Stage III objectives mastered	Percentage of Stage IV objectives mastered
Behavior				
Pre	97.4	52.7	7.8	1.0
Post	99.6	75.8	37.2	6.1
Net gain or loss	+2.2	+23.1	+29.4	+5.1
Communication				
Pre	94.0	53.5	13.0	
Post	95.7	81.1	41.9	7.3
Net gain or loss	+1.7	+27.6	+28.9	+7.3
Socialization				
Pre	93.3	60.2	9.8	
Post	98.2	84.7	34.8	4.0
Net gain or loss	+4.9	+24.5	+25.0	+4.0
(Pre)Academics				
Pre	96.2	66.7	18.0	1.5
Post	99.7	86.0	50.5	11.4
Net gain or loss	+3.5	+19.3	+32.5	+9.9

[a] Average treatment time, 27.3 weeks; range, 10–60 weeks.

The DTORF data in Tables 3–6 are grouped by stage at entry, thus showing the progress of children who began treatment at the same stage and subsequently completed treatment.

flected in every area across the stages. This is a construct essential to Developmental Therapy. Examination of the progress of the groups, by entry stage, reveals how this gradual progression reflects the unique characteristics of each stage.

Children Who Entered at Stage One

At the time of entry, the least developed area was communication. By termination the greatest gains had been made with the communication objectives, yet this area still lagged behind the other three areas in proportion to the total objectives to be mastered.

In contrast, more than half of the Stage One behavior objectives had been mastered by these children prior to entry. At termination, behavior was still the area with the greatest proportion mastered. In fact, the same relative position of all the areas to each other remained the same. At entry, the areas, in ascending order of proportion of objectives mastered, were communication, socialization, (pre)academics, and behavior. At termination, with gains in every area, the relative position remained the same. This finding is not surprising when you consider the type of child entering at Stage One. Lack of ability to use words in any meaningful way is typical. It would be an oversimplification, however, to conclude that Stage One children therefore might be functionally retarded. Consider the pattern of (pre)-academic and socialization objectives mastered by this group. By termination, they had achieved close to half of the objectives in these two areas at the stage above their entry stage and even a small proportion of the objectives at Stage Three.

Children Who Entered at Stage Two
The proportion of objectives mastered in the stage immediately below entry stage was above 93 percent in all four curriculum areas. At the entry stage, the least developed areas were behavior and communication. By termination, more than three fourths of these objectives had been achieved, with the greatest gains being in communication. As with the Stage One group, the relative position of the four curriculum areas remained the same at time of termination, even with the gains made. At termination, in ascending order of proportion of

objectives mastered, the areas were behavior, communication, socialization, and (pre)academics. This pattern follows the theoretical model of Developmental Therapy in which each of these areas draws upon the basic skills of the preceding area. It also supports the contention that Stage Two children have some communication ability and are generally having their greatest difficulties with behavior as they move out to explore and test their environment.

Children Who Entered at Stage Three
Virtually all of the objectives for Stages One and Two had been mastered by the Stage Three children at time of entry. At entry stage, the least developed area was socialization and the area of greatest development was academics. At

Table 5. Progress of Stage III Children (N = 30) From Entry to Termination[a]

Area of Developmental Therapy	Percentage of Stage I objectives mastered	Percentage of Stage II objectives mastered	Percentage of Stage III objectives mastered	Percentage of Stage IV objectives mastered	Percentage of Stage V objectives mastered
Behavior					
Pre	100.0	96.0	47.1	8.8	
Post	100.0	97.3	71.6	20.5	
Net gain or loss	0.0	+1.3	+24.5	+11.7	
Communication					
Pre	99.5	96.1	51.8	5.0	
Post	100.0	100.0	77.6	9.8	
Net gain or loss	+0.5	+3.9	+25.8	+4.8	
Socialization					
Pre	99.2	95.8	45.8	3.7	
Post	100.0	98.1	68.8	14.5	
Net gain or loss	+0.8	+2.3	+23.0	+10.8	
(Pre)Academics					
Pre	100.0	97.9	74.3	24.0	3.6
Post	100.0	99.5	91.2	44.3	4.2
Net gain or loss	0.0	+1.6	+16.9	+20.3	+0.6

[a] Average treatment time, 20.7 weeks; range, 10–40 weeks.

Table 6. Progress of Stage IV Children (N = 4) From Entry to Termination[a]

Area of Developmental Therapy	Percentage of Stage I objectives mastered	Percentage of Stage II objectives mastered	Percentage of Stage III objectives mastered	Percentage of Stage IV objectives mastered
Behavior				
Pre	100.0	100.0	93.0	41.8
Post	100.0	100.0	100.0	41.5
Net gain or loss	0.0	0.0	+7.0	−0.3
Communication				
Pre	100.0	100.0	100.0	52.8
Post	100.0	100.0	97.0	41.5
Net gain or loss	0.0	0.0	−3.0	−11.3
Socialization				
Pre	100.0	100.0	89.3	50.0
Post	100.0	100.0	96.5	24.0
Net gain or loss	0.0	0.0	+7.2	−26.0
(Pre)Academics				
Pre	100.0	100.0	97.5	47.0
Post	100.0	100.0	100.0	68.8
Net gain or loss	0.0	0.0	+2.5	+21.8

[a]Average treatment time, 22.5 weeks; range, 10–30 weeks.

termination, the same relative order existed even though socialization gains were considerable. This finding substantiates the need for program emphasis on the group process during Stage Three. This is the stage in which children are expected to have the necessary prerequisite communication skills and self confidence to begin learning skills for effective group functioning.

It is interesting to note that this group made a slightly greater gain in Stage Four academic objectives than with Stage Three academic objectives. In contrast, in the other three areas generally twice as many gains were made in Stage Three objectives as in Stage Four. The proportion of objectives mastered in academics at Stage Three (91.2) is the greatest among all of the areas, for all of the entry groups. This finding is somewhat surprising, considering that the area of academics does not receive major emphasis in Developmental Therapy. The type of academic objectives for Stage Three includes basic skills for reading, arithmetic, and communication, incorporated into group projects and games.

Children Who Entered at Stage Four
The number of children who entered Developmental Therapy at Stage Four is too small to warrant meaningful review. However, the results are included because they suggest a trend which has concerned those who have worked with entering Stage Four children—that is, regression.

Only five children have entered the program at Stage Four in two years. In each instance they have been bright children about 12 years of age. In most instances they had emotionally unhealthy home situations and unresponsive school surroundings. In discussions about the regression recorded for these few children, their treatment team voiced a number of concerns: (a) that the children might have been too old for Developmental Therapy; (b) that they might not have been in need of such a specialized program away from peers; or (c) that they had developed a high level of verbal sophistication which mislead the treatment team rating them for developmental objectives at time of entry.

Any one or all of these factors may have been at work; or possibly the small number has presented a unique sample. In any case, the results suggest that careful consideration should be given before entering a child at Stage Four.

LITERATURE CITED

Wood, M. M. 1971. Rutland Center Training during the Planning Year. University of Texas Staff Training Prototype Series. Vol. 10, no. 10. Austin, Texas.

Wood, M. M. (ed.). 1972. The Rutland Center Model for Treating Emotionally Disturbed Children. 2nd Ed. Rutland Center Technical Assistance Office, Athens, Ga.

chapter 4

HELPING CHILDREN GROW WITH MATERIALS AND ACTIVITIES

Mary Margaret Wood

Talk Time

Work Time

Exercise Time

Play Time

Special Time

P. Mooney Time

Yum Yum Time

Surprise Time

Music Time

Story Time

Art Time

Muscle Time   **Outside Time**

INTRODUCTION

The children are making hand puppets. Tommy makes a tall cylinder puppet with angel wings and silk fringe hair. He calls her "Mother." He makes another puppet, a faceless creation, from an old sock with holes. This is "Father." While the other children are finishing their products, Tommy carries his puppets to the window sill. The father puppet spanks the mother puppet and imaginary children.

"Father has to spank the children and spanks and spanks and spanks and spanks . . . The children are put in jail but escape by climbing out. They go home and mother and father are put in jail . . . Mother stands at the bars and father escapes by climbing up mother. Then mother says, 'Oh, oh, I better jump out and escape too.'

Then the family gets back together on the boat. The boat is sinking . . . 'Help, help' . . . Mother is tall enough to escape and drags father out because he is holding on to the base of mother.

The boat is underwater . . . It's painted 'I love you' and all decorated fancy . . . but the paint washes off."

In the use of materials children find an expression for themselves. By involvement in an activity they may act out a portion of their life experience which can never be expressed in words. And most important, with materials and activities, children grow.

Is it any surprise that children prefer TO DO, than be DONE TO? . . . That they gravitate to activities and materials which permit them to influence and command?

MAINTAINING A DEVELOPMENTAL OUTLOOK

You are planning for a new group of children with serious emotional problems. During the intake process each child received a developmental assessment. This information is the basis for grouping the children in your class. They are all at the same approximate stage of development in each of the four curriculum areas of Developmental Therapy. Grouping by developmental skills narrows the scope of individual variation in a group considerably. But even so, each child has a uniquely different pattern of abilities and problems and a particular family situation and life style. Your task as a teacher/therapist is to begin a program which can attract each child in his present condition and then move him forward, step by step, through a series of developmental milestones. Remember, too, that this growth must be accomplished within the boundaries of family acceptance and cooperation.

Expect many obstacles along the way. When a disturbed child begins to learn new ways of doing things, he may be his own greatest deterrent to progress. The process of change is usually painful. More than likely he will resist at first. And if you are not careful you, yourself, may be his second greatest obstacle to growth. He may present a barrage of strange or offensive behaviors which keep you at a distance or make you unable to respond therapeutically.

When using Developmental Therapy, keep in mind that your task is to help the child master particular developmental skills. The materials and activities you select should reflect this. It may be harder than you imagined. You will find yourself beginning to work for the elimination of particularly bothersome behaviors. Sometimes you will hang on to the same old materials and activities only because you want to bring the child around to participating. When this happens, you may have shifted in your thinking from a growth model to a deficit model of intervention. With your major attention on problems you may be less sensitive to the child's strengths and to new signs of growth.

There are several other important considerations in planning materials and

Chapter 5 contains many discussions about the impact of a teacher on a changing child. In Chapter 6 there is a section on problems teachers have with themselves.

No matter what the activity is, it should be planned to cover as many objectives for the children as possible.

63

activities for Developmental Therapy. The end goal is the child's personal assimilation of each developmental milestone, free from the need for contrived rewards or external controls. Guard against underrating a child's capability. Don't generalize about his disability; many of the things he does will be perfectly normal. And often he will be able to respond to more complex tasks than you have expected of him. Keep in mind the importance of having a wide variety of exploratory activities geared to each child's developmental objectives. Be certain there will be successful outcomes. Intermittently validate your selection of materials by introducing something new and a bit more complicated. You may be surprised at the frequency with which children are ready for a new step forward.

As an aid in helping a child organize himself, designate certain areas of the room for specific activities so that the child has a change in physical environment when an activity changes. This allows for physical movement between activities with clear distinctions in the settings. In this way, a child learns what kind of behavior is expected and appropriate for each activity. For example, "We sit for juice and cookies at the table." But "We play in this area of the room." Physical boundaries in the therapeutic classroom also simulate the physical boundaries and changes present in the real world, where a child is required to sit and eat at a table but can play games in another area of the house.

Plan activities which are closely related to a child's everyday experiences. Intersperse experiences which require a great deal of physical activity with those requiring both verbal and nonverbal communication, eye-hand coordination, and fine motor skills. Provide for quiet times when feeling tones of caring can be shared. Keep alive the feeling that it is exciting to master something new. Let your activities and materials create new sources of pleasure for the child.

Materials and activities should be vehicles for therapeutic interactions among child, group, and teachers. When a child controls the group activity, becomes "engrossed" in materials, or retreats from involvement, precious time is lost. Your program might then be called "maintenance therapy." Be constantly sensitive to the possibility that materials or activities may stand between you and the child. Materials and activities should never become a means for a child to keep you at psychological distance or as a substitute for your own participation when you are not up to the demands of your role as a teacher/therapist.

PLANNING YOUR DEVELOPMENTAL THERAPY SESSIONS

In order to select materials and activities which are effective, it is important to have specific information about each child. Here is a sample of the type of information you will need to obtain.

About the Child:

What interests the child?
What are his skills?
What can he do on his own?
With what does he need your help?
What are the child's prior experiences and skills you are building upon?
What attracts him? Holds his attention?
How long does his attention last?
How many variations of a task can he stand?
What difficulties will one child have which might influence a successful outcome for himself or the group?

When to schedule old favorite activities to reassure anxious children or where to use risky new activities is a delicate decision to make.

"Engrossed" is used here to describe a child's involvement in materials in order to retreat from the classroom reality. Some children deliberately use materials as a means to keep adults at a safe psychological distance by appearing to be deeply involved. Other children, usually at Stage One, become involved with materials in perseverative ways. For them the activity has little meaning.

Maintenance therapy is a program providing enough support and structure to prevent significant regression or deterioration but not offering enough therapeutic intervention to enable a child to make significant advances in his development.

About the Material or Activity:

What quality does it have to attract a child?

What sensory channels does it require?

What does the child have to do with it in order to achieve a satisfactory outcome?

What previous skills are needed in order to have a satisfactory outcome?

How much intervention, assistance, or instruction does it require from the teacher?

Will the outcome be something the child can recognize on his own?

Does the material encourage socialization and language?

What part does it play in the process which culminates in mastery of a particular developmental objective?

A guideline to aid you in planning for your group is outlined below.

1. Review all available information about each child, his family, school, and friends. Particularly helpful information tells you what he values, what interests him, what he can do, prior successes and failures, what he cannot do, how he copes with frustration, what form of discipline he has been receiving, how he responded, how he accepts limits, and how he communicates his needs and feelings. As you gather such information sort it out according to the Developmental Therapy objectives. You will begin to notice significant skills which cluster around particular stages of Developmental Therapy.

2. Plan a temporary, diagnostic teaching program for the first eight days. During this time you can begin to verify the children's developmental stages by providing a wide array of activities, permitting each child to reveal his full range of responses.

3. By the eighth day with the children, you and your treatment team should be ready to rate each of the children using the Developmental Therapy Objectives Rating Form (DTORF). Children at Stages Three and Four generally require the full eight days before they relax sufficiently to present an accurate picture of their skills. Children at Stages One and Two may show their full range of responses within a week.

4. From the individual DTORF's, compile one class DTORF, to show the objectives for all of the children. Many teachers have found this easy to do simply by taking an unused form and recording each child's initials by the objectives he will be working toward. By doing this for every child in the group, you can see objectives which several children have in common and objectives which only individual children may have. (As an example, a Stage Two class of five children is shown in Sample Form 1. This is the class DTORF for the group described in Chapter 8.)

5. Using the class DTORF, you can develop a schedule of general activities which includes the objectives for every child. As you estimate the length of time for each activity, be sure to include time for clean-up and transitions. With groups at all stages of Developmental Therapy, the time spent before or immediately after an activity should be considered a part of therapy and should include developmental objectives.

6. Consider the specific developmental objectives you will work for within each activity. While you are learning the specific objectives for each child in your group, review carefully each child's past objectives. Look for those most recently mastered. They may crop up again as a problem or may need careful support during crisis times.

In these beginning days, activities should be rewarding and comfortable for the children. Once they are "hooked" on the program, then more pressure can be placed on them to achieve their specific objectives.

Chapter 2 includes directions for rating a child on the DTORF.

Therapy can be conducted everywhere: while waiting for the bus to pick-up your class, on a nature walk around the center, or riding with the children to school.

When a new response suddenly emerges for the first time in a child, the teacher is faced with need for an instant decision to continue the group activity or to focus on the individual child and openly recognize the new response. Without some satisfying result, the response may be slow in coming again. With too much attention, the child may withdraw the response because he cannot cope with the results.

At Stage One the displayed schedule will only be valuable to the teachers. At the other stages the schedule is of immediate use to the children. Not only can it be made by them as an art activity and serve as a daily organizer but advanced classes also can change it as part of the group process.

No day will pass that all objectives are completely covered for all children. However, by constant referral to each child's DTORF (especially at debriefing right after class when everything is still fresh in the memory) then therapy will stay on target.

Consider also the objectives which will be coming up next. You may want to be alert to signs that a new skill is emerging. When you see this happening, you will want to be ready with adjustments in the activity to provide for these new responses.

Look for ways you can include a number of objectives within the same activity. You will find that incorporating objectives from each of the four curriculum areas in every activity tends to move most children through the stages of Developmental Therapy rather rapidly.

Analyze the cognitive, motor, and social-affective processes needed by a child in order to participate. Be certain that each child has the prerequisite skills. The developmental objectives (DTORF) can help you determine this. If a child needs instruction, assistance, or intervention in order to have a successful outcome, plan how it can be provided within the context of the group. If a child does not have the necessary skills, redefine the activity and the materials for lower level objectives. If he already has mastery of the objective, go on to the next one and incorporate it into the activity.

Figure 1 illustrates how you might think through this process of selecting materials and activities to accomplish a particular objective. You will want to consider what the materials and activities should accomplish, that is, the objective you are planning. You will need to identify the sequence of steps involved in mastery of the objective along with the processes and responses each step should evoke from the child. Finally, consider which activities, materials, and special conditions will make mastery of the steps easy, rapid, and pleasurable for the child.

Scheduling Activities

Children need to know what comes next and when to expect it. With a daily schedule of activities, displayed where the children can see it, you can provide them the security of a predictable routine. For children lacking internal organization and for those who test boundaries or have difficulties with reality, the routine provides security and some amount of external organization. The daily schedule also should allow you to introduce new ideas to stimulate the group's involvement and to make on-the-spot adaptations when a crisis develops. But, most importantly, the schedule should include daily activities which stimulate the mastery of developmental objectives in all of the four curriculum areas: behavior, communication, socialization, and (pre)academics.

By dividing your total class time into smaller time units, the same general activities can be consistently provided every day. Within these periods of time, specific objectives, activities, and materials may change from day to day, but the general schedule is maintained. A carefully prepared schedule is balanced to provide every child time to work on his individual objectives and time to participate in group endeavors. Even at Stage One, where children are scarcely aware of each other, their individual programs are designed to be conducted within a group setting.

In Table 1 you will find representative schedules for classes at each stage of Developmental Therapy. The greatest number of activities must be planned for Stage One, and the number decreases at each subsequent stage. For example, Stage One might have 12 activities; Stage Two, 10 activities; Stage Three, eight activities; and Stage Four, four activities.

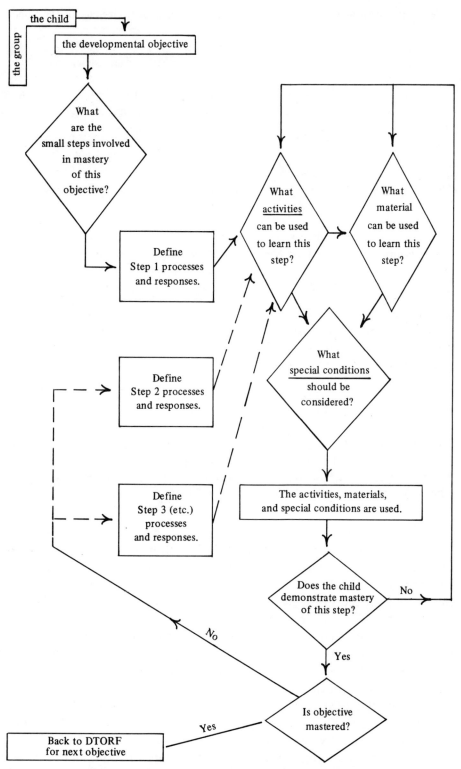

the group

the child

the developmental objective

What are the small steps involved in mastery of this objective?

Define Step 1 processes and responses.

What activities can be used to learn this step?

What material can be used to learn this step?

Define Step 2 processes and responses.

What special conditions should be considered?

Define Step 3 (etc.) processes and responses.

The activities, materials, and special conditions are used.

Does the child demonstrate mastery of this step?   No

Yes

No

Is objective mastered?

Back to DTORF for next objective   Yes

Figure 1. A schematic way to look at planning for a specific objective.

Table 1.   Representative Schedules of Activities for Classes at Each Stage of Developmental Therapy

Stage I class	Stage II class	Stage III class (beginning)	Stage III class (advanced)	Stage IV class
Inside play	Talk time	Talk time	Talk time	Academic work
Perceptual/motor tasks—I	Preacademic table work	Preacademic work	Academic work	Group project
Story time	Inside play	Group games	Outside recreation (game skills)	Snack time
Art	Story time	Story time		
Milk and cookies	Group art activity	Outside play (motor skills)	Milk and cookies	Outside recreation (physical game skills including swimming)
Bathroom	Outside play			
Sensory games	Milk and cookies	Milk and cookies	Special time (music, art, drama, or other group project)	
Exercise	Music	Music and art		
Outside play	Exercise or game time	Special time (group project)		
P. Mooney (language)				
Perceptual/motor tasks—II	Language			
Music				
Class time: 2 hr. daily	Class time: 2 hr., 4 days per wk.	Class time: 2 hr., 4 days per wk.	Class time: 1.5 hr., 3 days per wk.	Class time: 1.5 hr., 3 days per wk.
Average activity time: 10 min.	Average activity time: 12 min.	Average activity time: 15 min.	Average activity time: 19 min.	Average activity time: 22 min.

The decrease in number indicates that the children can sustain themselves in one activity through longer periods of time at each successive stage. It also substantiates the idea that intermeshing objectives from all four curriculum areas into a single activity is possible at the upper stages. Examples of this are included in a subsequent section of this chapter describing Stage Four activities.

Among Stage One and Stage Two classes four basic activities should always be included in some form: preacademic work time, play time, story time, and milk and cookie time. For Stages Three and Four at least three general activities should always be present: academic work time, group project or game time, and snack time.

A (pre)academic work time is important for all stages because it offers opportunities for developmental objectives related to attention, behavior, group process, listening, speaking, remembering, and the specific objectives in the academic area of the curriculum.

A snack time is included for all stages because food facilitates attention, participation, and impulse control and is an excellent way to stimulate communication and socialization skills. Over milk and cookies many significant forward steps have been taken in interpersonal and social relationships. Food also serves as an important source for nurturance. This is an acceptable way to nurture older children or those who have been so severely deprived of nurturing in their life experience that they cannot accept it in a personal form.

Some type of play or group activity is a necessary part of every schedule because it offers a child opportunity for independent exploration of materials, trying out newly learned skills, and venturing into social exchanges which invariably require language. Play also stimulates development, if planned well. There are several important considerations in selecting play equipment.

1. Does it stimulate communication? Does it require one child to speak to another in the course of play?
2. Does it stimulate socialization? Toys designed for isolated play should be avoided except at Stage One where organized solitary play is an objective, and precedes cooperative play at Stage Two.
3. Does it have a self monitoring feedback system? Does it develop a child's independence or foster adult dependency?
4. Does it arouse and stimulate the child to activity?

Teachers also consider the effect of play equipment on particular children. For example, a Stage One teacher removed a rocking chair even though the children needed and responded to nurturance, because one autistic child in the classroom isolated himself in it and rocked endlessly. The rocking chair seemed to be a way for this child to retreat. A "space-hopper" with its repetitive hopping motion may increase perseveration and is avoided in a class of children with this problem. However, it is used to provide an appropriate physi-cal outlet in another classroom for restless, aggressive children during play time.

Story time, which is used at Stages One and Two for communication objectives, may not be included at Stages Three or Four because development of language and communication skills at these stages can be enhanced through informal group projects, discussion groups, and Life Space Interviews. The Stage Four schedule is unique also in that the children themselves plan the activities.

The selection of stories is an important part of each planned program. Teachers of the lower stage classes emphasize the development of a child's receptive vocabulary by exposing him to many new words through stories, linking them to familiar experiences. As a child develops greater abstract skills, the emphasis changes to using stories to solve peer problems and to talk about feelings. It is important to choose stories in which the children participate emotionally and verbally. Stories also may be a source for nurturance because story time is a time when they get physically close to the teachers, sitting together on the "story rug." Through this physical proximity, they seem to share the feelings conveyed through the content of the stories.

These basic schedules permit you to incorporate any of the developmental objectives from each of the four curriculum areas into the daily activities. But the variations on these schedules are also important. In particular, music and art are highly effective for reaching all of the objectives and should be included as scheduled activities whenever possible. If time does not allow for these special activity sessions, use art materials or music in the activities you have already scheduled such as group project time, story time, play or special time.

In your program, include times for

The care a teacher shows for each child's needs during snack time is very important. For example, spreading peanut butter in equal amounts on each child's cracker should be routine. Giving a broken cookie is like saying "you are not worth a whole cookie." How to share the remaining juice fairly should be the teacher's concern, not dependent upon a child's demands for fair distribution.

When children feel that the teacher is looking after their interests, the need to agitate for fairness will be diminished.

At Stages Three and Four, story-time can be made more acceptable to older children by changing its title to ADVENTURE TIME, DISCOVERY TIME, or TUNE-IN TIME.

carefully structured instructional sessions. Equally important, however, are times planned around less structured activities which give children the chance to use newly learned responses on their own. Play and art are particularly effective activities for this. Such activities provide you with excellent opportunities to observe how well a child's mastery of an objective is holding up without your intervention.

The term "instructional" is used to describe any activity in which the teacher must participate actively in order that the child will participate.

Selecting Materials

In many instances, teacher-made materials seem to stimulate children to learning. For example, in a Stage Three class the teacher brought in cans, egg cartons, old pocketbooks, and cardboard boxes, labeled these with prices, and the children learned number concepts while having the social and communicative experience of playing "store." Also, children's work folders usually contain teacher-made worksheets on a child's individual level. When these materials are colorful and motivating, a child delights in knowing they have been made especially for him.

As you get to know your children, they can be the best source for ideas about effective materials. But from the few, or many, materials which interest the children, you will need to be very selective. Materials can be the catalyst for Developmental Therapy if well chosen. Here are a few guidelines for selecting materials:

Repetition and variation of activities takes different forms at different stages. A Stage One class might use a single brush and a different watercolor each day. The Stage Two class might explore many colors one day, use different size brushes the next day and then paint on colored paper for a third lesson. A Stage Three class might plan for a mural one day, paint it the next day and use it for scenery in a series of role playing for several weeks.

1.   The material should have qualities of its own to catch and hold the child's attention. The more children a material can attract, the more useful it will be to you in the group setting.

2.   Aspects of the material should be suitable to the developmental skills of every child in your group, so that each one can participate in an independent way.

3.   The material should encourage active exploration, in which the individual has opportunity to try out variations in the way he will use it.

4.   Involvement with the material should have a successful or gratifying outcome which the child can experience through the materials, not depending upon the teacher to provide a reward for involvement.

5.   The material should have a specific purpose in your planning for the Developmental Therapy objectives and should be a vehicle for accomplishing the objective in the least possible time. Often a familiar, preferred material may be used to introduce a child to a new activity. Or a new material, with qualities of extraordinary interest, may be selected to maintain a child's motivation while he is struggling to master a particularly difficult objective.

To accomplish one objective, you may plan to use the same activity with many different materials over a period of days, gradually increasing the complexity of each step and culminating in the mastery of a developmental objective. Another activity may depend upon the same material, day after day, while the children practice to become increasingly successful in independent use of the material. Such successful participation is a necessary condition for mastery of a number of the objectives, particularly those at the higher stages of Developmental Therapy where minimal teacher intervention is specified as a part of the objective. It is possible, also, that a single material or activity may provide experiences for many different objectives concurrently.

The number of materials used at each stage of Developmental Therapy de-

Table 2. How Materials Change Across Stages of Developmental Therapy

	Stage I class	Stage II class	Stage III class	Stage IV class
Content	Concrete; sensory	Semiconcrete; exploratory	Semiabstract	Abstract; symbolic; complex
Type of material	Special; arousing materials	Special adaptations of regular preschool materials	Regular (pre)school materials adapted to individual needs	Regular school materials, not adapted
Purpose	Used for individual mobilization	Used to stimulate individual skills	Used to increase individual effectiveness in group	Used as vehicle for group process
Source of control[a]	Teacher provides control of materials	Teacher assists child in control of material	Teacher assists group in controlling materials	Group develops, uses, and controls materials

[a]See Chapter 5 for a discussion of control of materials as a management technique for teachers.

creases as the skills of the children increase. At the lower stages, basic responses are being learned which require many simple, manipulative, concrete materials. These individual skills become the building blocks for higher, more abstract and expressive skills at later stages requiring fewer manipulative materials but more complex experiences.

Table 2 illustrates changes in several aspects of materials across the stages of Developmental Therapy. You will notice the similarity to the changes in teacher techniques described in Chapter 5.

Planning the Next Step

Process evaluation, with the developmental objectives as your reference point, should set the standard for planning each day. While an activity is going on, continually estimate each child's investment, attention span, the processes he is relying upon, and whether or not he is showing progress toward mastery of that particular objective. Consider whether he has had so much success that there is no new challenge or whether he has been exposed to so many new materials and processes that learning has been diluted.

If you follow closely the process each child is using with a material or activity, you will know what the next step should be. It may be to repeat the lesson with a variation, to drop back to a less difficult step, or to move forward to the next, more complex step.

The success of any one therapy session is not measured by its pleasantness nor how well the children behaved. Rather, progress toward mastery of a particular objective, no matter how small the movement may be, is the criterion for a successful day.

A situation that can entrap any teacher is to allow a great activity to continue past its high point. Always end on the peak of the lesson and begin the transition to the next activity on this positive note. Hopefully, this successful feeling will carry over for the group into the next activity.

Refer also to Chapter 5, which contains verbal techniques and management strategies for teachers.

Even though children are grouped according to developmental stage, there will always be a range of individual objectives from the stage below to the stage above. This means that activities and materials in any class will have the characteristics of the predominant stage but will also provide for individual objectives from other stages.

Chapter 7 provides a description of how an actual Stage One class is conducted.

Include in your plan ways for each child to receive ongoing feedback about his progress. This suggests immediate reinforcement, with redirection and correction as needed throughout every activity.

To the extent he can understand, each child needs to know his own current objectives. Show him *where he was before* (example, "Remember when you didn't think you could do this?"); *where he is now* (example, "You tried really hard today not to lose control."); and *what tomorrow will bring* (example, "The group had such a good music time today you should be ready to make a recording of it tomorrow.").

Always plan to have alternative activities and materials as back-up. Because the functional level of an emotionally disturbed child tends to fluctuate, continual readjustments in activities and materials may be necessary.

Sometimes activities need to be cut short or occasionally extended beyond the time you had planned. Plan to include each activity daily, even if for a brief time. If you find it impossible to have all of the daily activities because a particular activity has continued beyond the usual length, let the children know about the change and why it is necessary.

Motivation of children is always a challenge. Teachers find that presenting learning through games and activities that are developmentally appropriate, fascinating, and often teacher-made have provided the best results. Allowing children to guess or to take the initiative in using materials to make up a new game has been effective; for example, "I wonder how we can make a game out of this. We have two bean bags and a clock with no hands."

The following sections contain examples of activities and materials which have proved to be motivating and effective in Developmental Therapy at each of the four stages. Each of the sections is organized in a way which best fits the particular stage. At Stage One, the focus is the processes elicited from the child, particularly in behavior and communication. At Stage Two, modifications of regular preschool activities, particularly in communication, are emphasized. Because Stage Three activities involve regular primary curriculum and games, the focus is on the importance of the procedures the teacher uses, with emphasis on socialization activities. At Stage Four, activities center around group projects and interaction. The organization of that section is around a typical class schedule.

ACTIVITIES AND MATERIALS FOR STAGE ONE (RESPONDING AND TRUSTING)

Awareness. Responding. Sustained attending. Trusting. These are the basic processes to be mobilized in the Stage One classroom. The materials involve every sensory channel: tasting, touching, hearing, smelling, seeing. Children are encouraged to develop preferences for simple choices and to express these preferences in productive ways. They are taught to use language, at first using simple approximations, later linking words in phrases. There are many activities to stimulate eye-hand coordination and control of the large muscles of the body. Children also are encouraged to respond to adults and to toys.

Be certain that each activity you plan will produce a satisfying result for the child. Pleasure-in-doing is your goal. Definitely forget skilled performances as an outcome. You want your Stage One activities to simply create interest, involvement, pleasure, and trust. This may be the single greatest challenge for the

Stage One teacher. It means conducting completely individualized programs in a group setting.

The following ideas have been used successfully in Stage One classes. You will notice that the topics are not those usually thought of as curriculum activities. Yet for the children in Stage One these are essential processes. You will be able to create many exciting experiences for your Stage One children by using these activities as samples. The numbers following each activity refer to specific Developmental Therapy objectives (see Appendix). In each instance, the primary objectives have been listed first. Other objectives are included when applicable.

Activities for the Stage One Classroom

Learning to be Aware Physically moving a child into an activity or putting his hands on a material may stimulate him to a response. Particularly effective activities are "hiding" ("Peek-a-boo"); being lifted to the top of a short slide and being held for the trip down; books to touch and move; rhythm band instruments; finger paints; the sand and water table; balloons; and shaving cream (B-1, B-2, B-3; C-1, C-2).

For a child who will not respond to verbal arousal or to highly exciting materials, try a caress, a touch on his cheek; whisper next to his ear; put your hand gently under his chin and turn his face toward you; or take his own hand and touch his face. Then when you have his attention, be certain that there is a result from his response which brings him pleasure.

Learning to Attend for Longer Periods By intervening and redirecting a child to a next step in an activity, a teacher can increase the attention span in almost every instance. Children at this stage seldom are able to do this on their own. They tend to respond fleetingly to a stimulus, and then their attention is lost. Often they sit and perseverate or engage in restless motor movements, signifying that they simply cannot sustain attention without assistance. For example, a wooden hammer and peg set offers many possibilities for sustained attending by repetitive hammering to get the peg through (B-2, B-3; A-5). By asking the child to name the color of a peg as he hits it or by asking him to hit a peg of a particular color, the activity can incorporate communication and academic objectives (C-2, C-3; A-15). When a child is involved with this activity in a systematic way, he will also have demonstrated, in a basic way, socialization objective S-5, organized solitary play.

Imitating Activities involving imitating are important for a number of early Stage One objectives. By being the stimulus yourself, with a single word or movement you can gain the attention of several children at once (B-1, B-2; S-1, S-2; C-1). A variety of responses can be elicited by the nature of the stimulus, such as calling a child's name (S-3); giving a single direction, "stand up" or "do this" (S-4, S-7; B-3, B-4); or by asking a child to walk a tape line after you do it (B-4). If a child cannot sustain attention long enough to participate, you will need to move him physically through the desired response.

Learning to Use Words Many Stage One children cannot or will not talk. The ingredients you will need to begin this process are: (a) a desire on the child's part for something (a cookie, a toy, your attention, etc.); (b) a single word you provide consistently to associate with the desired object; (c) the child's attention when you say the word; (d) the child's understanding that you want him to imitate the same sound; (e) the child's understanding that he must attempt the

Of all the stages, perhaps Stage One requires the most careful sequencing of each small step in the learning process. When any material is shown and a response is expected, there are many small steps between. Because Stage One children cannot usually accomplish these steps spontaneously, the teacher often must move the child through the process.

To recognize any glimmer of response from a Stage One child the teacher must continually be tuned in to the child and the situation. This can be an exhausting demand.

The way a teacher verbalizes in a Stage One class can mean the difference between a child "tuning out" or wanting to respond because the voice is pleasurable and appealing.

In Chapter Seven, you will find a discussion about the importance of the teacher using a "controlled" vocabulary at Stage One in order to keep communication simple and explicit.

sound in order to obtain the desired object; (f) the child's feeling that you care for him and want him to attempt the sound to obtain the object; and (g) an extremely pleasurable or desired result when he makes the attempt. Each of these seven ingredients represents a sequence of small steps which must occur every time you attempt an activity to help a child learn to use words. If a child does not progress, evaluate each of these seven situations in slow motion. You can predict that there has been a breakdown in at least one of these seven steps. When you find it, focus on that particular element until it seems to be functioning. Then go back and try the seven steps again. They should produce results (C-1, C-2, C-3, C-4, C-5, C-7).

Self Help Activities Every Stage One child is helped to participate in clean-up after each activity. The clean up directions consist of only four words, "Time to clean up." Often the actual physical motions employed in bending, reaching, grasping, and putting may have to be taught (see "Physical Intervention" in Chapter 5.)

With Stage One objectives, keep in mind that the child's involvement is the essential element.

Other self help skills include participating in hand washing, putting on coats, turning door knobs, pouring juice, wiping the table, toileting, and using tissues for running noses or drooling.

The self help objective in Developmental Therapy emphasizes participation in the process of learning rather than in the skilled accomplishment of the task.

The QUALITY of cutting or pasting is ignored at this stage. PARTICIPATION by the child is the goal. Refinement of the gross motor skills will come with practice.

Rhythms and Song Through musical experiences almost all Stage One objectives can be learned. Drums, rattles, cow bells, and other rhythm band instruments arouse children, keeping them involved and participating (B-1, B-2, B-3, B-4, B-5, B-7).

Songs and vocal sounds stimulate basic language processes. With songs,

every communication objective can be used: vocalizing with others (unison), vocalizing by imitating others, vocalizing in response to others, using verbal approximations, using single words and sequences, and using words to get something from another (C-1, C-2, C-3, C-4, C-5, C-6, C-7).

By involving children in simple dance and rhythm movements you can keep their attention for extended periods of time (B-2). Walking, hopping, swaying, clapping, "stomping," leaning, and skipping are all effective rhythmic movements. Resistant children, seeing the others having so much fun, usually loosen up and respond (S-7, S-11). These activities also contribute to large muscle coordination (A-13), eye-hand movements (A-16), and knowledge of body parts (A-17).

Perhaps often overlooked but extremely important are the gains in socialization from music experiences. Children become aware of other children, often for the first time, as they are drawn together by the activity (S-1, S-2, S-4, S-7).

Learning to Use Scissors With a magic marker outline a large square on a 9 × 11 sheet of unlined paper. Perforate the magic marker lines with a pizza cutter. When the child begins cutting, the perforations fall apart easily. A preliminary step to this activity could be coloring the cube. The perforations tend to give a tangible boundary to touch. A step to follow after cutting would be pasting the shape on a sheet of colored construction paper (A-16, A-15; C-2).

Another simple activity is to use strips of bright construction paper about one inch wide. The child is helped to grasp the scissors correctly and make one cutting motion. The result is dramatic; he has severed the paper. The width of the paper strips may be widened as the child's skill increases.

Equipping the Stage One Classroom

As you may have concluded from the previous discussions of Stage One activities, it is the care, consistency, and simplicity with which each child's participation is handled that is most important. The same idea applies to materials. The Stage One materials have an unusually arousing quality and are selected to achieve responses from the children. The following lists are representative of materials which might be used in a Stage One class. Of course you might not have all these materials on hand at one time.

For Inside Play Time May satisfy socialization objectives S-4, S-5, S-11, S-12; behavior objectives B-1, B-2, B-3, B-4, B-6, B-7; academic objective A-13; and communication objective C-6.

Small wooden Jungle Gym and slide (Creative Playthings)
Large cardboard blocks
Blackboard with chalk (at children's height)
Books (previously used at story time)
Large barrel for climbing in and out
Medium rubber ball
Large wooden cradle
Large boy and girl baby dolls
Set of ethnic family dolls
Lacing shoes with wooden family
Old guitar
Bean bags
Puzzle form box (previously used for instruction)
Wooden puzzles with single shapes
Soft, cuddly stuffed animals to hold
Large stuffed animals to climb on
Tea set (previously used at milk and cookie time)
Wooden milk bottles in rack (Creative Playthings)
Wooden ride-on tractor
Wooden track and trains (Creative Playthings)
Play telephones
"Dapper Dan" (Playskool)
Cabinet (for all toys to be stored at children's height)

For Perceptual Motor Tasks May satisfy preacademic objectives A-1, A-2, A-3, A-4, A-5, A-7, A-11, A-16 and behavior objectives B-5, B-6.

Raisins (for fine motor exercise)
Individual work folders with teacher made worksheets
    Dot to dot
    Left to right movements
    Coloring simple shapes to learn colors and eye-hand coordination
    Tearing 1-inch strips of paper and pasting on colored paper
    Cutting 1-inch strips of paper and pasting on colored paper
    Cutting on lines made by magic marker
    Cutting shapes made by magic marker
Paste, one teaspoon on a scrap of cardboard
Kindergarten-size crayons
Scissors, left- and righthanded, blunt edge
Tape
Name tags on heavy cardboard written with felt tip pen
Small groups of objects for categorizing, counting, colors, memory games
Six pinch clothes pins attached around edge of medium size tin can
Small wooden cubes for stacking, counting, matching colors, and designs
Wooden beads for stringing (Building Bead Patterns, No. 6040, Ideal Co.)
Tactilmat No. 6225 (25 holes, Ideal Co.)
    No. 6220 (100 holes, Ideal Co.)

(to be used with large plastic pegs)

Wooden Preschool puzzles—SIFO No. 378, No. 106

    Playskool "I Learn to Draw and Paste"

    "My Toys"

Form box (Creative Playthings)

Montessori zipper, button, and snap boards

For Story Time May satisfy communication objectives C-1, C-3, C-4, C-5, C-7; socialization objectives S-1, S-2; and preacademic objectives A-6, A-14.

Bowmar Early Childhood Series:
    Little, Big, Bigger
    How Does It Feel?
    Me
    A Cowboy Can
    Where is Home?
    Telling Tails
    Through the Day
    Things I Like To Do
    Colors

(The) Great Big Fire Engine Book by Gergely (Big Golden Book)

Are You My Mother? by Eastman (French Beginner Books)

Picture cards of toys and foods (from Peabody Language Development Kit #P)

People In My Family (A Golden Shape Book, Sesame Street)

Three Little Pigs

For Sensory Experiences May satisfy behavior objectives B-1 through B-4; preacademic objectives A-5, A-7, A-10, A-11; communication objective C-2; and socialization objective S-4, S-5.

Box of textures (2 pieces each of: velvet, feather, rhinestone buttons, veiling, leather, burlap, sandpaper, vinyl)

Box of smells (onion, perfume, banana, lemon)

Water table with sand or water (Constructive Playthings)
    Plastic bottles and cups for filling
    Small plastic toys which float
    Shaving cream
    Soap flakes
    Stones and blocks

For Exercise Time May satisfy socialization objectives S-1, S-2, S-3, S-11; communication objective C-2; behavior objectives B-3, B-4, B-6, B-7; and preacademic objectives A-6, A-13.

Monsanto snap cubes (for jumping, climbing)

Walking board

Mat for rolling, somersaults

Tricycles and short paths made of tape

"Tall and Small" stretching game

For Outside Playtime May satisfy socialization objectives S-4, S-11, S-12; behavior objectives B-1 through B-4, B-6, B-7; communication objectives C-2, C-5, C-6; and preacademic objective A-13.

Climbing equipment: small cargo net, stacked railroad ties to platform

Walks to find stones, leaves, sticks, etc. ("treasure hunt")

A medium size utility ball

A ball with a bell in it

Mountain of sand to climb

Tiles in sand for stepping and jumping

A swinging basket for two or more (or a large rope hammock)

A small platform or tree stump to jump from (2 feet high)

Climbing equipment which brings good feelings such as the "Socia-Bowl," Octagon Donut," "Buddy Saddle," and "Big Blibbit" (Skill Development Equipment Company)

"Ring Around the Rosey" and "London Bridge's Falling Down"

For Language Time May satisfy all communication objectives, C-1 through

C-7; socialization objectives S-1, S-2, S-3, S-4; behavior objectives B-1, B-2; and preacademic objectives A-6, A-12, A-14.

Peabody Language Development Kit #P (P. Mooney puppet and props; picture cards of toys and foods)
Other hand puppets
Language Master, individual cards (Bell and Howell)
Cassette tape recorder
Picture concept cards (made by parents and teacher from magazines)
Teletrainer telephones (Bell Telephone Co.)
"Moods and Emotions" Teaching Pictures by Tester (Daniel C. Cook Publishing Co.)
Verbal Communication Picture Set III-A (Bowmar)

For Music Time May satisfy behavior objectives B-1 through B-4, B-7; communication objectives C-1 through C-6; socialization objectives S-1 through S-4, S-6, S-7, S-11, S-12; and preacademic objectives A-5, A-6, A-10, A-12, A-13, A-16, A-17.

Instruments and Equipment:
Record player or tape player
Guitar (teacher and children play)
Autoharp
Large drum (such as floor or tom-tom drum)
Rhythm instruments such as cowbells, sandblocks, tambourines, triangles, maracas, rhythm sticks, guiros, drum (Rhythm Band, Inc.)
Records:
More Learning As We Play (FC 7658), Ginglend and Stiles (Folkways Records)
Getting To Know Myself (AR 543), Hap Palmer (Educational Activities, Inc.)
Learning Basic Skills Through Music, Vol. I (AR 514), Vol. II (AR 522),

Vocabulary Vol. (AR 521), Hap Palmer (Educational Activities, Inc.)
Play Your Instruments and Make a Pretty Sound (FC 7665), Ella Jenkins (Folkways Records)
Songs:
"Let Everyone Clap Hands Like Me"
"London Bridge"
"ABC"
"Michael Row the Boat Ashore" (substitute different children's names and activities with sentences they know, i.e. "Tommy knows how to clap his hands . . .")
"Jingle Bells"
"This Old Man"
"One, Two, Three"
"Put Your Finger in the Air"

For Art Time May satisfy behavior objectives B-1 through B-4, B-7; preacademic objectives A-5, A-10, A-15, A-16; communication objectives C-1 through C-4; and socialization objectives S-1, S-2, S-3, S-4, S-11, S-12.

Fingerpaint (primary colors)
Fingerpaint paper
Powdered tempera
#12 brushes
White drawing paper (all sizes)
Dried beans, macaroni
Assorted color paper (construction and tissue)
Elmer's glue (4 oz. size for individual use)
Yarns, paper and cloth scraps, buttons
Wire (plastic coated)
Sand, gravel, birdseed
Playplax for 3-D structures
Playdoh and/or modeling clay
Paper chains (type that have glue on back and need to be licked)
Pastels
Craypas (for resists with watery temperas)
Food dyes

Styrofoam and toothpicks
Magazines and newspaper
Old shirts for "smocks"
Baby food jars (to hold water for each child when painting)

ACTIVITIES AND MATERIALS FOR STAGE TWO (RESPONDING TO THE ENVIRONMENT WITH SUCCESS)

Chapter 8 shows how Stage Two activities and materials are used with an actual class.

The activities and materials used at Stage Two are more demanding of a child than at Stage One. A Stage Two child has learned to respond; and now the program must see that his responses bring successful results. Keep in mind that you, the teacher, set the standard for what is success. This standard will have to reflect the individual skills of each child in the group. When you select activities and materials for Stage Two, remember also that the materials must be interesting and arousing or a child may not put forth the effort to get involved. The activity must require that the child give something of himself to make it work.

Simple, household materials can be exciting for Stage Two children. However, the manner in which the activity is presented will mean success or failure.

Perhaps the most important characteristic of a Stage Two child is his limited view of adults and other children, seeing them in categorical ways rather than as individuals. Stage Two children do not recognize group processes as the consequences of actions. They see problems solved by some outside power. This makes them responsive to exploring situations through story characters and magical solutions.

Several important principles for you to use as you conduct Stage Two activities are these:

Redesign games at Stage Two so that there are no losers. Stages Three provides ample opportunity for learning to be a loser.

Put feelings into words whenever a child expresses feelings through his behavior in an activity.

Insist on the participation of every child and encourage involvement with each other by selecting partners, noticing details of each child, and structuring activities for involvement.

Avoid activities which require long waits for a turn; with beginning Stage Two classes, have activities which do not require turns.

Have opportunities and expectations for every child to use words in all activities.

Select stories in which characters are children or animals in simple, specific situations with some familiar element for each child in your group.

Activities for the Stage Two Classroom

The following list offers a sample of activities which have been successful at Stage Two.

"I Like ——" Game Teacher asks who likes ——? She shows a picture of an object, toy, or TV character. The child who responds with the name (or the sentence "I like ——.") is given the picture to paste in his own scrapbook called, *I Like This* (C-8, C-9, C-12; S-13; B-9, B-10).

"How Does It Feel?" Game By modifying the game described above, using simple pictures of children's faces with explicit feelings of sad, happy, mad, scared, children can learn to recognize and label feelings in pictures (C-10) and details in pictures (A-19). Later children can go through their scrapbook with parents or other children and describe the feelings (C-12, C-13; S-18).

Reaching Into Surprise Bag The possibilities for activities and objectives are endless with a surprise bag: giving the answer to what they feel when reaching in the bag (C-8); one child tells another what to find in the bag (C-11); a child reaches in and tells the group what he feels (C-12); another child counts how many and tells class (A-21, A-23); another has success finding an object when described by its use (A-18). Any familiar objects with distinctly different shapes and textures can be used. For example, one particular "feeling bag" included marshmallows, jar rings, marbles, wooden blocks, and feathers.

Telephones Using pairs of telephones, each child telephones another with a specific message such as what he will do when he gets home from school today (C-8), giving directions to do a particular action (C-11). When used in dramatic play, telephones provide abundant opportunity to encourage communication with reticent children (B-8, B-11, B-12; C-13; S-15, S-17). Learning single-digit play phone numbers can be added to telephone activities as an incidental activity leading into the academic objective recognizing numerals to 10 (A-36), at Stage Three.

Puppets During talk time, a puppet can serve as a responding model for the children, in answer to teacher's questions. A puppet can also be the teacher, asking questions of the children. This is particularly effective for children who are resistant to adults (C-8, C-10, C-11, C-12, C-13).

Puppets can be used also as a preliminary activity to help children learn to participate in play, child drama, and story time (C-12, C-13; B-8, B-9, B-10, B-11; S-15, S-17; A-31).

Role Playing Teacher (or puppet) can serve as model initially. Incidents are selected around the children's actual circumstances. For example, teacher role plays a child struggling to put on her coat. She asks group, "What shall I say?" or "What shall I do?" Children contribute solutions. Then group thinks of another situation and a child can be the actor, asking the group the same question (C-8, C-11, C-12, C-13; S-18). Variations of role playing are many: acting out feelings in carefully structured situations such as "How do you feel when your mother won't let you go out to play?"; or taking on roles of persons needing help and special helpers such as policeman, fireman, grandmother, teacher, or TV character.

Role playing can go on during inside play time also. Make-believe with a box of hats or dress-up costumes is an excellent way to give Stage Two children socialization experiences. Such activities require an alert teacher who can move into the play to restructure it when it falters and then pulls back as the children catch on. It is also important to be alert to children who are not yet able to play this way. Considerable, subtle structuring of their play to encourage interaction may be necessary.

There are a number of ways teachers can structure role playing during inside play time to teach children how to play. Children playing alone with blocks or trucks can be given such assistance by being asked to "deliver the mail" to the children who are involved in role playing or dress up (S-13, S-15, S-16, S-17; B-13; B-11, B-12). The teacher may bring out a supply of hats for particular characterizations such as cowboy hat, fireman's hat, policeman's hat, army hat, hard hat, motorcycle hat, old lady's hat, or baby bonnet. Holding them up one at a time, the teacher asks "Who wears a hat like this?" Then the child who guesses it gets to put on the hat for role playing how that person acts. Variations of this activity may also include role playing familiar

Notice that each of the first te activities has an element of se expression requiring simple word to make a personal statement.

The outcome of these activitie never takes the form of a winner

animals while the group guesses the identity (B-9, B-10; S-14, S-18; C-9, C-11, C-13).

Role playing familiar stories is a good beginning for child drama (B-9, B-11, B-12). At a sample level all children have the same character part (S-13); later, children select the role they want and considerable interaction occurs (S-15, S-17; C-10, C-11, C-13).

Story Telling Perhaps more effective than reading a story is telling a story with simple sentence structure, feeling tone, and animation. The teacher can stop in the middle of a sentence and encourage a child to respond with the missing word or idea (C-8). She can ask "And then what happened?" or "What should — do now?" (C-12). Eventually the teacher can give the story telling role to each of the children (C-13).

Stories at Stage Two should be repeated frequently. When a story becomes familiar and the group is spontaneous in responding to parts of the story, child drama becomes an effective activity for encouraging spontaneous communication with one another (C-13).

Music Through music, Stage Two children can learn many behavior, communication, and socialization skills. Certain instruments in a rhythm band can give the "signal" to other instruments to begin playing, thus giving nonverbal children an opportunity to influence and command others. Children can take turns clapping a beat for the others to follow (S-15, S-18).

Making and using musical instruments such as tambourines, drums, and shakers builds confidence for participating (B-8, B-11; S-13, S-17; A-24, A-29). Marching and clapping in rhythm (B-11), when combined with the above activity, encourage socialization objective S-17, cooperative activity with others in play.

Musical chairs also encourages participation but at Stage Two should be done without removing a chair when the music stops (B-11; S-13; A-29).

Songs can ask questions which require an answer or a physical response (C-8, C-11). Songs can reflect feelings, "If you're happy . . ." (C-10). Children can select favorite songs for the group to sing (C-11, C-13). Each child can contribute a word, sentence, or refrain to a song (C-11, C-13). A "color" song can be used with cards of different colors; children hold up their card when that color is mentioned (A-22).

Feeling Pictures Children are instructed to draw a picture of what makes them happy or how they feel when mad, etc. The teacher can demonstrate through bright colors and wavy lines that she feels "happy" then, through dark colors and angular scribbles, that she feels "mad." This reduces the fear of failure surrounding representational drawing. Variations of this also can come from listening to short excerpts of "happy" or "mad" music and then doing art to express the feeling (C-10).

Group Recreational Activities (outside) There are any number of appropriate group games traditionally associated with kindergarten and first grade such as "Follow the Leader" (B-11; S-13, S-17), "Red Rover" (B-9, B-11; S-15, S-17; C-11), "Mother May I?", "Drop the Hankie," "Cat and Mouse" (B-9, B-11; C-8, C-11; S-17).

Treasure Hunt Children are given paper bags and individual lists with pictures of objects hidden in the room; when a child completes his list he brings it to a teacher to be checked and then helps another child (B-11, B-12; C-9, C-12; S-13, S-15, S-17; A-18, A-19, A-26).

Boats from Jar Lids Each child has a jar lid, a stick for a mast, and a piece of

Playdoh to hold it in the boat. Sails are colored, cut out, and stapled around mast. Boats are floated in a "lake" such as a large dish pan with blue coloring added to water (B-10; A-18, A-22, A-24). When children are put into pairs to make and sail a boat together other objectives can be added (C-13; S-16, S-18).

Making a Train Each child is given four rectangles and two circles cut from construction paper into sizes which will fit together to make a train car. After a child puts together the pieces and pastes them on an 8 × 11 sheet, crayons are available for decorating the cars. The teacher and children tape the cars on the wall to make a train and join the cars by bright colored yarn (S-13, S-15, S-16, S-18; A-24).

A train also can be made from cardboard boxes or orange crates, with a separate "car" for each child in the group. Deciding as a group where they will go and what they might see on a train trip will stimulate the beginning of group participation and can serve as a readiness for more involved role playing. It is usually necessary for the teacher to serve as "conductor" on the trip to encourage each child to see something from the train window, and to move the "passengers" back to the "station" when they reach their destination (S-13, S-14, S-17; C-19, C-12, C-13). By making train tickets beforehand, this activity can be extended for a fine motor coordination activity (A-24).

Wall Murals On butcher paper taped to a long wall, each child has an individual place marked. The mural can depict a story created by the class, a familiar story, or a series of parallel illustrations. Crayons, craypas, chalk, or cut-and-paste can be used. If the mural is spread on the floor, tempera paint can be used. In any case, for Stage Two children, each child

should have a specific task which he can successfully execute in a parallel but independent space (S-13, S-16, S-18; A-22, A-24, A-31).

Making a Styrofoam City With styrofoam pieces of varying sizes and shapes, and tooth picks to hold them together, each child is assigned a special type of building to make a group city. A large piece of butcher paper is spread on the table and roads and city blocks are laid out by the teacher with magic marker according to the group's plan. Places are designated for each building and children add their buildings on the "map" designating each child's place with his name. The styrofoam buildings can be painted with tempera if the construction is sturdy and the children able to handle the painting task. This makes a handsome product to display for parents and other teachers (S-13, S-14, S-15, S-16, S-18; A-24).

Variations of "I Spy" Teacher, puppet, or child initiates this activity by selecting some detail of another child (shirt, ribbon, sweater, shoe, etc.) while the other children guess who it is. For Stage Two children, it may be necessary to review each child's name in the group before the game starts. This is an excellent means of bringing children together at times when the group may be falling apart. Also it is excellent for beginning Stage Two children to start the socialization process by noticing individual details about others such as hair color, dress (S-13, S-14, S-15, S-17; C-11, C-13; A-22).

Giant Size Animal Puzzle (Any single object such as a house, car, etc., may be used.) Parts are cut out and each child is given a piece to contribute to putting it together (S-18; B-9, B-10; A-19, A-24, A-25).

A Giant Size Furniture Box Such boxes have a variety of uses for group

These latter activities provide essentially nonverbal experience, emphasizing fine motor processes simple group work, and cognitive exercises. Important foundation for self confidence and socialization are being built.

projects and for inside play time. Following teachers' directions, children can crawl inside, outside, over, around, through, and into as a means of learning these concepts (A-28). The box serves also as a playhouse, destination for a group trip, a rocket, airplane, mountain, ship, or store.

Picture Bingo Each child has a similar sheet with nine pictures (across and down). The teacher holds up a single picture card and calls out the name or use. The children all cover their corresponding picture with a marker (C-9, C-12; B-10; S-18; A-18, A-19, A-25). This activity becomes effective as a communication objective when children are selected to be the teacher, calling out the name of the pictured object for others to respond (C-11, C-13; S-18).

Traffic Game Used inside or out, with tricycles, trucks or walking, this game offers opportunity to work on behavior, communication, and socialization goals. A signal light (teacher made, Creative Playthings, or others) is necessary. A child can make it turn green or red. He is the "patrol" and can influence when the other children start and stop (C-11; B-8, B-9, B-11; S-15, S-17).

Names and Labels The beginning Stage Two child needs to know what belongs to him. Making a name tag for each child and labeling his individual chair at the work table gives a sense of security and self. Also, decorating a cigar box for each child's own crayons, scissors, and pencil increases the feeling of what belongs to that child. This is a carryover from Stage One (S-11) and moves the child toward recognizing and writing his own first name (A-27). As a Stage Two class progresses, the need for name labels on personal supplies decreases, and such activities would be inappropriate for a Stage Three child,

where sharing and group dependency is emphasized.

Work Folders Prepared individually, each folder should offer opportunity for independent success to develop confidence that there is school work a child can do. The work folder can contain any number of exercises or activities for number concepts, visual perceptual skills, colors, matching similar shapes, finding the different shape, and fine motor skills (such as coloring, cutting and pasting). If one side of the folder contains the newly prepared work sheets for the child and the other side has a place to put completed worksheets, the child has a concrete way of seeing the entire work time task before he begins and has a sense of completion in filing it away upon completion (A-24, A-25, A-26, A-28).

A child's first name should be clearly written on the outside of his folder in the handwriting style his school expects him to use. This should be a model to help him learn to write his first name (A-27).

Tools and Utensils The teacher brings out a box of household tools or utensils such as an egg beater, can opener, iron, hammer, screw driver. She asks "What is this?", "How do you use it?", and "What else do you need with this?" Be sure you have the necessary matching equipment such as a bowl for the egg beater, can for the can opener, tea towel for the iron, and screws, nails, and wood for the hammer and screw driver (B-8; A-18; C-12).

Equipping the Stage Two Classroom

Materials which will assist you in providing effective activities for Stage Two children usually should be adapted from regular toys and preschool curriculum.

The following lists are representative of the materials you might find in a Stage Two classroom.

For Work Time May satisfy academic objectives A-19 through A-28, A-30, A-31; behavioral objective B-10; communication objectives C-9, C-12, and socialization objectives S-14, S-18.

Individual work folders and worksheets

Cards with geometric shapes, alike and different

Cards with number groupings and numerals on back

Dominoes for number groups

Groups of small objects for counting and classifying: beads, buttons, spools, socks, gloves

Objects and pictures for matching

Same and Different Cards, DLM No. 254

Name tags (first names only)

Days of week chart, by month

Work materials:
  Kindergarten-size pencils
  Kindergarten-size crayons
  Catalogue and magazine pictures for cutting and pasting
  Kindergarten scissors
  Paste
  Magnets and metal objects
  Colored felt tip pens

Learning to Think Series—The Blue Book (Science Research Associates)

Sullivan Associates Readers (Webster Division, McGraw-Hill)
  Story Books 1, 1A, 1B
  Programmed Primer 1, 1A, 1B
  Film Strips No. 1, 2

Developmental Learning Materials
  Associate Picture Cards No. PP-156
  Motor Expressive Cards II No. P-160
  Spatial Relation Picture Cards, Series B, No. P-125
  Color Association Picture Cards, No. 158

For Inside Play May satisfy behavior objectives B-8, B-11, B-12; socialization objectives S-13 through S-17; communication objective C-13; and academic objectives A-18, A-24.

Doll carriage (Creative Playthings)
Play house (cardboard box)
Ethnic dolls, both sexes
Dress-up clothes
Box of jewelry and pop beads
Box of hats and purses
Mirror
Cardboard building blocks
Play telephones
Large wooden toy airplane
Large wooden toy trucks (Creative Playthings; Tonka Trucks)
Doll house
Doll furniture
Doll family
Magic Etch-A-Sketch
Blackboard at floor level; chalk and eraser
Stove, refrigerator, sink (Creative Playthings)
Large doll cradle
Plastic dishes
Stop signs (Creative Playthings)

For Story Time May satisfy behavior objective B-10; communication objectives C-9 through C-13; and (pre)-academic objectives A-19, A-22, A-25, A-26, A-31.

A Cowboy Can by Clure and Rumsey (Bowmar)
Best Friends by Cohen (Macmillan)
Big and Little, Up and Down by Berkley (Young Scott Books)
Big Red Bus by Kessler (Doubleday)
(The) Big Train Book by Kramer (McGraw-Hill)
Book of Shapes, Sesame Street (Little, Brown)

Play is the time to practice newly acquired skills or to experiment with new concepts of social awareness. Select equipment which allows these processes to occur.

In selecting storybooks for Stage Two children be certain that the topic is within the actual experiences of the children. You waste important time by using stories which do not involve the children in specific ways. Be sure, also, that story time becomes a vehicle for working on communication objectives.

(The) Bowmar Publishing Corp. Early Childhood Series

Changes, Changes by Hutchins (Macmillan)

David Was Mad (Holt, Rinehart and Winston)

Dr. Seuss's ABC's (Random House)

Fun for Chris by Randall (Albert Whitman)

Go Dog Go (Random House Beginner Books)

Goldie Locks and The Three Bears (Child Guidance Action Books)

Growl Bear by Austin (E. P. Dalton)

Happy Birthday by Izawa and Hijikata (Grosset and Dunlap)

How Many Teeth? by Showers (Thomas Y. Crowell)

If I Drove A Truck (Lothrop, Lee & Shepard)

Is It Hard? Is It Easy? by Green (Young Scott Books)

Let's Play House by Lenski (Henry Z. Walck)

Listen, Colors, Three Little Chicks (Bowmar)

Little Boy Who Lives Up High by Hawkinson (Albert Whitman)

(The) Little Brown Hen by Martin (Thomas Y. Crowell)

Little Chief by Hoff (Harper & Row, I Can Read Books)

Olaf Reads by Lexau (Scholastic Book Services)

Pop Up Animal-Alphabet Book (Random House)

(The) Real Princess by Izawa and Hijikata (Grosset & Dunlap)

(The) Sesame Street Book of Letters (Little, Brown; General Learning Corp.)

(The) Sesame Street Book of Numbers (Little, Brown; General Learning Corp.)

(The) Snowy Day by Keats (Scholastic Book Services)

Stop Stop by Hurd (Harper & Bros.)

Straight Hair, Curly Hair by Goldin (Thomas Y. Crowell)

Through the Day by Rumsey (Bowmar)

Timid Timothy by Williams (Young Scott Books)

Too Many Pockets by Levenson (Wonder Books)

(The) Very Little Boy by Krasilovsky (Doubleday)

What Time Is It? by Izawa (Grosset & Dunlap)

Will I Have a Friend? by Cohen (Macmillan)

Winnie the Pooh and the Honey Tree, book and record (Walt Disney Prod.)

Your Skin and Mine by Showers (Thomas Y. Crowell)

For Art Time May satisfy behavior objectives B-9, B-10, B-12; socialization objectives S-13, S-15, S-16, S-18; communication objectives C-8 through C-13; and preacademic objectives A-19, A-22, A-26, A-27.

Art activities are a major source for success at Stage Two. By avoiding activities which emphasize representational products, a teacher can provide unlimited success experiences for children. Several particularly effective projects are:

Crayons on sandpaper
String painting
Potato and vegetable prints
Chalk on wet paper
Smiling faces or designs painted on rocks
Tissue paper on waxed paper ("stained glass windows")
Weaving paper strips for placemats for a special snack time
Magazine collages
Paper strip designs
Paper maché on balloons
Tie and dye paper towel prints
Leaves and crayon stencil

At art time, a simple "model" should be provided by the teacher during the introduction of the lesson. This will help insecure and anxious children who often copy the example.

For Outside Play   May satisfy socialization objectives S-13 through S-17; behavior objectives B-8, B-11, B-12; communication objective C-13; and preacademic objective A-29.

Walking board
Tricycles or small bicycles
Sand mountain
Jumping pit
Climbing cargo net
An area for running and group games
Large and medium sized utility balls
Frisbees
Skill Development Equipment Company; Incline Mat, Octagon Donut, Merry Mountain, Socia-Bowl, Buddy Saddle, Big Blibbit

For Music   May satisfy behavior objectives B-11, B-12; socialization objectives S-13 through S-17; communication objectives C-8, C-11, C-12, C-13; and preacademic objective A-29.

Equipment
   Record player or tape player
   Guitar
   Autoharp
   Tone resonator bells
   Rhythm instruments such as sand blocks, tone blocks, claves, drums, maracas, tambourines, finger cymbals, guiros, triangles (Rhythm Band, Inc.)
Records
   American Folk Songs for Children (FC 7601), Pete Seeger (Folkways Records)
   Learning Basic Skills Through Music, Vol. I (AR 514), Vol. II (AR 522), Vocabulary Vol. (AR 521), Hap Palmer (Educational Activities, Inc.)
   Getting to Know Myself (AR 543), Hap Palmer (Educational Activities, Inc.)

Mod Marches (AR 527), Hap Palmer (Educational Activities, Inc.)
   Play Your Instruments and Make a Pretty Sound (FC 7665), Ella Jenkins (Folkways Records)
   Homemade Band (AR 545), Hap Palmer (Educational Activities, Inc.)

For Group Games   May satisfy socialization objectives S-13 through S-17; behavior objectives B-9, B-11, B-12; socialization objectives C-8, C-11, C-12, C-13; and preacademic objectives A-24, A-29.

People Puzzles (Developmental Learning Materials)
Bean bags and box target
Cassette tape recorder or record player
Polaroid camera
Picture Dominoes (Creative Playthings)
Playdoh or clay
Exercise mat

For Language   May satisfy communication objectives C-8 through C-13; socialization objectives S-13, S-14, S-18; behavior objectives B-10, B-12; and preacademic objectives A-19, A-25, A-26, A-31.

Peabody Language Development Kit, Level 1
Singer Education and Training Products, filmstrips and records (Society for Visual Education, Inc.)
Informal picture cards for vocabulary building
Language Master and individual cards (Bell and Howell)
Developmental Learning Materials, Expressive Language Pictures I, II; Sequential Picture Cards, No. P-161, 162; Sequential Picture Stories No. 242; Reaction Cards, No. 240
Felt characters for flannel board stories
Cardboard box with hole for hand to feel contents

Through music and games a child may find his first successful avenue for communication and socialization. Keep these objectives in mind when selecting materials and equipment.

Puppets (Creative Playthings)
Cassette tape player and recorder

ACTIVITIES AND MATERIALS FOR STAGE THREE (LEARNING SKILLS FOR GROUP PARTICIPATION)

When a child enters Stage Three, self control and self confidence are the keys to success. The most crucial of all activities and materials is the group itself. Each child must learn that he can be a successful group member, a unique contributor to the group. From Stage Two he has learned to value himself and to see himself as a person who can be successful. Now, in Stage Three he must go beyond a concern for his own success and become involved in the impact he makes on others. The Stage Three child responds to rules and routines. He finds it hard to accept changes in rules and expresses great concern over nonconformity in others. Anxiety is created by feelings that cannot be controlled or by feelings that cannot be fulfilled. During this stage the adult is seen as the person who solves problems and maintains the desired routines and procedures.

You as the teacher must be responsive to the feelings which this stage arouses. Help the children learn to share, control impulsivity, participate in planning group procedures and rules; and in general see that social cooperation and communication can be pleasurable and desirable.

Perhaps the most effective activities for Stage Three classes are group games, life-like toys and games, role playing, group art projects, and group music.

Games bring children together. If the rules are simple and there are opportunities for both success and failure, children at Stage Three gain the very important sense of "groupness." They learn

that their own success can come from being part of a team. They learn that to have a turn they must wait their turn. They learn that rules help to hold others in line as well as themselves. The purpose of games at Stage Three is a group process and a group product. The process can be the thrill and excitement of action and participation with others. The product is a group output. Avoid performance elements which break down into individual competition and rivalry. Redefine the games so that each child's score goes for the whole group rather than toward an individual score. In this way the group compares its group performance on one day with its performance at another time. This groupness also ensures success for every member.

For Stage Three, the procedures you use in conducting an activity are more important perhaps than the activity itself. You might think of each activity as having four distinct phases, each with particular Stage Three objectives.

Group Activity Phases

The Group Gets Ready for the Activity The group is offered choices of materials or games within the activity, giving opportunities for children to suggest (S-21) and to follow others' suggestions (S-22).

Children take turns helping get materials for the group (S-19).

The group discusses the procedures (rules) for the conduct of the activity (B-13). When suggested variations in an activity seem workable, the group has the opportunity to develop new procedures or change the old rules (B-14; S-21, S-22).

During the Activity Children share materials (S-20) and take turns at "having a turn" (S-19).

Each child is encouraged to talk

As an example of how Stage Three activities and materials are used, Chapter 9 contains a description of an actual Stage Three class.

The Stage Three group does not emerge instantly. It is through the verbal reflections of the teachers that the children become aware of the benefits of a group.

By always "talking through" the activity before it begins, the teacher insures that each child will understand the concept (even if over-simplified). This process is crucial to the success of an activity.

about his ideas related to the activity (C-16).

The teachers design activities which necessitate participation and involvement of every child with others (S-23).

An emphasis is maintained upon participating and complying with the procedures developed before the activity began (B-19).

Children are encouraged to verbally express feeling responses to the activity, materials, teachers, or other children (C-20).

Children are helped by the teachers to control impulses and destructive aggressions (B-18).

Almost all Stage Three activities involve some academic objectives such as using number concepts, writing numerals, writing name, reading labels or basic primary vocabulary, and responding to story telling or creating stories (A-35, A-36, A-37, A-40, A-43, A-44, A-45, A-48).

When Activities Go Wrong   Usually one or two children in a Stage Three group will have difficulty with any given activity. Early in Stage Three these incidents should be dealt with privately:

"What happened?" (B-15, B-16)

"What is another way you could have handled it?" (B-17)

"What can I do to help you so this won't happen?" (B-14)

Later in Stage Three these same questions can be asked of the group as a whole.

At the End of an Activity   Each child should be recognized for an accomplishment, either by the teacher or by another child (C-14). The teacher often must be the model for these children to learn the value of each other's contribution.

Each child is encouraged to make a gesture or statement reflecting pride in what he has done (C-19). This takes a long time to emerge with some Stage Three children.

The activity ends with recognition of the accomplishment of the group as a whole and with each individual's unique contribution (S-24).

By adjusting each of these procedures to the individual developmental objectives for the children in the group, you can see how a majority of the Stage Three objectives, in all four curriculum areas, can be woven into any activity you plan. The following lists offer sample activities which have been successful with Stage Three children.

Activities for the Stage Three Classroom

Story time   The teacher reads a story using various voice inflections to convey moods or characters (a mean, screechy witch voice; a deep, gruff voice; a whispery, scared voice). Children develop ability to recall characteristics of story characters according to the voice. They also quickly learn to produce these characterizations themselves (C-20; S-24; A-44).

Role Playing Rules   The teacher sets the scene for an imaginary event which might occur within the experience of every child in the group. "What will we do when we go . . . ?"

. . . to the movies? (set up chairs; make and buy tickets; make and sell popcorn; show film, preferably a video tape of the group itself in a child drama activity or role play)

. . . shopping with Mother? (use dress up clothes, wallets, pocketbooks, hats, play or child-made money; make different departments in a store for shoes, food, books, toys, clothes; price objects and make appropriate signs)

. . . to a restaurant? (Burger King, McDonald's, or other familiar spot;

At all times the Stage Three teacher encourages group involvement and individual contribution to mutual effort. Yet there is an implicit assurance that the teacher will not expect more than the members of the group can comfortably handle. This confidence is the basis for rebuilding from a crisis.

Stage Three activities are designed to promote an emerging sense of individual contribution to the group effort. Often, it is less uncomfortable for children to begin to do this by taking on the character of make believe.

make signs; make menus with a few choices either for make-believe, such as hamburgers and french fries, or for a real snack, such as peanut butter, graham crackers, popcorn, or cupcakes; set prices; teacher usually serves as cashier unless there is one group member with advanced skills for adding money)

These activities are excellent ways to teach Stage Three behavior objectives (B-13, B-16, B-17). They also permit all of the academic objectives to be incorporated into the role play and offer great opportunity for group projects.

Through the Stage Three activities, a child's confidence in himself grows and he begins to see himself as an accepted member of the group. This is the overall Stage Three goal.

Another variation for role playing expected behaviors is a simple situation initiated by the teacher and developed by the group without additional props. "How do you act when . . ."
. . . visitors come to school (or home)?
. . . someone stays for dinner?
. . . you visit a friend?
. . . you go to the dentist (or doctor)?
. . . you go to a ballgame?
. . . you have an accident?

While it is important to think ahead of time through each step which might occur in an incident, changes will occur while the children role play. Follow their new leads as long as the role playing situation remains relevant to the general topic (B-13, B-15, B-17).

The "trick" of entering into a group's role play, yet still remaining the teacher, is a difficult technique to master. By communicating these role changes with complete clarity and simplicity, it can be done.

Child Drama Use a familiar story, either a standard childhood tale, such as "Three Billy Goats Gruff" or "Red Riding Hood", a story read many times with the group or a story composed by the children themselves. Topics which have interested Stage Three children include:

"Fighting the Dragon" (the children have made a large cardboard and tissue paper dragon)
"Sailing Across the Ocean to Discover a

New Land" (in a connected series of boxes for a ship)
"Flying in an Airplane to Receive Awards for Constructing the Greatest Jet in the World" (same series of boxes arranged with wings)

During group art time, costumes (usually paper bag masks, paper hats, etc.) may be made; or the children may be able to get into character without costumes. In a beginning Stage Three class, the teacher often will define the positions and movements by role playing the central figure herself. This provides structure to the drama and helps prevent loss of control when a child indicates he might be carried away by the excitement. After a group has some success with child drama, the teacher should pull back from direct participation except to set the tone or to move in as a character when one child indicates that inappropriate behavior or loss of control is imminent.

Preparation for child drama often begins during role play at play time when the lead teacher moves in and out of the play to stimulate the children in a role or to get involved in play by assuming a role (B-18, B-19; C-16, C-20; S-21; A-44, A-48).

Travel Games Using butcher paper on the floor for roads, the children and teachers plan a trip and identify a particular destination (store, swimming pool, lake, mountains, picnic, home). They also plan what will be along the way, (such as stop signs, railroad crossings, forests, bridge, stores). The children can travel the road in accord with a predetermined plan. Crossroads can be added later, and children can make maps to guide them to the destination. When combined with role play or child drama these roads add structure by providing the plot and a place for each child along the way. When children are particularly reticent about interacting with others or have difficulty keeping a plot going, this activity works well.

If space permits, a "road" can be marked off permanently with masking tape from the work table to the supply cupboard. The child selected to get materials for the group "travels" this road and returns with the supplies (B-19; S-22; A-39). If the child is given a "supply list" written with basic words, another academic objective can be added (A-35 or A-45).

Modified Treasure Hunt The teacher hides parts of a large picture around the room, one piece for each child (a house, car, bicycle, motorcycle, etc.). As the group sits at the table, she gives a child a "clue," telling him where to walk, where to turn, etc. This continues until each child has had a turn and the group speculates on what the picture will be. When put together they paste the picture on another large sheet of poster paper (S-19).

This activity can be extended by having each member of the group contribute a word to make a sentence or story about the picture. The picture can be used also for a group game modifying "Pin the Tail on the Donkey" (B-19; S-19), with members of the group giving advice to the blindfolded child in order to get closer to the target (S-32). The target might be the wheel on the racer, the horn on the bicycle, etc.

Tape Recording A cassette recorder is useful for a number of auditory activities. Begin with recording sound effects until the group becomes skilled in selecting sounds and identifying the objects which make the sounds. Use paper crackling, emery boards or sand paper; rice, cereal, or beans dropped in a tin can or a plastic cup. Encourage the children to think of sounds and ways to reproduce them. By combining sound effects with role play activities conveying character and feeling through voice changes, the group can eventually have a radio show, complete with commercial (C-20; S-21, S-22, S-24; A-44, A-48).

Motion Games Each child is given a piece of colored paper. More than one child should have the same color. If colors are inappropriate, shapes, numbers, words, or pictures might be used. In song or by command directions are given, "Blue stand up. Green sit down. Yellow turn around," etc. The pacing can be modified to the ability of individual children to sit for a turn, to participate without excess motion, or to follow directions (B-19; S-19; A-21, A-22, A-34, A-35). This activity is particularly appropriate for beginning Stage Three. It tends to lose the interest of advanced Stage Three children; but by selecting such children to lead the activity, it regains their interest (S-22).

Telephone Book In separate booklets, each child makes a list of five people or places he likes to telephone. These may be friends, movie theatres, weather, time, relatives, or home (A-36, A-45; S-23, S-21; C-16).

This activity should be preceded by play telephone activities in which the children have a single digit phone number for individual play telephones. The children make a telephone list of the first names and the play telephone numbers of the others (A-36; S-19, S-24). During play time they "call" friends to give messages or directions. At first these may need to be suggested by the teacher, but later can be initiated by the children themselves (S-21, S-22, S-23).

The Address Chart To learn to write home addresses, children should have a model to which they can refer

As a Stage Three child begins to feel good about himself he can tolerate more from others. However, if he is expected to be supportive of others when he is unsure of himself, progress will come to a halt.

When Stage Three children have confidence that the teacher will not set expectations too high to meet and when the activities are interesting and varied, each child will participate with increasing enthusiasm.

when necessary. An address chart which includes the entire group provides another source for "groupness" in addition to assistance with the academic objectives (A-37; S-24).

Today's Date A large, blank calendar is placed on the wall or bulletin board on the first of each month with a bright star, sun, or other attractive symbol to designate the first day. Each day a different child is selected to write in the day and date. If a child cannot write, the activity can include small cards from which he selects the day of the week and tapes it to the board. To add communication experiences to this activity, the teacher asks individual children, "What day was yesterday? What day will tomorrow be?" (C-16; A-36, A-37, A-40).

Recipe Book Recipes can be modified experience stories. They can be created by the group using basic primary vocabulary and numerals, appropriate for individual academic objectives. While making custard, Jello, milk shakes, or popcorn, children contribute a sentence (word or picture) to describe each step. The teacher writes the steps on a chart. After the recipe has been completed and enjoyed, the children copy the recipe in their individual "Recipe Book." If there are nonwriting children in the group who cannot yet copy, that portion of the activity should be omitted for the entire group (B-19; C-16, C-19; S-19, S-20, S-22; A-33, A-35, A-36, A-38, A-43, A-45, A-48).

The "I Like ——" Game Ahead of time, the teacher cuts pictures from magazines by categories such as food, clothes, sports, cars, famous people, TV shows, etc.) Pictures are selected on the basis of every child's personal interests and ability. The pictures are spread out in the center of the circle if the children are sitting on the floor. Each child chooses a picture and begins "I like ——

(holds up picture) because ——." (C-16; S-19, S-24; A-44).

This activity is also helpful for children who are still behind in language concepts or other academic objectives at Stage Two (C-9, C-13; A-19, A-31). The activity is structured so that each child will have something tangible to hold as he speaks and something specific to which he can refer. Each child speaks briefly and is expected also to wait and listen to each other child.

Blackboard Activities A blackboard can solve a multitude of problems related to the transition from work time to another activity. Because children complete their individual work assignments at varying rates, provision must be made for attractive activities which are not too distracting to those still working but interesting enough to hold the attention of those who finish early. In no instance should the teacher give additional "work" to the child who has finished. A large blackboard, hung at children's height, provides excellent opportunity for carryover activities for one or two children. They often organize themselves, playing "school," "teacher," "tic-tac-toe"; drawing mazes for each other to follow; making dot-to-dot pictures; or illustrating a scene collaboratively (B-18, B-19; S-20, S-21, S-22, S-23; A-33, A-36, A-37, A-38, A-40, A-41, A-46, A-47).

A Class Scrapbook Polaroid photos of each class member are pasted into a scrapbook, "Our Class." Name cards can be made during work time and added. This book can be kept up to date by photographs of particular, special activities which the group does together (C-19; S-19, S-24; A-37, A-48).

Equipping the Stage Three Classroom

Stage Three generally uses ordinary school and play materials, with the mod-

Materials and equipment for Stage Three are already familiar to the children from home and school experiences. However, the memories are often of failure and frustration. For this reason Stage Three children often resist trying any activity.

ifications discussed previously. The following lists of materials are representative of what might be found in any Stage Three class.

For Art Projects May satisfy communication objectives C-14, C-16, C-19, C-20; socialization objectives S-20, S-21; behavior objectives B-13 through B-19; and academic objectives A-34, A-38.

Masking tape
Crayons
Felt tip pens (all colors)
Magic markers (all colors)
Modeling clay (white clay is paintable with water colors)
Construction paper (assorted colors and sizes)
Wheat paste (or made by children)
Elmer's glue
Scissors (left- and righthanded)
Dried beans, macaroni (for collages; can be dyed assorted colors with food coloring or used in natural form)
Butcher paper
Brown paper bags (medium size for masks; small size for hand puppets)
Toothpicks
Styrofoam (collected from drugstores, electronic firms, etc.)
Pastels and/or craypas
Tissue paper (assorted colors)
Wax paper, aluminum foil
Paper plates (for making clocks and faces)
Paper cups (upside down for standing figures)
Water colors
Powdered tempera paint
Alpha Colors (Webster-Costello)
Magazine pictures
Assorted size brushes (#1, #7, #12) for water colors and tempera
Newspapers and magazines
White drawing paper
Scraps of cloth, yarn, buttons, wire
Potatoes and other vegetables for printing designs

Washable ink, several colors, for printing and brayers

For Indoor Group Activities and Games May satisfy socialization objectives S-19 through S-23; behavior objectives B-13 through B-19; communication objective C-14; and academic objectives A-32 through A-36, A-38, A-42, A-43, A-46.

Rocket Darts (SportsCraft)
Toss a Cross (Ideal Company)
Ring Toss (Milton Bradley)
Space Hopper (Shell Oil Company)
Math Bingo (teacher made)
Bingo (usually teacher made)
Hot Wheel Cars (Mattel)
Battling Tops (Ideal)
Hands Down (Ideal)
Spill and Spell (Parker Bros.)
Twister (Milton Bradley)
Trouble (Kohner)
Playing cards
Balloon darts
Suction darts and target (preferably made by children)
Bowling
Assorted wood, nails, hammers
Tumbling mat (Atlas Company)
Record or tape player and popular records or tapes
Marbles and masking tape for ring
Bean bags (can be made by children); box to toss them in; score sheet for group
Growing a garden in paper cups
Popcorn and popper
Blender for milkshakes
Videotape for taping group projects
Blackboard game (tic-tac-toe)

For Indoor Play Time (Usually changes to game time at upper levels of Stage Three.) May satisfy behavior objectives B-13 through B-19; socialization objectives S-19 through S-24; communication objective C-19; and academic objectives A-32, A-35, A-36, A-40, A-42, A-43, A-45, A-46.

Store (built from boxes)
Wooden cash register (Creative Play-things)
Empty egg cartons, grocery containers
Play money
Play telephones
Baby carriage used as shopping cart
Pocket books, hats, wallets
Tinker Toys, Lincoln Logs, Leggo
Train track (can be child-made)
Wooden train

Selecting stories for Stage Three children is similar in most respects to the selection process at Stage Two. There is one important difference. Stage Three children can begin to assimilate more abstract concepts in a story and can generalize to themselves. Therefore, be certain that the stories have a relevant and generalizable theme. Remember, too, that stories should be a lead-in to communication objectives.

For Story Time May satisfy communication objective C-16, C-20; socialization objective S-24; behavior objective B-15, B-16; and academic objectives A-44, A-48.

Angus and the Cat by Flack (Doubleday)
Becky by Wilson (Thomas Y. Crowell)
(The) Blah by Kent (Parents' Magazine Press)
Blaze Shows the Way by Anderson (Macmillan)
Bowmar Monster Book Series (Bowmar)
Curious George by Rey (Houghton Mifflin)
George and Martha by Marshall (Houghton Mifflin)
Go Dog Go by Eastman (Random House)
Goggles by Keats (Macmillan)
Green Eggs and Ham by Suess (Random House)
Hop on Pop by Seuss (Random House)
(The) Loudest Noise in the World by Elkin (Cadmus Books)
Lucky and the Giant by Elkin (Scholastic Book Services)
Madeline's Rescue by Bemelmans (Scholastic Book Services)
Mr. Pine's Mixed-up Signs by Kessler (Wonder Books)
One Special Dog by Martin (Rand McNally)

Runaway John by Klein (Alfred A. Knopf)
Sam by Scott (McGraw-Hill)
Seven in a Bed by Sonnelworn (Viking Press)
Stevie by Steptoe (Harper & Row)
Talking Without Words by Ets (Viking Press)
Ten Apples Up On Top by LeSieg (Random House Beginner Books)
(The) Three Little Pigs (Child Guidance Action Books)
(The) Very Little Girl by Krasilousky (Doubleday)
(A) Very Special House by Krauss (Harper & Row)
What Do You Say Dear? by Joslin (Scholastic Book Services)

For Work Time May satisfy academic objectives A-32 through A-38, A-40 through A-43, A-45, A-46, A-47; behavior objective B-19; and communication objectives C-14, C-16, C-19.

Sullivan Associates Readers (Webster Division, McGraw-Hill) Story Books 2, 2A, 2B through Story Books 7, 7A, 7B; Programmed Reading Books 2–7; film strips No. 3–7
Elementary School Mathematics—Book 1 (Addison-Wesley)
Word Analysis (Macmillan)
Big clock face; individual clocks (child made)
Flash cards for words, numerals, and groupings to 10
File boxes or envelope for flash words
Individual "mail boxes" for children to review "letters" from other children and the teachers
Calendar for the month
Flannel board for number work, flannel counters
Individual work folders containing daily assignments
Supplies: pencils (#2), scissors, glue, tape, crayons, felt tip pens, rulers

For Language May satisfy communication objectives C-14 through C-21; socialization objectives S-19, S-24; and academic objectives A-34, A-35, A-44, A-45, A-47, A-48.

Language Master and cards with basic sight vocabulary, individual language master cards and special education set (Bell and Howell)

Flash cards with basic sight vocabulary

Fishpole with magnet on end of string

Paper fish with large staple or small paper clip for mouth; one basic sight word on each fish (or arithmetic problem)

Peabody Language Development Kit, Level 2

Developing Understanding of Self and Others (DUSO) D-1, Book 2, Units V-VIII (American Guidance Service, Inc.)

Hand puppets (Creative Playthings)

Classic fairy tales, film strips and records (Encyclopedia Brittanica Educational Corp.) "Animals of the Zoo" and "Little Beaver" filmstrips

Cassette tape recorder

Flannel board with flannel figures for story telling

For Outdoor Games and Recreation May satisfy behavior objectives B-13 through B-19; socialization objectives S-19 through S-23; and academic objective A-39.

Skill Development Equipment Company: Incline Mat, Spot Trainer, Thud Ball, Octagon Donut, Merry Mountain, Socia-Bowl

Large and medium utility balls for dodge ball, and modified soccer and volley ball

Frisbees

Softball and bat

Whiffleball and bat

Shuffleboard

Football

Basketball and basket

Tires for swinging and climbing

Tether ball

Long jump ropes for groups

Knotted rope from tree for climbing and swinging

A platform, or other defined area, for the group to congregate

Old automobile for imaginary trips (or old boat mounted on springs)

For Music Time May satisfy socialization objectives S-19 through S-24; communication objective C-20; and behavior objectives B-13 through B-19.

Equipment:

   Record player or tape player
   Guitar
   Autoharp
   Kazoos
   Snare drum
   Tone resonator bells
   Rhythm Instruments such as tone blocks, wood blocks, claves, guiros, maracas, tambourines, finger cymbals, drums (bongo, conga, hand drums) (Rhythm Band, Inc.)
   Materials for making "homemade instruments": cans, toilet paper spools, wood scraps, bottle caps, bolts, string, rubber bands

Records:

   Popular records such as The Four Tops (Motown), The Jackson Five (Jobete Music Co., Inc.), The 5th Dimension (Bell Records), Three Dog Night (ABC/Dunhill Records, Inc.)
   Whoever Shall Have Some Peanuts (SC 7530), Sam Hinton (Scholastic Records)
   Motivating Thought Processes Through Music, Vol. I (LPED 220A) (Stallman-Susser Productions, Inc.)
   Homemade Band (AR 546), Hap Palmer (Educational Activities, Inc.)
   Mod Marches (AR 527), Hap Palmer (Educational Activities, Inc.)
   Kimbo Educational Records, Early Childhood, Special Education Series

ACTIVITIES AND MATERIALS FOR STAGE FOUR (INVESTING IN GROUP PROCESSES)

Chapter 10 contains a description of an actual Stage Four class involved in typical Stage Four activities.

Stage Four activities and materials generally are more "sophisticated" than those of previous stages; the teacher must recognize the styles which are current within the peer group and build the program with these in mind. This may mean watching TV shows and movies which make a hit with the group. Visits to neighborhood recreation spots (afternoons and evenings) also will bring the teacher in closer tune with the action.

Stage Four of Developmental Therapy is a period of vacillation and change. The child is beginning the transition from childhood to adulthood, from dependence on others to dependence on self, from narcissism to valuing peer acceptance, and from self rejection to increased acceptance of self as a worthwhile individual. Such distinct changes produce considerable anxiety over the responsibilities of independence. This concern is manifest through intense interest in the roles of others, in exploring consequences, and in the ability of a group to change rules and exert control.

The organization of Stage Four activities can be best described as flexible. As a Stage Four teacher you will need to be flexible, too. Continue to be now-oriented but deal also with the recent past. In discussion, you can expect the children to recall recent events and be able to link these recollections to present situations. There are times when you will anticipate the group's need for adult leadership and assert your authority. At other times you will involve yourself only marginally.

During Stage Four, children are coming under greater self control and at the same time are responding to peer influence. A major challenge for you will be to assist each child in finding a balance between these two forces. These are real-life processes at work, and children at Stage Four are ready to meet the challenge. For this reason keep the activities and materials authentic and appropriate. Field trips and special projects are among the best means of doing this. Materials should be those which are admired and accepted or are so new to the children's experience as to represent an exciting challenge.

One way to look at activities for Stage Four is to consider the daily schedule and the wide range of options needed within each activity. In this way, you can plan to meet the Stage Four objectives. The following section contains general guidelines and sample activities to meet the various objectives. As in previous sections the most applicable objectives are listed first.

Activities for the Stage Four Classroom

Academic Work Time May satisfy academic objectives A-49 through A-53; behavior objectives B-21, B-24, B-25; communication objectives C-22, C-24, C-26, C-27; and socialization objectives S-25, S-28, S-29, S-30.

Individual work folder: includes a daily plan for individual academic work, usually developed jointly by the teacher and child.

Board work: has a group focus, but the teacher usually will be group leader in order to accomodate individual academic differences.

Group project: requires every child to contribute. Activities might include group story telling, writing and producing plays, constructing props (including play money, signs, charts, backdrops, etc.)

Individual projects: individualized projects should be kept to a minimum but do have a place in the schedule, especially for children who complete academic work before others. Individual activities might include measuring the room for dimensions, estimating weights of objects, making lists of materials needed for a project.

Regular school assignments: when necessary, work time should provide assistance to a Stage Four child in doing his regular school assignments. Close coordination with his regular teacher is essential if this is to be therapeutic in the limited time available.

Materials typically used at Stage Four work time might include the following:

Sullivan Associates Reader (Webster Division, McGraw-Hill) Programmed Readers, Books 8–14

Peabody Language Development Kit, Level 2

Edmark Reading Program

Road maps of city, state and region

Commercially made wall calendar

Microscope

Magnifying glass

Rulers, weight scales for postage, groceries, and people

Bank check books

Newspapers and current magazine articles

Arithmetic flash cards

Arithmetic work sheets

Individual loose leaf notebooks

Curriculum materials from regular school program

High interest, low vocabulary story books such as the Bowmar Company "Wheels Series":

   Custom Cars
   Drag Racing
   Drag Racing Funny Cars
   Dune Buggies
   Dune Buggy Racing
   Horses
   Karting: Fun on Four Wheels
   (The) Mighty Midgets
   Minibikes
   Motorcycles
   Motorcycle Racing
   Slot Car Racing
   Snowmobiles
   Surfing
   Teen Fair
   VW Bugs

Talk Time May satisfy communication objectives C-22, C-23, C-24, C-25, C-27; socialization objectives S-25, S-28, S-29, S-20; academic objective A-52; and behavior objectives B-23, B-24, B-25.

Activities selected for talk time should afford opportunities for expression of feelings and for both group and individual problem solving. Such activities can be dealt with successfully in the context of a warm, accepting, reality-based environment. The teacher promotes spontaneity of expression by making the children feel comfortable, asking questions about feelings, and sensitizing them to the need for verbal rather than physical expressions. The teacher encourages group members to recognize feelings in others in crisis situations and as they arise as a result of group activities.

Individual and group problem solving ability is crucial for Stage Four peer interaction. The teacher, who often serves as group leader, guides the group in their exploration of feelings, behaviors, and outcomes. The teacher also identifies strengths and weaknesses of group members and thus becomes a model for the children learning to praise and support others.

The teacher may use discussion sessions, audiovisual aids, group and individual Life Space Interviews, visiting public figures, sports stars, and other interesting people such as a scuba diver, musician, dancer, artist, and policeman.

Two activities which are particularly effective early in Stage Four for helping children develop basic discussion skills are described below.

"Instant Word" Game A one-word topic is given to the group and each member in turn gives the first, brief idea that comes into his head concerning the topic. Certain ground rules are developed by the group concerning length of time

Activities at this stage should stimulate the children to involvement and commitment. Because neither of these processes is developed at the beginning of Stage Four the teacher is the catalyst for initiating and sustaining the processes.

Separate, individual activities have no place in a Stage Four class. If the activities have been carefully selected on the basis of each child's individual objectives and the group tone is set around the individual worth of each member, the result will be children who are individually successful as members of the group.

any one person may speak (one minute is recommended at the beginning), the order turns will be taken, and whether or not group members will be permitted to engage in unstructured responding to each other's ideas.

Topics might include: *Sad, Storm, See, What, Color, Free, Fight, Sink, Cry, Love, Win, Gone,* etc. (C-22, C-23, C-26, C-28; B-21; S-28, S-29, S-30; A-52).

Discussion Club Discussion club is an extension of the "Instant Word" game. As the group develops skill in conversation longer discussions are encouraged. Topics then might include:

No Money: *"Why do people write checks that 'bounce'?"*
"What happens when they do this?"
"What other ways could they handle the situation?"

Nothing to Do: *"Why does this happen?"*
"How do you feel?"
"What could you do?"

Left Alone: *"What is it like?"*
"What do you do?"
"How do you feel?"
"How does it end?"

Nobody Likes Me: *"What gives you that idea?"*
"Why does it happen?"
"How do you feel?"
"What could you do?"

Feeling Dumb: *"What happens to make you feel dumb?"*
"What do you do about it?"
"How does it end?"
(C-22, C-23, C-24, C-26, C-27, C-28; S-28, S-29, S-30; B-22, B-23; A-52)

Group Project or Special Time May satisfy socialization objectives S-25, S-28, S-29, S-30; behavior objectives B-20, B-21, B-22, B-25; academic objectives A-52, A-53; and communication objectives C-24, C-26.

Group projects are the backbone of the Stage Four curriculum. They provide motivation for a child's efforts to maintain control when provoked. *"You did a good job of staying in control when Johnny pushed your chair. That let us keep going on with our plans for the trip."*

Group projects also provide for new experiences which a child may have previously avoided. Because of the warmth and acceptance of the group, such a child is often willing to risk himself in order to continue the good group feeling.

It is in such activities that there also are many opportunities for individual activities and people, such as in team selection, project partners, or group leaders. Members of a Stage Four group feel secure in that they know they will have many opportunities to be a leader and to follow.

Usually, group projects are the result of group selection and planning. Activities might include a number of elaborate or simple projects. For example:

A "club house" with:
Tape player and popular tapes
Guitars
Black light for making blacklight posters
Polaroid camera for group pictures
Scrap book of group activities
Popular posters
Popcorn popper
Table and chairs for "business meetings"
Cushions on the floor for informal sessions
Wall paint, rollers, and brushes for painting a preferred color
Commercial painter's hats

A "recording studio" with:
  Tape recorder and player
  Record or tape player and popular
  music
  A microphone (may be cardboard)
  Various rhythm band instruments
  A portable video camera, videotape
  recorder, and monitor for making
  "television shows"
  Signs, charts, cue cards, scripts, and
  title cards
  Stop watch
  Curtain or sheets for painted back-
  drops
  Spotlight for shadow plays
A "kitchen" with:
  Bowls, measuring cups and spoons,
  mixer, blender
  Paper Towels
  Hot plate (or stove)
  Sink with running water
  Dish washing detergent
  Refrigerator
  Easy-to-prepare foods such as Jello,
  custard, desserts, sandwiches, milk-
  shakes, peanut butter, popcorn
  Napkins, paper plates, forks, and
  cups
A "pet store" with:
  A "pet-of-the-month"
  Appropriate pet food
  Illustrations of similar pets
  Experience stories about this pet
  Chart of how to care for the pet
  Books about similar pets
  Tape recording of this pet's sound
  "Tours" given to younger children
  explaining the needs of this pet
  A make-believe story about an ad-
  venture with the pet
Field trips to:
  A local radio station
  The kitchen of a hamburger chain
  A local newspaper
  A television studio
  An artist's or potter's studio

The post office mail room
The hospital emergency section
A campsite for a picnic or cookout
A historical home open for tours
A professional sports team

Recreation, Sports, and Games May
satisfy behavior objectives B-20, B-21,
B-22, B-23, B-24, B-25; communication
objectives C-24, C-26; socialization objective S-25, S-28, S-29, S-30; and academic objective A-52.

Sports and games at Stage Four offer
great possibilities for behavior and socialization objectives. The activities should
foster physical skill building and adept
use of the body as well. It is helpful to
think of these activities in three categories, and plan your program with a balance among them.

Team sports: include familiar games with
  established rules and competition.
  Such games as touch football, softball,
  basketball, volleyball, modified soccer,
  and relay races would be included in
  this category.
Individual sports: flexible rules and in-
  tragroup competition. Included in this
  category might be dodge ball, whiffle
  ball, shooting baskets for points, running and standing broadjumps, shot-
  put, softball throw, running distances,
  tether ball, swimming, tumbling, and
  badminton.
Indoor activities: generally require impulse control, longer attention span,
  and more cognitive skill than do outside activities. In this category would
  be included card games such as "Go
  Fishing" "Hearts," "Slap Jack" and
  "War": group activities such as bean
  bag games, "ping pong ball blow,"
  "marble roll," a water gun with a can-
  dle flame as the target, horse shoes and
  charades; and commercial games such
  as Word Bingo, Math-O, Battling Tops,

*The teachers, working as a pair,
can provide a dynamic model for
Stage Four children learning effective transactional skills. Perhaps this is the most significant
contribution teachers make to the
Stage Four curriculum. Particularly in recreation, art, music and
dance the teachers' own responses
will determine the success or failure of the activity.*

and modified Monopoly. Games which require long periods of time to complete or which require contemplation are seldom appropriate because they lose the sense of social exchange which is an essential requirement for Stage Four activities. For this reason such games as Checkers, Scrabble, Chess, or Monopoly played by the regular rules are not usually effective.

Music Time May satisfy communication objectives C-22, C-23, C-25, C-26, C-27, C-28; socialization objectives S-25, S-28, S-30; behavior objectives B-20, B-21, B-25; and academic objective A-52.

Through music activities Stage Four children can be exposed to almost every Stage Four objective.

Instruments: children can plan and create their own individual instruments, play them in a group, take turns as band leader, and eventually learn to appreciate the possibilities of instruments for expressing themselves and understanding others.

Equipment
    Record player
    Tape recorder
    Guitars
    Ukuleles
    Autoharp
    Glockenspiel
    Tone resonator bells
    Chord organ
    Snare drum
    Rhythm instruments such as tone blocks, wood blocks, guiros, maracas, tambourines, finger cymbals, drums (bongo, conga, hand drums) (Rhythm Band, Inc.)
    Materials for making "homemade instruments": cans, toilet paper spools, wood scraps, bottle caps, bolts, string, rubber bands

Rhythmic movements and dance: with body movement activities many children find a source of recognition and success generally not available to them. Patterns of dance movements, reverse or mirror movements, interpretive movements, symbolic and dramatic dance stories, and forms of social dancing all require expression of self. When done in a group or in pairs the Stage Four socialization goal of participating successfully as a group member is easily accomplished.

Songs: for the Stage Four child, songs can be a most effective vehicle for communicating feelings and for learning to recognize the feelings of others. A child can select the songs which touch him, and with sensitivity a teacher can help expand this avenue of communication. With songs, as with drama and dance, children can explore new experiences vicariously. In this way many new feelings and situations can be experienced within the framework of a supportive group.

Records: popular records such as The Four Tops (Motown); The Jackson Five (Jobete Music Co., Inc.); The Fifth Dimension (Bell Records); Three Dog Night (ABC/Dunhill Records, Inc.)

Folk Dances such as "La Raspa," "Seven Jumps," "Troika" (Folk Dancer Record Service, Flushing, N.Y.)

Whoever Shall Have Some Peanuts (SC 7530), Sam Hinton (Scholastic Records)

Motivating Thought Processes Through Music, Vol. I (LPED 220A), Stallman-Susser Productions, Inc.

Mod Marches (AR 527), Hap Palmer, Educational Activities, Inc.

Books: *Great Songs of the Sixties,* Milton Okun (Random House, 1970)

Activities using materials listed above:
    Group singing of favorite songs (children use autoharp, guitar, etc. to accompany group)

Folk dancing, dancing to rock music, creative movement to music

Play instruments (children serve as group leaders; read musical notation when playing; create own musical notation; construct own instruments; create a musical play or skit)

Art Time May satisfy communication objectives C-25, C-28; behavior objectives B-21, B-25; socialization objectives S-25, S-28, S-30; and academic objective A-52.

Any art project that a child finds interesting can be used at this stage. Art supplies should be restricted only by the budget, facilities, and children's interests. Sophisticated art projects can be attempted such as batiks, acrylics, model building, carving, printing, and three dimensional constructions.

Stage Four children will tend to want to express themselves and the world around them in naturalistic forms. Because they are becoming conscious of a new reality apart from themselves, they may tend to degrade their own art expressions. For this reason, the teacher should respond to the feeling and expressive aspects of art projects.

To attempt to describe various art activities in this chapter would be too ambitious. A good art curriculum guide is recommended for teachers who do not feel comfortable with various art media. The following list of materials is offered as an outline for numerous art activities.

Drawing boards, drawing pencils
Charcoal
White drawing paper
Water color paper, watercolor sets
Assorted color construction paper, scissors
Paperclips, rubber bands, string
Model kits
Draftsman drawing kit
Balsa wood, airplane glue, straight pins
Plexiglass scraps, epoxy
Styrofoam
Scrap lumber, nails, hammers
Collection of "Old Master's" famous art prints
Muslin, coldwater dyes, beeswax for batik
Acrylics or oils, canvas and frames
Brushes and palates
Leather craft materials
Paper maché
Clay

Finally, the way in which the teachers relate to each other will have a significant impact on the Stage Four child's feelings about what kind of an adult he himself will become.

Perhaps there is no stage of therapy where there are greater demands upon the teacher to be an effective person. Materials and activities are merely vehicles.

ACKNOWLEDGMENTS

The author wishes to acknowledge the contributions of the many talented teachers at Rutland Center for their creative use of activities and materials with Developmental Therapy. Livija Bolster and Leslie Whitson made significant contributions to this chapter by systematically observing these teachers and collecting lists of the activities used. Nancy Cudmore prepared the descriptions of many of the Stage Two and Three activities for the chapter. In addition, Geraldine Williams provided the lists of art materials; Jenny Purvis, music materials; Carolyn Combs, storybooks; and Diane Weller, the equipment used in outdoor recreation.

Sample Form 1.
A Stage Two Class DTORF Illustrating the Cluster of Objectives
for Reg(R), Steven(S), Linda(L), Karen(K), Mindy(M)

Child's Name_____ Class Stage_____ Raters_____

Date _____ Type Rating (Check one)—Baseline _____, 5th week ____, 10th week _____

	Behavior	Communication	Socialization	(Pre)academics
STAGE I	____ 1. respond by attending ____ 2. respond by sust. attend. ____ 3. single mot. response ____ 4. complex mot. response ____ 5. assist in self help ____ 6. respond indep. play mat. ____ 7. respond w/recall/routine	____ 1. attend/speaker ____ 2. resp./motor beh. ____ 3. resp./verbal approx. ____ 4. init./vb. approx. ____ 5. recog. word/to adult ____ 6. recog. word/to child ____ 7. word sequence	____ 1. aware/adult ____ 2. attend/adult beh. ____ 3. resp. to name ____ 4. imitat. acts/adult ____ 5. solit. play ____ 6. resp. request/come ____ 7. resp. single request ____ 8. same as C-5 ____ 9. same as C-6 ____ 10. same as C-7 ____ 11. exhibit emerg./self ____ 12. seek contact/adult	____ 1. same as B-1 ____ 2. same as B-2 ____ 3. same as B-3 ____ 4. same as B-4 ____ 5. resp. fine/motor/24 mo. ____ 6. imitate wds./acts of adults ____ 7. resp. by simple discrim. of obj. ____ 8. same as C-3 ____ 9. same as C-4 ____ 10. short-term memory/ obj. & people ____ 11. resp. w/classif./simil. obj. w/diff. attri. ____ 12. short term memory/vb. express. ____ 13. body coord./3–4 yr. lev. ____ 14. match similar pictures ____ 15. recog. color names ____ 16. eye-hand coord./4-yr. lev. ____ 17. recog. body parts
STAGE II	____ 8. use play mat./appro. ____ 9. wait/no interven. ____ 10. partic. work time/ no intervention ____ 11. partic. play time/ no interven. ____ 12. spon. partic.	____ 8. answer/recog/word ____ 9. recept. vocab. ____ 10. label feel./pict. ____ 11. command activ./ simple wrd. seq. ____ 12. use words ex. min. info./adult ____ 13. use words ex. min. info./child	____ 13. paral. play/spon. ____ 14. same as B-9 ____ 15. init. min. move./child ____ 16. partic./sharing ____ 17. coop. act/child at play ____ 18. coop. act./child in organ. activ.	____ 18. recog. use of obj. ____ 19. recog. detail in pictures ____ 20. rote count to 10 ____ 21. count to 5 (1 to 1) ____ 22. name colors ____ 23. count to 10 (1 to 1) ____ 24. eye-hand coord./5-yr. lev. ____ 25. recog. diff./shapes, symbols, numerals, words ____ 26. categorize diff. items/ similar charac. ____ 27. write recog. approx. of first name w/o asst. ____ 28. discrim. differences (up-down, etc.) ____ 29. body coord./5-yr. lev. ____ 30. recog. grps. to 5 ____ 31. listen to story telling
STAGE III	____ 13. vb. recall rules/proc. ____ 14. contrib. to grp. ____ 15. vb. conseq. ____ 16. vb. reasons ____ 17. vb. other ways beh./ indiv. ____ 18. refrain when others not ____ 19. main. control & comply	____ 14. accept praise ____ 15. same as B-13 ____ 16. spon. describe work ____ 17. same as B-14 ____ 18. same as B-15 ____ 19. pride/words/gestures ____ 20. vb./feeling/resp. ____ 21. same as B-16	____ 19. turns w/o remind. ____ 20. share/min. remind. ____ 21. sug. to teacher ____ 22. partic./act. suggest child ____ 23. pref./child ____ 24. des. charac. of others	____ 32. recog. grps. to 10 ____ 33. left-right visual orien. ____ 34. recog. writ. names for color words ____ 35. recog. written labels ____ 36. recog. & write numerals for groups/1–10 ____ 37. write first/last name/date with sample

(Continued)

Sample Form 1., *continued*

	Behavior	Communication	Socialization	(Pre)academics
STAGE III				____38. eye-hand coord./6-yr. lev. ____39. body-coord./6-yr. lev. ____40. recog. & write numerals for grps./11–20 ____41. write alpha./simple words ____42. add-subtract/0–10 ____43. use ordinal/concepts verbally ____44. lstn. to story & resp. appro. ____45. read prim. vocab./sentences ____46. add-subtract above 10 ____47. write basic words/memory or dictation ____48. part. group. act./write, tell, mural
STAGE IV	____20. resp. appro./leader choice ____21. spon. partic./activ. prev. avoid ____22. implem. alter. beh. ____23. vb. express cause & ef. ____24. resp./provocation/ control ____25. resp. appro./ new suggest.	____22. vb. recog. feel/others ____23. vb. recog. feel/self ____24. verb. praise/others ____25. non vb./express./ feel./art, music ____26. spon. express. own feel./words ____27. express others feel. ____28. vb. express. exper./ feel./art, music ____29. same as B-23	____25. suggest. act./grp. ____26. same as B-20 ____27. same as B-21 ____28. diff. charac./others ____29. phys./vb. support/ others ____30. partic. grp. plng. & pb. solv.	____49. write name, ad., date/memory ____50. read, write/sentences ____51. read, write quant. words ____52. contribute grp. project/ expressive skills ____53. write indiv. exper. stories
STAGE V	____26. construc. suggest.	____30. maintain posit. rel. verb.	____31. init. & main./ interp. & grp. rel.	____54. write for commun. ____55. read/pleas. & info. ____56. write of feel. & attit. ____57. read/info. feel. & beh. of others

Progress Notes

chapter 5

MANAGEMENT STRATEGIES AND VERBAL TECHNIQUES WHICH BRING THERAPEUTIC RESULTS

Livija R. Bolster and Mary Margaret Wood

Praise and Rewards

Intervention

Confrontation

Reflection

Interpretation

Structure

Redirection

Removal from the Room

Rules

Body Contact

Holding

INTRODUCTION

Many techniques described in this chapter are already used by teachers. The important point is to know *when* to use the techniques. The best technique in the world will not produce results if used when a child is developmentally unable to respond to it. On the other hand, any number of techniques will produce the same emotional growth if used at the appropriate time in a child's development.

Children at each stage in Developmental Therapy have certain characteristics in common because of the presence or absence of particular developmental skills. Because children are grouped by developmental stages, a teacher can adjust her techniques to the needs of a particular stage and still be responsive to individual differences.

Finally, as a teacher masters the basic framework of Developmental Therapy she will be able to take her own style and techniques and apply them with a high degree of effectiveness within the developmental frame of reference.

COMMUNICATING WITH CHILDREN DURING THERAPY

When you, as a teacher/therapist, work with a group of disturbed children use the tools most readily accessible—your body and your voice. These two assets are more important than a roomful of materials.

With your body language you can reassure, convey security, nurture, redirect classroom movements, motivate, intervene in a developing crisis, decrease discomfort, reward, accept, and praise. If you rely only upon words to convey these messages you are depending upon the preferred adult mode of communication and may be missing a more significant means to reach children. Teachers often operate at communication levels far beyond a child's ability to respond, and in doing so force a child to rely on unspoken messages in body posture, tone, gesture, and expression. When these messages are not conscious on your part, you may be communicating more than you intend. So train yourself to use nonverbal communication. If you don't feel comfortable communicating without words, practice in private. As you increase your confidence in your own ability to convey these messages, practice with other staff members. Then try role playing in pantomime with groups of children until you and the children are able to communicate simple ideas without any words exchanged. This can be your most significant technique—use it. If you never have thought about using nonverbal communication, begin now.

After you feel comfortable conveying meaning to children without using words, consider the meanings you convey when you do use words. Try this simple exercise: Practice four different ways to say "Good morning": (a) all-business; (b) kindly but distant; (c) absent-minded; (d) intensely personal.

You may notice that the words you said are not nearly as important as how you said them. Did you find that you have sufficient control over your voice so that it will convey your desired meaning? Try another familiar expression. Practice saying, "You have to leave the room for hitting" four ways. Can you convey (a) support and confidence that everything will be all right; (b) all-business; (c) fear that the child may not leave without a fight; (d) rejection? These simple exercises are merely the calisthenics of staying in shape for therapy. Developmental Therapy requires that a teacher have an array of such nonverbal and verbal responses which can be called upon according to the immediate situation.

Many children rely upon "reading"

Make every minute of your contact with these children count—from the bus ride to the last goodbye. Enrollment in the therapeutic class should have meaning for each child and should pay off for the child with a series of new behaviors and developmental milestones rapidly mastered.

An abrasive tone will evoke a reflex response but seldom any positive emotional valences.

adults through facial expressions, voice modulation, and tonal quality, rather than listening to the words the adult uses. You should be aware of the effect your voice and face have on a child. Your voice can convey anger or tension inadvertently, and this might become the catalyst for a child who is close to acting out. When a child is upset, a slow and soothing tone lets the child know that *you* are not upset and can be trusted. An emphatic, matter-of-fact voice communicates that you expect a child to respond as requested. Some children will not respond even to a simple request unless you convey firmness. This does not imply shouting or demanding, but it lets the child know very clearly what is expected. If you do not convey clearly your expectations, a child is more likely to test your limits.

You also will find that by varying the volume and tone of your voice you are able to attract and hold children's attention. Few children can resist listening to a teacher when she suddenly drops her voice to a whisper, or when she conveys a questioning tone, surprise, or excitement in both face and voice. Vocal and facial animation, although used for all stages of therapy, is most effective with younger children, especially at story time.

Enthusiasm and warmth are important tonal qualities for teachers of all stages; how much you use will depend upon your group and their stage of therapy. You also must be aware of which tone or how much enthusiasm will be most effective for a particular child with a particular developmental objective.

Eye contact is another communication technique used by teachers for all stages of therapy. It usually indicates how comfortable a child is with others. Teachers should be confident in themselves and comfortable enough with each

child to look him straight in the eye. Older children especially are aware of this, and eye contact is effective in building trust with them. With a younger child, particularly at Stage One, a teacher may touch a child's chin and direct the child's face toward the teacher's. This technique is effective for helping a child attend to the teacher's verbal direction or to help a child who is learning to speak by imitating lip movement. However, this form of looking is not the same as eye contact which builds interpersonal relationships.

A few children, usually at lower developmental stages, cannot tolerate eye contact with the teacher. With such a child try to avoid direct eye contact until you notice the child beginning to watch you (S-2). Often some form of body contact is used by a child toward a teacher when he begins to trust her, and yet cannot bring himself to show it by overtly looking. In such situations make your glances brief, supportive, and non-demanding. Gradually lengthen the glance into a smile; and finally call the child's name and pause until he glances back at you (S-6). Be sure there is a meaningful, motivating activity as the vehicle for such exchanges, and you will suddenly see the child reaching out to show you his work or to call for help. A major developmental milestone at Stage Two, socialization objective S-12, is reached.

At all stages of therapy positive statements are more effective than negative ones. Instead of saying, "Don't run around" try rephrasing the idea into a positive statement, "You can come back and sit down." Identifying children who are ready for the next activity motivates more than naming children not ready. For example, "Nobody's leaving until Tommy settles down" creates a negative tone while "Hmm, I see two people ready to go" builds a positive feeling. Most children would rather be praised than ignored or degraded. Using positive statements in the class sets the tone and makes the classroom an enjoyable place to be rather than a punitive or oppressive place.

A child will let you know his reactions to you through his body responses—rigidness, fear, withdrawal, restlessness or enthusiastic participation, attention, and enjoyment, Above all whatever techniques you are using, be sincere and sensitive to the signals you are sending and the responses you are getting back from the children.

ADJUSTING TECHNIQUES TO STAGES OF THERAPY

Just as children in Developmental Therapy are grouped according to their differentiated developmental needs, the management techniques and verbal patterns you use should be differentiated according to the specific needs of children at each stage of therapy. Your responses to a Stage One child who needs arousal should be different from your responses to a Stage Three child who has mastered Stage One and Two objectives and now is expected to be a part of a Stage Three group. You may already know a number of techniques to stimulate, motivate, and control children; but in Developmental Therapy there are important distinctions concerning which techniques you should use for each stage. In order to apply techniques effectively, you must know a child's individual Developmental Therapy objectives and understand the developmental priorities of each stage. Then you must be able to respond with the appropriate technique to meet the needs of that developmental stage. Teachers who prefer

to use only one series of responses, saying "This is me," generally will be ineffective with Developmental Therapy.

Stage One teachers use a "controlled vocabulary" because most Stage One children do not have functional language. By using a limited language pattern to elicit a desired response, the teacher provides a simple model which the child learns through imitation and repetition. For Stage One children it is necessary to label (name) things (activities, materials, people) which are directly related to experiences in the room. At first the emphasis is on using a single word to get a particular result ("Juice. This is juice."). By repetition the teacher's statement is finally shifted to the child's statement ("I want juice."). Warmth and enthusiasm in the teacher's voice must be exaggerated in order to hold the children's attention and interest in speaking. As a child improves in his ability to use words to obtain what he wants, the teacher's verbal stimulation shifts. She now emphasizes using words in lieu of inappropriate behavior ("Tell me what you want . . ." instead of screaming.).

For Stage Two the teacher serves as the source of classroom organization. While this was primarily physical in Stage One it is essentially verbal by Stage Two. The teacher verbally structures activities and routines. Her verbalizations are used to bring the class together when they may not be able to do it yet by themselves ("Carol is doing her arithmetic; Charles is working on his number worksheet; Mark just finished his coloring. Everyone is working so quietly together."). At the end of the day the teacher gives closure to the class by recalling the day's activities, recalling good work done and giving a reminder of the next day's activities ("We had a really good day today. Everyone helped paint

Management techniques used by teachers in Developmental Therapy follow a pattern of decreasing physical intervention and increasing verbal intervention from Stage One through Stage Three classrooms.

The changing role of the teacher at each stage of therapy is outlined in Table 1, Chapter 1.

The major communication milestone for Stage One is C-7, "to produce a meaningful . . . sequence of words to obtain a desired response . . ."

This example of a Stage Two teacher's reflection of classroom activities illustrates the use of verbal structure to sensitize children to be aware that they are participating in an activity with others. She is working toward socialization and behavior goals in Stage Two: S-18 (to participate in cooperative activities . . . with another child . . .) and S-10 (to participate in activities such as work time . . . without physical intervention by teachers). Direct treatment focus on group investment does not occur until Stage Three.

the mural. I think this class is ready for a special art time tomorrow."). Such statements give a child the security and success he needs.

As a child's receptive and expressive vocabulary increases during Stages Two and Three, so does his ability to respond to verbal direction and support from the teacher. By Stage Three he begins to internalize the teacher's verbal structure and develop enough inner control of impulses that just a verbal reminder is enough to elicit constructive responses. Some verbal techniques cannot be used until a child reaches this stage in therapy because he must have certain verbal, social, cognitive, and behavioral foundations. For example, Stage Three teachers may generalize from a potentially stormy situation to universal peer norms, "Boys your age learn to write in cursive" or "Most boys get mad when someone calls them bad names." Such general statements can be used to set limits, motivate, or redirect, but only during the latter part of Stage Three and at

For Stage Three children, mastery of impulsivity with only verbal assistance from the teacher is a major developmental milestone, behavior objective B-19 (to maintain self-confidence and comply with group procedures).

At Stage Four, the teacher's questioning is a means of working for a major developmental milestone in the areas of behavior and communication, B-23 and C-29 (to verbally express cause and effect relationship between feelings and behavior).

In short, as a child's needs change the teacher's style changes; but in all stages she serves as the major model by providing effective verbal and interpersonal responses for each child for his particular developmental needs.

Stage Four. It is at these stages that a child cares enough about what peers do to identify with them.

By Stage Four the teacher's focus is on helping a child put his feelings into words, to look for relationship between what he feels and what he does. She might prod a child with questions, "What happened?" "Why did he hit you?" "What were you doing?" "How does it make you feel when he does that?" A child may need this stimulation as a stepping stone to eventually put his feelings into words spontaneously. Stage Four children are involved in organizing and conducting their own group activities, and the teacher uses verbal techniques to redefine group processes when needed.

Table 1 summarizes the most frequently used management techniques and how they change in form and use at each stage of therapy. By reading across this table, you can follow the changes a teacher must make in her use of a technique with children at different stages of

Table 1. Most Frequently Used Techniques in Developmental Therapy[a]

Teacher techniques	Stage I	Stage II	Stage III	Stage IV
1. Body contact and touch	3	2	changes to physical closeness — 1	0
2. Physical intervention	3	2	1	0
3. Removal from room	0	1	2	usually voluntary — 1

(Continued)

Table 1., *continued*

Teacher techniques	Stage I	Stage II	Stage III	Stage IV
4. Removal from group (removal from room)	1	2	1	0
5. Classroom structure and rules	3	3	2	group develops 1 rules
6. Control of materials by teacher	3	2	1	children control 0 materials
7. Verbal interactions between lead and support teachers	1	3	3	1
8. Redirection	2 usually physical	3 changes to verbal	3	1
9. Reflection	1	2	3	1
10. Interpretation	concrete 0 referent	1	2	3
11. Confrontation	0	chiefly 1 verbal	chiefly 1 verbal	2 chiefly verbal
12. Life Space Interviewing	0	0	3 individual LSI	3 group LSI
13. Praise and rewards	2 sensory rewards	2 individual activities	2 group activities	2 peer recognition

[a]3, used as a major technique; 2, used frequently; 1, used occasionally; 0, seldom or not used.

Developmental Therapy. By reading down the column for any particular stage, you can find the pattern of management techniques most frequently used for a particular stage. The first six techniques involve physical forms of intervention. The remaining seven are essentially verbal forms of intervention.

The remainder of this chapter describes the application of each of these 13 techniques in Developmental Therapy.

BODY CONTACT AND TOUCH

A teacher's body should be used to convey positive messages to the child—encouraging, motivating, caring. Body contact and touch from the teacher are used to nurture a child, to let him know he is doing a good job, to calm him down, and generally to tell the child that the teacher likes him. The type and amount of body contact changes from Stage One to Stage Four. It also will vary widely according to the needs of each child. At Stage One, the teacher often keeps the child in psychological contact with the classroom by body contact and touch. Patting, hugging, holding, touching are all used by the Stage One teacher. At Stage Two, touch is used to a greater extent than direct body contact. Body contact is used at Stage Two only when a child regresses or is in need of unusual amounts of nurturance. By Stage Three contact changes to physical closeness, an arm around the child or a touch on the shoulder. Older children cannot tolerate being held in someone's lap, but some older children still need and respond to physical closeness. By Stage Four neither body contact nor touch are needed.

Occasionally, you will find children in Stages One through Three who do not trust their environment, people, or the

Physical nearness may be the one most powerful, nonverbal technique a teacher uses. It is effective at all stages of therapy and can convey the entire range of messages between a teacher and child.

Body contact or touch may have a paradoxical effect with some children.

As long as a teacher takes an authoritative stance, standing over children and directing them, children will tend to react in one of two ways: passive (or passive-aggressive) compliance or combative resistance. Neither response is conducive to emotional growth. Cooperation is genuine when the child is responding out of his own volition not when he is forced to do so by an adult.

teacher enough to tolerate any physical contact at all. For these children, body contact triggers impulsivity and acting out instead of calming them down or rewarding them. Often the child who cannot tolerate any contact is severely emotionally deprived and associates physical contact only with abuse or severe punishment; or it may be more personal attention than he is able to handle. For such children contact has to be given verbally, in a low key, and without much personal focus. The teacher may pat the child on the shoulder as she walks around the room saying, "Good arithmetic page, Tommy," and quickly go on to another child. Nurturance for such children is provided through stories, food, and physical nearness.

A teacher's physical nearness at all stages of therapy can control and encourage a child in an activity. Physical proximity communicates to a child that you care about what he is doing and in this way often prevents inappropriate behavior before it happens. By sitting next to the most impulsive children in a group you can prevent much acting out because you are in a better position to react quickly before things get out of hand. But more important, by your physical presence you are telling the child you are interested and care, so the child does not need to act out to get attention. Especially effective at Stage Three, physical nearness conveys, "I am here to help if you need me."

It is easy for a teacher to use physical presence negatively. When near a child try not to stand over him: kneel, stoop, or sit. Standing over a child communicates: "I'm the authority around here and I'm not going to let you get away with a thing;" whereas being on eye level with a child says: "I trust myself to control the situation, and I trust you not be take advantage of it." Another negative example is, "If you two can't behave I'm going to move your seats near mine" or "Now that I'm here you won't be able to act up."

Physical closeness or proximity shows that you care about what a child is doing, but you must also be aware when closeness stifles a child and becomes so overwhelming that he will act out to get away. You may be violating his psychological boundaries. For example, a Stage Three boy was throwing crayons across the room and the teacher stopped him with her hand, "Crayons are for drawing not throwing." They both struggled for control of the crayon. Realizing what was about to happen the teacher let go, stating, "You can put them up" and walked away. The boy put the crayons away without further incident. Walking away let the boy know that the teacher was not challenging him but instead expected him to follow through. She allowed him to save face by not standing over him to make sure he did it.

PHYSICAL INTERVENTION

Within the Developmental Therapy context, permitting a child to participate with responses inappropriate to his developmental stage would be to perpetuate or extend the period of his disturbance. For this reason, great emphasis is put upon expecting appropriate responses, communicating these expectations clearly, and intervening to teach a response when it is not forthcoming.

The use of physical intervention, that is, physically moving a child through an activity or physically controlling a child, follows the same pattern as body contact—the need and use of it decrease the higher the stage of development. Physical intervention is a major

technique for Stage One, used frequently at Stage Two, occasionally used at Stage Three, and not used at Stage Four. In Stage One the teacher will bodily move a child through an activity, hold a child to keep him with the group, or physically move his arm and hand in response to materials. Such physical intervention should be accompanied by a specific word or simple statement related to the activity. By associating physical intervention with positive, supportive words, the child will begin building responses for future verbal intervention. For example, "We pick up toys at the end of play time," as the Stage One teacher physically moves a child through the activity. In Stage Two the teacher uses this technique but not as often. When a child is in a Stage Three classroom this kind of intervention should be very limited and rare. Instead, the child should be able to respond to verbal intervention because he has developed the necessary language skills and impulse control. At Stage Four the technique is not needed.

At any stage, whether the teacher is physically moving a child through an activity, stopping him from throwing a toy, or holding him through a rage, the child must always feel that the teacher cares. She should hold him firmly but gently and supportively. In the midst of classroom activity (sometimes chaotic), it is easy for a teacher to slip into the pattern of moving quickly to intervene, and too often she will just grab at whatever part of the child is closest. This is where physical control becomes negative and no therapeutic gain can be made from the incident.

What do you do with a child who seems to be physically out of control (kicking, screaming, hitting, spitting, throwing himself on the floor, or running away)? Should you restrain him physically or try verbal controls? Often,

How much physical intervention should be used? The teacher can be guided by asking herself, "What is the least amount of intervention I need to use in order for this child to respond according to his developmental objectives?"

Physical intervention is an essential technique for severely deviant behavior. Don't permit deviant behavior to continue. Intervene. When such behavior is allowed to continue it may hurt the child in a number of ways: (a) the behavior may become a fixed response through repetition; (b) the child may see himself as "different" and lose what little confidence in himself he has acquired; (c) others may see him as "strange" or as a threat to their own comfort; therefore they will avoid or antagonize him.

a child may seem to be out of control because he is frustrated, needs attention, or is so anxious that he must test limits. If the crisis seems to be a manifestation of such an urgent, unmet need, a child usually will respond constructively to verbal techniques or some form of supportive physical nearness appropriate to his developmental stage.

If the crisis seems to have developed to the point where a child seems unable to respond to changes in the situation and does not pull himself together, physical restraint may be necessary. Some very disturbed children actually lose the ability to control themselves. It is the teacher's responsibility to determine this and respond accordingly. If physical restraint seems to be the only way to protect the child from detrimental results, contain him with your body—crossing the child's arms in front of him and holding his back against you. This kind of position communicates to the child he doesn't have to be afraid because you can help him with control. The other essential element in holding is a warm, comforting tone, "It's all right. You can calm down." This communicates to the child the expectation that he can do better and you will help.

What about a child who reacts with increased violence to physical holding? With a younger child, a corner of a room or some other physically enclosed place is effective in containing him without holding. By positioning yourself at the entrance in a supportive, unthreatening way, you can contain him and provide emotional support. An older child should be removed to a Quiet Room without furniture and extraneous equipment so that he can be contained without being held. An exception to this might be a Stage One child who generally would not be removed from the classroom under any condition.

Try to differentiate between diffused and channeled acting out. The latter can usually be approached rationally.

Never restrain a child if there is another alternative technique to which he will respond.

Removal is based upon the assumption that the child is invested enough in the activity or the group so that he will want to come back. If a child is not motivated by the activities going on in the classroom removing him will not be effective.

Be sensitive to the tone you are conveying nonverbally as you remove a child from the room. Is the removal punishment? Is it the result of your frustration? The last straw? Abdication of your role as the dependable, helping adult? Or is it quiet confidence? Assurance that things will be better? Trust that together you can work things out?

REMOVAL FROM THE ROOM

There are times when a child is so out of control that he must be removed from the class. The criteria for removal are fairly stringent: (a) if a child is so out of control in the classroom that he cannot be managed or will do harm to himself or others; (b) if a topic is so private that a child cannot discuss it in front of the group but needs to discuss it alone with the teacher.

Removing a child from the classroom, even for a short period of time, is not a technique which is useful for all children. Stage One and Stage Four children seldom need removal, for very different reasons. Few Stage One children are invested enough in what is going on for removal to be effective. In contrast, by the time a child is in Stage Four he feels that he is part of his group and he has developed enough verbal skills to talk about what is bothering him within the group.

Removal is particularly effective for children in Stage Three because they have some skills to be successful, they have some ability to be verbal, and they are motivated to the classroom activities. Removal from the room at the time of crisis provides a good opportunity for the teacher of Stage Three children to work on objectives, particularly in the areas of behavior and communication.

An available Quiet Room, away from class, is a necessary resource if you are a Stage Three teacher. When you remove a child from the room do it with as little talk as possible. Be swift and firm. Plan to stay with him in order to use the crisis to help him grow emotionally. You must know which developmental objectives he is working on in order to avoid expectations beyond his developmental mastery level. Have an arrangement with the treatment team to take over your activities in the classroom while you are out. This will free you to spend as much time as needed to work through the crisis with the child.

If a Stage Two or Stage Three class has a number of violent children, you will probably need to plan for a back-up teacher to come in to assist the treatment team while you are in the Quiet Room. During the time in a Quiet Room a child often goes through three dynamic phases: aggressive, regressive, and compliant.

When a child is first taken to the Quiet Room after a crisis, some type of aggression usually is exhibited. This may be physical or verbal aggression toward teachers or peers. Verbally aggressive outbursts can be handled best during the first phase by ignoring them. Attempting to stop a child from verbal aggression or focusing on it will serve only to take the focus away from the precipitating crisis and cause the child to take a longer period to calm down. During a physically aggressive outburst, a child may need help controlling himself and may need to be held. This should be done only in the most extreme circumstances—when the child may hurt himself or you. If you have to hold a child move in quickly and restrain him only until he can control himself. Limit your talk. Verbalizations used during this type of situation could be: "I won't let you hurt yourself (or others)." "No one hits here; hitting hurts." "I'll have to help you now but I think you can control yourself in a minute." Always be positive. If the child continues to attack you physically, help the child control himself by firm but supportive restraint. *Never get into a fight with a child.* Be matter-of-fact about holding. Watch for physiological signs that the crisis is passing: relaxed muscles, decrease in body rigidity, or a more regulated breathing pat-

tern. As soon as possible terminate your holding. You may want to ease your hold gradually. Holding a child should be a supportive technique. Never hold a child in a rough or demeaning way. Remember you want him to walk away from this crisis feeling good about himself and you.

To terminate any type of physical holding, give verbal cues as to what is expected ("When you seem ready to control yourself I can let you go."). Be careful of the question "Are you ready to control yourself?" Sometimes a child is not able to tell you, or he will say he is when he is not. When the physical or verbal aggression subsides the child usually will move into the next phase, regression.

The second phase will find a child reverting to earlier patterns of response, sometimes exhibiting behavior of a much younger child looking for nurturance. The child will be reaching out to you for some support physically (moving close to you) or verbally ("You don't like me."). The seige is over. The child has gestured toward you and you must respond. Create a nonverbal bond of support. Sometimes silent acceptance is the best way to support a child. Occasionally, a child will need a reassuring touch. But remember, too much touch or talk can set things off again at this phase. Watch for the time when the child indicates he is able to talk about what happened in the classroom, and at that point begin the Life Space Interview. Children who are developmentally at Stage Three but essentially nonverbal can be helped to use words to express feelings by the sensitive management of the Quiet Room time. With the teacher supplying simple phrases to describe the most basic, nonjudgmental parts of the crisis, the child will learn to describe what happened in a few phrases. Without fear of

Holding a child with firmness while conveying support is an art. Grabbing at a child's arms is not holding and will only provoke combat. Holding involves complete body control and is discussed also in this chapter under the section on Physical Intervention.

You may need to catch your own breath before beginning any talk with a child in crisis. Take the time you need. You must be able to convey that the situation is under control.

If a child has mastered the Communication objectives of Stage Two, he will be able to respond to Life Space Interviewing techniques. (See the section on Life Space Interviewing in this chapter.) If not, the teacher uses reflection to provide simple, descriptive statements of the central issue. By restructuring the situation, the teacher sets up a few basic responses which the child must make in order to return to the classroom.

judgment from the teacher, his capacity and willingness to talk will increase rapidly.

Often the most difficult part of removing a Stage Two child from the room is actually getting him back into the class. The child cannot be expected to move rapidly from loss of control to model behavior. You must structure the situation so that it will end positively, allowing him to save face. Because he has so few verbal skills, the Life Space Interview is not usually an appropriate technique for this stage child. Make minimal expectations for the child (according to his developmental objectives) and do not be distracted by other behavior. Each step toward the expected behavior should be praised: "When you stop kicking and hitting you can go back to the class. Good, your arms are still and relaxed. I'll let go of them. I can see you'll be ready in just a minute."

REMOVAL FROM THE GROUP (BUT REMAINING IN ROOM)

A highly effective variation of removal from the room is to remove a child from a group or activity but keep him in the room. This technique is used primarily at Stage Two where children have developed some amount of interest and motivation to participate in group activities. This interest generally does not continue if a Stage Two child is removed from the room. By removing him to another area of the room, he can still see and hear the activity—a reminder of what he is missing. Used selectively, this technique can help eliminate inappropriate behavior. For example, a Stage One child who is aware enough to know when he is being silly can be taken to a corner for a very short period of time and told, "When you calm down, we can go back." It is

Structure also includes consequences. In Developmental Therapy, the term "expectations" may be a more useful way to think of consequences. The teachers define expectations for each child according to his developmental objectives, accepting only responses from the child which are appropriate for mastered objectives while teaching responses to new objectives. Responses inappropriate to the specific developmental expectations are not accepted, and therapeutic intervention is used continually until the expected response has been mastered. Expectations reflect the full range of developmental objectives, some as basic as simple motor responses, others as complex as maintaining interpersonal communication when members of the group are under stress.

your responsibility to make the "time out" as brief as possible. In Stage Two, where children are developing behavioral controls, it can be used in much the same way to eliminate hitting, upsetting other children, and "messing around." At this stage you should begin verbalizing action and consequences, "You're here because you hit Tommy. We don't hit because it hurts. When you calm down you can go back to the group."

This technique seldom works with a Stage Three child because he is so aware of the group that he will try to incite others to join him in the acting out.

CLASSROOM STRUCTURE AND RULES

Classroom structure refers to the expectations and limits for children in the classroom. The schedule of activities, routine procedures, rules, expected behaviors, and amount of teacher control are parts of the structure. Used meaningfully and selectively, structure provides security to a disturbed child by conveying what will occur and what he can depend on. Structure entails letting the child know exactly what activities are planned each day and what kinds of behavior are expected of him. These expectations must be changed to suit the goals of each activity and each stage of therapy.

Through the stages of Developmental Therapy, the design and enforcement of the classroom structure follow a pattern from chiefly physical structure in Stages One and Two to verbal structure in Stages Three and Four. For example, in Stage One, the lead teacher claps hands to music while the support teacher physically assists children in imitating the clapping; in Stage Two, "We sit for story time;" Stage Three, "When you hit you have to leave the room;" Stage Four, "Some of the group are mad; let's stop the project and talk about the problem."

Structure conveys order, predictability, and security. When a child learns that he can cope with what is planned he can trust the therapeutic classroom to be a place for success. If he has ample opportunity to experience, respond, and cope in the classroom, constructive, comfortable responses can be learned.

Several forms of structure are a part of every classroom at all stages of therapy. Each class posts a schedule of activities for the day so that each child will know what comes next and when to expect it. Such routine builds security into a classroom and provides some external organization for a child. The technique is especially effective with brain-damaged, schizophrenic, hyperkinetic, and autistic children, who lack internal organization and respond to external structure. At Stage One, the teacher works to make the schedule a remembered routine; at Stage Two, the schedule is anticipated by the children; at Stage Three, it is reviewed and recognized in written form; at Stage Four, it is developed and changed by the group process.

Another aid for helping a child organize himself is designating certain areas of the room for certain activities so that the child has a change in physical environment when the activity changes. This allows for some physical movement between activities, and the child also learns what kind of behavior is expected and appropriate for each activity. For example, "We sit for juice and cookies at the table" but "We play in this area of the room." Physical boundaries in the therapeutic classroom also simulate the physical boundaries and changes present in the real world, where a child may be required to sit and eat at the table and play games in another area of his home. Used therapeutically, structure is not static; it is different at all levels and for all children. It is the teacher's responsibility to set the structure and to adjust it to individual and class needs. For example, part of every class structure is that all children finish their work before they go on to the next activity. However, if a Stage One child is extremely upset, the teacher might take his hand and make the expected movements; the Stage Two teacher might redefine the task; the Stage Three teacher might say, "Sometimes boys are too upset to work. Something's really on your mind today. Let's go talk about it before you try to finish." And the Stage Four teacher might involve the entire group in a discussion of the task and its problems. In each of these situations, the teacher has restructured her expectation to meet the child's most important need at that moment. When the crisis has been relieved, the teacher can again restructure her expectations of the child by defining the class procedure, "Now you can finish your work."

Building Rules

It is helpful to think of rules in several ways. First, there are building rules. These are rules applying to all children on the premises. Such rules are clearly conveyed by the principal, secretary, bus drivers, and teachers. These should be very few, simply stated, and enforced consistently by all staff. Examples of building rules, for children at all stages of therapy, might be:

"No one hits; hitting hurts."
"Furniture and books are for using not for breaking."
"Everyone is important; respect their feelings."
"On the bus everyone sits in his seat."
"The edge of the playground is the limit; everyone stays inside the limit."

The number of different classroom activities decreases with each stage of therapy while the amount of time spent with an activity increases. In Stage One there may be as many as 16 activities for a two-hour period. On the other hand, a Stage Four class schedule may include only four activities, determined by the group.

Remember, every moment should be planned for a therapeutic purpose. Juice and cookie time is not a coffee break for the teacher but a time to work on communication and behavior objectives. Play time is not free time for the teacher but an opportunity to stimulate and support each child's independent socialization.

A strong caution: make the structure meaningful and mobile for the children. If the teacher sets up a procedure that the children must return to the table to sit before they go home, there must be a purpose in it. For example, in a Stage Two class the teacher and children review the day's activities at the table before they go home. The objectives: a short term memory exercise (academic objective A-10), remembering the classroom routine (behavior objective B-7), participation in group activity by taking turns talking (communication objectives C-12 and C-13; socialization objective S-18).

Classroom Rules

In addition, within each classroom, the teachers and children have a number of formal, procedural classroom rules conveying clearly and concisely what will happen and what is expected of the children as members of that class. These rules directly reflect the stage of therapy for the group. Classroom rules should be viewed as a means of building security and trust within the classroom. Most importantly, the rules should reflect developmental objectives. When clearly conveyed and meaningful to the progress of the class, the children assimilate rules into their own inner control systems. Examples of how classroom rules change at each stage might be:

"We sit on the rug for story time" (Stage One, behavior objective B-7).

"When we pass the cookies, we only take one at a time" (Stage Two, socialization objective S-16).

"We take turns working the record player" (Stage Three socialization objective S-19 or behavior objective B-13).

"If someone makes you mad tell him instead of hitting him" (Stage Four, behavior objective B-24).

An emphasis upon "visual" instead of "implied" may help remind you that you convey more by what you actually do (nonverbal rule enforcement) than by the words you use to talk about rules. Most importantly, the classroom procedures and rules should be developed mutually between you and the children, except at Stage One where children have little ability to organize even themselves. And finally, never make up rules to control children from moment to moment. This form of gamesmanship leaves children feeling helpless and uncertain—a poor setting for therapy.

Interpersonal Rules

There is another set of rules used within the classroom. These are the informal, interpersonal rules. Unspecified, flexible, and generally unspoken, these rules are guidelines for adjusting your expectations for individual children based upon their individual, developmental needs. If the established classroom rules are not extensive and if you are effective in conveying each individual expectation nonverbally, then the interpersonal rules can operate without conflict. Examples of a teacher's use of interpersonal rules might be:

Accepting eye contact as the first positive response to the stimulus "Say 'Cookie'" (Stage One, communication objective C-3).

Giving a restless child first chance to reach out and touch the fuzzy picture during story time in order to maintain his attention (Stage Two, behavior objective B-9).

Changing a planned activity at the suggestion of a child who has never volunteered a preference before (Stage Three, socialization objective S-21).

Stopping a group project in order to explore with the group what effect their feelings toward each other are having on the project (Stage Four, communication objective C-29).

Interpersonal rules really represent the expected performance you hold for each child for his particular developmental objectives. When a child regresses or loses control of himself, you may have to redefine your expectations for him in terms of a lower developmental response. These interpersonal rules also help the teachers respond with flexibility to such needs, permitting a child to change and grow by responding in new ways. Two techniques often used by teachers in implementing the interpersonal rules are ignoring a behavior and nonverbally conveying that "every person is important." If you use these two techniques with skill you will find few areas of conflict between the spoken classroom rules and the unspoken interpersonal rules. You will find also that your classroom will have a dynamic tone in which the rules do not require children to respond in a stereotype.

CONTROL OF MATERIALS BY TEACHER

The teacher's control of materials decreases as the children move into higher stages of therapy. It begins with almost total control in Stage One, where the teacher's role is the provider of pleasant and satisfying things. She passes out the paper, the work folders, the juice and cookies, brings in the mat or walking board, the guitar, the puppets. Children in Stages Two and Three are given progressively more control of materials, getting and putting up their own work folder, pouring juice, helping to put up the mat, getting games for play time. However, since inner controls are not yet completely established, the teacher sometimes has to reinstate her own control of materials to calm a group or prevent a child from acting out. By the time a child is in Stage Four of therapy he has enough control, so that he often chooses the materials and activities as a member of his group, planning and being responsible for the outcome.

At every stage there should be some opportunity for the free exploration of materials by the children. During such periods it is important to convey to the children that this is a time for freely exploring the possibilities in the mate-

rial. Then monitor your own responses or you may find yourself teaching, assisting, and redirecting. By doing this, you turn a creative opportunity into another directed session.

VERBAL INTERACTION BETWEEN LEAD AND SUPPORT TEACHERS

The verbal exchange between members of the teaching team serves as a significant interpersonal model for the children. Verbal interaction between lead and support teachers may be used to neutralize an explosive situation, stimulate interest in an activity, reinforce a procedure, or provide sex role models when the teachers are male and female. The requirement, of course, is that the two teachers be able to work together well and discuss differences before and after class. Because it serves so many purposes, this technique is useful for teachers of all stages above Stage One. Here is only one example of how this interaction can be effective. A Stage Two class is becoming disorganized during the transition from one activity to another. The lead teacher has the material for the next activity in a box but cannot get enough attention from the children to begin. She and the support teacher sit at the table, jiggle the box and converse:

> Support: *"I wonder what's in that box."*
> Lead: *"It's something we used about a week ago."*
> Support: *"A week ago! Let me think. Is it hard?"*
> Lead: *"Listen!"* (She shakes the box.) *"It sounds hard."*
> Support: *"It surely does; maybe you can give us a hint."*
> Lead: *"Well, it's three different colors."*
> Support: *"Three different colors! Help me

Control of materials follows the same general changes from physical control in Stage One to group determination and management in Stage Four.

During times for free exploration of materials, it is important to be a careful observer. You may see emerging spontaneously new responses which you had not expected.

A full discussion of the roles of lead and support teachers is contained in Chapter 6. However, the interaction between the two members of a treatment team is such an important technique for managing behavior and bringing therapeutic results that it is included in this chapter also.

guess, David. What did we use a week ago that's hard and had three colors?"

One by one the children will be enticed into the guessing game that started out as a conversation between lead and support teachers. Because their responses lead quite naturally into full participation, this technique has a productive outcome. On the other hand, had the teachers tried to control with commands of "Get quiet," "Sit down," or with punitive threats, the outcome would have been nonproductive.

Often the Stage Two class is simply not able to participate in a new activity until there is something to model. By slipping into the role of a child and providing a response model, the support teacher can give responses which are expected from the group. As the children begin modeling the support teacher's responses, it is important for the support teacher to pull back by directing her attention to the lead teacher. When the group begins to lose interest, the support teacher can remotivate by her facial expressions and body responses to the lead teacher. You will find that teaching children to participate by verbal interaction models will be a major technique used with Stage Two classes.

There will be less need to teach children this way at Stage Three because they are developing their own set of verbal interactions. While still used frequently, the content and purpose change. Now the lead and support teachers use verbal exchange to provide models for interpersonal responses while working with the Stage Three objectives in socialization and communication. The teachers' relationship to each other is watched carefully by most Stage Three children. A considerable number of disturbed children have had disturbing experiences with adults. No small part has been disturbed relationships between

two significant adults with the child as the third party. It is essential to provide a model for consideration, team work, respect, and cooperation. Many times, children who have successfully manipulated their parents against each other bring these skills to the therapeutic classroom to test the teaching team. Watch for this. When you see it tried, you may want to put particular emphasis on the relationship of the team. Occasionally, this will be an important element in a Stage Four class. The major difference between using this technique at Stages Three and Four is in the pairing of interpretation with verbal interaction at the latter stage. In team work at any stage, the important, overriding message must be that both members of the team are in complete agreement that collectively and individually the well-being of the child is first.

REDIRECTION

Redirection is guiding a child back to a task through an alternative motivation. It is used to show a child a more productive response than what he is doing. It can be used to refocus a child's attention or to avoid unnecessary confrontation. For a child in Stage One, redirection is chiefly physical. The teacher may change the child's physical activity patterns by moving his arms and hands in a more constructive way or by presenting the child with a toy when he is engaged in nonconstructive behavior. Physical redirection is combined with verbal redirection for a child in Stage Two, to help the child learn to respond to verbal cues. For example, during play time a child who has great difficulty controlling his aggression may become quite agitated while he is involved in using his truck to crash into blocks other children are using. The teacher takes several blocks and

Just as the teachers' roles change for each stage of therapy, so the nature of the teachers' interactions change. The Stage Two support teacher provides participating responses to the lead teacher for the children to model. In contrast, the Stage Three teachers work as an interpersonal team to provide verbal exchanges at a more complex level for children to model, while in Stage Four the team offers two individual models for interpersonal and sex role identification.

Redirection usually is followed by restructuring. A teacher can intervene and redirect a child to a more productive situation. However, to obtain a sustained involvement or to make it clear that the change is not the result of a child's manipulation, careful restructuring is needed. A discussion of this is included in this chapter under Classroom Structure and Rules.

quickly builds a road for him saying, "This is the superhighway for your emergency vehicle. Your truck has the right to speed on this road to get to the next town." (The block road leads in a direction away from the other children's buildings.) Further restructuring may be needed by involving another child in building the new town or in a play adventure when the truck gets to the end of the road.

At Stage Three a teacher might say, "Here's the wastebasket," and push it toward a child who is about to throw a ball of paper across the room. Or a teacher might respond to a child's question with another question in order to redirect the focus of the conversation. For example, a child asks, "Why do you comb your hair that way?" The teacher says, "Have you noticed how many people wear their hair in different ways? Let's look around at the others." This technique will turn the situation toward socialization objective S-24 "to recognize and describe characteristics of others . . ." This avoids burdening the child with personal information about the teacher which in itself is not important. An example of redirection used in the academic area is when a child asks, "Is this right?" The teacher answers, "Let's see, will 9 and 9 make 17?"

By the time a child enters Stage Four of therapy, just a verbal reminder usually is sufficient for redirection. "The wastebasket is over there," or the question "Is there anything more you could add to that picture?" should be enough to redirect the child into appropriate behavior or remotivate him to his task.

REFLECTION

Reflection is the practice of verbally stating what a child is doing, saying, or feeling, or it may be a statement of events. Reflection is one of the most valuable tools a teacher can have. "When in doubt, reflect" is a guideline told to student teachers. Reflection tells the child that the teacher is noticing what he is doing, yet no judgments or demands are set forth.

With reflection the teacher serves as a mirror for the child, reflecting SUCCESS ("Carol did a good job on the walking board."), FEELINGS, ("It makes you mad when someone hits you."), and ACTIVITIES ("Charles is building a tall garage with the blocks. Maybe Mark's car could park in it.").

Reflection by the teacher helps define in words how a child feels when he may not be able to put it into words himself. This communicates that the teacher cares and understands that feeling. Reflection also may verbally link children in a group as an encouragement for cooperative interaction. (After a session where several Stage Two children assist other children in cleaning up from art time the teacher reflects, "It's nice to have friends to do things for.") At times reflection should be depersonalized ("Sometimes it's hard for girls and boys to sit in chairs while waiting for the record to start" instead of a personalized response such as, "Sometimes it's hard for you to sit in your chair while waiting . . ."). For a young schizophrenic child who has difficulty identifying himself, the teacher should be careful to use personal pronouns in her reflection ("I see you rocking the baby to sleep now.").

Reflection can be used at any stage of therapy. At earlier stages the teacher uses reflection to sensitize children to expect a verbal but nonemotional response to critical incidents and feelings. At Stage Two, reflection offers children a verbal model for putting simple experiences into words. In Stage Three, the teacher expands the use of reflection by

Reflection requires no response from a child but serves to sensitize a child to anticipate that the teacher will notice.

Reflection is a basic technique for beginning a Life Space Interview with Stage Three children. It is important to use with manipulative children instead of ignoring their testing behavior.

By reflecting what you have seen, in a matter-of-fact way, you convey that you are aware and choose to ignore. By reflecting in a concerned and personal way, you convey that you are aware, understand, and accept.

encouraging children to reflect, in non-judgmental ways, the characteristics of themselves and others. During Stage Four these skills are further expanded into helping children recognize and express feelings in themselves and others.

INTERPRETATION

Interpretation is a means to connect a child's behavior with his feelings. It is a major technique for helping children master communication objective C-29 and behavior objective B-23 in Stage Four. However, interpretation begins during Stage Three by simply connecting your reflection of a child's feelings to an evident behavior ("Look at Carol's face—was she kidding?" "When I see you walking into class like that I know you are discouraged."). Thinking of a child's ability to handle interpretation from a developmental point of view, you will notice that he must have certain prerequisite skills. In particular, a child must have mastered the Stage Three, communication objective C-20 "to use appropriate words . . . to show feeling responses . . ." Until a child can do this you should not move ahead with interpretation.

As a child masters this objective, provide more and more motivational labels for his behavior.

"You wish you had someone to play with . . ."
"It's hard to be quiet when you have to wait . . ."
"It makes you mad when you can't get the one you want . . ."
"When things don't go right you just want to throw them away . . ."
"You want to win so you open your eyes . . ."
"It feels good to do it right . . ."

"Sometimes you're not interested and you wish you didn't have to do it . . ."
"You get mad when the teacher makes you take turns . . ."
"Sometimes it's scary to try something new . . ."
"It's hard to stop when the activity is so interesting . . ."
"It's hard to try when the work looks tough . . ."
"You were feeling upset so you tried to get David into trouble . . ."

By the time a child is in Stage Four he can provide much of the interpretation himself and can respond to a direct approach. "What were you doing?" "Why did you do that?" "What were you trying to do?" When a child can answer such questions he is ready to explore alternative behaviors to meet his needs. This leads to mastery of another Stage Four objective, behavior objective B-22 "to implement appropriate alternative behavior toward others . . ."

Consider the following exchange between a teacher and a beginning Stage Four child as a result of an incident.

Bob climbed out a window onto a porch, ran out of the building and up and down the front steps, hitting other classroom windows to attract the attention of other boys.

Teacher: *"What happened?"*
Bob: No verbal response; looks away.
Teacher: *"Let me tell you what I saw. You seemed to be having trouble staying in the classroom today. You were running up and down the steps. Some people might think you wanted to play chase."*
Bob: *"No! The work is too hard and there's too much. The others have easy work."*
Teacher: *"It's discouraging when you think there is too much to do."*
Bob: *"I have a lot of work at school and then I come here and have a lot of work."*
Teacher: *"You would like us to understand how much work you have."*

Interpretation should not be used until Stage Three and then it should not require a response from the child. If your interpretation strikes a sensitive chord, he will let you know it, usually by denial or increased anxiety. Be ready to respond by restructuring the interaction between you for a positive outcome, leaving the door open for future discussions about feelings and behavior.

At first, Stage Four children may react to the teacher's questions as requests for evidence that will be used against them. So, the teacher should be extremely careful to convey support and acceptance in her tone and posture.

In this exchange the teacher redefines the child's running as wanting to play chase. Her purpose, to open a face-saving avenue so that she can get to the central issue and eventually consider alternative behaviors.

Bob: *"Yeah. But you don't understand."*

Teacher: *"You feel like you shouldn't have as much work here because you have so much at school."*

Bob: *"Yeah. I've got three tests at school tomorrow."*

Teacher: *"Sometimes when kids feel like they have too much on them they climb out of windows and run out to play chase."*

Bob: No verbal response; begins cracking knuckles; looks away.

Teacher: *"Lots of people play games to get troubles off their minds."*

Bob: No verbal response; looks briefly at teacher.

Teacher: *"Besides playing games, what is another way you could let me know how you feel?"*

Bob: *"You wouldn't care."*

Teacher: *"We could decide upon another way to let me know when you feel like it's too much . . . like a private code . . ."*

Bob: *"If I let you know, what would you do?"*

Teacher: *"There is a special word for emergencies at airports like 'team 2-1-2.' We could use that to mean 'It's time to get together to work it out.' Let's give that a try today when we go back to finish your work."*

Bob: *"Okay but it probably won't work."*

Teacher: No verbal response; puts arm briefly around Bob's shoulder.

Interpretation is the major technique for Stage Four. Its careful use can move children rapidly toward mastery of all of the Stage Four objectives in behavior, communication, and socialization. You will find many examples of interpretation by teachers and children in the Stage Four class described in Chapter 10.

CONFRONTATION (AND HOW TO AVOID IT)

Confrontation brings a teacher and a child face to face over an issue. Possibly no other technique has more potential for interpersonal devastation or emotional growth. Confrontation is used to convey the limits and the dependability of the teacher to enforce these limits. When a confrontation focuses upon a significant issue and is used for a particular developmental objective, it can be therapeutic. On the other hand, if you inadvertently slip into a confrontation over an insignificant issue you may find that you have exposed the child to an extent where he has no alternative but to retaliate or retreat. Either way, you have both lost something. You have lost his trust and he has lost face. Watch for signs of a potential confrontation and adjust your techniques so that it does not happen unless you are certain of a therapeutic outcome.

Confrontation at Stages One and Two will be primarily physical. Stage One children lack functional language and are seldom aware of issues. Confrontation for Stage Two children generally involves physical intervention with associated verbal responses. Refer to the discussion under Physical Intervention for confrontation techniques appropriate for these stages. By Stage Three, children have functional language and are beginning to learn inner controls. Verbal confrontations with such children generally produce physical acting out. If you feel that you can sustain such a confrontation to a therapeutic conclusion, you may want to use this technique occasionally at Stage Three. Used selectively it can help a child grow emotionally.

When a confrontation or crisis does occur with a Stage Three child, an essential part of the conversation between you and the child must be to convey what is expected of him. Verbal or nonverbal cues must provide a way for the child to resolve the situation. Something embarrassing, meaningless, or too difficult would just set the child up for an-

The teacher sidesteps Bob's excuse of too much work in order to stay on the central theme of running. She conveys support and understanding by reflecting that playing games is a universal solution to trouble. The child's nonverbal response and brief look are accepted as a mutual understanding that he ran because he feels anxious. He tests her one last time with "You wouldn't care" and she responds with a possible way they could team up on his behalf.

A confrontation implies bringing a child into direct contact with the reality of consequences. Be certain that the confrontation is legitimate and one the child is developmentally ready to meet. To create a confrontation over contrived or supercilious incidents is to convey to the child that this is important to you.

Ask yourself "Is this confrontation really essential for the child's progress?"

other confrontation. If a child spills his juice accidently hand him a paper towel and say "Accidents happen; let's wipe it up." If a child is out of his chair and reaching for a cookie, you might hold the cookie tin beyond reach and motion with your hand that he must come back to his chair before he is allowed to take his cookie. If a child breaks a window, part of the ensuing discussion with you must resolve how the situation will be corrected. Before the child returns to his group, there must be a discussion of how he can make retribution. A child feels bad when he has spilled his juice or broken a window, and so your expectations conveyed verbally or nonverbally give him security in knowing what will be expected of him. No gain results from an extracted apology.

Significant growth through confrontation usually is limited to Stage Four. By this stage children have developed enough impulse control so that a confrontation does not need to deteriorate to physical acting out. These children also have a capacity for abstract thinking which enables them to learn to respond to verbal problem solving and choose independently between alternative solutions.

You probably have concluded from the preceding discussion that verbal confrontation is not the most generally useful technique. At the same time, you recognize that potential confrontations are the continual diet of the therapeutic classroom. Perhaps a discussion of ways to make therapeutic gains by avoiding unnecessary confrontation would be useful to you.

Often your most casual question may be interpreted as confrontation by a child. Consider the question "Are you finished with your work yet?" This often receives a "No! And I'm not going to." Rephrased, "I see you are almost finished with your work and ready for play time." This might be sufficient to motivate and redirect the child to his task. Statements rather than questions avoid conveying to a child that he is being interrogated or challenged. This is a good technique when a child has few verbal skills for expressing his feelings. For example, a child walks into the classroom after recess, knocks the books off his desk, grabs another child's crayons, and begins cursing. The teacher can respond with understanding, "Tommy, you seem to be upset about something. I'll help you pick up your books and we can talk about it." A less productive alternative might be a confrontation, "Who do you think you are coming in here creating such a ruckus? What's the matter with you? Give back those crayons, pick up those books, and SIT DOWN!"

A teacher often can avoid unnecessary confrontation by selectively ignoring behavior which is merely trying to elicit a reaction from the teacher. Selective ignoring is chiefly used with children in Stage Three of therapy because at this stage children are beginning to develop inner controls. In judging whether or not to ignore a child's action, you must be aware of how secure the child's controls are, whether he trusts your judgment, and how motivating the activity is. You must be confident in your knowledge of whether the child is testing you or is actually in crisis and cannot help himself.

By ignoring a child's behavior you take away his audience. You also communicate to the child, "I know you can stop that by yourself and you don't need me to stop you." For example, one boy in a Stage Four class sat on the window ledge during an art activity and threatened to climb out. The teacher commented, "You can come join the group," and proceeded with the art lesson completely ignoring the boy. He soon joined the group in productive activity. Had the child continued this inappropriate behavior the gamble would be lost and the teacher would have to back track, usually to intervene physically. But each time the gamble is taken and won, the child has strengthened his own controls and grown a little bit more.

Ignoring can backfire with some children. Ignoring a child who is acting out for your attention may result in intensified behavior, a desperate attempt to have you respond. A child also may respond to ignoring by interpreting it as vulnerability on your part. He may see you as someone who lets things get by or who is not swift enough to keep up with children. Such an interpretation on a child's part (true or not) inevitably will produce a series of confrontations as the child attempts to test your limits to find out what sort of person you really are. You will save considerable time in therapy if you convey your expectations so clearly that testing does not have to occur for that purpose.

Another way of avoiding an unnecessary confrontation is by giving a child alternatives instead of commands. This allows a child to choose his own course of action and have some control in the situation rather than just buckling under to adult authority ("Where would be the best place for that special toy you brought, in your pocket or on the shelf?"). Alternatives provide a structure, setting limits while giving a way for choice.

There are times during a class period when children will request things or opportunities they know belong to others. A confrontation may be avoided by reminding the child, through a question, what his role had been. For example, a child says, "I want to pass out the scissors." Teacher: "I know you do; what job did you have today, Tony?" Another example: "I'm going to sit in front today." Teacher: "What day is it your turn to sit in front?" In this way the teacher has communicated that she understands what the child wishes, is concerned about it, and assures the child that he will have a turn again.

Another technique which helps a child conform to limits and learn new behavior patterns without unnecessary confrontation is depersonalizing the limits by referring to the universal condition or the editorial "we." If a child hits another child the teacher might intervene with a statement of a building rule: "In this school the rule is 'We don't hit because hitting hurts.'" By invoking a classroom rule: "We sit for work time," the teacher communicates that all children are expected to act this way instead of communicating "*You* have to stay in your chair."

Previous success experiences can be used to challenge the best in a child or a group ("I remember how you stayed in control that day when everybody had such a hard time, and I bet you can do it today even though you are upset."). This technique uses the relationship between teacher and child. The child trusts the teacher to require of him only what he *can* do. Challenge to a group based upon a previous success is particularly effective at Stage Three ("This group stayed in control all day yesterday; I bet you can do it again by helping each other today.").

When the children in a class are not responding to other verbalizations, sometimes they will respond to something in their own vernacular, phrases that are part of their everyday language. A casual comment such as, "OK, guys, cool it!" might calm them down instead of an expression such as "let's settle down" or

A successful outcome of ignoring depends upon an accurate assessment of the child's developmental stage. A Stage One or Stage Two teacher would not have ignored such behavior, knowing that children at these stages may not have developed adequate reality awareness, impulse control, or motivation to participate in the class activity without assistance from the teacher.

Reflection, combined with redirection, is an excellent technique for handling incidental acting out behavior without confrontation. By reflecting what has happened, the teacher lets the child know that she is aware of it; but by redirection, she provides a face-saving way out of the dilemma.

When a child KNOWS that you will be consistent in follow-through and KNOWS you care about him, it is easy to avoid insignificant confrontations. However, several major, significant confrontations may be necessary between you and a child before he KNOWS.

Make the assumption that street language is the same from place to place and you are lost!

"I'm waiting for you to get in control of yourselves." This is especially useful when a child is in crisis, because the familiar is more meaningful and responding to it may be second nature. "Something's bugging you. Tell me about it" may make more sense than "You're upset about something." Caution must be exercised to avoid overusing or misusing this technique.

Using high impact words or long, unknown words may be useful for children in Stages Three and Four. Some children are easily motivated when they think what they will be doing is important or exciting. That is the connotation behind the choice of a "conference" rather than "talk." Often children will show interest in making a "collage" or a "design," when making a "picture" would be out. High impact words are especially effective in the management of a crisis situation. "Let's give pause," said in a dramatic way, might calm a group down enough to redirect them or entice them into a task. "You boys are going through contortions," or "Bill is trying to be facetious" are other expressions which might serve to divert a possible crisis. These same words can be turned into a game when one of the children asks, "What does 'facetious' mean?" You can structure it into "Instant Word Game" where each child reacts instantly to what association "facetious" has for him. There does not have to be a correct answer. The purpose is to bring the group together, participating in verbal exchange.

Humor is another effective way to neutralize a potential confrontation. Humor communicates to a child that the teacher is comfortable with a situation. This generally makes the child more comfortable. It is a difficult technique to use but is applicable occasionally to children in Stage Two and frequently is used

Teachers using humor as a management technique must be careful to avoid sarcasm and other forms of "put down." Keep in mind that your purpose in using humor is to convey a comfortable relationship with a child. Be certain he can handle your humor with a successful comeback.

for Stages Three and Four. One example might be a big child refusing to leave the room with the teacher and defiantly declaring, "Make me!" She might respond by saying, "What would it look like, with me trying to move someone as big as you?" With a grin and a friendly touch, she can continue to paint a verbal picture. The end result is a relaxed child and a relaxed teacher, ready to go out and talk.

Remember, whenever you have successfully avoided a crisis or confrontation, in your mind review your own verbal content and look for clues as to what you said and how the children responded. Store these details away. You can use them for the next potential confrontation.

LIFE SPACE INTERVIEWING

The Life Space Interview (LSI) was developed by Fritz Redl and extended by William Morse and Nicholas Long (Long, Morse, and Newman, 1971). They have defined it as ". . . a style of teacher-pupil interaction to deal with many issues" (p. 484). They recommend that the LSI be used for the "clinical exploitation of life events" or for "emotional first aid" (p. 475).

The LSI can be used with individual children or with groups. In Developmental Therapy, the LSI is most effective at Stage Three with individual children and at Stage Four with a group.

In general, the LSI requires some amount of expressive language and conceptual ability on a child's part. These skills are not adequately developed until a child is moving into Stage Three. For this reason, the LSI is not used before a child has mastered a majority of communication objectives for Stage Two.

For teachers of Stages Three and

Four, the LSI is a significant, therapeutic tool. If you have not already developed the technique, begin by carefully reviewing Long, Morse, and Newman (1971). Then learn the steps outlined by Dr. Morse. If possible, ask for supervision from someone who uses this technique. Such supervision is important if you want to perfect your skills in LSI.

To begin, however, there are a number of things you can do on your own. Remember, your role at this time is to be a mediator between a child and a particular issue. Remember also that the LSI is not a one-time shot but a series of interactions between you and the child around issues that arise while working with developmental objectives. The purpose is to help him gain more insight into his own behavior, the feelings that promoted the behavior, and the consequences of the behavior. Ultimately, the two of you are working for changes in his behavior which will promote more satisfying responses from others. To do this you have to be trusted by the child, have a developing relationship, and convey acceptance.

At the beginning, wait. See what elements you are dealing with in the situation. How upset is the child? Is he angry and acting out? Needing restraint? Needing emotional support? Needing firmness? Be calm and put the pieces together in your own mind. Most important, take your cues from the nonverbal messages you are getting from the child.

Teachers sometimes expect the child to bring his anxiety under control and talk right away. Don't push too much. Use reflection. If a child is crying, or cursing, you might say sympathetically, "Things are pretty bad, aren't they?" Don't expect an answer. It is essential for you to convey dispassionate compassion. When the child's physiological proc-

esses are restored to normal (breathing, muscle tone) try to obtain the child's perception of the situation. Don't tell the child what you perceived. Give him the chance to tell it his way and accept his perception. Sometimes you will have to start it off by reflecting what you saw or interpreting a possible feeling behind a behavior ("Something happened during juice and cookie time. Bob was trying to make you feel bad in class.").

Responses you might get from a child during this part of a LSI are:

Child won't talk.
He may digress to other subjects and try to lead you away.
He may distort reality.
He may attack you either physically or verbally.
He may blame you for the situation.
He may regress.

Sometimes the situation will have to be reconstructed from the beginning to pin it down. At this point in the LSI, don't be concerned with uncovering "the real truth." Rather, focus upon how the child sees it. Question. Show interest and sensitivity to feelings but do not judge. If the child changes the subject, you might want to reflect what he is doing and possibly interpret the feeling behind it. In any event, keep the exchange focusing back on the situation. Sometimes it may be necessary to arrive at a temporary resolution and stop.

If you continue into the next phase, try to find out what is important to the child. You will need to listen intently; try to pick up cues from his nonverbal communication, and remember what seems to be important from his point of view. You may need to use such information later in the LSI. Many times a child will lose control during this phase because he feels badly and cannot put it in words. He may need to lean on you

Reflection is a technique used at Stages Two and Three to "ready" a child for the LSI. If a child already has learned that you can reflect his feelings when he is not able to do so himself, he can easily move with you into the LSI.

The LSI can help a child with all of the Stage Three objectives in behavior, communication, and socialization. However, the LSI has its greatest effectiveness helping Stage Four children master behavior objectives.

Reading body language is a skill all teachers should have. It is essential for an effective LSI.

for emotional strength until he can recover enough to handle it himself. Your support may be through words or physical contact. If he starts to draw back let him. As the LSI progresses, you will find your role changing, from providing nurturance to an attitude of "we'll-work-on-it-together."

The next step is to use what the child has given and put it together in a reality context around the central issue. This may be related to a specific, obvious incident for Stage Three children or may be a quite complex, emotional issue for Stage Four children. Again, reflection and interpretation are techniques to help you. Having the child admit his guilt is not the object. You want to continue the process of awareness of behavior, the feelings behind them, and the consequences. It is important that you avoid implying judgments or opinions.

If the child seems ready to consider changing his responses, move the discussion to alternative ways he could respond to the situation. There are many alternative responses, some more productive than others. Let the conversation consider a number of these responses, weighing the possible outcomes. Among fairly specific choices, work with the child to select an alternative that will assist him in dealing more successfully with the central issue. It will be important for you to keep in mind the Developmental Therapy objectives for the child as you guide the LSI to its conclusion. Selecting alternatives which are beyond his current ability to accomplish will certainly mark the child for failure, while modifying an alternative to a more realistic level will help the child in the process of constructive change.

Once a resolution has been reached, you and the child should talk about what is going to happen when he returns to the classroom. "Do you want to tell the teacher about this?" If he does not want to tell the other teacher, you might respond with "Okay, some things are private." If he wants to talk to the teacher you might respond with "She'll be going downstairs with you to wait for the bus after class, and that would be a good time to talk." In some situations you might offer to talk to the other teacher and give him the choice of participating or not.

If a child is not ready for change, you may have to give him several specific alternatives to chose among. In such situations, set up a fairly specific circumstance and end the LSI with the idea that you and the child will continue to work together again. "As soon as we talk about it, you can go back to your classroom."

Some final cautions about using the LSI:

If you try to wind up with an appropriate resolution on the first interview, you are lost.

Don't expound at length on the reasons behind the incident.

Too much teacher talk will dry up an interview.

Too little teacher participation will result in an interview which dissolves from lack of direction.

Do not be judgmental.

Get your inputs from the child's nonverbal behavior.

Be flexible. Don't be certain you "have it all together" before the LSI begins.

PRAISE AND REWARDS

Letting a child know he is doing a good job is an important part of any therapeutic program. Praise is essential for reflecting children's successes for them to see because disturbed children seldom see their own successes. When you help them see themselves as being able to do, they will gather the courage to venture to the next challenge, trying something new. Rewards vary according to the stage of therapy. With some children a successful outcome, a sense of mastery and accomplishment is the reward. For others, recognition by a significant adult is the reward. Don't use gifts, objects, money, or individual privileges which create a climate for competitiveness. Rewards should lead to internalized motivation on the child's part.

The progression from physical to verbal techniques, which is so characteristic of other techniques in Developmental Therapy, is used also for praise and rewards. A child in Stage One receives much praise physically, through body contact, hugging, touch, rubbing, and other pleasurable sensations. Used initially to arouse and elicit responses, these forms of contact soon become a form of praise and reward for spontaneous responses.

By Stage Two, the mobilized child is responding to highly motivating, individualized activities for which the pleasure of doing is the reward. The teacher verbally reflects the successful aspects of a child's participation as she helps him master fundamental skills for successful participation in a task. Often, abundant verbal praise must be used at Stage Two and accompanied by physical contact. Very small accomplishments need to be recognized, as there are very few things a beginning Stage Two child can accomplish successfully by ordinary standards.

During Stage Three, children have progressed to a level where verbal praise is usually enough to communicate your recognition of their accomplishments and the good feelings you share with each child over his situation. Responding to praise without loss of control or in-

appropriate behavior is the first communication objective for Stage Three (C-14). This milestone usually is necessary before a child can use words to praise his own work (C-19). Because participating successfully in group activities is a major goal of Stage Three, your reflection of success and redirection of responses to successful outcomes are significant techniques which precede praise and reward. By drawing upon each child's strengths, you can make praise legitimate. Your own credibility with the Stage Three child will increase; and he will begin to internalize feelings of being a successful person. At this point the child will depend much less on you for praise, indicating that he is moving into Stage Four.

Peer recognition is a major motivating force in a Stage Four class. Praise and rewards should come from group interaction and have an authentic, real-life meaning. The Stage Four group can work to make their own rewards by learning what options will bring the results they want. A major challenge for the teacher at this stage is to avoid superimposing a preconceived reward system on the group. To be truly effective, the motivation for group effort must be defined by the group itself.

Stage One children may respond to sensory rewards such as food, touch, holding, and other arousing experiences. In contrast, Stage Two children may be held back by the continued use of Stage One rewards when they could respond to higher level rewards such as social exchange, play, success, and attention from a significant adult.

At Stage Three, the rewards are group activities, so that a child learns that good and "fun" things happen because he is a member of a group.

Rewards and motivation should be inseparable by the time a child is well into Stage Four.

LITERATURE CITED

Long, N. J., W. C. Morse, and R. G. Newman (eds.) 1971. Conflict in the Classroom. 2nd Ed. Wadsworth, Belmont, Cal.

ACKNOWLEDGMENTS

The authors wish to acknowledge the contribution to this chapter by Patricia McGinnis for the section on managing a child in crisis. Originally prepared for staff training at Rutland Center in 1970, her material is included in the section, Removal From the Room.

chapter 6

DEVELOPING THE SKILLS TO BE EFFECTIVE USING DEVELOPMENTAL THERAPY

Diane Weller

Failure

Feelings

Reality

Success

Conflict

Anger

Aggression

Rejection

Guilt

Deprivation

Abuse

Trust

Accomplishment

Concern

INTRODUCTION

Teachers of disturbed children need to be prepared to face the assault of bizarre behavior, attitudes of rejection, and verbal and physical acting out by the children they are to teach. They need to understand and work with psychiatrists, psychologists, and social workers who also have responsibility for the treatment of such children and their families. They must be prepared to educate in the domain of social-emotional development. They are confronted with varying social standards and expectations from the families and communities of these children. They often see the compounding effect of severe cultural deprivation on potentially normal emotional responses.

The essential forces these teachers face are reality, rules, social expectations, motivations, drives, feelings, anger, conflict, successes, and failures. They must understand these powerful pressures, and they must understand their own responses. They must learn that they themselves are the catalyst in the therapeutic process. Often they are the major agents for change in the life of disturbed children. They must know where they are headed in therapy, what their goals are for these children, and what steps they must follow to reach these goals. They must be able to recognize the accomplishment of a developmental objective. They also must know when new procedures could expedite the mastery of an objective.

Such skills are not developed easily or rapidly. The process requires considerable insight into oneself. Most importantly, it requires a depth of emotional maturity, self confidence, and empathy for others.

LEARNING TO REACT AND INTERVENE

Often, persons who desire to teach emotionally disturbed children are without knowledge of the nature of serious emotional disturbance or how children's behavior effects the emotions of adults. Without actual experience, they are unaccustomed to "what disturbed youngsters are really like." One statement made by a master's degree candidate in Special Education at the conclusion of her course work is characteristic: "I have spent one year learning about children in the abstract."

Other teachers have exotic, sometimes exaggerated views of disturbed children whom they have seldom seen, describing them as fragile "flower children," "withdrawn," "spaced-out," "violent," "temperamental," "confused," or "hyperactive." All of these may be descriptive of disturbance, delayed development, or seriously disordered behavior, but even these characteristics are generally intermingled with normal behaviors. A simplistic account of one morning at the center illustrates this important point. The secretary described her experiences upon entering the building as follows:

When I walked up to the front door a shower of small rocks and debris was coming from the roof of the building. A child was on the roof angrily shouting and throwing rocks and debris at anyone within range. A teacher calmly leaned against the tree, making supportive comments to him. I left for the back door in a hurry.

In the side yard I was greeted by another shower—water from a hose. This child, happily laughing, was playing with the garden hose while his teacher maneuvered into closer range. When I finally reached my desk inside the building two children were in the hallway. They were really excited about their weekend experiences, and both greeted me with "Hi, Lady." A third child walked past slowly and barely moved her hand in a gesture of greeting, at the same time quickly averting her eyes. By this time the child who had been on the roof was walking stormily past with his teacher, pausing long enough to shout at me, "I'm going to spit in your face."

Later that day, when leaving, that same boy stopped by my desk and said, "I had a good time playing kickball in class; I really had fun today." And a teacher told me that the boy playing with the water hose had written an experience story that day about growing a garden in his yard.

All of these children attend therapy classes, but their outward behaviors reflect both appropriate and inappropriate actions; normal and maladaptive functioning can be inferred to be within the same individuals. This is one of the important assumptions inherent in Developmental Therapy and must be understood prior to any attempt to use Developmental Therapy in the classroom.

With Developmental Therapy the teacher responds to a child's normal processes as well as his maladaptive ones.

Developmental Therapy in the therapeutic classroom might be thought of as the outcome of *decisions* based upon a teacher's awareness of developmental stages and objectives, a child's individual pattern of development, and behavioral dynamics merging at a specific moment in time. These ongoing decisions are commonly called "interventions" and may be verbal or nonverbal. Such decisions enhance a child's developing skills, but may evoke direct confrontation or cause regression.

The most difficult decisions are those which cause temporary discomfort to the child. But if a crisis, large or small, will produce growth it is not only desirable but essential.

The effective teacher of disturbed children is constantly monitoring her own feelings concerning herself and her competencies. Not only must she respond to the children, but she must also evaluate their effect on her and the effect of her responses on them. This is a continuous process; it should never cease. During the first year, feedback from a person experienced in Developmental Therapy is essential to help develop self monitoring skills. The exactness of skills demanded for good therapy can be personally taxing for a teacher. Without support and extensive feedback, a trainee can develop rigid and negative feelings toward her own abilities. Many persons possess the qualities to become skilled teachers if given supervision. However, few develop effective skills without supervision. The following episode in a Developmental Therapy class illustrates the type and quality of intervention which is typical of a teacher beginning training in Developmental Therapy. The teacher in training in this excerpt is a support teacher.

Karl is a five-year-old boy who is a member of a group of six Stage Two children. It is Karl's birthday, and a birthday cake is to be provided for his group at snack time. Karl's behavior in the group is characterized by constant, deliberate testing of limits. He has thrown toys, refused to complete tasks and sporadically exhibits immature behavior such as crying and lying on the floor. He has difficulty during transitions from activity to activity but responds to the physical and verbal support of both teachers in the classroom.

For no apparent reason during story time he says, "I already had a birthday party at home yesterday." Neither the lead nor the support teacher comment back to him. Later, near the end of play time Karl begins throwing blocks toward the area in which they are to be stored. The support teacher, in the course of her overall supportive statements to the children says, "Karl, you can stack the blocks in the corner," and moves toward Karl. Karl slumps to the floor and lies motionless, his head away from the teacher. A small grin spreads across his face. The teacher does not notice this. She quietly kneels beside Karl, places her hand on his back, and urges him to stack the blocks in the corner. Karl complies. The teacher moves away from Karl and involves herself with helping other children. While stacking blocks Karl hears the lead teacher say, "When all the toys are put away, we will have our snack time with a special cake." He begins to stack blocks in a very directed manner.

The lead teacher and five children by now have moved to the table in the room. Each child is praised for his specific effort in cleaning the play area: "Jerry drove all the trucks to the garage," and "Donna put away three hats and two dresses." The support teacher, observing that Karl is about to finish putting the blocks away, leaves him and joins the group. Karl soon finishes. On his way to his seat, he looks at the open toy cabinet doors and carefully goes to close them. Then he looks at the support teacher, a very large, open smile on his face. No response. Both teachers are by now engrossed in the conversation of the children at the table. Disappointed, Karl proceeds to his designated seat at the table and sits quietly, listening to catch threads of meaning from the conversation.

At least one significant therapeutic moment was lost during this period of time. When Karl was able to risk himself openly by seeking recognition for his constructive act, the support teacher did not respond. Karl's outward expression of trust, positive self mobilization, and appropriate feelings of pride in closing the cabinets were overlooked. So often such small, beginning signs of growth are overlooked by children and adults alike.

If handled by a skilled teacher, the incident described above could produce therapeutic changes over a fairly short period of time. Karl's behavior during this particular day gave cues for anticipating his behavior. Difficulties have arisen during transitions and activity periods. As time drew near for his birthday cake, the teacher could expect heightened anxiety and increased restlessness. Karl's statement, "I already had a birthday party at home yesterday," is significant and calls for interpretation and response on the part of the teacher. We can assume that the teacher is aware of his parents' rejection and Karl's ambivalent feelings toward his parents. Karl, in making the statement, may be protecting himself from an expected failure to earn a birthday cake in class through good behavior. Or the statement

may have been a response to confusion or insecurity on his part and might be interpreted as, "Am I going to have a birthday cake?"

In either case, no response was given by the teachers, who seemed unaware that the remark was made. This lack of response might reinforce Karl's negative feelings about himself as being unworthy of a cake because of his "bad" behavior, or it might produce ambivalence toward the teachers with associated feelings of insecurity (Maybe she will make something good happen for me; maybe she won't.).

On this particular day Karl needed support in making the crucial transition from play time to snack time. Based upon his previous behavior and ability to respond to help, one could anticipate that he would respond to praise. The teachers possibly assumed that no response was necessary since the birthday cake was next, and Karl would be anxious to be the first child at the table. When intervention was needed it was given in terms of a directive statement, "Karl, you can stack the blocks in the corner."

Movement toward Karl produced his falling on the floor, an old coping behavior. Physical contact or movement on the teacher's part was needed to provide Karl support, at the same time evoking a constructive response. The moment was salvaged when the teacher placed her hand on Karl's back and urged him to complete the activity. Karl's compliance in getting up and independently finishing the task indicates high Stage Two skills— willingness to trust the adults in his environment and ability to complete tasks without physical intervention.

In focusing on the group rather than on Karl, the support teacher lost the opportunity to reinforce his appropriate

Even though this episode portrays an outcome which was appropriate by ordinary standards, an opportunity for greater growth was lost.

In Developmental Therapy this small expression of positive growth, and the many which occur during each therapy session, typify important intervention points for which teachers must develop heightened awareness. Intervention at such times often makes the difference between maintenance therapy and growth.

Anxiety, caused by fear of possible loss of affection or fear of failure many times motivates a child's behavior in the classroom.

actions and feelings. In closing the cabinet doors he mobilized himself for positive action. With his smile he openly expressed pride in himself. Karl also exhibited strengths in his ability to join the group at the table and in his attempt to join the conversation. Acknowledgment of his actions by the teachers, either verbally or nonverbally, would have secured some small, positive gain.

This incident illustrates in a microcosm some skills you will need to be an effective teacher using Developmental Therapy. Additionally prior to classroom placement, you should feel a commitment to operate within the parameters of the Developmental Therapy model, should be able to demonstrate knowledge concerning the theories and assumptions of Developmental Therapy, and have the ability to grow by utilizing feedback from supervised experiences.

Observation of groups of children in the treatment program is an important step. While you observe you should be actively participating, in the sense that you learn to connect behavior to particular developmental objectives. Look for developmental characteristics rather than deviant behaviors. Question. Watch the teachers' responses, and examine your own feelings concerning what is transpiring in the classroom. The end result of observation should then be heightened awareness of children's behavior and an understanding of the changing elements in the treatment model at each stage of therapy. It is essential also that you develop understanding of your own reactions to what is actually happening in the classroom. Since feelings of teachers generate a variety of behaviors in children, it is essential that this type of self examination begin before you actually enter the classroom. If you know that something can evoke an emotional reac-

Observing children and looking for developmental characteristics is a first step in preparing to use Developmental Therapy.

The other side to observing children is observing the responses of their teachers and peers.

To make observing profitable, examine your own reactions to what you see and then connect your conclusions to the Developmental Therapy framework.

tion in yourself, plan ways to work through or circumvent it. In short, you must be able to subjugate your own needs if necessary, in order to move children successfully toward treatment goals. For example, consider again the case of Karl, the five-year-old, Stage Two child on his birthday. A small group of trainees was observing this class with an experienced supervisor.

Karl and his group are at the table eating birthday cake. Karl has eaten some of his cake. He expresses great pleasure at having a cake. "Oh, boy, it's a birthday cake for me."

The teacher reflects warmly, "This is your birthday cake." Shortly after that Karl stops eating and tries to listen to the conversation at the table. After glancing at the support teacher he leans forward, pushing his face into the cake on the table. The support teacher gently pulls Karl back into a sitting position and moves the cake away. Karl says petulantly, "I want my cake."

The teacher responds, "Karl, it is really exciting to have a birthday cake, but you can eat the cake with your fork." Karl laughs and makes faces, attracting the attention of others in the group. Karl is given a napkin with which to wipe his face. He complies, is given his cake again, and starts to eat. The lead teacher mentally notes that the class period is nearly over and that others in the group are finishing. She states, "We have a little more time to finish eating the cake." Karl again plunges his face into the cake. Again the cake is removed and Karl is helped to sit upright in his chair. The support teacher says, "You wonder what will happen when you put your face in the cake."

By this time the lead teacher states "Snack time is over, and now it's time to go home." The class period ends and the other children in the group are ready to clean up. The food, including Karl's remaining cake, is removed from the table. Karl's eyes follow the cake from the table to the shelf. The teacher says seriously, "It was really a nice birthday, Karl. You made everyone feel good." Karl looks at the teacher and reaches up to take her outstretched hand. As all of the children leave the room Karl looks back once more at his uneaten piece of cake.

The response from the trainees observing the group was unanimous. "Poor Karl, it was his birthday. The cake really meant a lot to him, and he didn't get to finish." They were mildly astonished to find that outside the classroom Karl had spontaneously hugged both teachers and stated that "It was a nice birthday party."

Some of the trainees then commented, "Well, maybe the cake wasn't that important." They had responded to the situation purely on an emotional level, possibly based upon their own experiences. Their remarks in response to questioning as to what they would have done if they had been the teacher illustrate how their emotions dictated their judgment. Their solutions centered around taking the cake home, finishing it after class, or finishing it the next day. Upon meeting with the two teachers and discussing the incident, they heard the lead teacher's reasons for her procedure. Karl's needs for nurturance and acceptance were real and were met through provision of the birthday cake. He was aware that the teachers cared. They had provided a material symbol of caring (the cake). They demonstrated that they cared about what happened to him by helping him maintain his position at the table as a constructive member of the group.

By reacting to their own personal feelings, any one of the observers could have made a critical error in treatment. This type of self understanding is basic to becoming an effective teacher of disturbed children. Guided observation of incidents such as this can help you determine whether or not you can exercise

enough control over yourself to meet the demands of the various teacher roles in Developmental Therapy.

There are a number of personal qualities which seem to foster the mobilization of forces for effectively teaching disturbed children. Perhaps most important is the conviction that children can change. Other important qualities are: flexibility of expression and thought, intelligence, warmth and cheerfulness, honesty, objective self examination, desire to succeed, empathy with children and adults, and a personal sense of security.

Other special competencies which are desirable for effective therapy are difficult to define but generally appear to be the same as for excellent teachers in regular schools. The following is a partial list of abilities which seem to be necessary for teachers using Developmental Therapy:

1. Ability to plan experiences from Developmental Therapy objectives.
2. Ability to adjust own style of communicating to a child's receptive language level.
3. Ability to use own body to convey messages to children.
4. Ability to understand child's experiential world, including fantasy.
5. Ability to anticipate child's behavior and respond within the context of the child's stage of development.
6. Ability to understand motives for children's actions.
7. Ability to convey calm dependability and competence under stress.
8. Ability to subjugate own needs to those of children.
9. Ability to immediately adjust own actions and procedures and to alter classroom experiences to foster change in children.

This incident underscores the importance of people rather than things. But the idea is more difficult to deal with than you might imagine. Disturbed children have disturbed relations with people. They tend to convey that they dislike practically everyone. When they seem to prefer things to people they may be covering up the painful truth. They are afraid of being rejected.

10. Ability to serve as a model for a child's parents and regular school teacher.

11. Ability to work effectively as a member of a treatment team.

LEARNING SKILLS TO BE A SUPPORT TEACHER

Classroom training begins with learning to be a support teacher, an integral member of the treatment team. Each member of the team has distinct functions, but each is dependent upon the others for information and back-up. You will find that a support teacher is by no means a junior team member or lesser therapist. Highly significant aspects of therapy are the responsibility of the support teacher.

Learning to be a support teacher is the beginning of a process of *inner* and *outer monitoring* of your own actions toward children. You must learn to use verbal and body language with dexterity. You must learn also to adjust your responses to the developmental stages of each child. Being a good support teacher is a mental process rather than a mechanical exercise in the classroom. You will be dealing with behavior which is especially taxing physically and emotionally. You must be prepared to meet personal failure, master your own feelings, and remobilize your own responses while you keep the children moving toward mastery of Developmental Therapy objectives. One of the hardest things to accept is the constant feedback from others on the team. Often, even things which you feel that you have done well could be done differently or better. Many times you may feel that you are doing everything wrong. This is when it is easiest to give up and become critical of the people you work with or the system you work in. If you can over-

come these feelings by working through them rather than repressing or denying them, you will be able to make the changes which others are suggesting to you.

As a beginning support teacher you will probably be assigned to different morning and afternoon treatment teams. For each, you will be expected to prepare materials for the daily classroom activities, participate in a 30-minute pre-planning and preparation period with the lead teacher, fulfill the support teacher role on the treatment teams for two hours in a morning therapeutic class and again in the afternoon. Following each class you will participate in the daily debriefing sessions with the treatment teams. In addition, you will have responsibilities such as housekeeping tasks, weekly staff training sessions, and participating with the lead teacher in regular school contacts.

RESPONSIBILITIES

Your most important responsibility, however, is to develop the skills to fulfill the support teacher's part in the therapeutic process. Here are thirteen important first steps for the beginning support teacher.

1. Meet children entering and leaving the building.

2. In the classroom maintain strategic locations for each activity, planned in advance with the other members of the team.

3. Be physically alert to move as needed.

4. Learn how each child responds to stress and success.

5. Redirect children to the lead teacher, into group activity, or toward materials they are using.

6. Make positive statements; reflect

The Developmental Therapy model has been demonstrated on the basis of a three-member treatment team consisting of a support and a lead teacher and monitor. Each member has a special function. Teachers generally train for all three positions sequentially, beginning with the support teacher role. The skills needed in these positions are cumulative; that is, a lead teacher's skills are built upon support teacher competencies. Monitor skills grow from effective lead teacher skills.

Even if you are teaching disturbed children without benefit of a treatment team, you may want to think through the requirements of each position as outlined in this section. More than likely you have found yourself responsible for the conduct of all three positions.

outcomes of children's behavior in positive terms.

7.   Talk as is necessary, but be careful not to talk too much.

8.   Assume a pleasant attitude verbally and nonverbally and use it to help children move ahead. Look and act interested and pleasant.

9.   Know thoroughly the daily routine, materials which will be used and where they are stored.

10.   Take a real interest in the children; learn their strengths and weaknesses; see yourself as each child's advocate, rather than being concerned with your own performance.

11.   Know the Developmental Therapy objectives for each child in the group.

12.   Plan individual programs based upon the objectives.

13.   Learn the objectives at stages immediately below and above the present levels of functioning for each child in the class.

If you can do these things decisively and positively you will establish credibility with the children in the group and will be a valuable member of the treatment team. In an effective team, the support teacher complements the lead teacher, keeping children involved in the activity which the lead teacher is conducting. Your movements and verbalizations usually involve one to three children rather than the total group. Often, you will be the one to deal with the child in crisis, the resistant child, or the child with a special need. By responding to the individual needs you free the lead teacher to continue the group process. But in doing this, be certain that your efforts are toward redirecting the children to the lead teacher, activity, or materials.

During the first few days of classroom training the support teacher must learn basic body movements and intervention strategies. Having a few effective verbal and nonverbal responses is important. *Reflection* and *answering-a-question-with-a-question* are two verbal techniques which are easy for a trainee to learn immediately. Learning basic intervention and verbal strategies is most easily done by modeling the lead teacher. However, extending your skills to include all of the techniques described in Chapter 5 takes considerable time and experience with a number of stages of therapy.

Awareness of Developmental Therapy objectives is the basis for intervention in the therapeutic classroom. Intervention is necessary to promote and reinforce the child's progress toward mastery of the objectives. Since Developmental Therapy is an experiential program, the activities and how they are organized and presented are of paramount concern. Also, good techniques will diminish in effectiveness without the substance of developmentally appropriate activities. Each objective which applies to a particular child should be examined and memorized for classroom usage. Remember that the objectives are your guideposts for both curriculum activities and techniques. They also serve as your resource in crises, when you ask yourself, "What should I do in this situation?"

Plan specific activities and prepare appropriate materials and procedures around objectives. Begin by planning individual academic sequences in reading, writing, spelling, and arithmetic. These are easier to sequence than activities in socialization, behavior, and communication. Although the lead teacher will conduct many of the activities, your involvement in planning and preparation will be an important step in learning to use the Developmental Therapy objectives.

One frequently mentioned problem

A major difference which arises between early childhood educators and those who work with disturbed children concerns the extent of intervention by the teacher. Without highly skilled intervention a disturbed child will not utilize opportunities to participate. Waiting for growth to occur in an impromptu way earmarks the child for an even greater development lag.

Some teachers prefer to learn the support role for different stages of therapy before going on to learn the lead teacher role. One benefit of this approach is learning developmental objectives for all stages. This will provide a clear idea of the behavioral manifestations of each objective and the approximations leading up to it. Then when a child's behavior changes she will be able to recognize it as growth or regression and will know the appropriate objective.

in regard to learning the support role is: "I don't know when to move in to handle problem behavior," or "I don't know what to say." These are realistic questions and may mean "I don't know what the child needs." This points up a major responsibility for the support teacher, that is, directing your actions to meet a child's immediate needs while moving him toward Developmental Therapy objectives. Sometimes support teachers are so anxious about being in a classroom situation that they become more concerned with management than child objectives. They may think that if a class is quiet and orderly, children are progressing and they are doing a good job. This is not necessarily true. If you have found yourself in that position, separating issues of classroom control from the developmental needs of children may be a most difficult task for you. You can overcome it by defining why you react to children who present management problems. Expand upon the positive aspects of your response and change those which are detrimental to developmental progress. Be personally secure enough to accept daily suggestions for improvements from your team as well as to make your own suggestions for treatment. Communicate feelings about yourself or the children to the team, but be able to confine them in the classroom and eventually internalize needed changes. Develop a feeling for the delicacy of interactions with children and a feeling for growth and change. No teacher is successful when she is so wrapped up in her performance that she conducts a superficial, self gratifying program in the classroom. Although it is natural to want to be liked, you should not be concerned with whether the children like you or not. What is important is that you view these children as individuals who can develop and change, regardless

Some children are so insecure in their abilities that they do need to know that "ever little thing" is correct. Global comments such as "you did a good job" are not quite enough to satisfy their overwhelming feelings of anxiety. Ultimately, the success of completing tasks such as the one mentioned in the example will serve to decrease these feelings. Until then the teacher must plan to lend her support to the child in specific ways.

of your personal feelings toward them.

Before going on to become a lead teacher, a support teacher may work in many different classes to fully develop her skills. Some become so expert that their lead teachers are able to maintain a therapeutic group process most of the time. If all of the children in a group are participating in an activity, you know there has been much skilled work on the part of the support teacher.

The following is an account of an interaction between a support teacher and an individual child. It illustrates the activities of an effective support teacher.

Example of Support Teacher Interacting With One Child

Bernard, nine years old, is enrolled in a Stage Two class. He is aggressive and frequently shouts, curses, and bites when upset. He is negative toward school, has a poor self concept, poor socialization skills, and difficulty reading. He is large for his age and has a poor body concept. After he has been physically aggressive he becomes remorseful. Often he has sudden mood swings. Work time is a sensitive area because of Bernard's poor academic skills. During work time the teacher watches Bernard's actions closely. She knows that reading is particularly difficult, but success has been achieved with encouragement and reflection of each accomplishment by the support teacher. Bernard has completed his math work and now works slowly on an initial consonant recognition sheet. The support teacher comments specifically "Yes, the C matches cookie." She times her comments to come when he has finished a problem rather than in the middle of a process. Some children in the class finish and go on to the next scheduled activity, play time. But Bernard is still working with the support teacher sitting on his left at the end of the table.

As the lead teacher leaves the work table to join the group in the play area she says, "Your work is almost finished. I'll be waiting for you." Bernard begins to stare at his paper. The support teacher says, *"As soon as you match the D and the R, you will be finished."*

Bernard shouts, *"Shut up, you have bad breath, I ain't finishing."*

The support teacher reflects, *"You wonder what will happen if you don't finish."* She knows he has the capability to finish because he has succeeded with previous reading activities. She feels that he is testing limits as his frustration over finishing increases. It is difficult for him to be the last child finishing his work. No physical move is made toward Bernard, but the teacher conveys nonverbally that he is expected to finish his paper. Suddenly, Bernard's body tightens. The support teacher senses more frustration. Bernard tears his paper and wads it into a ball, *"Take your —— paper! I ain't doing it."*

The support teacher takes the wad of paper, reflects, and restates the expectation. *"Bernard, you want to see what would happen if you ripped up that paper. You can put it back together, and then you can finish. You can do it."* The support teacher is careful not to move physically toward Bernard at this moment. Instead there is a confident pause followed by her restructuring of the task. *"There are two more problems. Then you can go to play time."*

"Ain't doing it . . . You're dumb, you stink! And you're ugly and your breath smells like old dirty socks." Bernard himself feels dumb and ugly. He stands up and runs to the end of table.

The support teacher quickly moves toward Bernard who is now yelling toward the other children in the play area, *"Hey, look at her. She's dumb! She stinks!"* The support teacher puts her arm around Bernard's waist and moves him out of room to the quiet area.

The lead teacher says *"You can come back to the room when you are able to finish."*

On the way out, the support teacher keeps in mind that she must ignore personal comments made toward her. Bernard's derogatory comments are made partially to test the teacher's limits and partially to express his own frustrations. If not carefully treated the remarks can become self derogatory and lead to more detrimental feeling about himself as inadequate and "bad." She is aware that she must act quickly to prevent this from happening. That is why he is taken from the room. Bernard is working on Stage Two objectives in behavior

and communication. As they leave, the support teacher reviews to herself the objectives and estimates his ability to respond.

Bernard himself feels stupid, fat, and unsavory and projects this into what he is saying, loudly, but not yet out of control. As the support teacher and Bernard reach the quiet room, the support teacher immediately releases Bernard.

Support teacher, not looking at him directly: *"Bernard, we must have walked up 50 steps to get here. Do you think it was 50 steps?"*

Bernard: *"I ain't talking to no ugly old bitch. It was only 7 or 8."*

Support teacher, still looking away: *"Last Monday we had a good conference in the grown-ups' conference room. Remember, we decided that you were grown-up enough to talk in there. Boys who can control their behavior can talk in the grown-up room."* Bernard listens. He likes the image of being associated with the grown-ups. The support teacher has reduced Bernard's feelings of anger toward himself as a first step. She develops a positive alignment with Bernard as a second step.

Support teacher, looking at her watch: *"I think that the people who were working in there left five minutes ago."* This enhances the fact that grown-ups actually do use the room. *"We could talk in there. You are in control enough to go right now."*

Bernard: *"Yeah, I went down there Monday."* His body language says he is ready to go. He appears relaxed. The support teacher makes no further comment.

Both go to conference room and sit down at a table.

Support teacher, in a businesslike manner: *"Now Bernard, you did your math and most of your reading. Sometimes work goes slowly; and boys rip their papers to see what teachers will do."*

Bernard: *"I knew I was going to tape the paper back together."*

Teacher: *"That's an excellent idea. We may be able to get you back and finished with your work with a little time left to play."* This was necessary in order to restructure the expectation the child might have about what happens next.

Bernard and the support teacher walk back

Old coping behaviors surface in the wake of frustration. When a crisis such as this will produce opportunity for growth it is allowed to occur.

The support teacher asks a neutral question to estimate the child's ability to respond verbally. Because he did answer her question she judged that he would not act out aggressively, was not out of control, and could respond on a verbal level. Therefore, a rapid reentry to the classroom was desirable as soon as a resolution to the work crisis could be made.

The teacher begins this conference with a positive statement, reviewing the child's accomplishments in a simple, honest way.

The lead teacher's interjection at this point is an important part of team work. It conveys that the lead teacher is in agreement with the expectations and consequences communicated to the child by the support teacher. This comment also provides the support teacher and the child with a positive goal for reentry.

The entire tone of this exchange conveys a positive alliance between child and teacher. Real expectations are communicated in a way which avoids confrontation. The unspoken message to the child is "You are a person I have confidence in."

to classroom. The support teacher puts her hand on Bernard's shoulder. As they reenter, the support teacher says to the lead teacher and the group, *"Bernard is going to tape his paper together and will come over to play time as soon as he finishes."*

Lead teacher: *"We need someone who can pump gas for the cars and run the gas station."*

Bernard is able to finish his work and successfully participate in play time.

LEARNING SKILLS TO BE A LEAD TEACHER

As a lead teacher you must have personal qualities and competencies which will allow you to generalize from what you learned as a support teacher to any stage of Developmental Therapy. Your knowledge of Developmental Therapy objectives and individual behavioral dynamics should be proficient to the point that you can conceptualize the strengths and weaknesses of a child within the developmental framework across stages of therapy. This type of continuum of thought allows for the widest range of therapeutic input and ongoing program adjustment. It complements the assumption that behavioral change may be very rapid but often uneven among the four curriculum areas. It also provides for needed changes when children in crisis revert to a lower level of functioning.

As the lead teacher you will be the catalyst for individual and group progress. You must already possess the skills necessary to deal with individual behavior, both normal and deviant. Management techniques and program planning should by this point be solidly based upon knowledge of Developmental Therapy precepts, objectives, and behavioral dynamics. As a novice lead teacher, you have the opportunity to extend your skills with responsibility for planning and implementing Developmental Thera-

One of the major role changes from support to lead teacher is that of learning to motivate the entire group. The lead teacher is responsible for the group's collective interest and the objectives which they have in common.

The lead teacher is aware of each child's individual way of behaving in the group. In motivating the group she hopes to gain each child's attention and direct it into a successful, constructive experience.

py for an entire group. Additionally, you will share the responsibility for planning a coordinated program of intervention in each child's school, home, and community with the other members of your treatment team. You will find yourself constantly formulating new strategies for providing experiences to meet children's needs; to do this you will draw on your own resources as never before. Each class day represents a new challenge in planning daily activities which will supersede the past day's activities in terms of their impact upon children.

As a lead teacher you should be able to predict behavior on the basis of your knowledge of each child and his developmental objectives. You will need to understand a child's method of gaining emotional needs, ways of interacting with peers, length of attention span, ways of dealing with frustration, interests, and his response to various classroom activities. Consider a typical Stage Two child, six-year-old Betty. Her major avenue for meeting emotional needs (nurturance, attention) is crawling into the teacher's lap or clinging to her. Interactions with peers are mainly rejection, pushing, and stating "No" when approached. Her attention span is approximately five minutes, given intermittent support. Outward signs of frustration are thumb-sucking, staring, and chewing on her clothing. Frustration is dealt with through withdrawal, usually physical, as in the form of flight. Some of her interests are food, dolls, cuddly toys, and physical activities. She usually participates in classroom activities if encouraged or if the activity involves materials which are manipulative in nature.

Stage Two objectives are appropriate in Betty's case and should be translated into techniques and experiences which will help her to progress. Her short attention span, nurturance needs, interests and response to activities lend themselves readily to progress and change. It is more difficult to change Betty's methods of dealing with frustration. Her withdrawal might involve running under the table, around the room, or out of the room. This is a highly contagious behavior in a Stage Two class. What it actually represents is a method of coping for Betty, a means to control others. However, being able to control others, especially adults, can have a frightening effect on a Stage Two child. It should not be allowed to happen. When it does occur, it usually does not reflect a classroom "control" problem but a lack of awareness on the part of the teachers to signs of impending frustration and unmet needs. It can be resolved through a teacher's decision to act when the symptoms such as thumb-sucking occur. In Betty's case this decision has to be made frequently, often physically, but always with the goal of less physical intervention as time passes and her verbal communication skills increase.

Types of Intervention

At each stage of therapy the techniques and interventions you will need as a lead teacher are essentially the same as for a support teacher but oriented to reach all children in the group. You are the instigator of all classroom activities. The group members need to be aware of your attitudes, structure, and expectations as the lead teacher. If your expectations are reasonable, children will respond to meet them; if they are low, children will also respond to meet them. Your actions in the classroom must be carefully executed. Many times Stage Three children have commented that the support teacher does all the hard work like looking after equipment, and the lead teacher does all the talking. This may be an

oversimplification but essentially accurate. In well run Developmental Therapy classes the children usually comment that "We had fun today," or "We did good on our project." Seldom is a comment made regarding preference for one of the teachers, which would denote a dependent bond with that person. The teachers are viewed by the children as a caring team which provides experiences that are meaningful, profitable, and enjoyable. The team communicates to each child, "You are important."

You must produce the classroom atmosphere and experiences which foster this type of thinking. Your relationship with each child is expressed through the types of intervention strategies you use. Such strategies may range from affection to firm physical restraint. Most importantly, your relationship is always geared to free a child from overwhelming, personal dependence on you. Keep in mind the long range effect of your intervention upon the child as well as the immediate effects. Chapter 5 deals at length with management strategies at each level of therapy and can be used as a guide for amount and type of intervention. Quality of intervention is more difficult to define but approximates an overall attitude of "dispassionate compassion" on your part. Gentleness, firmness, calm logic, humor, fantasy, disdain, excitement, or other feelings and stances must be communicated to the child with genuine affect, but to do this you must necessarily conceptualize objectively the feelings.

In situations where you are unsure of what type of intervention is appropriate, a deliberate risk is a more appropriate action than an impulsive response. A risk may involve your breaking out of a role which is having adverse effects on the child, and moving quickly to restructure the situation. To do this you must be

The lead teacher in a Developmental Therapy class is seen as being "in charge" by the children. Yet the quality of the teamwork between lead and support is the important issue. This interaction provides a model for the children, showing how consideration, mutual cooperation, and social exchange can be conducted.

In general, the lead teacher keeps the group process going, initiating each new activity, and continuing an activity for the group even when a crisis has occurred.

able to play many different roles and draw upon the child's experiential world. For instance, during play time at Stage Three, many children are learning to interact with other children using play materials. There is a good deal of simulation of reality through the materials, and limits are placed upon use of the materials (no hitting, throwing, or destroying toys). On many occasions specific limits are imposed by the lead teacher. If the group is playing with blocks and soldiers and the "war" shows signs of giving way to rampant impulsivity, she may intervene in a role as the General-of-all-the-Armies ("The battle is over and all of the trucks and planes are ordered back to the barracks immediately. Roger. Over and out!"). Or she can maintain the classroom teacher role, reflecting and restructuring ("All the soldiers are getting excited and fighting hard. Captain Joe, Major Sam and Lieutenant Bob can go back to camp for a rest now, and the other soldiers can fix their trucks and jeeps."). In both of these situations the teacher has entered the experiential world as a participant in the child's fantasy and is prepared to continue the role in order to create a successful play situation. Her affect in intervening is one of firmness in the first case (the General as the authority figure). In the second situation she reflects their excitement and leads them to calmer activity as their group leader.

The lead teacher might also have intervened in the above situation as a mediator and elicitor of feelings if she felt that the group could manage this and if it were appropriate for meeting objectives. In that case, the dialogue would reflect the teacher as a concerned helping adult, and the fantasy aspect of the play situation would be utilized to help the children express actions and feelings. The exchange might follow this course:

Lead teacher: *"When fighting and battles happen there is a way to stop them. What is it?"*

Boys respond: *"We talk about it."*

Lead teacher: *"Yes, that's right. After battles there are peace talks and negotiations. Let's talk about what's happening in this war."*

The teacher and group then go on to discuss what transpired in the battle, how they felt and were affecting each other, and what would happen during the remainder of the "battle." The group is encouraged to make some decisions concerning their own actions. Such involvement usually results in more investment in the outcome, as well as greater understanding of themselves and others in the group.

Group Interactions

Two of the most difficult areas for teachers involve strategies for dealing with group dynamics and for dealing with primitive and aggressive children in groups. Group dynamics has been extensively written about in professional literature. It is recognized as a sensitive and complicated endeavor to analyze and interpret individual and group relationships and to predict their interaction effects. A lead teacher must have knowledge of group dynamics in order to be effective at any stage. However, this knowledge is not used as a major technique until Stage Four.

At Stage One, there is so little awareness of others that group interaction can be viewed in a fairly uncomplicated way. That is, one child's behavior may or may not evoke a response from another. When awareness of others is evident, it usually takes the form of a physical contact such as touching, poking, biting, or scratching, a verbal response such as jabbering, or a scream of frustration when a

The whole concept of helping children to grow in Developmental Therapy is based upon the teacher's being able to remove restrictions on behavior, rather than creating more restrictions and limiting children to fewer behaviors.

When a teacher moves into the midst of play, she must be sensitive to the time to withdraw. Keep in mind, the purpose is to influence the group. When this is accomplished the teacher should not continue to play.

Each of the three types of intervention just described may be proper for a particular group at a point in time and illustrates how an effective teacher can change her own methods of responding to the same situation.

The nature of group interactions changes distinctly at each stage. The teacher must also change her responses or she may find herself responsible for a rapidly deteriorating situation.

personal need is unmet. These responses are usually indicators of social awareness and should be viewed as the signal to begin teaching a new way to interact.

At Stages Two and Three the foundations for group interactions are being laid by developing individual skills which will foster growth within the group setting. A close look at Developmental Therapy objectives at both of these stages reveals that interpersonal relationships between children are extremely limited. Constructive movement among members of the group is usually generated through the teachers' planned activities. Chapter 4 contains a number of suggestions for promoting group interactions. While the skilled lead teacher of Stage Two or Three directs, encourages, and molds interactions, she also creates a classroom atmosphere which allows children to express themselves.

Stage Two classes, by nature of the developmental objectives, require that you maintain a posture simulating a group leader, a focal point for expecting participation and minimal group interaction. This is because children are learning to participate in activities with others. Eventually you will be able to elicit statements from the group regarding your expectations for behavioral limits and classroom participation. To this extent you control the group. Successful participation is the necessary outcome and is accomplished through masterful interpretation of developmental skills and individual needs by the teachers.

In contrast, individual assertion of self is a necessary occurrence in Stage Three classrooms. When this happens you must react in a manner which is nonjudgmental and fair. Many times this type of assertion is in the form of manipulation or hostile-aggressive actions, both physical and verbal. It may be directed toward you or another child. View this behavior as a temporary but significant sign of emerging autonomy. You will need to convey your understanding and dependability regardless of the type of intervention you choose.

Since you must lead and encourage children at Stage Three toward communicating with their peers and subjecting their needs to the group, you must be a dynamic, not overwhelming, presence in the classroom. The goal always is to make the individual feel successful while participating as a group member. Methods of constantly reflecting progress and accomplishment in the group become important. Timing of activities, the ability to drop back to a lower order of classroom structure, and the ability to consistently but flexibly set limits and convey expectations are absolutely essential. You must continually estimate each child's ability to interact and plan procedures and experiences accordingly. Perhaps the most difficult part of this is being able to adjust procedures to accomodate individual problems without losing consistency or credibility.

At Stage Four, group problem solving, individual recognition of the effects of behavior, spontaneous verbal expressions of feelings, and modifications of behavior toward the group are paramount. In order for this to happen the teachers must pull back and allow the group process to begin. An excellent example of this is contained in Chapter 10. Keeping the developmental objectives for each child in mind, the teachers are careful observers of the process. When it falters and outcomes seem to loom bigger than the group can resolve, the teachers interject direction or responses which refocus the process. It is essential that the group process not be detrimental to the progress of each individual. This is the challenge for Stage Four teachers.

At every stage of therapy, deviant

behavior must be allowed to occur at various points in therapy if it has been an emotionally important or predominant behavior through which a child has coped with his environment. If allowed to occur it can be dealt with and changed over a period of time. When it occurs, the message is given in various ways to the child that it is known that he behaved in a nonproductive manner; that nothing bad will happen to him; that nothing harmful to others will be allowed to occur; that he can change his behavior; and that when he does, better things happen.

When a teacher clearly conveys recognition of a deviant behavior and responds to it with confidence and support for the child, it alleviates guilt; the child draws upon the teacher's confidence and skills until his own controls take over. Often the teacher must teach the child a new way of responding which brings about a happier result.

In order to facilitate behavior change you need not be overly concerned with controlling each child in your group all of the time. Be flexible enough to move children in positive directions; anticipate responses from the cues they give. Stage Two groups particularly seem to be chaotic at times. It may be difficult to deal with all of the problem behavior at once, but this can be expected because of the children's development at this stage. Much of the chaos can be eliminated through simplification of procedures, consistency, clear limits, motivating appropriate activities, and immediate intervention toward containing or redirecting inappropriate behaviors. You must remain in control of yourself and be prepared to intervene in order to help all of the children in a group when inappropriate behavior becomes contagious. This denotes more than simply controlling groups so that the day's activities run smoothly.

A monitor provides outside information to a treatment team by her direct contact with persons in the child's environment outside the Developmental Therapy class. Without this information the team would be operating in an artificial environment. Information from home and school is essential to the treatment program.

As a lead teacher you will be responsible for recognizing an impending crisis or confrontation and usually make the decision when intervention is needed. However, it may be the support teacher who actually intervenes. This enables you to continue the activity as the lead teacher with the other group members.

Close teamwork is essential. Sometimes such teamwork is accomplished through open, verbal exchange between lead and support, and sometimes by nonverbal cues and body language.

LEARNING SKILLS TO BE A MONITOR

The monitor in the Developmental Therapy model is the third member of the treatment team. A monitor, lead teacher, and support teacher are assigned to a group of children, their parents, and their regular school teachers. It is the team's responsibility to move the children toward more adequate functioning at home, school and at the center, as rapidly as possible. The lead and support teachers conduct the daily treatment program directly with the children. A monitor's major responsibilities are to (a) serve as team captain for coordination of all aspects of each child's program; (b) conduct programs for parents of children in the group; (c) observe the class in order to provide feedback to the team; (d) supervise a trainee on the team; and (e) serve as the crisis back-up when needed in the classroom. Coordination of all of these activities is the responsibility of the monitor. Table 1 provides a sample of a typical daily schedule.

Before becoming a monitor, you must have broad understanding and experience in the use of Developmental Therapy. You should also have a high level of expertise in using Developmental Therapy with children and have demonstrated this through successful accomplishments as support and lead teacher. Most persons work in the classroom for at least one year in these positions before becoming a monitor. Even then, not all choose to train to be a monitor.

You should successfully demonstrate the following as an effective monitor:

Table 1. A Sample Daily Schedule for Treatment Teams[a]

	M	T	W	Th	F
A.M.: *a Stage II team*					
8:30–9:00	Team planning	Team planning	Lead and support spend morning contacting regular teachers and visiting schools	Team planning	Team planning
9:00–11:00	Lead and support in class; monitor does parent work	Lead and support in class; monitor observes class		Lead and support in class; monitor does parent work	Lead and support in class; monitor observes with parents
11:00–11:30	Team debriefing	Team debriefing	Monitor has time off to compensate for evening schedule with parents	Team debriefing	Team debriefing
11:30–12:00	Lead and support prepare for next day	Lead and support prepare for next day		Lead and support prepare for next day	Lead and support prepare for next day
P.M.: *a Stage III team*					
12:00–1:00			LUNCH		
1:00–1:30	Team planning	Team planning	Monitor attends intake staffing for new children or does parent work	Team planning	Team planning
1:30–3:00	Lead and support in class; monitor does parent work	Lead and support in class; monitor observes class		Lead and support in class; monitor does parent work	Lead and support in class; monitor observes with parents
3:00–3:30	Team debriefing	Team debriefing	Lead and support do school contact work	Team debriefing	Team debriefing
3:30–4:30	All staff meeting	School contacts		School contacts	School contacts

(Continued)

Table 1., *continued*

	M	T	W	Th	F
7:00–8:00	Monitor makes home visits		Monitor makes home visits	Monitor makes home visits	
7:30–9:00		Parents' group meetings with monitors at center			

[a]The treatment staff is not ordinarily assigned to the same teams in the mornings and afternoons.

1. Thorough knowledge of the philosophy behind Developmental Therapy and the ability to communicate it to others.
2. Thorough knowledge of the implementation of the Developmental Therapy model including the use of the developmental objectives and evaluation procedures.
3. Thorough knowledge of procedures which support the treatment program, such as the referral and intake process, community contacts, treatment consultation procedures, relationships with other agencies, and termination and follow-up procedures.
4. The ability to plan and conduct effective child treatment programs using Developmental Therapy.
5. The ability to plan and conduct effective programs to help parents of disturbed children.
6. The ability to plan and provide effective school intervention programs.
7. The ability to identify and mobilize community resources which will benefit a child and his family.
8. The ability to work in the classroom as both support and lead teacher.
9. The ability to work in a leadership capacity with peers.

Persons who are monitors have varied professional backgrounds, such as social work, education, guidance, psychology, or music therapy. Although professional background is important, certain other attributes have made it possible to succeed as monitors. Some of these attributes have been discussed in sections of this chapter on learning to be a support and lead teacher. The additional outstanding characteristic of monitors is their ability to provide leadership for a treatment team.

Heading the Developmental Therapy Team

In the capacity of team captain, you must be able to communicate effectively with both experienced and inexperienced lead and support teachers, parents, and regular school teachers. Effective communication often makes the difference between excellent and mediocre child treatment. You must be able to help the team in making day-to-day decisions by providing information on home or school situations, treatment techniques, child development principles, group or family dynamics, observational evaluation data, or information from the child's permanent clinical file. Strategies for involvement with home and school must be developed through the leadership of the monitor. Child treatment has little impact if it is only geared toward improvement in the special setting, such as center or clinic. Strategies which will enable the child to develop skills in the home, school, and neighborhood must be incorporated into the treatment program. The monitor provides this linkage.

You need to be understanding in working with the lead and support teachers. You have a responsibility to help them enlarge their knowledge of Developmental Therapy, develop techniques for therapeutic results, and develop confidence as therapists. This is done by knowing each team member's strengths and weaknesses. The type of approach best suited to each individual at a particular time will vary. Sometimes you may be encouraging, and at other times, demanding or critical.

As team captain, you also must see that the team follows specified procedures for rating each child on the Developmental Therapy objectives every five weeks. The team makes a joint decision on mastery of each objective and decides what each child's major developmental objectives will be for the coming five-week period. In doing this, you must ensure that each member of the team has input into each rating.

If the treatment team includes a lead or support teacher who is a trainee, as the monitor you will be the primary supervisor. Through observation and the debriefing sessions described in the following section, you can help the trainee learn her role as quickly and fully as possible. Occasionally, a trainee will bog down and need additional time with the team in order to work through difficult situations. Again, be as sensitive to each team member, trainee or not, as you are to the children.

A team is only as effective as each member, and as the monitor you play a major role in creating and maintaining a climate of productivity and effectiveness for them. In order to do this, you need to be able to take on many roles such as child advocate, teacher or parent advocate, lead or support teacher, crisis teacher, counselor, parent educator, bus or playground attendant, regular school teacher aide. You must also be able to teach these roles to others in training.

Working with Parents

Another major responsibility you will have as a monitor is to conduct programs for parents of each child in the class. A session with parents and the monitor is viewed as an exchange of information between persons concerned with the child's well-being. It is important to obtain parents' perceptions of problems, goals, growth, and changes in their child. Some parents may freely offer information about their child, but in some cases you may have to ask questions or otherwise draw the parent into the conversation. In order to facilitate this type of dialogue, the general tone of the conference should be congenial, friendly, and concerned. In other words, parents should be made to feel comfortable enough to talk about their child.

Whatever type of session is used, it is essential that an exchange of information occur and that you and the parents establish specific objectives. In the

A monitor plans the proportion of time daily and weekly to be spent in observing the therapeutic class and in working with parents of children in the group. However, daily debriefing with the lead and support teachers immediately following class is a necessary part of sustaining a dynamic and effective treatment program.

A full description of parent work conducted by a monitor in conjunction with Developmental Therapy is found in Chapter 12.

Each child's parents, if possible, are contacted once weekly by the monitor. A mutually satisfying meeting time is agreed upon by the parents and the monitor. This time might be during the class period or possibly during the evening.

Many times children progress more rapidly in the treatment class, exhibiting more growth than they do at home. This is a natural outcome of therapy and may be distressing to parents. Once change is seen in therapy, the parents must be helped to create situations at home where this same progress can be seen. Without this, parents can become very discouraged and a negative cycle is created.

Classroom training for parents is one of many ways for parents to improve their interactions with their child. Such experiences should be planned to insure success. Chapters 7 through 10 give illustrations of other types of parent programs.

The children in a group know the monitor as an important part of the team because of home visits. The monitor also serves as a standby to help out on special projects or in times of crisis.

Children in Stages Three and Four are aware that the monitor may be observing and in some instances are invited to briefly view the classroom from the observation room with the monitor.

course of an appointment, several questions should be kept in mind to provide a direction for the exchange of information:

1. What are the objectives and reasons for the conference? If the objectives can be stated clearly, parents can be helped to see a purpose more clearly.

2. What are the child's current developmental objectives?

3. How are the objectives being met in the center classroom? At home?

4. How have the teachers' and parents' techniques changed since the last meeting?

5. How has the child's behavior changed since last time?

6. Have these changes been noted at home?

7. Which objectives are parents working on at home?

8. What activities are the parents using to meet these objectives?

9. Why are the teachers using certain techniques to accomplish specific objectives?

10. How comfortable do the parents seem?

11. What elements in the program do they respond to?

12. What tends to cause parents to withdraw from open exchange?

13. What were the high priority problems originally identified by the parents at the time of referral?

14. To what extent are these problems increasing or decreasing with each visit?

15. What techniques do the parents see as reasonable for them to use at home to solve specific problems?

Most monitors meet with parents either in their homes or at the center during the time when the class meets. This procedure enables parents or teachers to observe the class with you. Often

parents are asked to participate in place of the support teacher for particular activities in the classroom. It will be your responsibility to prepare the parent through a series of observations which emphasize how the support teacher responds to the children during the activity. Your observation of the parent during his time in the classroom is essential. Taking notes of the parent's specific successes and problems is also important. When the parent comes out of the room after the activity is completed, use your notes as the basis for a feedback session. This session usually is conducted while the lead and support teachers complete the day's scheduled activities. Ordinarily the parent leaves at the end of the class with his child. This frees you to meet with the treatment team for the debriefing session.

Working with the Class

The third major area of responsibility for a monitor is observation of the class for feedback to the team. In this capacity, you will need to observe the class regularly through an observation mirror and assist in daily program planning with the team. By watching the class, you can provide information of value to the team in making necessary adjustments for individual children or for the group. Particularly important elements to look for are:

1. *Group elements*
    A. General trends in class functioning such as transitions, group tone, group structure, interactions, timing, and length of activities.
    B. Appropriateness of materials, physical environment, and activities in each curriculum area for the stage of Developmental Therapy of the group.

2. *Individual child elements*

   A. Relationship of each activity to the specific Developmental Therapy objectives for each child.

   B. How the child and group needs are blended.

3. *Teacher elements*

   A. Type and quality of teachers' verbalizations.

   B. Type and quality of physical interactions between teachers and children.

   C. Creative and responsive listening from teachers.

   D. Emotional reaction of teachers to individual children.

   E. Teachers' roles for the particular stage of therapy.

   F. Consistency and appropriateness of individual and group limits, rules, and procedures.

In this way, you help the team focus upon whether the children are being moved toward Developmental Therapy goals. Notes from observation are discussed with the lead and support teachers during debriefing immediately following class. It is your responsibility to lead the debriefing sessions. Make sure that all persons who were working with the class that day attend the debriefing. This might include art, music, or recreation teachers and also might include a child's regular class teacher or parents. The debriefing session usually lasts 30 to 45 minutes. Your role is that of facilitator of the exchange of information and decision-making regarding the children's programs at the center, home, and school. The focus of debriefing may change from day to day but always includes a review of that day's classroom activities, with planning for modifications in the next day's activities. Other focuses might be a review of observational data with the evaluator, an exchange of information with a parent or teacher, planning a specific experience (such as a field trip), or discussing feelings team members have about working with a particular child or each other. If a regular teacher or parent is present at part of a debriefing, the treatment team will have prepared for their visit. The discussion at debriefing then takes on more of the form of a conference focusing upon a child's progress in treatment and helping to plan more effective school or home programs.

In order to help the treatment team improve the therapy program, use a variety of means to stimulate discussion with the team. During the discussion you might refer to notes which you took during observation. An example of one format for monitor's note taking is shown in Figure 1.

Feedback to the lead and support teachers is usually given immediately after class. At this time they are still aware of the impact of the day, of their insights and feelings about the class. These feelings are important and need to be discussed while they are still fresh.

Class _____   Date _____

Teacher _____

Monitor _____

Observation and comment

1. Appropriateness of experiences for children. (Do they meet Developmental Therapy objectives?):
2. Body language (major messages given children):
3. Physical intervention (group and individual):
4. Verbalizations:
5. Activities:
6. Materials; preparation:
7. Motivation of children:
8. General classroom tone:

Figure 1.   Sample format for monitors to use during observation and debriefing.

Teachers of disturbed children who do not have benefit of a treatment team for ongoing consultation might use this format for reviewing their own daily programs. Or it may be possible to ask someone else on the school faculty to come into the classroom periodically to observe, using this format as a basis for discussion following the observation. This might be especially beneficial in identifying a specific problem area.

You might want to begin the debriefing with several questions:

What was the main thing which happened to make the day go well?
What was the major message the children picked up from you today?
What behavior change did you see in ——?
Why did it happen?

Other discussion formats could include a review of the clinical file for a child, a review of each child's work folder to evaluate the appropriateness of the daily materials for academic objectives, a detailed examination of the activities conducted and the children's responses to them, or a talk about the teachers' feelings toward the children and the teachers' own skills. Another useful idea for debriefing is role playing of classroom situations and alternative teacher behaviors. References, audiovisual presentations, or consultants might be used if the team feels that more information is needed about certain techniques or materials.

The final responsibility of the monitor is that of crisis teacher in the classroom. If a group of children cannot be therapeutically managed by the lead and support teacher because of severe, acting out behavior, you will be needed in the classroom. This might happen when the support teacher leaves the room with one child or if the entire class shows signs of losing control. In most crisis situations, it is usually more effective for a monitor to assume the support teacher role rather than dealing with individual children outside the classroom. The support teacher, who works continuously with children in the group, is then free to have the major therapeutic input with individual children. This type of crisis back-up is usually planned by the team in advance so that it will not interfere with your scheduled parent work.

The discussion topics during debriefing are direct outcomes of whatever occurred in the classroom. Experienced teachers have found that debriefing is profitable because of their increased understanding. It should not be assumed that an experienced teacher will not profit from discussing the day's classroom experience.

Unless a monitor has effective skills already developed for classroom intervention her effectiveness in a crisis will be seriously limited. For this reason monitors should have successful experiences as support and lead teacher prior to becoming a monitor.

Each teacher must individually judge how much she can give away in psychic energy without some personal return from a child. A person who continually feels that she has little energy may have the type of personality which needs more pleasant responses from children than they are able to give.

Some persons have the ability to become excellent teachers for mildly or moderately disturbed children but not for seriously disturbed children. It is a mistake for these persons to continue to struggle and experience feelings of failure with seriously disturbed children.

PROBLEMS TEACHERS HAVE WITH THEMSELVES

Considering the severity and range of disorders presented by emotionally disturbed children, it is not surprising that teachers of these children encounter a variety of challenges, pleasures, and problems themselves. Severely disturbed or disordered children are by nature unwilling and unable to meet the emotional needs of the teachers who are attempting to assist them. These children cannot provide supportive, pleasant responses for the teachers. Many times even the most skilled teacher must mull over a classroom incident for hours in order to discover the painful truth of her errors, with the consolation that she will be better able to handle a similar situation the next time it arises. Fortunately, progress toward a teacher's personal skill goals and movement of children in therapy is usually parallel. It is likely that this type of success generates in the teacher enough interest, satisfaction, and challenge for her to continue learning more skills. For those persons who are truly skilled, but aware and open to change, the pursuit of Developmental Therapy with children represents new learning, new avenues of experiences and satisfaction.

Many problems encountered by teachers of disturbed children are related to their inability to feel and think as children do and to understand and anticipate behavior. Some teachers have this ability; others develop it; a few never do. It is a necessary ability because children change at varying rates and do not usually communicate their problems or progress in words. This leaves the teachers with innumerable daily decisions and only their own careful preparation as the sole resource. Many times the positive effects of intervention are not apparent in a child until days or weeks later. The teacher must still be convinced that the course which she has embarked upon with a particular child is correct. She must have an idea of what the end behavior for the child will be. For example, many Stage One children exhibit serious pathology. Lack of response to play materials may be symptomatic. The teacher, in the daily play period, may use various luring and stimulating methods simply to encourage a child to grasp appealing, sensually arousing toys for a short period of time. The objective is that the child one day will spontaneously pick up the toy. The teacher's actions are appropriate in continuing to stimulate and lure the child but may not generate the desired response until a later time. It would be a mistake to stop such activities because the child did not readily respond to the toys, nor would it be appropriate for the teacher to force the child to hold the toys.

The team must ultimately share in a successful therapy program. Effective teamwork in the class helps to prepare the child for his environment. Planning school and home programs sensitizes and mobilizes resources on his behalf. The successful team realizes that therapy is only part of the program. The team must be equally effective in helping the regular school teacher and the parent to function more effectively in their relationships with the child. Each member of the team must be able to clarify growth to the other team members and give suggestions which may be conveyed to school and home. At the same time, particular home and school problems must be incorporated as part of the therapy program. If a teacher is only concerned with classroom therapy, or cannot communicate with her team, the progress of the children will be minimal. The treatment team should be able to discuss their own feelings about what was effective in class, what needed to be changed,

what growth occurred, and current problems related to the teacher's personal competencies.

Personal Conduct

In one particular class, a support teacher possessed great sensitivity and many competencies which were effective with children. In the class, she was able to perform her role adequately, but children responded to her redirection and verbal input less and less. The monitor noted that the teacher was dedicated, bright, aware, and knowledgable. Her voice was consistently very soft and barely audible to children other than the one to whom she was speaking. Each member of the team recognized this characteristic, but it had not been discussed in terms of the problems in the classroom. All were feeling increasingly uncomfortable about her effect on the children, but they discussed other methods of circumventing the children's behavior so as not to hurt her feelings. This situation, if allowed to continue, could have had many detrimental effects on the children and the therapy team, although it seemed to be the easy way out at the time. When the monitor brought it out openly, and yet supportively, the team worked out strategies to help the support teacher develop more effective verbal communication skills. The support teacher initially felt that she might not be able to change her voice and felt very self conscious when she tried different tones. But she learned, through role play, to effectively convey a number of different messages. The situation illustrates the point that growth and change for teachers many times involve a personal change which can be painful to the teacher and to the team which is committed to a common cause.

Many effective teachers using Developmental Therapy have endured changes

Role playing is an effective method for working through teaching problems and personal characteristics which are ammenable to change. It provides the person with an opportunity to desensitize themselves to the change and to see how it feels before they attempt it in the classroom.

in voice, appearance (including clothing), manner of movement, outward affect, and personal habits to facilitate therapy, without changing or giving up their personal standards or freedom. This must be done in many cases because a teacher's most effective resource for helping children progress is herself. She must outwardly portray to the children a composite of realistic, desirable traits, with the utmost clarity. She must simplify and clarify her messages to children by using her voice and body. In many groups the teachers become models which the children can imitate, learning skills which strengthen them for life experiences. For these reasons, a teacher must dress with the reaction of others in mind, confine her speech to succinct verbalizations, physically move in a free but nonseductive manner, change her affect and demeanor when appropriate, and convey values which are compatible with those in a child's environment.

Children tend to model or imitate what teachers do rather than what teachers tell them to do. In this way a child integrates some of a teacher's value system into his own value system.

The Developmental Therapy classroom should reflect the teachers' concern for the child. In its neatness, arrangement, displays, and atmosphere, the classroom should create a supportive climate. This fact must be recognized by a teacher. If she personally places little emphasis on housekeeping in her own life, she should see that her personal preferences do not carry over into the classroom.

These problems are controversial in nature. Some teachers are really adament regarding being able to "do their own thing" in terms of their appearance and relationship to others. Some feel that if they can relate well and reach other persons, then how they do it or how they look is unimportant. This discussion of problems stemming from "doing your own thing" serves to point out some of the possible effects it may have on very disturbed or confused children.

The following problems illustrate superficially some of the personal issues which some teachers might be inclined to express and their possible detrimental effects upon children who are disturbed.

Use of Slang Terms or Sarcasm, including Joking or Teasing Children Disturbed children have difficulty developing adult and peer relationships. Many children have learned to relate only with controlling, manipulative behavior. Sarcasm, teasing, or other ways of veiling messages may leave a child helpless to respond constructively. Others are left in limbo because the message given through teasing or excessive use of slang can be nonsupportive or derogatory. This approach to children should be eliminated as a general way of relating. Occasionally, teasing or slang may be useful in particular situations solely as a management technique.

Unprofessional Dress, Revealing Clothing, or Generally Unkempt Appearance A child may be unnecessarily stimulated, especially older children, by the sight or physical contact of a scantily clad teacher. A child may feel that this type of dress is acceptable (as it is in many places), but it may create a direct conflict between the teacher's values and those of the child's group or family. This may be putting the child in the middle of an unnecessary conflict.

School personnel and parents may object to an unkempt, unprofessional appearance on the part of the treatment team. It undermines their confidence in the ability of the agency to help their child and may impede communication if the parents and treatment team have different values and standards for dress and appearance. Teachers can safely and effectively conduct therapy and conferences while dressed in "conventional" outfits. Care for one's own personal appearance has value in conveying a message of caring to the children. When meeting parents or other members of the community, teachers should be careful that what they do, how they look, and what they say will enhance acceptance and communication.

Displaying or Condoning Antisocial Values (those which may conflict with the child's value system) Examples: religious or political beliefs; condoning stealing, smoking pot, illicit relationships; cursing; excessive emotionality; losing one's self control, etc.

A child already confused in his values may feel that these actions are appropriate for meeting his needs; or if he possesses a rigid value system, he may feel betrayed and hostile. These values are definitely found and condoned in various sectors of society, but their expression is contraindicated in the Developmental Therapy framework. Expression of personal values or beliefs by the therapist should never occur in the therapeutic classroom or through contacts with parents, teachers or other professionals in the community. If a teacher is inclined to use the classroom as a showcase for "doing her own thing" or for deriving vicarious satisfaction through children's acting out behavior, a serious situation exists. The teacher should be removed from the classroom until her own adjustment problems can be resolved or isolated from her work with children.

The above-mentioned situations may or may not indicate basic personality problems on the part of a teacher. All are concerned with the way in which a person expresses herself and are not mentioned here as entirely negative personal attributes. The point to be made is that a teacher must alter some expressive behavior in the classroom to help disturbed children who have not reached a point where they can be responsible for their own decisions regarding values, personal expressions and the consequences of their decisions.

Coping in the Classroom

Other areas of difficulty in teaching emotionally disturbed children lend themselves more easily to change through open discussions during debriefing. Many problems are related to lack of experience on the part of a teacher or lack of understanding of teaching techniques and can be changed with little emotional duress on the part of a teach-

er. One large group of problems falls under the general heading of responding to aggression. Many teachers are traumatized to inaction if a child suddenly or gradually becomes aggressive, even if they are expecting such behavior.

Consider the situation of the teacher who must physically restrain a child who is out of control for more than an hour, with the knowledge that the same restraint may be necessary the next day. Consider the teacher's feelings as a child hurls a chair and obscenities toward her. Overwhelming anxiety can very well be the teacher's response, but she must mobilize herself enough to catch the child or the chair and let the verbal attack bounce off. Above all, the teacher must protect the child from physical and psychological harm. Usually, a few experiences with aggression are enough to convince a teacher that she is physically stronger than a child. She finds also that the child is attempting in his own way to elicit help for his problems. If a teacher can weather such a crisis with a child in a firm but supportive manner, a bond of trust is established. The child will learn that the situation precipitating the aggressive act is the crux of what will be discussed between the teacher and himself when the aggressive phase has diminished. The teacher recognizes that she has nothing to fear. She must expect, however, that such an experience will be physically and emotionally draining for both her and the child.

Another common problem relating to aggression in children is the teacher's feeling of helplessness which is generated by manipulative, controlling children who are not being outwardly aggressive. If a teacher is aware that a child is controlling others in the group, thereby setting an inappropriate tone for the classroom, the problem usually can be solved through good teamwork. If the teacher is unaware of this, she may resort to a very

A discussion about management of aggressive behavior is contained in Chapter 5.

Punitive reactions by a teacher to a child's aggression are destructive to the therapeutic process.

rigid stance, using more classroom rules and becoming increasingly negative in her actions toward the group. As this happens, the teacher increases her demands for strict adherance to classroom rules and employs punitive measures to enforce adherence to these rules. Removal of children's privileges or removal from the group usually results. This produces anger on the part of the children, which in turn generates more anger and rigidity by the teacher. A senseless cycle is created. This type of problem calls for intervention by someone outside of the classroom, such as the monitor, to help redefine limits and plan new strategies. The teacher must examine and understand her actions and feelings toward the children and devise activities which are motivating and require fewer restrictions. In this way, the situation is changed from negative to positive as quickly as possible. Additionally, the teacher must contain any hostile feelings of her own if she is to be effective in breaking the cycle.

Another problem results if a teacher cannot cope with the many interactions occurring in a group. She may develop "tunnel vision" and deal with only certain children in a therapeutic manner while ignoring others. She usually fails to see those who are attempting to control the situation or group. This is different from planned ignoring of a child. The teacher in this case must be given suggestions as to how she can comfortably and effectively deal with all children in the group. The response pattern which she has developed must first be pointed out. One specific way of handling this problem is for one teacher to give the other teacher direct cues regarding children's actions and behaviors. Another technique is for the teacher to sensitize herself to making psychological contact with every child in the group every few minutes.

Teachers who are punitive provide the child with an excellent model of aggression. Frequently such teachers stimulate uncontrollable, hostile feelings within a child.

To overcome the problem of inadvertently ignoring a child, you might train yourself to ask this question about each child in the group, "How does —— feel right now about what is happening for him?" If you develop a habit of asking yourself this question continually and answering honestly, you are sure to increase each child's involvement.

Mass confusion in the classroom and a host of therapeutic evils can arise if the teacher "lets down" or relaxes into free or ambiguous structure for the children. Disturbed children usually become frightened and disorganized if they are exposed to this type of looseness. Teachers may allow this to happen because of fatigue, lack of consistency, or lack of understanding of the need for continued, positive behavior in the Developmental Therapy program. Each teacher must learn to provide a therapeutic climate which allows children to function at their optimum levels.

One last problem worth mentioning, because it frequently occurs with inexperienced teachers, is that of the whole area of personal emotions and body language. Overwhelming frustrations, fatigue, pressure to conform, fear of failure, aloneness, are feelings all people experience from time to time. Keeping these feelings out of therapy can require considerable effort and self knowledge. A teacher's emotional state is usually detected by children through her body language and voice tone. If a teacher is anxious, she must make a conscious effort to convey exactly the opposite to her group of children. She should always be aware of why she is touching a child, such as for his nurturance, redirection, or reinforcement, and not for her own needs. Impulsive, jerky movements should be avoided. Calm, deliberate movements instill confidence. A low soft voice says "Everything is all right," while a rapid speech pattern can signal an alarm to the group.

There are times when past experience can completely dominate an otherwise effective teacher. Several issues occur frequently, to which many teachers seem vulnerable: the problem of being unattractive or overweight; being the scapegoat of a group; fear of invading privacy; and hostility toward parents teachers, or schools. If such issues have not been resolved, they can so dominate a teacher's perceptions and responses that therapy cannot progress.

In conclusion, most problems a teacher has with herself are within reach of solution if she is constantly aware of her feelings and motives and has the desire to improve. She should be open enough to rely upon others to aid in solutions if her own solutions do not produce positive changes or growth in the children.

Each day that a teacher spends in the classroom should be an opportunity to help children improve their functioning. The day's progress will be linked directly to her personal outlook and her professional skills.

Occasionally, you may hear a teacher speak in a derogatory manner about a child's inability to participate. What she is really saying is that she has not found an approach which works. As monitor, you should encourage her to keep seeking a solution.

chapter 7

THE STAGE ONE CLASS, A PLACE FOR RESPONDING AND TRUSTING

Ann Reed Williams, Lead Teacher

Autism

Severe Functional Retardation

Delayed Development

Brain Damage

Childhood Schizophrenia

Severe Behavioral Disturbance

Language Disorders

INTRODUCTION

Here are gathered perhaps the most bizarre children in the community. They repulse and anger those who live with them and those who see them for only a time. For these children the world is a frustrating, confusing, and painful place. They are not understood nor can they understand. Most of them gave up responding a long time ago or have never learned to respond at all. Their retreat from the world of constructive behavior is complete.

Suddenly they are given the Stage One experience. Something very arousing yet reassuring is added to their lives. They are dealt with so consistently, but so warmly, that they begin to trust this class and these teachers. It is a place which is so luring that they are enticed into responding. They find that old behaviors, infuriating and pain-producing to themselves and others, are no longer useful. They are not rejected for these behaviors but are reorganized and redirected to new responses which bring them pleasure. Within the first 10 weeks, these teachers will cross a gulf of confusion, reach out to hold, comfort, and arouse. They pull new life from within these children that were once so immobilized.

Children's names are fictitious but the material presents as accurately as possible actual children and classroom situations.

At the time of referral, none of these children were testable with any standardized instrument.

THOUGHTS BEFORE CLASS

It is the first day of fall classes at the Rutland Center for Severely Emotionally Disturbed Children. We are waiting for the children to arrive. My support teacher, Peg, and I sit around the work table in the Stage One classroom. We think we have everything in order but we check around the room to be sure all needed materials are available. We review the seating arrangement at the table to be sure that the children needing the most physical intervention are closest to us. I make sure that all the materials needed at the table are right inside the cabinet, close to my chair. This way I won't have to leave the table to pass out crayons, scissors, puzzles, or other materials.

As we look around the room it seems obvious this is no ordinary preschool classroom. Most play and work materials are out of sight. There are not the usual pictures and posters strung across the room. These children would only be confused by the clutter. Yet the red shag carpet and hot pink walls look warm and inviting.

About 10 minutes before class is to start, we both go out to the parking lot to be sure we meet the children and their parents as they arrive. As the first child arrives, I go into the classroom with him.

The support teacher visits with his mother briefly while waiting for the other children to arrive. There will be five children in this Stage One class. Let me tell you briefly about them.

DONALD

Donald is seven years old and unaware. He often just sits and stares and doesn't seem to hear or see anything around him. When he is aware he can talk in sentences but refers to himself as "you." Occasionally he repeats TV commercials or says bizarre things that don't make sense. His attention span and understanding of what people say to him are so limited he cannot be maintained in a regular classroom. However, with assistance Donald can read and write and do simple math problems. Donald has a four-year-old sister who doesn't seem to have problems. His parents try to cope with Donald but he is so erratic and unresponsive that they often just leave him alone, watching out only for his physical needs. He has never been to school. At the time he was enrolled, Donald's specific problems noted by both staff and parents were:

ritualistic
resistant to discipline
careless, unorganized

There are eight activities for this Stage One class during the two-hour morning program:

Play time
Work time
Exercise time
Art time
Milk and cookie time
Sand time
Yum-Yum time
Music time

The same schedule is followed each day, but the time for each activity varies according to the ability of the children to stay involved. With some groups of Stage One children, there may be as many as 16 activities planned for a two-hour period. Within this schedule, activities to meet each child's Developmental Therapy objectives are included.

The children are grouped for this class because they are working on Stage One objectives according to the Developmental Therapy rating procedure described in Chapter 2.

lacks comprehension
immature
unusual language
listening difficulties
difficulty expressing feelings
repeats
echoes
little eye contact
unaware
avoids participation with adults or children

The psychiatric diagnosis is childhood schizophrenia with autistic characteristics.

The Developmental Therapy objectives set for the first five weeks of class for Donald are:

Behavior

B-1 to respond to sensory stimulus by attending to source of stimulus
B-2 to respond to stimulus by sustained attending to source of stimulus
B-4 to respond with motor and body responses to complex environmental and verbal stimuli
B-6 to respond independently to play materials

Communication

C-1 to attend to person speaking
C-6 to produce a recognizable word to obtain a desired response from another child
C-7 to produce a meaningful, recognizable sequence of words

Socialization

S-4 to imitate simple, familiar acts of adults
S-5 to engage in organized solitary play
S-10 same as C-7

S-11 to exhibit a beginning emergence of self

(Pre)Academics

A-1 same as B-1
A-2 same as B-2
A-4 same as B-4
A-6 to imitate words or actions of adult upon request

EMILY

Emily, a four-year-old, doesn't participate in activities. She usually sits with her fingers in her mouth and squirms and pulls away when someone tries to involve her. The language she uses is more like a two-and-a-half-year-old. She needs much encouragement to ask for things she wants. She acts as if she can't do anything, but occasionally there are glimmers of understanding and performance that point to normal potential. Emily's father is extremely withdrawn, spending no time with Emily or her baby sister. Her mother has few skills for taking care of the children and often finds it difficult to get up in the morning. She frequently leaves the children alone. Emily has been found by neighbors and police wandering far from her home.

Problems noted by her parents at the time she was enrolled were mainly in communication:

immature language
unusual language
speech problem
difficulty expressing feelings
manipulation of others

The staff noted many more problems:

short attention span
distractible
perseverative

ritualistic
resistant to discipline
careless
unorganized
lacks comprehension
does not follow directions
silliness

The psychiatric diagnosis is adjustment reaction to childhood, resulting in marked delayed development.

The Developmental Therapy objectives for the first five weeks are:

Behavior

B-4   to respond with motor and body responses to complex environmental and verbal stimuli
B-5   to actively assist in learning self help skills
B-6   to respond independently to play material
B-7   to respond with recall to the routine spontaneously

Communication

C-3   to respond to verbal stimulus and single object with a recognizable approximation
C-4   to voluntarily initiate a recognizable verbal approximation to obtain a specific object or activity
C-5   to produce a recognizable word to obtain a desired response from adult

Socialization

S-4   to imitate simple, familiar acts of adults
S-5   to engage in organized solitary play
S-6   to respond to adult's verbal and nonverbal requests to come to him
S-8   to produce a recognizable word to obtain a desired response from adult

(Pre)Academics

A-6   to imitate words or actions of adults upon request
A-7   to respond by simple discrimination of objects
A-8   to respond to verbal stimulus and single object with a recognizable approximation of the appropriate verbal response

FOSTER

Six-year-old Foster wanders aimlessly around the room. If something catches his eye he might grab it, or punch it, or throw it on the floor. He has no language and often just stands, rocks, and jabs the finger tips of one hand with the open palm of the other. He is afraid of some stuffed animals and any new people. Even to adults he knows, he gives only fleeting eye contact and rarely touches them. He is aggressive toward other children, hitting and throwing objects. His mother is very concerned about his head banging and disregard for danger as well as for the safety of her other two children when Foster lashes out. He has never been away from home for any preschool program.

At the time he was enrolled, Foster's specific problems noted by staff and parent were:

ritualistic unusual behavior (repetitively
   rocking his body and flailing his arms)
aggressive toward children
no speech
self aggressive (severe head banging)
avoids eye contact
tends to avoid adults

The psychiatric diagnosis is brain damage caused by lead poisoning, resulting in mental retardation and severe behavioral disturbances with autistic characteristics. The Developmental Therapy objectives set for the first five weeks of class for Foster are:

Behavior

B-1 to respond to sensory stimulus by attending to source of stimulus

B-2 to respond to stimulus by sustained attending to source of stimulus

B-3 to respond with motor behavior to single environmental stimulus

B-4 to respond with motor and body responses to complex environmental and verbal stimuli

Communication

C-1 to attend to person speaking

C-3 to respond to verbal stimulus and single object with a recognizable approximation of the appropriate verbal response

C-4 to voluntarily initiate a recognizable verbal approximation

Socialization

S-1 to be aware of adult

S-2 to attend to adult's behavior

S-3 to respond to adult when child's name is called

S-4 to imitate simple, familiar acts of adults

(Pre)Academics

A-1 same as B-1

A-2 same as B-2

A-3 same as B-3

A-4 same as B-4

CARLA

Carla is five years old and screams a lot. She has language like a three-year-old, refers to herself as "Carla", and often repeats word for word what others say to her. She is very resistant to what the teacher asks her to do and will give shrill, ear piercing screams when kept to a task or when approached by children in the class. Sometimes in the middle of an activity she will sit and stare. The teacher's touch gets her attention back to what's happening. Carla's father has been away from home off and on for three years. Her mother takes extremely good care of her physical needs but is more comfortable reading a book than responding to Carla's emotional needs. She has never stayed long in any kindergarten or child care center.

Problems noted by parents and staff at the time of enrollment at Rutland were:

restless
overactive
perseveration on words and ideas
ritualistic
unusual behavior (cares for imaginary rabbit)
resistant to discipline
easily frustrated
temper tantrums
immature behavior
echoes other's speech
lacks self help skills
avoids participation with adults or children

The psychiatric diagnosis is childhood schizophrenia. The Developmental Therapy objectives for the first five weeks for Carla are:

Behavior

B-2 to respond to stimulus by sustained attending

B-4 to respond with motor and body responses to complex environmental and verbal stimuli

B-5 to actively assist in learning self help skills

B-6 to respond independently to play material

Communication

C-6 to produce a recognizable word to obtain a desired response from another child

C-7 to produce a meaningful, recognizable sequence of words to obtain a desired response

Socialization

S-5 to engage in organized solitary play

S-6 to respond to adult's verbal and nonverbal requests to come to him

S-9 to produce a recognizable word to obtain a desired response from another child

S-10 same as C-7

(Pre)Academics

A-10 to indicate short term memory for objects and people

A-11 to respond with classification of similar objects with different attributes

A-14 to match similar pictures

A-15 to indicate recognition of color names with the correct response

SAMMY

Sammy is almost five years old. His skills are about on the two-year level. He has been enrolled in a class for retarded children for six months but was such a behavior problem that he was expelled for the remainder of the session. He rarely participates in the routine but constantly pushes other children down. In a one-to-one situation, Sammy proves to have some functional language but in a group situation he is practically nonverbal. His father is not living at home and Sammy's mother works long hours in a local dry cleaning store. During the time she spends with Sammy she requires little of him. She had been told he is retarded and had accepted it. At the time he was referred, the staff had the impression that Sammy was a little boy who wanted very much to give and receive affection. However, he has no skills to meet this need.

Problems noted by staff and mother at the time of enrollment were:

demands excessive attention
short attention span
distractible
restless
overactive
resistant to discipline
aggressive toward children
immature verbal behavior
speech problems
lacks self help skills

The psychiatric diagnosis is mental retardation with severe behavioral disturbance.

The Developmental Therapy objectives for Sammy for the first five weeks are:

Behavior

B-5 to actively assist in learning self help skills

B-6 to respond independently to play materials

B-7 to respond with recall to the routine spontaneously

Communication

C-5 to produce a recognizable word to obtain a desired response from adult

In the Stage One class, play time is the first activity of the day. This gives the teachers opportunity to reorient the children each morning to the expectations and realities of the room.

Play time is important for practicing new skills. After a new activity or toy is introduced during instructional time, it will be put in the toy cabinet. This permits the children to explore on their own the toy's potential and practice a newly acquired response to it.

The Stage One teachers use a "controlled vocabulary" technique in which a limited number of words are selected which have direct reference to the classroom (e.g., milk, cookies, paste, work time, play time, etc.). The teachers limit their vocabulary entirely to these few words and sentences. In this way, the teachers' simple, consistent language patterns serve as models for the children to imitate. Because Stage One children characteristically are confused and have no functional speech, the teachers' controlled vocabulary is essential to progress.

There are three forms of the controlled vocabulary:

1. Statements: no responses required from child
2. Commands: require specific behavioral responses
3. Questions: require specific verbal responses

This format for describing the Stage One teachers' language patterns was developed by Nancy Cudmore, a Rutland Center preschool teacher. It is the result of her extensive observation and recording of the teachers' language patterns. Her findings are summarized in a paper for the University of Georgia, Division for Exceptional Children, "Effective Language Patterns for Use With Disturbed Children" (1973).

Commands are used to convey a required response or to redirect the child to a desired response. "Sammy, we don't push children." "Sammy, you can push the pig." (Socialization objectives S-3, S-5; Behavior objective B-3.)

C-6 to produce a recognizable word to obtain a desired response from another child

C-7 to produce a meaningful, recognizable sequence of words to obtain a desired response from adults or children in the classroom

Socialization

S-5 to engage in organized solitary play

S-8 to produce a recognizable word to obtain a desired response from adult

S-9 to produce a recognizable word to obtain a desired response from another child

S-10 same as C-7

(Pre)Academics

A-10 to indicate short term memory for objects and people

A-11 to respond with classification of similar objects with different attributes

A-12 to indicate short term memory for verbal expressions

A-13 to perform body coordination activities at the three/four-year level

THE CLASS BEGINS

The schedule on the inside of the classroom door designates play time as the first activity, but at this point the schedule is merely a reminder for the therapy team. (The children don't respond to it.) Once inside the door, I move down on my knees and into Donald's line of vision and announce with animation *"It's play time!"* Donald is familiar with the room and routine from the summer program so he moves over from the door with Carla, Sammy, Emily, and Foster, who are all greeted individually with touches and smiles and the phrase

"Carla's here," "Sammy's here," and *"Foster's here."* Sammy allows a quick hug and then sits on the rug. Carla pulls away from the hug but tolerates the teacher's hand on her back. Emily is still cowering by the door with her head down and fingers in her mouth. Peg stoops to her level, puts an arm around her and tells her quietly about a doll in the cabinet. With her arm gently around the child Peg begins to move her over to the play area.

The play area is designated by the red shag rug. Except for a small wooden jungle gym and a large barrel on a wooden frame, most of the toys are in the toy cabinet. Foster begins to wander away from the play area, rocking from foot to foot, jabbing one hand into the other and making a throaty noise. I call his name, but he doesn't seem to hear so I move to him, put my hand on his back and lead him gently back to the play area saying, *"Play time is on the rug."* When we pass near the jungle gym I move his hands out to touch it saying, *"You can climb."* He starts climbing.

Peg has finally moved Emily to the toy cabinet and she encourages her to open the cabinet. After several unsuccessful attempts Peg puts the child's limp hand on the knob and pulls with her. When Emily sees the doll she squeals and shakes her arms aimlessly but doesn't reach for it. Peg brings the doll close to Emily and says *"Doll. This is a doll."* Finally Emily reaches for the doll and Peg then says *"Say, 'Doll' Emily."* After several repetitions Emily attempts *"daw"* and immediately Peg gives her the doll and a big hug, saying *"Good, Emily. You said, 'Doll'."*

Carla is now sitting on the floor staring at the wall. I move over to her and emphatically say her name while I rub her back. She still doesn't seem to hear me so I blow in her face. She is startled and looks at me. I am still calling her name. Then I say, *"It's play time."* I put a fuzzy white ball in her hands, whispering *"This is a ball. It feels soft."* She starts rubbing the ball and begins to roll it around.

As I turn my head I see Sammy giving Emily a big push into the cabinet door. Emily starts to cry. I comfort her. Then I take Sammy's hands firmly, saying *"Sammy, we don't push children!"* I move him over to a big stuffed animal and say, *"Sammy, you can push the pig."* And I help him start to push the toy across the room.

Donald is lying on the floor, his eyes half open, repeating bits and pieces of a TV commercial, completely oblivious of anything outside his own body. I intercept him immediately saying, *"Donald, sit up."* I take his hands to give him encouragement but not to do the task for him completely. Once he is sitting, he is now aware of me but needs motivating to begin to respond to the toys. I say *"Donald, do you want to play in the barrel?"* He nods his head and I say *"Tell me."* He then says, *"I want to play in the barrel"* and moves to the toy. I've been working on helping him refer to himself as "I" during the summer program. I do not give him what he wants or let him do what he wants until he uses the right pronoun. I supply him with the words he needs if he can't say it himself.

During play time as well as for all the other activities in the Stage One classroom, the lead and support teachers have to operate as a highly synchronized team. We have to be aware of what each child is doing all the time. While I hold one child in my lap I stroke another one, direct simple comments to another, and watch a fourth across the room. Simple sentences are used by the teachers to constantly reflect each child's physical behavior. For example, *"Carla has the ball." "Emily has the doll." "Donald is in the barrel." "Sammy is pushing the pig." "Foster has the tractor."* It is important to touch each child as you speak to him and keep your voice animated and stimulating.

Each child must be aroused to respond to his environment and must be adequately (physically and verbally) reinforced for those responses. Children engaged in aimless or repetitive (perseverative) activities must be constantly redirected (given a more appropriate experience). For example, when Foster picks up a tractor he spins the wheels with his other hand. I have to stop his hands saying, *"Not for spinning"* and help him push the tractor on the rug while I make motor noises to entice him. Then I say, *"The tractor goes on the rug!"*

After being in the play area for as little as 10 to 15 minutes, the children become increasingly difficult to redirect to the toys and their own specific problems (symptoms) appear with more frequency. I become increasingly aware that the children are ready for a new activity and so I give the warning *"Play time is almost over."* To be sure that each child hears me, I touch each child and repeat the simple phrase. In another minute or so I announce, *"Play time is over. It's time to put up the toys."* The support teacher and I move in quickly and physically assist the children who need help. This may be the first time many of these children have been expected to put away what they play with. This is usually a pretty confusing time in class until the children understand this routine. We repeat a simple phrase to each child directing him to where his particular toy goes. We are particularly careful to use the same phrases with specific children every day. This simple repetition seems to contribute greatly to their understanding. Almost always at Stage One the children have to be physically moved to put up the toys. After touching Foster and giving him the simple command *"The truck goes in the cabinet,"* the support teacher sees that he is not going to put up the toy. She gently places her body behind him and extends her hands down to him, helping him bend and grasp the toy. Then she helps him move to the cabinet while repeating *"The truck goes in the cabinet."* After the task is completed, she warmly reinforces his movements with a squeeze and *"Good work, Foster. You put the truck in the cabinet."* After many repetitions of this procedures, Foster will begin to put away toys on command.

After the toys are up, I announce *"Now it's WORK TIME. We sit at the table for work time."* These phrases are sufficiently repeated with accompanying physical movements to get each child to the table and in his chair. Very often during the first weeks of a Stage One class, these transitions take as long as some of the activities themselves. Today Sammy and Donald begin to move to the table after my first statement and a slight touch on the back. However, Foster is standing in the play area rocking and jabbing his hands together. I put an arm around him, taking one of his hands in mine, and lead him to the table. Suddenly Sammy runs for the door. Peg strategically places her body between Sammy and the door and stoops to his eye level saying, *"We sit at the table for work time."* She places an arm around his back and guides him to his chair. Emily and Carla have returned to the play materials so Peg moves over to them saying in her most animated and luring voice, *"Play time is over. Now it's work time!"* She takes the girls' hands and walks them back to the table swinging their arms playfully.

Meanwhile I sit at the table and reach for the materials at my side. Since this is the first school-type experience for many of these children, the preacademic materials must be highly motivating. It's difficult enough just getting them to sit in their chairs; there must be some reason for them to want to stay. Crayons, coloring sheets, and construction paper are bright and often decorated to grab their attention.

Sammy has trouble holding scissors. I help him place the scissors in his hand and give him a bright thin strip of paper that he can sever with one whack. He is delighted with his accomplishment and grins each time he cuts off a piece.

Foster has a simple puzzle to do. After I give him the puzzle he begins to jab at the shapes. I put my hand on his and help his grasp and take out the pieces. Once motivated he begins to replace the parts. I pat him on the back saying *"Good work. Foster is putting the puzzle together."* Then I turn to another child.

Carla is staring away from the table. I have to stroke her arm and call her name to get her attention. She screams and says, *"I don't want to sit down."* She starts to get up so I move around to her and replace her in her chair. She screams again and again but I stoop down beside her and gently hold her in the chair saying, "Carla, we sit for work time." She continues to scream and I motion for Peg to pass me the crayons. I start to outline the big flower on her paper and make a silly sound with my voice while keeping one hand on her gradually relaxing body. She begins to quiet down and looks at the paper. I slip the crayon in her hand; she imitates my movements and starts to color.

Emily is sitting with her head tucked down and fingers in her mouth. I hand Peg some bright shiney beads and a knotted shoe lace and Peg says, "Emily, look what I have. Beads." Peg rolls them into Emily's line of vision and taps them together to get her attention. Emily gradually is lured into attending to the beads and

reaches for one. Peg holds the string and directs her, "Put it here." The child giggles as the bead falls down the string. After several such repetitions, she seems sufficiently interested so Peg moves the string into Emily's hand and continues to assist her until she can manipulate the beads and string.

Donald is staring at his hand and singing a familiar TV commercial. I interrupt him quickly as he seems out of contact with what is happening in the room. *"Donald, it's work time."* I try to make my voice inflection more interesting than what he has devised for himself. This technique doesn't work so I clap my hands sharply. He bounces slightly in his chair and his eyes are no longer fixed on his hand. Again I repeat, *"It's work time"* and thump my fingers on his work sheet. Since Donald reads but his comprehension is limited he has several sentences to complete like *"My name is ——."* *"I have —— fingers."* I assist him in answering these questions because his knowledge about his own body is very limited.

As the children become accustomed to the work time procedures, we begin to expect them to ask for the materials they want. I always say the word (such as "scissors," "paper," "paste") as I give the object to the child. As a child begins to make the connection I hold the object a little out of reach and repeat the word. *"Emily, say 'beads'."* Once she is sufficiently aroused to want the material, she will attempt an approximation of the word. Then I immediately give her the object, give her some physical contact and say *"Good work Emily. You said 'bead'."* When this procedure is continually repeated throughout each activity, even nonverbal children will attempt some speech.

Work time may last only 10 minutes because attention spans are so short; and the children tolerate only short periods at one task. I plan the materials so that each child's specific task takes about the same amount of time.

Again I prepare them for the end of the activity by saying, *"Work time is almost over."* Peg and I help each child have a successful finish with the materials. Every minimally positive move made by each child must be recognized and reinforced.

Then I announce, *"Work time is over; now it's EXERCISE TIME. Let's sit on the floor."*

The success of most Stage One activities can be attributed directly to this arousing, attracting nature of the activity and to the teachers' involvement in showing the child successful responses.

The teachers know when to accept a particular response and when to expect a higher level response. This knowledge comes from the Developmental Therapy objectives for each child.

A child's ability to attend to a task may vary from day to day and from activity to activity. The teachers continually stretch the activity to a maximum for productive involvement, and then pull back and end the lesson before interest and motivation lag.

Again we physically guide the children who need help in getting to the activity. Since these particular children are all somewhat behind in gross motor coordination, this activity is planned to help them move their bodies with greater assurance as well as to give them training in following specific verbal commands.

A new support teacher, in training at our center, comes in to help with this activity. Every child in the group needs specific physical guidance to complete the exercises. I start to sing, stand up, and clap my hands enthusiastically, *"Now it's time to stand up, stand up, stand up."* I repeat the simple, made-up tune until each child has been assisted to stand up. We are careful to give each child only the minimal amount of physical assistance he needs to do the task. Then I proceed through a series of gross body movements such as sitting back down, lying down, jumping, rolling over, standing on one foot. After several minutes we are all breathless, and the children seem physically aroused and ready to dart out in any direction. A teacher's hand is placed on each child who looks as if he might become disorganized, and I say, *"Exercise time is over; now it's ART TIME."*

Art time is across the room on the wooden floor. We are careful to plan activities so that quiet activities alternate with more physically active ones. The body positioning required by each activity should change: free movement, sitting at the table, moving around again, sitting on the floor. These changes are arousing and help the children maintain attention.

I move over to the art area with my arms around Emily and Sammy and announce again, *"It's ART TIME."* I keep my hands lightly on the backs of these children and say, *"We sit for art time."* As they sit down I praise their movements and rub their backs again, while calling to the other children to come. Peg is trying to get Donald off the floor. He has rolled over; his eyes are closed and he is unresponsive to her voice. Meanwhile, Foster has reached over to Carla and pinches her arm. She starts to scream and Foster runs to the far corner of the room. It's hard at a time like this to know what to do first. I generally move to the child in most distress first and if possible try to make contact with more than one child at a time. Carla is still

screaming and is obviously very frightened. Quickly I approach her and she screams even louder. Now everyone seems threatening to her. I slow down and move to my knees for the last few steps and reach out my hands to her. As I touch her she screams again but gradually quiets down as she realizes my contact is conveying calm and reassurance. She feels, through the touch, that I will not harm her. I hold her and comfort her for a few seconds and look around just in time to see Sammy dart out the door and into the hall. My impulse is to run out to get him but I know I will lose Carla if I do. I also count on the monitor or crisis teacher assigned to our team to intercept Sammy. So I take Carla's hand and tell her, *"It's art time, let's go sit on the floor."* She starts to scream again but I still move her gently and help her sit down. Peg now has gotten Donald off the floor. She had to shake him, speak his name loudly to get his attention, and offer both her arms to him. Once mobilized I call his name and say again *"It's art time"* and he begins to move over. Peg moves to the corner to get Foster who has started to bang his head against the wall. She steps up her pace, in fact she runs, and holds his head against her body to restrain him from hurting himself. By this time, Peg feels that Foster no longer remembers what he did to Carla, and since his understanding is so limited she just leads him back to the activity saying, *"It's art time."* With children at Stage One, their specific behaviors, aggressive and positive, must be dealt with immediately in order to make any connection for them at all.

During this time I am sitting with the children and starting the art activity. When Peg gets back with Foster, I send her out in the hall to get Sammy. With one hand I reach out to Foster. He looks as if he might get up again. I rub his knee and say, *"Paper. I have paper."* I hold up huge sheets of colorful construction paper for all the children to see. I shake the paper to make a noise and sway it before each child's view. Carla starts to reach for the paper. I say, *"Carla, say, 'I want paper.'"* I realize she is going to repeat my words exactly. I shake my head, holding the paper near her, and say, *"I want paper."* She reaches again, and I say again, *"I want paper."* Then she repeats the phrase. I give it to her quickly and say *"Good work,*

Here the transition falls apart. The teachers must remain calm, keeping their voices unexcited and moving in physically to re-organize the children for the next activity.

The teacher must discover, often intuitively, how and what to do to help a child in crisis. The teacher must first really care how the child is feeling. She must feel that distress in order to communicate the necessary warmth and reassurance.

Each activity has a great potential for individual variations in performance and many different Developmental Therapy objectives can be included. This exercise time activity is a good example. It is used for Donald and Emily to work on the developmental objective in academics (A-6, to imitate words and actions of adults). The same activity is used for behavior objectives B-4 for Foster, Carla, and Donald (to respond with motor and body responses to complex environmental and verbal stimuli). For Sammy this activity assists in mastery of academic objective A-13 (to perform body coordination activities at the three/four-year level).

Notice how each child is managed in an individual way. The teacher must assume a different approach for each child to be effective.

It is the lead teacher's responsibility to provide the motivation and leadership for the activity. In times of crisis, the lead teacher continues the group activity, drawing children back to the materials, while the support teacher responds to the individual child who is diverted from the group.

This Art Time activity is another example of the way one activity can include many individual objectives. For Foster the objectives are in communication C-1 and C-3 (C-1, to attend to person speaking; C-3, to respond to verbal stimulus . . . with a recognizable approximation. In behavior, his objectives are B-2 and B-3 (B-2, to respond to sensory stimulus by attending to source . . .; B-3, to respond with motor behavior to simple environmental stimulus).

For Emily, the objectives are B-6 in behavior (to respond independently to play materials), C-3 in communication (to respond with a recognizable approximation of the appropriate verbal response), and socialization objectives S-4 and S-5 (to imitate simple, familiar acts of adults; to engage in organized, solitary play).

Sammy's objectives for this art activity are the same as Emily's, in behavior, B-6 and in socialization, but his communication objective is S-7 (to produce a recognizable sequence of words . . .).

At Stage One, it is essential to make an activity so exciting that the children can't resist becoming involved, regardless of their pathologies.

If this had been one of Carla's better days, the activity might be used for objective A-15 in academics (to indicate recognition of color names . . .). But on this particular day, the objective had to be at a much lower level, behavior B-2 (to respond to stimulus by sustained attending . . .). This is an objective she has made progress on, but she still cannot meet the criterion of mastery (90 percent of the time).

In a Stage One classroom, the teacher must be alert to every modality for stimulating interest.

Milk and cookie time is most valuable for communication and behavior objectives. The major objectives to notice in this description are:

Foster: *C-3 to respond to verbal stimulus . . . with a recognizable approximation*
   B-2 to respond to stimulus by sustained attending . . .

Donald: *C-7 to produce a meaningful . . . sequence of words . . .*
   B-2 to respond to stimulus by sustained attending . . .

Carla. You asked for paper!" Meanwhile Peg is back with Sammy. She tells him to sit down and rubs his back as he sits. Then she reaches out to the children whose attention seems to be straying, touching those who look like they might get up.

I go through the same procedure with each child, expecting each to give some approximation of the word *"paper,"* or the phrase or just physical reaching. Foster can only make the "p" sound. Emily approximates *"pa—er."* Donald says, *"You want paper."* Finally he says, *"I want paper."* Sammy approximates the phrase *"I ont paua."*

I bring out a large cup of water and pour some on my paper. Then I spread it with obvious pleasure. I repeat the same routine I did with the paper and get each child to make some verbalization to get the water. I repeat the same routine for the large paint brushes. Then I begin to shake dry tempera paint on the wet paper. The paint runs and mixes together, looking very exciting. The powdered paint falling from the can is also stimulating. Even Foster watches this procedure. Once the children are sufficiently fascinated, I get them to ask for the paint too.

We continue to pour on the paint, helping each child to keep his brush moving and on the paper. Sammy wants to put the brush in his mouth. Foster's hand must be guided to the paper as he does not yet discriminate between the paper and the floor. Carla and Donald begin to stare and must be aroused back to painting. As their interest wanes, I announce *"Art time is almost over."* Then we help each child get another round of paint before the activity ends.

Now I announce the end of art time and say *"Wash hands for MILK AND COOKIE TIME."* Each child is directed into the bathroom adjoining the classroom. Peg lingers behind to quickly pick up the art materials and remove them from view. In 10 seconds or so she joins us in the bathroom and is helping with the hand-washing procedure. Time is too valuable in the therapeutic classroom for a teacher to waste it being away from the children because of housekeeping procedures.

Washing hands can be an arousing and stimulating experience for these nonresponsive children. When Emily's hands touch the water she squeals and grins. It feels good. Sammy likes the bubbles I make with the soap. This gives me the idea to help him say the word *"bubbles."* Since this is something he wants, I know he will attempt language for it. It's important to be aware of what each child might be responsive to.

As the children come out of the bathroom, I tell them individually to sit down for milk and cookies. Again we physically help the children who can't get into their chairs without assistance.

For the first few weeks of class, another staff member will place our milk cartons outside the door as neither of us can be spared to leave the class. Peg's chair is close to the door so she reaches out to get the milk and gives it to me.

I hold up the milk saying, *"I have milk; who wants milk?"* The children are hungry and thirsty now, so food is an excellent arouser. Foster grabs for a carton. I immediately place my hand on his, saying *"Foster, say, 'milk'."* He looks confused so I say *"milk"* several times. Then I realize he cannot say the whole word. I repeat the "m" sound, touching my lips to draw attention to the sound. He starts to rock back and forth in his chair and jabs his hands together. I quickly grab his hands and hold them, not with force but with affection saying, *"Foster, say 'mmm'."* He can't do it yet, but he watches my face intently, so I give him the milk repeating the sound again and again. Throughout the activity I come back to Foster saying "milk" and making the "m" sound while touching his carton. In a week or two he will be able to say "mmm."

Donald is jabbering something about *"a good deal on a Ford"* and is staring into space. Peg calls his name forcefully and slams his milk carton down on the table. He looks at the milk and reaches for it. Peg says, *"Donald, do you want milk?"* Donald repeats *"You want milk?"* Peg says, *"Say I."* Then he corrects his own statement saying, *"I want milk."* Quickly she gives him the milk, a hug, and a smile.

Emily is sitting with one hand in her mouth and the other hand in her pants. I pull her hands gently to the table and place them around the cool smooth carton. She looks at me with some pleasure, and I say, *"Emily do you want milk?"* She pulls away, putting her fingers back in her mouth. I open the carton and smell it saying, *"Mmm, the milk smells so good!"* I lift the milk to her nose and repeat the phrase. She smiles and reaches for the milk. I decide not to press her for language today. I know she can approximate the word, but she seems especially anxious now. If I push she might not say the word and might stop even her physical response (reaching for the milk). I give her the milk and rub her back gently, then I let my arm rest around her body. She desperately needs this warm contact. In a Stage One class I make it a point never to let my hands rest on the table. My hands and arms are always needed to stroke or hold or redirect.

Carla is screaming. She had gotten up from her chair and Peg had helped her sit back down. She struggles to get up again so Peg moves over by her chair and gently replaces her in her chair. Her scream is grating but Peg doesn't respond with impatience. She realizes this is the way Carla controls situations at home. So here in class we never let this behavior change our routine. Peg repeats, *"Carla, we sit for milk and cookies."* Then I hold up a carton to Carla saying, *"This is chocolate milk. It tastes so good!"* As she begins to attend to what I'm saying, she reaches for the milk still screaming. I say *"Carla, stop screaming"* and hold the milk closer. She gets quieter but I repeat the phrase until she stops. Then I give her the milk, while Peg rubs her back. Now I say *"Good work, Carla. You stopped screaming."* During this sequence, I felt that her screaming behavior was the most important thing to deal with. As her screaming decreases in the next few weeks, I will expect language in its place.

Sammy has grabbed Emily's milk. Quickly I retrieve the milk and give it back to her. I realize Sammy had to wait longer than he can tolerate so he impulsively reached for the closest carton. Although he has some language, he functions as a nonverbal child who uses his body rather than language to get what he wants from other children. I see no need to deal with his offense against Emily, but rather I must teach him how he can get what he wants. For the next few days I'll be sure to intervene with him sooner to get some language attempt before he uses the same, nonproductive way of getting what he wants.

Now I get out the graham crackers and peanut butter. We use the food to elicit speech from some children and to redirect specific behaviors in others. I announce when the activity is almost over, giving every child a chance to have a last cracker. Then I say *"Milk and cookie time is over; now it's SAND TIME."*

Each child is individually assisted (physically and verbally) by one of us to get up, put his milk carton in the trash can, and come to the sand table.

The waist-high, metal-lined sand table has a top which I quickly remove to show the mound of white sand inside. Sammy and Foster plunge their hands into the sand. Carla looks with disgust at the boys. She's not comfortable getting her hands dirty. I take one of her fingers to draw a design in the sand. She looks intrigued and begins on her own to touch the sand to see what will happen. Donald had his hands in the sand but is staring at the opposite wall. He is not in touch with us. I grab his hands saying, *"I'm going to pull you, Donald."* I pull him towards me, across the table, until his belly bends a little over the table. He likes this, looks at me and smiles. Then I say, *"Let's build a mountain."* I start scooping up sand with a large plastic cup and pouring it out in one spot. Then I give him the cup and say, *"Now you pour the sand."*

Peg has put Emily's hands in the sand and moves them around. Once she realizes it feels so good, she begins to play spontaneously. Every couple of weeks I will change the sand table from sand to mud, to water, to soapy water. Whatever I think would be exciting I try.

During sand time Peg takes each child individually to the bathroom. I stay with the rest of the children to keep them involved. With each child she requires specific behaviors (pulling down own pants, flushing commode, and language to help each one learn the routine of toileting).

When everyone has had a turn in the bathroom and as interests start to wane, I announce *"Sand time is almost over."* Then after several minutes I say, *"Sand time is over, and now it's YUM-YUM TIME."* During this activity I explore some single food usually starting with sweet fruits; I peel and offer a slice to each child. They are intrigued and for several it is

Emily: *C-4 to voluntarily initiate a recognizable verbal approximation to obtain a specific object...*

B-4 to respond with motor and body responses to complex environmental and verbal stimuli

Carla: *C-7 to produce a meaningful... sequence of words to obtain a desired response from adults*

B-4 to respond... to complex environmental and verbal stimuli... through completion of verbal direction; minimal participation in in the routine...

Sammy: *C-5 to produce a recognizable word to obtain a desired response from adult*

C-6 to produce a recognizable word to obtain a desired response from another child

The consistency with which the teacher verbally prepares the children for the end of one activity and the beginning of the next provides continuity and security during transitions. It also prepares a child for behavior objective B-7 (to respond with recall to the routine spontaneously).

The teacher must constantly use her imagination to think of new ways to arouse the children and sustain their attention. Sensory experiences work particularly well.

The teacher often is a model for play as well as for language. She must enjoy the materials and communicate that enjoyment, enticing the child to respond.

Stage One children need a certain amount of repetition with the same materials in order to be comfortable enough with them to attempt to use them. The materials should be varied when they no longer stimulate the children, when interest wanes, or when old symptoms reappear.

their first experience with such foods. As with other activities, I want to get each child's attention. As the weeks progress I expect to get sustained attending, then simple concepts and associated language.

Our last activity is MUSIC TIME. When Peg brings over the guitar most of the children are stimulated. They have never been this close to a big instrument. When I start to strum even Foster looks up from his rocking and hand jabbing and attends. Peg sits close to the children using simple touch or body closeness to keep the children attending. I sing a simple tune with each child's name in a verse. I show them how to strum and each child has a turn. This is such an exciting experience that I expect them to be reaching for a turn in a matter of days and using some speech within five weeks.

Two hours have passed. I announce *"Music time is over; it's time to GO HOME."* We help each child get to the door. I get on my knees to give them a goodbye hug and repeat, *"It's time to go home."* Again we make physical contact and lead them out of the building to their waiting parents.

Peg and I walk back in to debrief with our treatment team monitor. We feel excited and good about this first day. A lot has happened to each child in that two-hour period. Our monitor, watching through the one-way mirror, has many observations to share with us and with each of the parents. We expect to have at least one set of parents observing the class every day with the monitor. It is this sort of cooperation which makes us confident that these children will progress.

After parents have observed with the team monitor, often they are asked to take the support teacher's place on the treatment team for specific activities. In this way, they develop management skills by modeling the way the teachers touch and speak to the children.

TENTH WEEK NOTES

Donald

At the end of 10 weeks Donald is attending more to classroom stimuli, but this goal must continue to be a major focus (B-1). He is also more aware of the adults in the room because we have constantly required his attention when we speak (C-1). Yet he has not mastered this objective. He is not yet responding independently to play materials (B-6). He seems to be learning specific responses to various toys when assisted by the teacher. Because he is so close to mastery, we will pull back from physical contact and will try to verbally elicit desired responses to the materials. Recently, Donald has begun to ask spontaneously for his milk, but he still prefers to use only one word (C-7). He is still unaware of the other children and has not yet learned to use a word to get what he wants from them (C-6).

We are ready to ask his mother to come into the classroom one day a week to learn the support role and thus techniques for managing Donald at home. He's still pretty out of it. We have a long way to go.

His Parents Mrs. A. had taken Donald to practically every special service available in the state. Each had given her a new diagnosis and new techniques. It was very difficult to get any real investment from her using our techniques. She communicated that things were going well at home and was rarely able to admit her real difficulties in managing him. Extensive participation was planned, but Mrs. A. usually was unable to meet the monitor for observation. When specific techniques were suggested for dealing with Donald's behavior at home, Mrs. A. would report that this certain behavior was no longer a problem. Finally, the monitor found that by discussing only one specific behavior and technique, writing it down to take home and reviewing the notes the following week, some progress was made in her resistance. By the end of the 10 weeks, it is still difficult to evaluate the amount and quality of intervention Donald is receiving at home, and Mrs. A. is not yet ready to have us visit in her home.

Foster

Foster has mastered the first behavior objective (B-1), attending to specific activities and stimuli most of the time. However, the length of his attending behavior is still brief. In the next 10 weeks we will work on sustained attending (B-2). Foster is also aware now of the person speaking to him (C-1). He has discovered, as most children do in this classroom, that the adults speak simply and that their language and behavior are consistent and predictable. He watches adults closely and responds when his name is called (S-1, S-2). He can now verbally approximate five words and is spontaneously producing two of those approximations to get what he wants (C-3, C-4). For the next 10 weeks we will attempt to get him to increase the number and frequency of those approximations.

His aggressive behavior has decreased but is still evident both at home and at school. We must focus again on this, making sure that the teachers give simple verbal requests and consistently move him through the required task (B-3).

His Parent One of Mrs. B's most urgent problems had been to find someone to keep Foster during the day while she worked. Because of his aggressive and unpredictable behavior, no one wanted to keep him for long. Our first accomplishment was to get financial assistance for Mrs. B. so she could stay home. She had wanted to try staying home but was afraid she too would be unable to control him all day.

Extensive intervention was planned. Mrs. B. came in on a weekly basis to observe Foster in class and to learn new techniques for management at home. The monitor also helped Mrs. B. deal with her negative and angry feelings toward Foster and his bizarre behaviors.

We worked with Mrs. B. in identifying the critical management problems at home. Then we encouraged her in trying some of the same techniques used by the teachers in the therapeutic classroom.

By the end of the first 10 weeks, Mrs. B. felt that she was better able to control Foster and that many of the home management problems had disappeared. In many of our sessions with Mrs. B., we also discussed Foster's future needs, including periodic visits in a residential program to give her relief.

Carla

At the end of the first 10 weeks, Carla is having only one or two brief screaming episodes a week (as compared to several hour-long episodes every day). Her attending increased for sustained periods of time during every activity (B-2). She also learned the routine and how to respond with motor and body responses to complex environmental and verbal stimuli (B-4). She had only occasional accidents in toileting at home and none at school (B-5). She has also learned to respond independently to play materials after minimal encouragement by the teacher (B-6). Her echolalia has decreased but must continue to be a focus (C-6, C-7). She seems to be beginning to trust the teacher and will tolerate her touch. Occasionally, she will now sit spontaneously in the teacher's lap (S-6).

For the next 10 weeks we will focus on communication and socialization objectives, especially C-6, C-7, S-5, and S-9.

Her Parents Extensive intervention had been planned for Carla's parents. Mrs. C. came in to observe Carla in class on a weekly basis, and Mr. C. was able to observe several times during the 10 weeks. The teacher and monitor gave them some new techniques for dealing with Carla's screaming, as this was identified as the first priority at home. Her parents were open to new suggestions from the team, even though their previous attempts to deal with her strange behaviors had been a source of conflict between them. We helped them set up a daily schedule that Carla would follow. Carla was expected to complete certain tasks and was rewarded with Kool-Aid, which seemed to be important to her. Her screaming behavior was to be ignored and they planned ways to keep from giving in to it. Techniques used for toilet training were also discussed. Throughout the 10 weeks, the monitor supported the parents in dealing consistently and firmly with Carla. Also, Carla's need for acceptance and nurturance were emphasized. Her parents have noticed much less screaming behavior and toilet training is practically accomplished. They are now focusing on the problems arising from the more subtle behaviors she exhibits when she wants to be understood.

Emily

Emily is participating much more in the routine (B-7). As she comes into class she still initially tends to avoid responding (B-4). However, this period of adjustment to the classroom is shorter and her new modes of responding are sustained for a longer period. Her self help skills have improved but, here again, it is more a matter of motivating her into becoming involved rather than having to teach her the actual responses (B-5). She is now responding independently to play materials and is beginning to show organization in her play (B-6, S-5). Her verbal approximations to get what she wants have increased dramatically but should remain a focus because this still represents an area of major difficulty

(C-4). For the next 10 weeks we will help her learn to use those approximations with other children as well as with adults (C-5, C-6).

Her Parents In this 10-week session, the main goal with Emily's mother has been to increase Mrs. D's awareness of the potential dangers of leaving her children unattended. Mrs. D. came in to observe and talk on an every-other-day basis. She and the monitor planned her home routines so that she felt she could cope with the basic needs of her family. By working with her daily routine, the monitor was able to help her remain aware of the physical needs of her children. Mrs. D. was not resistant but rather oblivious that her actions endangered her children. The monitor found that Mrs. D. responded best to specific suggestions for child care. Then the monitor was careful to fully support Mrs. D's attempts to follow these suggestions. During the first 10 weeks, new techniques for child management were not emphasized; rather, child care routines were delineated. As a result, Mrs. D.'s own awareness of her responsibilities toward her children was greatly increased. As our next step, we plan to focus on helping Mrs. D. learn to meet more of Emily's needs for nurturance.

Sammy

Sammy's involvement in learning self help skills improved a bit (B-5). He can now button and unbutton his pants and zip them, too. He has learned to respond to the play materials and is beginning to organize his play (B-6, S-5). As his ability to play has increased, his aggressiveness toward the other children has decreased. He has learned that his aggressiveness is not permitted in the classroom, and he has learned to use a few words to express his needs to the teach-

Table 1. Length of Treatment and Subsequent School Placement

	Total weeks enrolled in Stage I	Present school placement
Donald	23	Public school, primary EMR (Educable Mentally Retarded) class
Foster	36	Community day care center for the retarded
Carla	34	Regular second grade
Emily	20	Regular private kindergarten
Sammy	24	Public school, TMR (Trainable Mentally Retarded) class

ers (C-5). He can now remember where to move for each activity and is using words spontaneously to get what he wants from other children (B-7, S-9). He also can use a sequence of words to get what he wants from adults (C-7).

We think he is ready to attend again his other school in addition to his participation in class.

His Parent Since Sammy's mother did not understand his expulsion from the school for the retarded, our first goal was to help her see his aggressive behavior when he was in a group setting. By observing the class through the one-way mirror, Mrs. E. was able to see the problem for herself. At first she was angry to see Sammy behave aggressively, but gradually she began to understand his behavior and feelings.

Our second goal was to help her learn how to elicit language from Sammy. Through observation of teacher's techniques and discussions with the monitor, she began to model the teacher's behavior and language patterns. The monitor reviewed the phrases used by the teacher with Sammy at snack time so that she could use the same phrases at home.

The monitor also helped Mrs. E. set up a consistent bedtime procedure. This was especially hard for her because Sammy became resistant and difficult to manage when she began this routine. She still needs much encouragement to enforce this limit firmly without getting angry and resorting to physical punishment.

EPILOGUE

These children now are all participating in some other school program. The length of time they spent in treatment, their rates of progress, and their subsequent placements vary greatly (Table 1). Donald is still enrolled, but he is in a Stage Two class and also participating in a public school program for the educable retarded. Carla subsequently participated in both Stage Two and Stage Three classes and now is terminated. Periodically, the teachers visit her home and school for any follow-up consultation which may be needed. Emily continued in Stage Two for 16 weeks more and is no longer in need of special help. Sammy has made a good adjustment to the school system's program for the trainable retarded.

The elements they share in common are their progress in mastering normal developmental milestones, their increased capacities to respond to educational programs not open to them before, and their acceptance as contributing members of functioning families and peer groups.

Without the special intervention they received, one can only guess what might have been the condition of these children and their families.

chapter 8

THE STAGE TWO CLASS, WHERE CHILDREN LEARN INDIVIDUAL SKILLS

Andrea Lomax, Lead Teacher, and
Marylyn Galewski, Monitor-Parent Worker

Reactive Disorder

Learning Disability

Depression

Mental Retardation

Chronic Brain Syndrome

Obsessive-Compulsive Reaction

Passive-Aggressive Personality

Deprivation

Antisocial Reaction

Adjustment Reaction

Aggression

INTRODUCTION

Unlike Stage One children, those at Stage Two *do* respond, but their responses don't produce the successes which help most children grow. Without success, a child feels bad about himself.

He may act out—kicking, screaming, cursing, resisting, or destroying. He may act out within himself—withdrawing, showing little feeling, talking very little, avoiding others, passively resisting, or controlling. These are responses of children who do not like themselves or the world around them.

They enter the Stage Two experience . . . a time when a child's failure-producing responses are replaced, redirected, changed to new, successful behavior which makes a child say, *"I can do it!"*

The teacher helps each child begin to experience success by learning to talk, work, and play in new ways. These new skills bring success, give new confidence, and work better than a kick or a shrug.

Five children met and grew together in this Stage Two class: Steven, Linda, Reg, Karen, and Mindy. They are typical of children who are not quite to Stage Three, even though they have mastered a few Stage Three skills. What they say to us as sensitive teachers is this, *"So far things have not been so good. We feel bad about the way we are and we don't know how to make things better."*

Our job is to make things better.

STEVEN

The sharp rap of Steven's heels against the floor filled the hallway as I struggled to remove him from his first grade classroom. He clutched at the slick concrete walls trying to stop our progress toward the exit door and my familiar car. "I'll be good. I won't do it again. I didn't do nothing." A vicious kick aimed at all he hated yet meeting none of it.

"I know you really want to stay, Steven. I know you really feel awful. But it helps to leave school early when you are having such a hard time."

"I don't wanna go . . . don't wanna go."

Tears streaking his soft brown face. Eyes heavy with fear, anger, defeat, self hate, fury, panic . . . all written on that one small face.

Snickering kids peeking out of other classrooms. Teachers' eyes leering from shaking heads, "I told you so, told you so . . ."

The janitor speaks to his empty bucket, "I tole you dat boy was crazy." The janitor had told me that too, months before when I pulled Steven down the hall toward his first grade class.

Steven is seven years old. His behavior is extremely disruptive and aggressive. When provoked by failure, fear of failure, or not being able to have his way, Steven is liable to erupt into violent loss of control. He kicks, hits, and screams. Usually an episode ends with regressive crying. At other times when highly anxious, Steven sexually acts out toward the teacher or other children. Steven considers himself inadequate to handle school work. His frustration tolerance is low and he becomes extremely anxious and aggressive if he feels his work is too hard for him. Visual perception problems, poor fine-motor coordination, and borderline retardation compound the problem. Numerous incidents occur throughout any day which cause his anxiety to mount and wreak havoc with his flimsy behavioral controls.

Upon referral, specific problems noted by staff, teachers, and parents were:

demands excessive attention
distractible
apathetic
overactive
aggressive toward children
crying

silliness
immature
academic problems:
    reading
    arithmetic
    hand coordination
    verbal skills

The psychiatric assessment reports mental retardation associated with chronic brain syndrome of unknown causes, suspected socioeconomic deprivation, learning disability, and aggressive reactions.

The Developmental Therapy objectives for Steven are:

Behavior

B-9   to wait for his turn without physical intervention by teachers

B-10 to participate in activities such as work time, story time, talking time, juice and cookie time without physical intervention by teachers

B-11 to participate in activities such as play time, mat time, games, music, art time without physical intervention by teachers

B-12 to spontaneously participate in routine without physical intervention by teachers

Communication

C-10 to label simple feelings in pictures, dramatic play, art, or music: sad, happy, angry, afraid

C-11 to use simple word sequences to command or request of another child or adult in ways acceptable to classroom procedures

C-12 to use words to exchange minimal information with an adult

C-13 to use words spontaneously to exchange minimal information with another child

Socialization

S-6   to respond to adult's verbal and nonverbal requests to come to him

S-14 to wait for his turn without physical intervention by teachers (same as behavior objective B-9)

S-17 to participate in cooperative activities or projects with another child during playtime, indoors or outdoors

S-18 to participate in cooperative activities or project with another child during organized class activities

(Pre)Academics

A-22 to name colors (black, purple, orange, green)

A-23 to count with one-to-one correspondence to 10

A-30 to recognize groups of objects to five

A-31 to listen to storytelling

LINDA

"But I didn't do nothing, I don't wanna leave the room . . . you're always picking on me . . . you never make the other kids go out. Reg made me do it. Just leave me alone. I'll tell my grandmother . . . wah-ah-ah-ah . . ."

"Linda, I know you feel really bad right now. You don't like to be out of class. When you're not crying then we can talk about it."

I sit and wait, thinking it will take her awhile to stop crying and even longer for her to talk about the things that happened before I took her from the classroom. She sits crouched in the corner; the tension seems to be leaving her body.

Her fists suddenly hit the wall. Plaster falls from the wall above where her fists hit. Another small chunk crumbles on the floor as she hits again. I wrap my arms around her, holding her hands in the process.

"I hate this place and I hate you . . . I'm going to tear this building down with my own hands and then I'm going to run down the street in front of a car and kill myself . . . and you shut up."

At the age of five Linda was abandoned by her parents and left with unprepared and unwilling grandparents. Now seven years old, Linda fears rejection. Her life is dominated by extreme anxiety. This anxiety results in behaviors at home and school which alienate her from her peers and make her extremely difficult to manage.

At school she demands constant attention, talks continually, cannot attend to tasks, has difficulty following directions, and resists any work which could entail even a remote possibility of failure. She whines, screams, and has crying tantrums when demands are not met. Her teachers find her behavior intolerable and openly show their dislike for her. Linda's sensitivity to their negative feelings only serves to heighten her anxiety and increase her feelings of rejection.

Socially, Linda often ingratiates herself with her classmates and is scorned in return.

At home she also feels rejection and lack of approval. Her grandparents feel their own personal lives and plans have been disrupted by Linda's sudden appearance in their household. Feelings of exasperation and hostility surface readily.

Upon referral, specific problems noted by staff, teachers, and parents were:

demands excessive attention
unable to concentrate
distractible
restless, overactive
resistant to discipline
careless, unorganized
lacks confidence
fears failure
immature behavior
talks excessively
manipulative
academic problems:
    reading readiness
    arithmetic

The psychiatric diagnosis is adjustment reaction of childhood with the possibility of a personality disorder (hysterical reaction).

The Developmental Therapy objectives for Linda are:

Behavior

B-9   to wait for turn without physical intervention by teacher

B-10   to participate in activities such as work time, story time, talking time, juice and cookie time without physical intervention by teacher

B-11   to participate in activities such as play time, mat time, games, music, art time, without physical intervention by teacher

B-12   to spontaneously participate in routine without physical intervention

Communication

C-11   to use simple word sequences to command or request of another child or adult in ways acceptable to classroom procedures

C-19   to use words or nonverbal gestures to show pride in own work, activity, or to make positive statements about self

C-20   to use appropriate words or gestures to show feeling responses to environment, materials, people, or animals

Socialization

S-14   to wait for turn without physical intervention by teacher (same as behavior objective B-9)
S-15   to initiate appropriate minimal movement toward another child within the classroom routine
S-17   to participate in cooperative activities or projects with another child during play time, indoors or outdoors
S-18   to participate in cooperative activities or projects with another child during organized class activities

(Pre)Academics

A-25   to recognize differences among shapes, symbols, numerals, and words
A-29   to perform body coordination activities at the five-year level
A-30   to recognize groups of objects to five
A-31   to listen to storytelling

REG

"I don't care if it wasn't your fault. You deserved that whipping anyway. Now go to your room."

"Seems like every day he does something he needs to be whipped for. Don't get me wrong. I loves that boy like he was my very own. I raised him, I works hard for him, but he can't stay out of trouble no matter what I do for him. I gets up at five every morning to make money to keep that boy in clothes. Now what was it you wanted?"

"I just wanted to tell you that Reg's teachers told me that he had done very well at school this week. He finished all his work and got along real well with the other children."

"He better do well. No sense in that boy acting like he does. Everyday it's something else. I tell you I can't put up with it much longer."

"Reg, come in here. Bring your teacher those school pictures you got today."

"Thanks, Reg. You know, this is a fine looking boy."

"He was a lot better looking when we first got him. Seems like now his head's too skinny and his lips stick out too much."

Reg sat crouched in a corner, face to the wall, but he could not conceal the tears.

Reg is insecure and highly anxious. At the age of eight he has lived in three different foster homes, none of which has met the normal needs of a growing child. Reg describes his present home as a "scary place." He feels inadequate about his own abilities and harbors much hostility caused by the neglect and abuse he has experienced. His anxiety presents itself primarily in school where he demands constant attention—banging on tables, provoking other children, crawling under desks, refusing to complete tasks, sulking, demanding. He is a disruptive influence, which teachers find intolerable. Enrolled in classes at the center, the same sorts of behavior present themselves but with a fury yet unleashed at his school. He presents a strange combination of a child who has superficially adopted the very moralistic codes of his present parents, but who underneath is a torrent of primitive anger. This child has tried to please them with the proper words: "Please," "Thank you," "Yes

Ma'am," "May I help you?". But when his insecurity and anxiety rule, he is feared by his foster parents, avoided by his peers, and has to be physically restrained by center teachers.

Upon referral, specific problems noted by staff, teachers, and parents were:

resistant to discipline
aggressive toward children
aggressive toward property
self aggressive
does not complete tasks
careless, unorganized
lacks comprehension
does not follow directions
easily frustrated
silliness
lacks confidence, fears failure
seeks failure for attention
immature behavior
talks excessively
listening difficulties
unable to express feelings appropriately
moodiness, overly sensitive, sad
untruthfulness
regressive behavior
repeats unnecessarily
echoes other's speech
avoids eye contact
tends to avoid participating with children in groups
tends to avoid adults
daydreams, unaware
avoids difficult or new situations
irresponsible
manipulative
academic difficulties in:
    reading
    writing
    verbal communication
    spelling
    written communication

The psychiatric diagnosis is reactive disorder with possible depression and suspected learning disability.

The Developmental Therapy Objectives for Reg are:

Behavior

B-8   to use play materials appropriately, simulating normal play experience

B-10 to participate in activities such as work time, story time, talking time, juice and cookie time without physical intervention by teacher

B-11 to participate in activities such as play time, mat time, games, music, art time without physical intervention by teacher

Communication

C-12 to use simple word sequences to command or request of another child or adult in ways acceptable to classroom procedures

C-16 to use words spontaneously to describe own ideas, activity, work, or self to another adult or child

C-19 to use words or nonverbal gestures to show pride in own work, activity, or to make positive statements about self

Socialization

S-13 to participate spontaneously in specific parallel activities with another child using similar materials but not interacting

S-14 to wait for his turn without physical intervention by teachers

S-15 to initiate appropriate movement toward another child within the classroom routine

S-18 to participate in cooperative activities or projects with another child during organized class activities

Academics

A-24 to perform eye-hand coordination activities at the five-year level

A-26 to categorize items which are different but have generally similar characteristics

A-27 to write a recognizable approximation of first name, without assistance

A-30 to recognize groups of objects to five

KAREN

It has been a good day. The kids have been waiting for the party for almost a week and despite the excitement of costumes, games, party food, and even a visiting magician, none of the kids has "blown." They are getting better. All our efforts *have* made a difference.

Karen turned her round face toward the end of the table; her eyes were slits glaring through her glasses. She looked like a bitter old lady when she opened her mouth, "Is this all? Is this ALL you're going to do for our party?" With one sentence she skillfully cut through the teacher's good feelings, a reminder that the job was not yet finished.

Her mother sat in the observation room. "That's what I mean. She knows just what to say to make you feel horrible. Sometimes it's hard to love a kid when you get nothing in return. No matter what I do she doesn't appreciate it. You know, if Phillip and I separate, I want to keep the other two kids, but I think Karen would be happier with him."

Karen is large for her seven years, somewhat overweight, a very round face behind thick glasses. She appears unattractive, even dull looking, but she tests in the very superior range of intelligence.

She is a child with a poor self concept, restricted, immature, and withdrawn. Karen's responses in class are mechanical. She rarely shows enthusiasm. She cannot relate with peers and seeks excessive attention from adults, wanting to be hugged and carried by them. She often sucks her thumb and in moments of extreme withdrawal curls up in a fetal position on the floor. In contrast to this immature social behavior, Karen is sophisticated in her communication. She is a master in the art of passive-aggressive behavior. She is the first to point out mistakes others make, particularly adults, and the last to acknowledge that an activity has been enjoyable. Her intellect and the aggression she feels give her the verbal sophistication to strike at what she considers the heart of a matter. "Nothing you do can make me happy," or "The only reason you want me to look pretty is so other people won't think you have an ugly kid. I'd rather live with Daddy anyway."

The inadequacy which Karen feels often vents itself through a strong desire to control situations. Karen insists that things go her way, or else. She always has to be the teacher, the mother, the person in charge. She is bossy and authoritarian. When she cannot get her way she becomes whiney and withdrawn. Generally, children are not eager to play with her, thus increasing her social withdrawal.

Specific problem behaviors noted at referral by parents, teachers, and staff were:

immaturity
moodiness
regression
lacks confidence
resistant to discipline
self aggressive
frustrates easily

The psychiatric diagnosis is adjustment reaction.

The Development Therapy objectives for Karen are:

Behavior

B-11 to participate in activities such as play time, mat time, games, music, art time without physical intervention by the teachers

B-12 to spontaneously participate in routines without physical intervention

B-14 to contribute to make group expectations of conduct and procedures

B-15 to verbalize consequences if group's expectations are not reached

Communication

C-14 to accept praise or success without inappropriate behavior or loss of control

C-19 to use words or gestures to show pride in own work activity, or to make positive statements about self

C-20 to use appropriate words or gestures to show feeling response to environment, materials, people, or animals

Socialization

S-15 to initiate appropriate minimal movement toward another child within the classroom routine

S-16 to participate in a verbally directed sharing activity

S-17 to participate in cooperative activities or projects with another child during play time indoors or outdoors

S-18 to participate in cooperative activities or projects with another child during organized class activities

Academics

A-51 to read and write quantitative words for measurement of distance, time, money, fractions

A-52 to contribute to group projects requiring expressive skills

A-53 to write individual experience stories

MINDY

Mindy's hands dart from knob to knob on the dashboard. Windshield wipers, defoggers, radio (AM and FM), cigarette lighter, all activated in a brief 30 seconds.

"Mindy, it's hard to drive when kids play with the knobs. See if you can get that seat belt fastened again."

"God damn, I plays with what I want."

"You must really be tired after all that work you just finished."

"He made me do everything. You'd be tired too."

"I tell you what, Mindy, you've had a hard morning and you've already missed your lunch at school. Let's stop and get a hamburger before you go back to class."

Before the car stops Mindy is out of the car running gleefully in. We bring our hamburgers back and settle down for a picnic on the grass. She seems elated with this unexpected treat. She finishes her hamburger, looks me straight in the eye and says, "Thank you."

I pat her back lightly and leave my hand briefly on her shoulder. She looks at me intently and with great deliberation purses her lips to spit. Her aim is good. Saliva runs slowly down my cheek.

Mindy is an extremely aggressive, hyperactive child with a primitive lack of self control. She often erupts into frenzied rages which cause her to be feared by her peers and the adults around her. She also exhibits a constant suspicion of other people, even to the point of terror. She gets herself into situations where her aggression provokes hostility from other children and then she is immobilized with fear by their aggressive responses. Mindy has a need for nurturance but her suspicious nature and lack of trust toward others cause her to reject the nurturance she needs.

She acts out sexually by exposing herself or by being verbally provocative. When her provocation meets with a sexual response she runs shrieking and clinging to her teacher, regressing far below her six years.

At school Mindy is highly resistant to any routine imposed by her teacher. She cannot sit at her desk, refuses to do school work, and physically and verbally assaults teachers and children. She also is highly manipulative and makes every attempt to maintain complete control over situations.

The specific problems identified by her first grade teacher and center staff at time of referral were:

demands excessive attention
short attention span
distractible
apathetic
overactive
perseverative
resistant to discipline
aggressive to property
careless, unorganized approach to task
lacks comprehension
does not follow directions
easily frustrated
immature
talks excessively
listening difficulties
irresponsible
jealous

academic problems in:
    reading
    arithmetic
    writing
    verbal communication
    spelling

Somewhat in contrast, her mother identified only eleven problems:

short attention span
distractible
apathetic
forgetful
resistant to discipline
aggressive toward children
cries easily
talks excessively
academic problems in:
    reading
    arithmetic
    spelling

There are multiple psychiatric diagnoses: adjustment reaction, inadequate personality with aggressive-hostile reaction, and associated learning disability. Suspected socioeconomic deprivation and generally delayed development are noted also.

The Developmental Therapy objectives for Mindy are:

Behavior

B-9   to wait for her turn without physical intervention by teacher

B-10   to participate in activities such as work time, story time, talking time, juice and cookie time without physical intervention by teacher

B-11   to participate in activities such as play time, mat time, games, music, art time without physical intervention by teacher

B-12   to spontaneously participate in routines without physical intervention

Communication

C-11 to use simple word sequences to command or request of another child or adult in ways acceptable to classroom procedures

C-12 to use words to exchange minimal information with an adult

C-13 to use words spontaneously to exchange minimal information with another child

C-16 to use words spontaneously to describe own ideas, activity, work, or self to another adult or child

Socialization

S-14 to wait for his turn without physical intervention by teachers

S-15 to initiate appropriate minimal movement toward another child within the classroom routine

S-17 to participate in cooperative activities or projects with another child during playtime, indoors or outdoors

S-18 to participate in cooperative activities or projects with another child during organized class activities

(Pre)Academics

A-17 to recognize own body parts

A-22 to name colors

A-24 to perform eye-hand coordination activities at the five-year level

A-25 to recognize differences among shapes, symbols, numerals, and words

THE DAY BEGINS

Here comes Steven ... oh man, it's gonna be a wild day with Steven unless we can help him feel better. Watch him as he comes up the stairs. Block him. He'll get more and more anxious if we don't control him now. That's it,

arms around him from behind. *"It's okay, Steven, it's okay."* Calm him down. Something must have happened on the bus. Glad he got here early ... gives me a chance to get him together before the rest come.

"Let me go you god-damned f—— " Ignore language. It's not an issue at this point. This will take awhile with Steven today. Steven needs to calm down in the quiet room. Where's the monitor, Marilyn? Darn, she's out helping get Reg and Linda in. This is more important right now. I'll have to get the support teacher in from the bus area.

"Steven, it's okay. I know it was hard on the bus." Reflect his feelings. Soothe with your voice. *"I'm going to let Mr. Johnson help you so you'll be ready to join the class."* Let him know what to expect. *"Secretary, could you get Bob Johnson? He's on the porch helping kids in."* Watch it, Steven's kicking. Save your shins.

"Don't want no help you white bitch. I'm ready to come in. I'm in control." Watch out, he bites. Remember if he hurts you, the guilt will make him feel even more anxious ... and here comes the support.

"Mr. Johnson, I think Steven had a real hard time on the bus. When he feels better and is in control we'd really like to have him in class for talk time." Let Steven know we want him in the room and what comes next in class. Also cue in the support teacher to the probable cause of his behavior.

"Aaaaaaaaaaa Aaaa"

"Mr. Johnson, Steven came right in the building today without running around." Praise Steven for any positive behavior.

"Hey, Mindy, good to see you. Look at that pretty dress. Slow down, kiddo! I can't get a good look at that dress at high speed." She sure doesn't waste any time getting in here—and already into her worksheets. So far that's about the only activity she's been successful with. It's the security of the concrete activity, I think.

"Where's all my work, god-damn you, you promised me lots." Move over there with her so that in her impulsivity she doesn't tear up what's there and make success even more difficult. It'd be nice not to have to worry about their next moves all the time.

"I remember you asking for more work,

Physical control of a child should be the last alternative in intervention. It should only be used to prevent a child from physically injuring himself or another person or to prevent a child's behavior from "spiraling" to the point where damage is done to the child's feelings about himself.

Voice tone and control is an extremely important device used by teachers. The teacher's voice at this point should convey calmness, strength, and security—those things which the child does not feel. At Stage Two the teacher lends much of her own self confidence.

Do not respond to his surface communication. Make judgments based on his affect and body language.

Limits set are not authoritarian.

The teacher must be able to anticipate the child's actions to avoid possible failure.

Mindy, and I know you like a whole bunch." Let her know you're aware of her needs. Reflect feelings. Good, her face brightened a little. Move in and redirect her. *"Mindy, how many fingers on your right hand?"* Good, she's looking at her right hand; her left-right confusion is clearing up. *"Ok, count 'em up."* A secure, concrete activity, guaranteed success.

"One-two-three-four-five"

"Right! And you know what, Mindy, that's just exactly how many worksheets you have today—a big ole pile! And after talk time you get to do every one." Praise her success, then let her know when she can do them. *"Here's your chair. We have talk time at the table. It's gonna be a surprise."* Positive redirection. Works better than saying, *"Sit down!"* Also lets her know expectations, and the lure of a surprise helps her be successful in meeting them.

"Mindy, here comes Karen. Hey, cutie. Good, Mindy's in her chair and Karen will be in her chair in a minute." Linda is helped into classroom by the monitor.

"He was my friend. Before we made a 'greement we'd be friends, but he took my pocketbook and went through all my stuff and now he's not my friend 'cause he tore all my papers up that I wanted to show . . ."

"Hey, Linda. Sounds like you and Reg . . ."

"He tore up all my papers that my teacher said I did kinda good on and now we're not friends no matter what and I don't like coming here 'cause I get nervous."

Better help her get settled while the monitor goes out to find Reg. Let Linda know expectations and then reflect her feelings. Also keep Mindy and Karen involved.

"Linda, Karen, and Mindy are gonna try and think of the surprise for talk time. Now think, Karen and Mindy, of what's purple and orange and pink and you've seen it in here before. Linda, when you're ready you can think too." Help her in the chair. Hold her some or she'll be running out soon. Never saw a kid so anxious. A regular "little old lady."

"When you guess it, keep it a secret. Put your hand on your mouth, Mindy and Karen." Help them stay with activity.

"It's okay, Linda, it's hard riding in the car with other kids sometimes. You feel so nervous, don't you? Good, now you're sitting down just

like Karen and Mindy." Soothe her, reflect her feelings, praise her for appropriate behavior, and use other children as a model. That will help them too.

"Yeah, I just feel . . . nervous. Everybody makes me feel nervous. My stomach hurts and my paper's all messed up and I feel like crying all day." She's more under control now and is trying to manipulate for more attention. Give her a little more support and move on into activity.

"Sometimes when you sit really quiet it helps you feel better. It's okay now." Ruffle her hair. *"You look so pretty with that smile."*

Mindy's just about to leave us, gotta move quickly into activity. Darn, wish they would get back with Steven and Reg. Reg must be around the building by now. What a start.

"Did you guess what's purple and orange and pink? Wait, say it to yourself. We're gonna whisper it in my ear. It's hard to wait, huh, Mindy?" Reflect Mindy's feelings . . . helps her wait longer.

"This is so easy." Wish I could get Karen to loosen up and enjoy something. So hard to keep her motivated when she's so much brighter than the others.

"You like hard work, huh, Karen?" Reflect her feelings.

"Now when you all whisper in my ear, I'm gonna whisper back and tell you if you got it." Kids like to whisper. Makes it magic and it's a good way to get in a little nurturance. Creates a quiet tone too.

"God-damn you and your whispering. Don't get your filthy face near me." Sometimes it's so hard for Mindy to accept being close to a teacher. She's so ambivalent about forming relationships. OK, hold off on her. Go on to Linda. Hold her head gently as she whispers. Let Mindy see that interaction with Linda will be enjoyable.

"Did you say telephone, Linda? You have a good memory. That's RIGHT!"

"Hey, Steven, you're just in time for talk time. Glad you made it." Bob did a good job on him. He looks better. Praise him now. Welcome him back and let him know what we're doing. Involve him.

"Did you all see Steven find his chair so fast? What a man!"

"Hey, Steven!" Mindy has been really friendly with Steven. I wonder what she will do with the relationship today?

"Steven, we're trying to think of something we've seen in here before that's purple and orange and pink. Linda just finished whispering her guess in my ear and Mindy has her mouth all ready to go. Good, Mindy, get your mouth right up to my ear." Now pray she doesn't spit or yell. Go easy with her. She doesn't respond to touch as well as Linda.

"Mr. Johnson, while I'm listening to Mindy, let Steven whisper his guess to you. And then it will be Karen's turn." Steven needs involvement now.

"Right, Mindy! It is the telephones we made. You remember well. You've got such a nice soft whisper too!" Praise her for modulating her voice.

Now baby Karen. She needs to be a little girl. She acts like an old lady when she's in the group. Tweak her on the cheek and hope for a smile. "Right, Karen, you've got it. And I like that big, pretty smile on your face." Reinforce her about her appearance.

"Do you know what? Everybody got the right answer on the first guess. Everybody knew it was the telephone we made yesterday. You kids are so smart!"

"You don't have to be so smart to guess that." Karen's passive-aggressiveness coming out. Don't fall into the trap of responding to her bait. Say something so that Karen's comment doesn't alienate her from the others. "I guess it was pretty easy for you, huh, Karen? It's neat to have so many kids in here that always know the answers."

"Reg didn't get to guess, huh, teacher? 'Cause he was running around outside. Sometimes he gets me to run with him but he's not my friend now and I'm not listening to him anymore 'cause he..." Cut in on it before she gets worked up again. Touch her. Good, Bob's supporting Mindy and Steven. Karen's just sitting as usual. Touch her with the other hand. Now... support Linda for not allowing Reg to manipulate her and let her know that when Reg comes in the room it's going to be okay.

"Linda, it's really neat... you came right in the room. You're really growing up. I think you're worried about when Reg comes in. We will help him sit down and then he will do his work. I bet you think he'll be mad at you... but Mr. Johnson and I will help both of you. It will be okay." Now, it's up to me to make sure it will be.

"Mr. Johnson, the kids have been waiting so long. Could you get the telephones? Do you kids remember your phone numbers?"

"I'm #1."

"Right, Steven."

"Gimme a phone!"

"Don't worry, I'm going to give you each your phone."

"Mindy's #2, Karen's #3, and Linda's #4."

"Hurry up!" "Number two is doo-doo!"

"It's so hard to wait, but they're doing a good job, huh, Mr. Johnson?"

"OK, now, #1 call #2 and tell her to call Mr. Johnson."

"Dial Mindy's number, Steven. Good. R-rrrrring."

"Hello"

"Hello"

"OK, Steven, now tell her to call Mr. Johnson."

"Call Mr. Johnson."

"Steven, watcha call me for. Want some booty, huh?"

Here we go. I was wondering when Mindy would start the sex thing with Steven. Try redirection first.

"Mindy, Steven wants you to call the teacher."

"Nooo way, he call 'cause he want some booty, huh, Steven." No deal, she's going to keep it up and Steven won't hold much longer.

"Mindy, it bothers Steven when you put his hand there." This needs physical intervention.

"Mr. Johnson, could you help Mindy put Steven's hand on the table?" It's too late, Steven's on Mindy.

"Mindy's my girl and I'm gonna get her booty."

"Mr. Johnson, Steven's having a hard time staying in control. Could you help him sit in his own chair?"

And now Mindy's crying. She knows just what to do to set Steven off sexually and then when he comes at her, she's terrified and runs straight for me. She has a lot of trouble understanding that what others do is a result of what

Turn a child's negative response into a positive one.

Let a child know what to expect.

This activity builds communication and socialization skills.

Anticipate behavior by knowing how much the children can tolerate.

During a crisis situation try and be aware of all the children's reactions so that they can be dealt with therapeutically.

she does. Meantime Linda's giggling hysterically and Karen's strict attitudes are in for a shock. It is the first time I've seen her interested in anything though.

"Mindy, it's okay now. Mr. Johnson is helping Steven and I'm helping you. Mindy when you say things like that to Steven and put his hand there, it really bothers him and then he jumps on you and you get scared. It's gonna be okay. I think you can remember next time."

"Yes, I'm ready. I've been ready."

And finally here comes Reg with the monitor. *"Reg had a hard time coming in today but he's ready now and said he wanted to be here for talk time."*

Now help him in . . . make him feel comfortable. *"Hey, Reg, really glad you came . . ."*

"He tore up all my papers and now he's not my friend and . . .

"And next time I'll tear up your little ass too."

"Reg, here's your chair."

"It's okay, Linda."

Now . . . make it okay!

Ignore profanity. It is done to gain attention. There are much more significant issues to be dealt with at Stage Two.

SUCCESS IS THE STAGE TWO SPRINGBOARD

Beginning teachers often comment that they feel success is "contrived" in a Stage Two classroom. True. It may be created from a flimsy incident or from the most meager response. But somehow the cycle of failure must be interrupted and reversed.

Assess individual strengths within the group. One child's strengths might be used to help another child grow. In this instance, Reg was quite imaginative during play. Interaction between him and Steven was encouraged to help broaden Steven's play experiences.

The dialogue you just finished reading is TALK TIME—the start of a very typical day for a Stage Two class. As you probably noted from the teacher's thoughts and the way she interacted with the children, the most important goal to keep in mind at Stage Two is that the children experience success. If they do not experience the sense of self worth which comes from successful interaction, they will not continue to progress. It is up to you to provide situations so that the child will be successful. There are a number of techniques which you can rely upon to help children be successful at Stage Two. Among these are positive verbal redirection, praise, a structured, consistent classroom, supportive reflection of feelings, touch, and verbal interactions between lead and support

teachers. In addition, the teachers must be tuned in to the responses of each particular child so they will know which developmental skills contribute to the child's success and those which are lacking and produce failure.

Steven, for instance, has an extremely low frustration tolerance in doing academic work. It is important that his work be nondemanding and limited to one or two problems per page with constant physical and verbal support and intervention. Because of his impulsivity and aggression it is important that he sit next to a teacher and as far away from other impulsive, aggressive children as possible. Initially, it was also necessary to provide Steven with a highly structured situation during free play in order to offer him appropriate models for behavior in a group situation.

More like a Stage Three child than the others, Karen has high academic ability and is facile with language. She had started at the center in a Stage Three class. During the eight-day prebaseline period, her socialization was so acutely lagging that she was changed to this Stage Two group in the hopes that she would begin to interact with children with similar socialization needs. Karen is passive and socially inhibited with peers and directs most of her social behavior toward adults. She needs a very structured, teacher-directed activity during free play time in order to help her begin successful movement toward peers. She does not have the social skills or self confidence to interact on her own initiative.

Mindy, an impulsive, aggressive child, has needs much like Steven's. In addition, she is a child who needs concrete experiences in order to be successful. Directions and explanations must be very clear. She has little understanding of cause and effect, and it is necessary to explain consequences of behavior to her frequently. Emphasizing the positive consequences of constructive behavior seems to work more effectively than focusing on negative consequences. Socially, she often chooses not to interact with peers, so that, as with others in the group, it is necessary to provide her with numerous structured situations which encourage her to interact successfully.

In Reg's case, in order to ensure success, it is first necessary to get him in the building and finally in the classroom. He is the most skillful of "runners" and without daily physical intervention he would easily have missed the first half hour of each class. It is necessary for the support teacher to escort him from the bus to the classroom daily. His chair at the work table is farthest from the door and next to the support teacher. Lacking the basic readiness skills, Reg is "turned off" by academic work, especially reading, and the whole idea of "school" elicits few positive feelings from him. Reg enjoys situations related to construction work, farming, and animals. The teachers plan activities which link experiences in these areas to school related activities with successful outcomes.

Success for Linda comes in an atmosphere which is calm and in which expectations are clearly stated. When she fears failure she often makes aggressive or resistant statements. In these instances she responds well to the teacher offering her an out such as, "You are the biggest teaser I've ever seen," or "You say the funniest things," to which she would respond, "Yeah, I know," and do what she had just flatly refused to do. She becomes highly anxious when other children lose control and runs aimlessly and frantically around the room. At these times she is physically removed from the room by the support teacher. The emphasis at such times is on increasing her

self confidence in her own ability to successfully cope with the classroom expectations.

EVERYTHING SEEMS TO GO BETTER WHEN YOU'RE ORGANIZED

It's not a large room, and that seems to be important with these Stage Two children. The size of the room places boundaries on the children's behavior. The physical boundaries seem to actually assist with controls.

"Run away!" There's not enough space to go.

"Hide from others!" There are others always close.

Both for the child who is not fully in control of his impulses and for the child who is restricted and withdrawn, the small size of the room can help him move toward more appropriate action.

The room is well organized because this helps the child organize himself. The work table and chairs are at one end of the room. Individual desks are not used. Work folders are placed in reach of the children. Necessary and frequently used work supplies are arranged in separate, labeled boxes—pencils, scissors, crayons. If it is a beginning Stage Two class, each child will have his own personal materials and the teacher will hand them out. If children are ready for socialization objective S-18 (to participate in cooperative activities with another child . . .), then the materials should be in boxes which the children share. Likewise, play materials are kept in boxes which are stored out of sight in cabinets.

There is a certain place in the room for every activity. For some of the activities, like PLAY TIME, which might demand more behavioral controls from children the area is marked off with masking tape on the floor. The schedule

Confrontation is usually an unprofitable technique with a Stage Two child. Offer children positive alternatives to the behavioral traps they build for themselves.

Individual desks are never used in Developmental Therapy. Because socialization is a major area of difficulty for all disturbed children, therapy time should not be spent alone.

of all activities is placed so that it is easily seen by the children, and picture cues are used to help them remember it. These same picture cues might be placed also in the areas where each activity is to take place.

Questions often arise as to how to display the work that the children do. Sometimes Stage Two teachers make the decision to show finished work right after it is completed and then store it in a folder. Some children are distracted by art placed around the room. Others destroy their own or another's work if it is left out. When work is displayed, it should be neatly arranged and not allowed to become old and tattered before it is removed. If the teachers show that the things the children make are to be valued and protected, the children sense this and feel, "I did something of value." With the warmth of sensitive response from the teachers the children will begin to feel, "I am something of value."

A well arranged schedule is another device which helps the Stage Two child experience success. In addition, the right choice of activities will encourage optimal growth toward the developmental objectives. Talk time, portrayed previously in this section, is a good activity to start the day. It is primarily a time for communication and socialization, but it is important in that it helps the children settle down at the table when they arrive and does not demand that the whole group start in unison.

Often, activities which could be used at talk time are telephone communication activities, using construction paper telephones which the children make; homemade puzzles, which the children can fit and glue together; homemade games, centering around academic objectives, which two children can play together and complete in a short time; discussions of activities at home or

In Chapter 4 numerous activities and materials for Stage Two are provided.

Lack of competition allays children's anxiety and helps prevent failure.

school; discussion of interesting objects brought in by the teacher; or very simple activities which would stimulate discussion about something which may happen later in the day (i.e., cut out pictures of ice cream if children are having ice cream at special time later).

After talk time, the teachers might move into WORK TIME. Usually at Stage Two individual folders are used. Work sheets are teacher-made and tailored for each child. Often, work time activities will be done with the group but with minimal group interaction. Activities centered around the Language Master, ITPA materials, Peabody or Duso Kits are useful for numerous objectives during work time. Other possibilities for group work time might center around specific developmental objectives such as recognition of body parts, counting, colors, letters, and numbers, discrimination activities, etc. Initially, the teacher leads the activities and encourages the children to take turns in responding and participating. Later, to encourage more child-child interaction, the children themselves take turns playing the role of teacher.

After work, the children will probably have been at the table for half an hour and need a break. Outdoor play offers an opportunity for physical activity and a change of scenery. Games should have simple directions, encourage body movement, and bring success. Rules of familiar games should be changed to eliminate competition and ensure that all children can participate at all times. Thus, games like dodge ball where children are eliminated from the group, would be inappropriate. Sometimes, teachers hesitate to take Stage Two children outside because the freedom of space encourages impulsivity. If the teacher carefully plans and structures her activity, this does not have to be problem. As an example, Steven, Reg, Mindy, and Linda were impulsive and difficult to contain outside. Management strategy centered around finding a theme which would be so stimulating that it would outbalance the children's impulses to run away and at the same time could structure the running into an appropriate activity. The answer turned out to be a unit lesson on race car driving. The children made cardboard steering wheels and racing helmets out of old rubber balls cut in half. A race track was roped off outside where the children were able to run their "cars." Green flags, checkered flags, stop signs, pit stops, and a teacher in charge of the races were all devices used to control the activity. It worked, and subsequently the roped off area became a horse pasture, farm yard, house, outlaw hideout, ad infinitum. Eventually, as the children began meeting some of their developmental objectives in behavior, the rope was not needed; the children used their own controls and stayed with the group.

Since being outdoors also has the disadvantages of having a difficult transition in returning to the building, it is important that a very attractive indoor activity follow. SNACK TIME seems to be the clincher. Snack time is an excellent opportunity for communication and socialization objectives (S-14, S-15, S-16; C-11, C-12, C-13). The enjoyment of the food and supportive interpersonal relationships loosens the children up and relaxes them. At first, milk and cookies should be passed out by the teacher. Later, a chart designating the "milkman-for-the-day" could be used. If the children progress rapidly in sharing materials, they should be encouraged to pass the snacks among themselves. It is a good time to help prepare the children for the next activity. Because cooperative play is so difficult for Stage Two

children and yet so essential to the socialization process, many Stage Two teachers plan for indoor play to follow milk and cookies. Toys which are in the play cabinet can be discussed, and selections might be made before the children leave the table. If role play or child drama is used, the teacher can begin setting the stage through her conversation at snack time.

Free play seems to be most difficult for the Stage Two child, perhaps because of the lack of a structured activity and the fact that children must use their own resources and controls. During the first week of the class just described, free play was such an explosive and anxiety-producing activity that it caused the rest of the day to go badly. Children destroyed materials, were disorganized, could not involve themselves in meaningful play, or were extremely aggressive in their play. It was decided at that point to have group games instead of free play in order to offer the children needed structure. However, the children were not able to tolerate this substitute either because it involved much waiting and turn taking. They also began to compete with one another, despite the modifications made in the games to avoid this, and a failure cycle rapidly developed.

The remedy proved to be child drama during play time. The lead teacher provided a dramatic situation for the children to act out in order to arouse their interest. She played the lead role in the drama, and in this way provided structure, set limits, and applied pressure to the children to respond. One of the first successful dramas centered around the "mean old witch" who constantly was stealing children from a little house in the woods. This solution not only helped the children bring some immediate organization and success to their play but also helped them to develop skills

A Stage Two child often needs to rely on the teacher for support and security. One way to achieve this during free play time is to provide highly motivating opportunities for success and pleasure.

Child drama provides the freedom to express and explore within the safe boundaries of make-believe.

which could be used in successful free play later.

A modification had to be made in the schedule to overcome the difficulties presented by this adaptation of play time. It was decided that the children would be more successful if the play time were shorter, and so a story time was added to the schedule. This was a pleasant contrast, a quiet time when the children could settle down and receive much needed nurturance and reassurance. A considerable amount of physical touch was used and the children responded well.

Story time should be held on the floor where children and teachers can be physically close. Stories should be well illustrated and should not tax the children's attention spans. Most importantly, story time should involve the children in communication. Alternatives to reading from a book include the children telling the story, flannel boards, film strips, or records.

Special time is the last activity of the day and is usually a group, fun activity: either art, music, role play, cooking, or treasure hunting. For extra-special times, guests such as firemen, policemen, jet pilots, skin divers, or football players can visit with the children. It should be something so special that the children look forward to it. You may have secret messages hidden in a mystery bag or surprise box telling what the special time will be.

Throughout these activities the teachers make every attempt to help the children feel good about their participation and individual contributions. If a child cannot do his work the teachers support him verbally or physically help him through the activity. Minute progress toward completion is praised either verbally or through body language (a wink, a touch, a nod). If a child cannot

bring himself to talk with others, the teacher plans strategies to elicit the child's talking. She may initially give the child the appropriate words or phrases to use in situations where previously the child had relied on body language. Games or activities are planned which require language. An example would be the telephone game played at talk time. If a child does not play with other children, the teachers find out what "turns that child on" in play. By letting him drop back to solitary play with that activity and encouraging another more outgoing child into parallel play, the groundwork is laid for interaction. With a teacher's help two cars may crash together. Or, "You run a gas station, Steven? Why, Mindy's car is out of gas. Mindy, ask Steven to fill 'er up!"

In Stage Two the teacher lends much of her own emotional strength, her own security, and her own sense of "good feeling" about the world to the child. This, coupled with a program which creates success, stimulates reality, alleviates failure and gives order to disorganization, helps the Stage Two child grow. He begins to rely less and less on the teacher and more on his own good feelings about himself. For all of this to happen, the teachers must remain sensitive to growth in a child and allow a child to use his own resources as they emerge.

EACH CHILD HAS DUAL WORLDS: HOME AND SCHOOL

Steven

His Parents   It was recommended that parent services be extensive for Steven's family because he was experiencing serious difficulties in school, and his home situation was extremely unstable. His parents were having marital problems

Each child has individual needs and must be responded to differently within the context of the group.

Teachers walk the fine line between suffocating a child with controls and allowing a child so much freedom that he fails. Sensitivity and understanding of the child's developmental needs will help find the balance.

The terms extensive, intermittent, *and* minimal *are described in Chapter 12 and are used to indicate the amount of parent involvement needed.*

and his father had left home. However, the father continued to support the family and came each Friday with rent payment and groceries. On each of these occasions, his mother became extremely upset and got into serious fights with his father. This also upset Steven and he openly resented his mother. To help stabilize the situation, the monitor began discussing with the mother how it affected Steven when he heard them fight and why he rejected her for this. The monitor began to plan with Mrs. A. what she needed to do to make the situation tolerable for Steven. For example, she began to go to the back porch or into the bathroom until the father left on Friday, in order to avoid a fight. She also had not allowed her husband to touch the baby before but began to allow it now.

Steven had been derogatory of his mother and accused her of driving his father away. Hurt by this, she would respond by paying attention to the other children. The monitor attempted to help her understand why Steven did that and to provide other ways for her to respond so that she did not increase his anxieties. She learned to treat Steven like the child he was, not burdening him with her problems. At the same time, the monitor began to direct her toward cleaning the house and spending effort on herself, things which made her feel better about herself and for which the monitor effusively praised her.

Although it was not a specific goal to help the parents reunite, as the mother changed her behavior, her husband began to visit her more often. Conferences were held with Steven's father to help arrange time to spend with him. He began to visit the house, taking him for rides, and buying him clothes and medicine.

While working with these parents, the monitor met resistance from other relatives; this slowed the process. At first, while his mother was working, Steven stayed with his grandmother, who shared her house with his aunt. The aunt in particular did not understand the center's purpose, thought Steven was crazy, and tried to disrupt his participation by throwing away his medication and trying to persuade his mother to withdraw him. His mother was easily manipulated by her relatives. The monitor, having gained the mother's trust, attempted to strengthen her ability as a parent to do what was needed for Steven.

The monitor also realized that it would be necessary to get the grandmother's trust. She was the dominant power in the family. To do this, the grandmother was involved as part of the therapy team. She participated in planning sessions which reviewed Steven's emotional needs and developmental objectives. She began to see the importance of Steven receiving his medication on schedule. She became so responsible for Steven that she would override any attempts of the aunt to throw the pills in the toilet. The grandmother also came to the center to observe Steven's class and attended parent training sessions in the evening once a week.

The aunt had been averse to Steven's taking medication because she was often ill, had many operations, and was afraid of drugs. At one point, when the aunt went into the hospital, the monitor went to visit her, asking if there was anything she needed done. The aunt said that her mama had not been to visit her because she did not have transportation. Within a half hour the monitor brought her mother to see her. From that point on, the aunt did not interfere with Steven's program any further; every member of his family was working with the treatment team on his behalf.

Although aware that Steven's mother had serious problems herself, the monitor chose to put her efforts initially into improving specific situations which would enhance the family's daily routine.

Relationships within a family are revealed gradually, as the family members come to trust the monitor and have confidence in the program.

His School While the monitor was involved with Steven's family, school services also were very intensive. In a 10-week period the lead teacher made 32 contacts with the principal and teacher. When Steven enrolled in first grade it was such a disaster that the principal met with Steven's parents concerning their son's highly disruptive behavior. The principal explained to Steven's parents that he was not expelling Steven but recommending that he not continue to experience the anxiety and sense of failure he was obviously feeling at school. In short, Steven did not have the skills to cope with first grade. The principal suggested that Steven return to school as soon as intervention from the center was available to help him better cope with the public classroom.

Long periods of suspension from regular school make reentry extremely difficult for child and teacher.

Steven remained out of school for six weeks and attended only center classes. Efforts at this time centered around mastery of the preliminary Stage Two objectives, stabilizing his medication for hyperactivity, and preparing school personnel with management techniques for his re-entry. Weekly conferences were held with the first grade teacher and principal during this time. Discussion centered around helping them to gain an understanding of his behavior, the importance of a predictable routine, consistency and limit setting, and methods for enhancing his chances for academic success.

Arrangements were finally made for Steven to attend first grade for one hour a day. One half hour of this time was spent in the lunchroom. He was accompanied by the lead teacher and went to school immediately after class at the center.

Careful planning with the school to ensure Steven's success was essential for his continuing progress.

A week before he returned to school, the team began preparing him for his return. He reacted with no overt signs of anxiety and seemed to look forward to going back. On the Monday that he was to return, Steven erupted into a violent fit of panic. He was extremely aggressive and said he would never go back to school. Finally he began pleading with the lead teacher not to take him. Reacting to Steven's impassioned plea and to the thought of a grand spectacle on his first day back, the teacher assumed he was not ready. However, after debriefing that day, the team began to see that in not sending Steven they had allowed him to make a decision he was not equipped to make. As a result, he manipulated the whole treatment team out of a decision which previously had been considered therapeutic and correctly timed. It was quite understandable that Steven would feel panic on reentering and would express this anxiety by acting out as he had done.

The next morning Steven again "blew his controls," but this time he was physically carried to the car and buckled in. In the meantime the school was called to let them know of his highly anxious state. Steven cried all the way to school. By the time he arrived he was only whimpering. But once he saw the building, he again broke into a tantrum and had to be dragged to the cafeteria. The important concern was to move him through the activity, letting him know without signs of ambivalence that he was going to return to school, that he would be supported there, and that he could have successful experiences there.

Once Steven saw the other children, he stood up and only passively resisted his return. He would not eat, but he did walk through the line and seat himself. During the one half hour he spent in the classroom he engaged in all the activities and he looked as if he was enjoying himself. The other children and his teacher were warm and responsive to him. As they drove away from the school, Steven looked up at the lead teacher and said, "You know what, I didn't think they wanted me there!"

Gradually, Steven's time in school was increased. The lead teacher drove him to school but waited in the teacher's lounge for him. Later he began riding the bus to school and the lead teacher picked him up. Eventually he was allowed to ride the bus home. Steven began to view staying in school as a privilege. Often he would resist leaving, suggesting that he should stay longer. But the team had learned an important lesson about leaving these decisions to a young, Stage Two child. It was important to have him leave while he was still successful so that "good feelings" would go with him.

Gradually his sessions were lengthened, through careful planning with his first grade teacher and principal. After three months Steven was remaining in school from 11:30 to 2:30. Arrangements were made with the principal so that if Steven began having problems which the teacher felt she could not handle therapeutically in the classroom, the center would be called to help him through the crisis. This intervention, usually occuring about every 10 days, took the form of removing him from school for the day, reflecting his feelings, and reviewing for him the behavior which had precipitated his removal. Infrequently, if Steven had a particularly hard time controlling himself and had been aggressive with other children, the principal would request that he be removed for several days. During these times, classes at the center continued for Steven.

With a responsive, understanding, and flexible school staff and with intensive intervention from the center staff, Steven's reintegration into his school classroom was successful. This is not to say that he now attends school problem free, but it is to say that he is there, that

his behavior can be tolerated, and he is one step closer to the normal life style for a six-year-old.

Linda

Her Grandparents Intermittent parent services were planned with Linda's grandparents. Objectives included working in four major areas: (a) feeling put upon by the natural parents to care for Linda, (b) hostility toward the natural parents, (c) hostility toward Linda, and (d) Linda's voicing preference for her natural parents. Another major focus was helping her grandmother learn and implement constructive management techniques.

It was her grandmother who came in to the center for conferences and observation of the class. She experienced the major difficulties with Linda and the grandfather could rarely get off from work. The grandmother found it difficult to express her bad feelings toward Linda at first but began to welcome a chance to discuss them. In the course of these discussions, the monitor reflected the grandmother's feelings and helped her understand them. She also began to understand Linda's feelings and behavior. At that point, they began to discuss things that the grandmother might do to improve her relationship with Linda.

The grandmother had been doing things for Linda that would let her know she cared about her, but Linda would not reciprocate or return her affection. With encouragement by the monitor and a new understanding of why Linda had difficulty expressing affection, the grandmother tried again to cook with Linda and do other things she enjoyed. She also tried to praise Linda when she was helpful. The monitor at first provided much support for the grandmother so that she would continue this behavior;

When a principal feels that a child cannot be managed in school, the child's treatment team continues to work with the family, child, and school, using the suspension as a catalyst for therapy.

The quicker the cycle of negative feelings and hostile responses in a family can be broken, the sooner positive relationships can begin.

but eventually Linda began to respond, enjoying the activities and reaching a point where she could tell her grandmother she loved her. This reciprocal relationship further diminished the grandmother's feelings of hostility and helped to decrease Linda's anxiety as well.

At the same time, the monitor helped the grandmother develop consistent management techniques so that she was not manipulated by Linda's protestations of preference for her natural parents nor other complaints. This helped to further decrease the grandmother's hostile feelings, because she felt more competent to control Linda's behavior.

Linda has become much more responsive to her grandparents, and their love has grown to the point that they do not want to consider ever giving her up. Even though their relationships with Linda have become more pleasant and their parental skills more effective, the grandparents continue to need support periodically.

Her School Services to Linda's second grade teacher usually took the form of visits to the school by the lead teacher, with classroom observation followed by a conference after class. Linda was referred late in February, and negative behavior patterns between Linda and her teacher were well entrenched by the time she was enrolled at the center program. Her behavior in the classroom was marked by extremely high anxiety. She constantly and inappropriately demanded the teacher's attention. She talked incessantly. She was resistant to limits and she could not (or would not) complete any work assignments. She had an extreme fear of being rejected, and this seemed to result in her constant demands for attention. Her teacher, unfortunately, fed right into this problem; she rejected her. The teacher admitted open-

ly that she disliked Linda and found each day with her hard to tolerate.

Considering the fact that this negative relationship had been in the making for the past six months and that there were only three months left for Linda to remain in the class, to hope for sweeping behavior and attitude changes from the teacher would be unrealistic. Strategy centered around helping Linda and her teacher cope with each other for the next three months. The teacher was given a chance to ventilate her feelings toward Linda about once every two weeks, and the focus of each meeting was one behavior which the teacher found particularly hard to tolerate. Suggestions were made for management of only that particular problem. At the first meeting, the teacher said that Linda would not leave her alone long enough in the morning to take care of the business of the day such as collecting lunch money or taking orders for school supplies. Linda constantly interrupted by demanding attention and asking that her own individual needs be met. Her teacher usually responded by ignoring Linda; this only made matters worse. For this problem, it was suggested that the teacher make a point of meeting Linda outside of the classroom every morning. With a warm greeting and as much nurturance as the teacher could muster, she was to tell Linda that she knew that Linda had lots of important things on her mind and that she really wanted to hear them. In fact, as soon as homeroom business was over, she would have a special time to listen to all the things Linda had saved to tell her. During the second visit the teacher admitted that she had consistently used this approach and to her astonishment it had worked.

Perhaps the most important result at this point was that the teacher saw by not rejecting Linda and by establishing

Expectations for change in both children and teachers must be realistic. In this instance the simplicity of the expectations for the classroom teacher produced positive results.

structure which would help her delay gratification for attention, Linda's behavior patterns could be altered.

Two more behaviors were altered in the classroom in much the same way, and by the end of the three-month period the teacher was able to say that her feelings for Linda had changed for the better. Linda, on the other hand, proved even more malleable than the teacher. She had proclaimed a dislike for Mrs. B. when she began her program, but during the last week of class she asked the lead teacher how to write "I love you, Mrs. B."

Reg

His Parents Before intensive intervention with Reg's parents, Reg went through a constant cycle of misbehavior followed by physical punishment and verbal degradation at home. Invariably, when Reg had trouble at home he carried his anxiety with him to school and had more problems there. Eventually, the school threatened Reg with suspension for the remainder of the year. Until this time, Reg's parents had been uncooperative in working with the center staff. They would not come in for observations and were not at all receptive to home visits. The mother expressed her feelings succinctly when she said, "Us black people treats our kids different than you white folks does."

When faced with Reg's possible suspension they had no place to turn but the center. The team then met with the principal and Reg's teacher and discussed the anxiety which Reg brought with him every day from home. If the parents could change the way they dealt with Reg, his behavior at school probably would improve. Now that we had some leverage in working with the parents, the school agreed to suspend Reg for only one week, provided that the center provide crisis intervention in the school.

Once this arrangement was made, the parents began to feel that we could offer them some help. Home visits were made once a week to discuss Reg's progress in the school and at the center. Visits were also made following any crisis which occurred in the school. At this time, appropriate punishments were worked out, such as missing television for that night, rather than the whippings and tongue lashings which usually ensued.

During the many home visits it became increasingly apparent that Reg experienced much covert and open rejection at home. His parents openly discussed Reg's adoption in front of him, ·with the mother's response being that it had been her husband's idea and that she hadn't really wanted him. When really angry she threatened to send him away to a home for boys. In discussing how they made Reg feel, the mother said that Reg knew she loved him and didn't mean those things. Eventually, after the parents began to realize how much rejection and insecurity Reg had already experienced before even living with them, they began to realize how sensitive he was to any possible hints of rejection.

Intervention with this family was intensive. Both parents had many feelings to work out concerning the disappointment Reg had been to them, the imposition he had been, and their rejection of him. Because of these feelings, it was very difficult for them to see Reg's positive characteristics and the progress he made.

Additionally, the parents were elderly and had difficulty managing his behavior. At the same time that they rejected him, they also overprotected him, not allowing him the normal privileges and responsibilities of a nine-year-old boy. Thus, he was deprived of experiences

The crisis of suspension provided the parents motivation to cooperate. Then it was up to the treatment team to reflect the positive changes, in specific ways which the parents could appreciate.

This statement by Reg's mother is an articulate caution to monitors not to impose different values on a family.

which would have helped him adapt in school.

His School Helping Reg maintain himself in school demanded intensive efforts from both his teachers and the treatment team. Reg did not express himself easily, so that it was important that the team talk often with his teachers. His teachers were able to describe what had happened throughout the school day. Often these experiences gave the team clues as to why Reg seemed particularly upset or out of control on certain days.

The lead teacher met regularly with Reg's teachers in the school. In addition, teachers called the center immediately when Reg could not be managed in the classroom. At these times a member of the treatment team went to the school and worked with Reg outside of the classroom.

Reg responded best to firm, consistent setting of limits. He needed to know exactly what was expected of him. Since he had three different teachers in the school, it was important that they work together to maintain consistency, so as many joint meetings as possible were held.

There were times when Reg was so disruptive that he was brought to the center for crisis intervention. An example of such intervention follows.

The school called the center at noon saying that Reg had fought repeatedly with children in class and had been sent to the principal's office seven times that morning. Each visit was followed by continued provocation of other students in class. Reg's center teachers were not immediately available; therefore, the art therapist, whom Reg had known in class, was sent to pick him up at school and bring him to the center. The lead teacher returned 10 minutes before Reg's arrival and met Reg and the art therapist at the

door. She attempted to convey warmth and understanding and at the same time to communicate that the situation was quite serious. Her conversation with the art therapist centered around letting Reg know that she was highly concerned. Questions were directed toward getting at any background information which might be helpful in conducting the crisis intervention which was to follow.

Reg was taken to a classroom (which was not being used). The teacher began by reflecting Reg's feelings, "Sounds like it was a really hard day. You seem to feel so bad now." This along with supportive statements such as, "It's good you're here so I can help you. You're really in control of yourself now," seemed to set the tone for the session and relaxed Reg somewhat. But he remained unresponsive and reluctant to talk about the morning's incidents. The teacher decided that Reg needed still more time before the issues could be discussed. She asked the art therapist to bring something they could make Reg's lunch with, since he would miss his lunch hour. The making of sandwiches offered more time for Reg to feel comfortable.

After eating, Reg was more relaxed but refused to discuss the school incident. He left the table. The teacher, knowing that Reg would eventually seek contact with her because of their previous relationship, reflected, "Sometimes it's really hard to talk about things like that," and "Sometimes a boy just needs to think things over for himself." Furthermore, knowing that Reg had a strongly developed conscience burdened with much guilt concerning the morning's behavior, she said, "Reg, on Wednesdays I usually clean up the room to get ready for the children to come tomorrow. I'm going to straighten things up while you think." After this, she began to straighten up a shelf, ignoring Reg

Only the closest cooperation between school and center enabled Reg to eventually have a successful adjustment at school.

This incident illustrates the team work among staff necessary for the smooth conduct of therapy at times of crisis.

but feeling that he would eventually help in the clean-up.

In less than two minutes Reg was hard at work straightening the shelf with her. She remarked about how nice it was to have such good help and generally reinforced Reg for his appropriate behavior. Reg's attitude changed from sullen, ashamed withdrawal to one of cooperation and enjoyment of the activity at hand. After cleaning, he suggested that he and the teacher read a story together. She agreed.

The good feelings which Reg had about helping his teacher clean up the room were still not enough to enable him to discuss his morning, much less give him the strength to return to his classroom. Time was on the teacher's side. "Take the time," the teacher told herself, "and make him more confident about walking back into the classroom. Make him feel better about himself before you push for discussion of the incident."

Reading, fortunately, was a good activity for doing just that. He could be reinforced for his reading skills and given much nurturance at the same time. They decided to read the story on the floor side by side. The teacher touched Reg frequently during the story, and a natural, warm interaction ensued.

As soon as the story was finished, the teacher moved around in front of Reg. Sitting facing him, she reviewed his behavior from the time he walked into the room until the present moment. Emphasis centered around all of the appropriate behavior which Reg had exhibited, particularly that behavior which would enable him to function better in school, for instance:

Walking in the door of the center
Greeting the teacher politely
Walking straight to his own chair in the classroom
Helping the teacher clean up the room
Cooperating in a reading activity
Sharing food supplies
Listening and talking in a friendly way

Reg smiled broadly; he felt much better about himself than he did when he had walked in the door 40 minutes ago. He was also quite ready to forget that he had even had any trouble earlier in the day. This was symptomatic of Reg's behavior; he rarely learned from his experiences.

The teacher knew that now was the time to go back to the problem that had brought Reg to the center that day. She said, "Reg, I know you're ready to go back to school now, but before you go we need to talk about what happened in school this morning."

Reg talked, tested limits, and eventually discussed some of his general behavior that morning. Because Reg was not ready to discuss alternative behavior himself, the teacher helped him by suggesting other ways he could have behaved. To end the session, she and he used role play to practice alternative behaviors.

The teacher accompanied Reg back to school and stayed in his classroom for the rest of the afternoon. His behavior was consistently appropriate.

After school, a conference was held with his third grade teacher. She described Reg's behavior during the morning, and the center teacher shared what had occurred during the crisis intervention. Together they developed greater insight about Reg's needs and strategies for meeting them.

Karen

Her Parents Intermittent intervention was planned for Karen's parents because, although they were extremely cooperative, they were also involved in private

At this point some would say that the boy had successfully redirected the teacher from the issues at hand, specifically his problem in school that morning. But she realized that in order to get the child successfully back into school that afternoon, two things had to occur:

1. The boy's self confidence had to be reinforced so that he would feel worthy and strong enough to reenter his class room.

2. The incidents which occurred had to be discussed and alternative behavior had to be considered.

Throughout this session the teacher realized that there was no one specific issue at school which caused him to act out; it was a day when his anxiety ruled him, and he needed an extraordinary amount of support to maintain himself.

These strategies used with Reg to help him profit from the crisis at school illustrate an effective approach with older children who are finishing Stage Two and beginning to function at Stage Three.

marital therapy. It was agreed that the center would focus on improving both parents' interaction with Karen. Her mother was the disciplinarian in the family but provided no nurturance. As a result, Karen received most of her mother's attention for negative behavior, whining, and not helping when asked. The main objective of the center with Karen's mother was to help her give positive attention to Karen—to be more nurturing, to give praise when Karen acted appropriately and to compliment her on her physical appearance. Her mother also observed the techniques of Developmental Therapy used for Stage Two children through a one-way mirror in the classroom, with the monitor. Almost immediately Karen began to respond to her mother's praise, making it easier for her to continue.

Her father was extremely nurturing but had difficulty setting limits. This caused Karen to play one parent against the other, increasing their negative feelings about her and her feelings of insecurity as well. The center's objective with the father was to help him set limits for Karen and stick to them. In spite of the marital difficulties, he realized that Karen needed him to set limits. He also observed Stage Two management techniques through the one-way mirror.

Two things that particularly bothered Karen's mother were thumb sucking and overeating. The team agreed to work on these in class. The lead teacher discussed these problems with Karen knowing they would be difficult to overcome. They agreed on a signal to remind her about the thumb sucking and her eating and planned to substitute another behavior which would be gratifying to her. The monitor and Karen's mother also discussed how the same signals would be used at home. Mutual work on this

problem which had caused such negative feelings in the mother resulted in eased tensions between mother and daughter.

Toward the end of the 10-week period, Karen's parents separated. While this required additional adjustments, it ultimately created an easier atmosphere for Karen because the conflict between the parents no longer surrounded her. As the only parent, Karen's mother began to be more nurturing and allowed herself to show affection. She continues to need support and to attend the center regularly to observe therapeutic techniques. She also enrolled in the group parent training course offered by the center one evening each week.

Her School   School intervention for Karen was minimal. She had been referred by her parents, and the school reported no high priority problems. Karen's second grade teacher was contacted once every three weeks. The first conference was particularly fruitful. Her teacher had been so impressed with Karen's superior academic performance that she had overlooked Karen's immature and withdrawn social behavior. The teacher realized that Karen tended to be moody and rarely interacted with other children except in a structured academic situation. When opportunities arose for games or informal discussion with children, Karen chose to read.

Her teacher was able to use management techniques for Karen's sulky, moody behavior, and the techniques were effective. First of all, she made Karen aware of her own behavior and then reflected her feelings. The teacher provided nurturance through physical contact and attention. She helped Karen seek alternative behaviors and insisted that she participate in all group activities.

Mindy

Her Parents Intermittent intervention was planned for Mindy's parents because her problems occurred mainly at school and both her parents worked. Because the center did not have their new, unlisted phone number, letters were mailed inviting them to come to the center at specific times. None of the letters received a response, and the monitor began making home visits but never found the parents home. Discouraged, the monitor felt that these parents were being resistant. Finally, on one occasion, Mindy's mother was home and very cooperative in arranging an appointment. She was also extremely congenial and cooperative in future conferences. Most conferences were held at home with the mother since she did not have a car. Appointments were sometimes made after work so that the father could be involved as well. Every few weeks the monitor brought the mother to the center for observation of the class.

The same developmental objectives used at the center were appropriate for Mindy at home, particularly communication objectives so that she could use words appropriately to gain needs. These objectives, in time, helped to decrease her cursing and sexual expressions. Mindy's mother felt that she did things with Mindy from time to time such as playing games with her, cooking, and cleaning. She soon realized that she also needed to pay more attention to doing something with her every day. Many perceptions that the parents had seemed to be accurate and constructive, such as seeing that Mindy responded to affection and praise, that she liked to draw, and that she cared about her appearance. The monitor spent much time discussing and reinforcing these things with the parents.

On one visit to Mindy's home the monitor noticed several of Mindy's school papers displayed on the walls. The monitor and Mindy's mother discussed this idea and how she showed pride in Mindy's work by hanging it on the walls at home. She also agreed to display Mindy's work done at the center. On the next visit the monitor brought Mindy's pictures and her mother displayed them on the walls.

Because of the parents' work schedules, the monitor often made contact by phone to discuss progress and problems. In this way, the parents could praise Mindy's progress and work on difficulties in ways consistent with the Developmental Therapy program at the center.

Her School Mindy's first grade teacher was very threatened by her hyperactive, impulsive, and aggressive behavior. She was very defensive about her inability to control the child in her classroom. She resented and was suspicious of the center teacher's first attempts to talk with her. Initial strategy was to tell the teacher that we, too, found Mindy exasperating and very difficult to manage. We related some of Mindy's most disasterous incidents at the center. This let the teacher know that she did not have to feel so inadequate in dealing with Mindy. It was difficult even for people who had been trained to deal with this type of child.

Observation of Mindy in the Developmental Therapy class was postponed until her teacher felt comfortable in dealing with us. Instead, we asked the teacher to talk to us about Mindy's behavior. It became apparent that the teacher definitely disliked the child and had difficulty seeing any positive behavior at all. A particularly helpful technique was to have the teacher go through the daily schedule, starting from the time Mindy walked in the door in the morning until she left in the afternoon.

Be careful not to mistake a parent's lack of availability for disinterest. Parents often need a demonstrated result before they trust the center sufficiently to make themselves available.

It is a general policy at the center that children's work does not go home because others in the children's environment may not value it. In Mindy's situation this policy was not followed because her mother placed a value on Mindy's work.

If a child's teacher has strong, negative feelings about the child, it is usually best to approach the situation initially through strategies for helping the child adjust successfully to the teacher's routines.

This technique helped to pinpoint not only Mindy's problems, but also helped the teacher to see that there were times when Mindy did well in class. During these discussions, we became familiar with the teacher's basic management strategies and praised her for those strategies felt to be most effective in working with Mindy.

Some progress was made in improving the teacher's attitude and management of Mindy, but most success came in working with the school's resource teacher, who helped Mindy in the afternoons. She was most receptive and eager to learn effective ways of dealing with Mindy. She found that lowering her expectations of Mindy, simple directions, concrete activities, positive redirection, praise, and positive, consistent setting of limits were useful techniques. Eventually, the resource teacher became invaluable in helping Mindy's teacher.

EPILOGUE

All of these children have made strides in their adjustments both at home and in their schools (see Table 1).

Steven was terminated from the program after completing first grade. He entered second grade the following year. That year he received help from the learning disabilities teacher in his school and required very little intervention from center staff. He has been successfully reintegrated into a normal school environment. However, the monitor continued to work with his family after Steven's termination.

Linda continued to have some problems in school, although her second grade teachers found her much easier to manage than had her first grade teachers. Her grandparents have worked through much of their resentment and are beginning to feel a sense of pride in contributing to Linda's accomplishments. She continues at the center in a high Stage Three class.

Reg moved into a Stage Three class during his fourth grade year. He made tremendous gains in his ability to express feelings and in his self confidence. During the summer he participated in Boy's Club activities and in a relatively unstructured recreation program. In both of these activities he demonstrated a maturity which had not emerged before. He

Table 1. Length of Treatment and Subsequent School Placement

	Total weeks enrolled in Stage II	Present school placement
Steven	32	Regular second grade
Linda	20	Regular second grade
Reg	10	Regular fourth grade
Karen	19	Regular third grade
Mindy	35	Regular second grade

showed an increasing ability to get along with children his age. Because of the progress seen in these new situations, center staff began investigating the possibility of a new school situation where Reg would not be subjected to the pressures of negative peer group and teacher expectations at his previous school. Reg's parents continued in their attempts to be more consistent and fair with their management techniques at home. They gradually began to show more acceptance of Reg as he continued to improve. They also began to allow him opportunities which helped him in his growth. This is evidenced by their giving him permission to attend the Boy's Club and recreation program, something they had not permitted in previous summers.

Karen was terminated from the program during her second grade year. She was showing pride in herself, was making friends in school with her teacher's help, and was indicating interest in joining a Girl Scout troup. The following summer she was enrolled in a program which encouraged creativity in gifted children. Reports from that program indicated that she had responded in a spontaneous, socially well adjusted manner. Her parents divorced after going through a tenuous separation during Karen's third grade year. The resolution of this conflict seemed to further strengthen Karen.

Mindy's behavior in school improved dramatically when she entered second grade. Her new teacher was firm, consistent, and provided a very stable source of nurturance and approval for Mindy. She was terminated from the center since she was doing so well at school. During that year she received no intervention from the center other than periodic visits with her teachers to check on progress.

chapter 9

THE STAGE THREE CLASS MEANS LEARNING SKILLS FOR GROUP PARTICIPATION

Cynthia Cook, Lead Teacher, and
Ola Jennings, Monitor-Parent Worker

Deprivation

Reactive Disorder

Learning Disability

Inadequate Personality

Slow Learner

Behavior Disorder

Aggression

Hostility

INTRODUCTION

It is difficult to write an introduction to a Stage Three class. Probably these children exhibit more acceptable behavior and more outrageous, rebellious behavior than children at any other stage of therapy. They fool most people with their shyness or sophistication. They can also fool people with the most primitive, raw behavior imaginable. To their parents, teachers, and acquaintances they are frustrating paradoxes of good and bad. For instance, they make up rules, and then ask to be personally exempted from them. They reject overtures of friendship and then seek to repair the same friendship. They refuse to tell you when they are upset but will tell the child sitting next to them. This happens at home, at school, and in the Developmental Therapy class.

A poet could write beautifully of the paradoxical nature of these children projecting a bleak image of isolation. In any case, they are struggling to fit into a society composed of groups with rules. They belong to their outside world just as much as they belong to the treatment group. That is why the emphasis in Stage Three is placed on groups and expectations.

Helping these children to fit in requires considerable sensitivity, sincerity, time, and hard work. Going out at night to settle family disputes, taking a child to the doctor, or trying to adjust the school curriculum is just as much a part of treatment as conducting the Developmental Therapy class. Somehow, just about the time you begin to question yourself and your program strategies, the children begin to adapt and communicate effectively with others. Suddenly, they have mastered Stage Three objectives and are ready to move to Stage Four or leave the center.

VICTOR

A third grader, Victor has a history of school absences, untruthfulness, denial of behavior, and aggression toward children. He cannot relate to his peers and manipulates demandingly for his teacher's attention. Victor can do academic work at his grade level but does not seem to find adequate satisfaction in this form of achievement.

Victor is an alert, verbal, and friendly boy. He has an awareness of his own feelings but lacks appropriate ways of dealing with his frustration, anxiety, and anger. He believes his feelings are more important than the feelings of others and often tries to justify his hitting, pouting, or verbal abuse of another child.

His absorbing need seems to be for adult approval. Roots for this longing may be in his parents' divorce and his subsequent separation from his natural father. Also, ensuing struggles for acceptance from a traveling stepfather may have magnified the problem.

High priority problems checked by his parents, teachers, and the center staff at the time of referral were:

short attention span, unable to concentrate
distractible
aggressive toward children
aggressive toward property, rules
does not complete tasks, careless, unorganized approach to assignments
hand writing and coordination
talks excessively
untruthfulness
moody, overly sensitive
sad, irritable
irresponsible
tries to control others (critical of others, influences others, manipulative)

The psychiatric assessment is a reactive disorder. He is enrolled in a Stage Three class, where emphasis is upon acceptance of each individual as a valued and contributing member of the group. Victor's verbal skills are recognized as a strength which can be directed toward explorations of his own feelings in relation to other people.

The developmental objectives set for Victor the first five weeks are:

Behavior

B-15   to verbalize consequences if group's expectations are not reached

B-16   to give simple reasons for expectations

B-17   to verbalize other ways to behave in a given situation

Communication

C-19   to use words or nonverbal gestures to show pride in own work, activity, or to make positive statements about self

C-20   to use appropriate words or gestures to show feeling responses to environment, materials, people, or animals

C-22   to verbally recognize feelings in others

Socialization

S-20   to share materials, activities

S-22   to participate without inappropriate response to activity suggested by another child

S-23   to indicate developing friendship by preference for a particular child or children

Academics

A-44   to listen to a story and respond with appropriate answers to questions

A-48   to participate in group activity for writing experience stories, dictating to teacher, or working on murals

A-52   to contribute to group projects requiring expressive skills

LEWIS

Lewis is an old timer at the center. He is now 11 years old and has been re-referred by his fifth grade teacher. He was first referred for severe behavior problems when he was in first grade. At that time he had progressed through Stage Two and was provisionally terminated during his second year in school.

A "slow learner," Lewis reacts poorly to both home and school expectations. A low frustration tolerance and a high level of anxiety continue to plague and isolate him. Although attractive in appearance and seemingly self confident, Lewis remains on shaky ground. He is self conscious about his performance of tasks and denies his problems in academic areas. When angry with himself, he strikes out at his group or an adult who is in a helping role. He often attempts to sabotage the group's success. He needs approval and works hard for praise but regresses rapidly when left on his own. Other children fear his disruptive behavior and hostile acting out. This fear, combined with his verbal skill, makes him an influential leader in his group. In contrast, he conveys detachment and an apathetic attitude toward organized community activities.

Lewis' mother suffers periods of severe depression sometimes requiring hospitalization. She has raised him alone with the general attitude that tomorrow may not be any better than today.

Problems noted by the staff, parent, and school at the time of re-referral are:

lacks interest
resistant to discipline, directions, and/or structure
restless
immature behavior
unable to express feelings appropriately
obscene language, cursing, sex talk

moody
irresponsible
tries to control others, critical of others
influences other's behavior, manipulative
reading and math deficiencies

Lewis' psychiatric assessment reports a reactive disorder manifest through hostile-aggressive behavior, learning disability and environmental deprivation. He was reenrolled in a Stage Three class.

The developmental objectives for the first five weeks include:

Behavior

B-16 to give simple reasons for group's expectations
B-17 to tell other, more appropriate ways to behave in a given situation; individual focus (may not be able to implement alternatives)
B-18 to refrain from inappropriate behavior or breaking group rules when others in the group are losing control
B-19 to maintain self control and comply with group procedure

Communication

C-19 to use words or nonverbal gestures to show pride in own work, activity, or to make positive statements about self
C-20 to use appropriate words or gestures to show feeling responses to environment, material, people, or animals
C-22 to verbally recognize feelings in others

Socialization

S-19 to take turns without verbal reminders from teacher
S-20 to share materials, activities (minimal verbal reminders from teachers)
S-22 to participate without inappropriate response to activity suggested by another child
S-23 to indicate developing friendships by preference for a particular child

Academics

A-47 to write basic words from memory or dictation
A-48 to participate in group activity for writing experience story, dictating to teacher, or working on mural
A-49 to write full name, address, date from memory

KENDRA

Kendra is 12 years old. This is her first referral to the center. Her sixth grade teacher describes her as being very aggressive, constantly fighting with peers, and verbally abusive to teachers. She has been suspended from school four times this year for fighting. Previously, the school had suggested a special education placement because of her severe academic problems, but her parents would not agree to this.

Physical complaints are common with Kendra, possibly because of her weight problem. Eating is her main outlet when frustrated. However, there is basis for concern because she is on medication for grand mal seizures. There are indications also that Kendra may have petit mal seizures, manifest by prolonged periods of staring or hesitation.

Her mother sees Kendra as shy and dependent. Yet Kendra is expected to shoulder most household tasks, including care of two younger brothers. Her relationship with her father is not good. Supposedly, he neglects Kendra in favor of her brothers. There is a feeling existing in the family that her father is ashamed of Kendra due to her weight problem.

Kendra's home environment is not one in which a great amount of healthy development can take place. Her parents have innumerable marital problems. More than once Kendra has seen physical violence between her parents. On one occasion, her mother was hit on the head with a metal table leg and was unconscious for more than 30 minutes.

The major problems identified at the time of referral are:

demands excessive attention
short attention span
distractible
forgetful
resistant to discipline
immature behavior
unable to express feelings appropriately
untruthfulness
aggressive toward children
lacks comprehension of assignments
crying spells
lacks confidence
regressive behavior
daydreams
stealing
suspicious
academic problems:
    reading
    arithmetic
    verbal communication
    spelling
    written communication

Initial psychiatric diagnosis is reactive disorder with suspected retardation manifest in severe learning disability. There is concern that brain damage exists also, and further diagnostic studies are needed. Recommendations are for enrollment in a Stage Three class and serial EEG's to determine appropriate medication for suspected petit mal seizures.

The developmental objectives noted for her on the baseline DTORF are:

Behavior

B-12 to spontaneously participate in routines without physical intervention

B-15 to verbalize consequences if group's expectations are not reached

B-17 to tell other more appropriate ways to behave in a given situation

B-18 to refrain from inappropriate behavior or breaking rules when others in the group are losing control

Communication

C-11 to use simple word sequences to command or request of another child or adult in ways acceptable to classroom procedures

C-12 to use words to exchange minimal information with an adult

C-16 to use words spontaneously to describe own ideas, activity, work, or self

C-19 to use words or nonverbal gestures to show pride in own work, activity, or to make positive statements about self

Socialization

S-20 to share materials, activities

S-21 to suggest to the teacher activities or preference for play materials for group activity

S-22 to participate without inappropriate response to activity suggested by another child

Academics

A-35 to recognize written labels

A-45 to read basic primary vocabulary words spontaneously in sentences

A-47 to write basic words from memory or dictation

A-48 to participate in group activity for writing experience story, dictating to teacher, or working on murals

BRAD

Brad sits in the waiting room looking as if the problems of the world rest on his shoulders. He seems self effacing and unloved, a child whom others use for emotional support.

Brad is nearly 11 years old. He has been referred because of inappropriate and aggressive behavior. He has temper tantrums and crying spells at school, especially after separation from his older brother, Eddie.

Brad wants to be liked. He attempts to make friends, but children avoid him because he cannot fit into their groups. He retaliates by picking arguments, and Eddie usually rescues him. Brad is a manipulator, often complaining of physical ailments in hopes of escaping from frustrating predicaments or attracting attention.

Brad's father has recently left home and moved to another state with a young woman. Declaring that she would not be able to keep a home going by herself, Brad's mother has developed severe depression.

Brad's outstanding talent is the work he can do with his hands. He is skilled in constructing model cars.

The psychiatric assessment for Brad reported a reactive disorder resulting in an academic lag. The top priority problems identified by his mother, teachers, and center staff are:

demands excessive attention
overactive
resistant to discipline
lacks confidence
temper tantrums
immature
untruthful
avoids new situations
academic problems in:
    reading
    arithmetic
    verbal communication

Brad is enrolled in a Stage Three class. The treatment objectives on the baseline DTORF are as follows:

Behavior

B-11 to participate in activities such as mat time, games, music, art, without physical intervention

B-12 to spontaneously participate in routines without physical intervention

B-13 to verbally recall group rules and procedures

B-14 to contribute to making group expectations of conduct and procedures

Communication

C-14 to accept praise or success without inappropriate behavior or loss of control

C-16 to use words spontaneously to describe own ideas, activity, work, or self to another child or adult

C-19 to use words or nonverbal gestures to show pride in own work, activity, or to make positive statements about self

Socialization

S-13 to participate spontaneously in specific parallel activities with another child using similar material but not interacting

S-15   to initiate appropriate minimal movement toward another child within the classroom routine

S-20   to share materials, activities

S-21   to suggest to the teacher activities or preference for play material for group activity

Academics

A-32   to recognize groups of objects to 10

A-43   to use ordinal concepts

A-47   to write basic words from memory or dictation

A-48   to participate in group activity or writing experience stories, dictating to teacher, or working on murals

MARIA

Ten-year-old Maria comes bouncing through the doorway of the center, screaming in a very loud voice at another child, "You'd better leave me alone, boy! I'm gonna tell Mama on you." The boy is her brother, David, and he continues chasing her. In a jumble of arms and legs the two of them fall to the floor, hitting and yelling profane, street language.

Maria's troubles began when she first entered school, encountering expectations and pressures beyond her coping skills. She has average ability for academic work but exhibits poor judgment in social situation. She yearns for nurturance and tries to meet this need through possession of material objects. She has poor impulse control and fears failure. If Maria has any doubt about a particular task, she refuses to do the work in a manner so defiant and aggressive that

removal from the room is often necessary. On many of these occasions, the center teacher has to physically restrain her. She loses control, screaming, thrashing and crying "Mama." As long as 45 minutes have been necessary to calm Maria and to provide the nurturing support that eventually helps her regain control and return to the classroom.

Maria lives in a housing project with her mother and five younger brothers and sisters. As the only source of support, her mother works long, hard hours and returns home exhausted in the evenings. Maria is expected to assume all domestic responsibility and the mother role.

High priority problems reported by her mother, teacher, and center staff on the referral checklist are:

demands excessive attention
short attention span
distractible
restless/overactive
aggressive toward children
easily frustrated
silliness
tries to control others, manipulative
immature behavior, verbal and nonverbal
unable to express feelings appropriately
obscene language
regressive behavior, verbal and/or nonverbal
physical complaints

Psychiatric examination gives an initial diagnosis of character disorder, with aggressive-hostile and predelinquent behaviors and socioeconomic deprivation.

Maria is enrolled in a Stage Three class. The baseline developmental objectives for her are:

Behavior

B-17   to tell other, more appropriate

ways to behave in a given situation

B-19 to refrain from inappropriate behavior or breaking group rules when others in the group are losing control

Communication

C-23 to recognize and acknowledge feelings in self

C-24 to use words to praise or personally support others

C-26 to use words to express own feelings spontaneously and appropriately

Socialization

S-16 to participate in a verbally directed sharing activity

S-19 to take turns without verbal reminders

S-20 to share materials, activities

Academics

A-47 to write basic words from memory or dictation

A-48 to participate in group activity for writing experience story, dictating to teacher, or working on murals

A-51 to read and write quantitative words

A-53 to write individual experience stories

HOW CAN A GROUP EMERGE?

Before the class arrives, you will find the lead and support teachers in the classroom with the monitor, mulling over the activities planned for the day. They review the previous day and the specific ways the developmental objectives will be used today. The monitor discusses which parents will be contacted and those who may

come for observation of the class. The lead teacher lists again the expectations for individual class members and does a mental check that each expectation realistically reflects a child's present capacity to be successful. When new challenges are planned, the treatment team is ready to help.

Just before the bus arrives, the support teacher goes to the entrance of the building, waiting with a warm welcome. She either accompanies the children up to their room or sends them on alone in order to remain with any who may need support. The monitor is nearby if need arises for extra support and encouragement or just to say "Good Morning."

The bus arrives and in they come. Victor struts by, smiling and saying something to everyone he sees. His comments are smug and haughty. The girls, Maria and Kendra, come in together and rush to hug the support teacher. Lewis cocks his hat over his plaitted hair and sits at the reception desk. Sending the others on their way upstairs, the support teacher moves over to Lewis just as he turns on the electric typewriter. She puts her hand on his shoulder, smiles and gives him the individual greeting that he has been waiting for, *"Hey, how you doing?"* He gets up. She reminds him to turn off the typewriter and push in the chair. They go upstairs together without further delay. Brad dawdles in, alone. The monitor greets him and they go together to an office. Arranged by the team, this procedure gives Brad opportunity to vent his feelings about members of his family and situations at home. This daily conversation enables Brad to find immediate relief for his anxieties about his family and better focus on the group activities when he enters class.

In the classroom the lead teacher greets each child, "tuning in" to the feelings they have brought with them. Usually such observations are used to make adjustments in the strategies the teachers will use and may or may not be brought out in the open.

The children cluster around the lead teacher at the table and discussion time begins. She directs the group toward a discussion of planning a special project for the group. When Victor suggests swimming, the direction of the discussion turns to what actually is involved, step by step, and what rules would be impor-

This daily, preliminary planning gets the team off to a good start. The monitor is able to keep the parents informed about the current program and the teachers are able to keep the day's activities close to the objectives.

Riding the bus may be a major problem for these Stage Three children with weak behavior controls and few social skills. Discussion time is used for unwinding and calming down. It also provides excellent opportunity for working on communication and socialization objectives.

Reflection of feelings and progress is important for all of these children. The teachers empathize with them and verbalize the more abstract, hidden, or unrecognized meaning of relationships.

"You're upset because Brad marked ink on your arm."
"You're doing a good job staying in control."
"That was generous of you to share your red paint."
"Lewis likes your picture. He wants to copy it."
"That makes Kendra feel bad when you call her fat."

The lead teacher always finds situations where children practice skills they are learning. Here, Kendra is able to show that she is moving toward mastery of communication objective C-16 (to use words spontaneously to describe own ideas, activity, work, or self).

tant. The lead teacher indicates that such an excursion is in the realm of possibility for this group, pointing out successes they have experienced in group effort. Kendra responds only when the teacher touches her or asks her a direct question. Brad enters during the discussion, and the lead teacher uses this opportunity to ask Kendra to summarize the discussion for Brad. She does so with little prompting from the teacher.

Brad and Lewis are excited and hop out of their chairs, but they are verbally redirected and reseat themselves. Maria is negative and cuts down the whole idea. Victor raises his voice at her, and she attempts to hit him. The lead teacher uses the incident to begin a discussion of feelings and says, *"Everyone is excited, everyone in this group is excited about swimming . . ."* Victor is still shouting at Maria.

The group is highly motivated to go swimming, but they fear Maria's explosiveness, her tantrums. Each knows if she loses control, it will be harder for them to control themselves. They immediately rely upon the teacher to provide the intervention which will make it possible for them to maintain self control and reach their goal of going swimming. She assumes the role of group leader and draws their attention away from Maria.

While talking the lead teacher has her hand on Maria's arm and is looking directly at Brad and Lewis. This relieves their anxiety and they begin to listen. Victor stops shouting and turns away from the group. When the teacher realizes that she has their fleeting attention she quickly stands up, raises her hand to her forehead, turns away from the group, and then quickly looks back to them. This happens within a few seconds. Not certain of what is coming, all the children look at her. She continues: *"It reminds me of the time when John Kennedy was a boy and wanted to go for a boat ride. Do you remember who John Kennedy was?"*

Victor, Kendra, and Brad all respond, *"Yeah, he was President of the United States."*

Maria chimes in, *"No he wasn't; he was stupid."*

The teacher provides a neutral, impersonal question for Maria. She uses the least amount of intervention possible to bring Maria back as a group member.

"Yes, you remember him. Well, he had two brothers who wanted to go on a boat ride with him. He was going fishing in the boat. But they were afraid that he wouldn't take them because they had been fighting with John that morning about who was going to play with some model racing cars . . . or something like that. John got really mad at them and told their mother. Anyway, their mother said that they couldn't do anything else that day if they were going to argue and fight about it. Does that sound a little like what's happening to us?"

Victor responds, *"Yeah, but Maria doesn't want to go. She can just stay here. I don't want*

The teacher's comments provide a framework for working on developmental milestones in the areas of behavior, communication, and socialization:
B-18 to refrain from inappropriate behavior or breaking rules when others in the group are losing control
C-22 to verbally recognize feelings in others
C-23 to recognize and acknowledge feelings in self
S-19 to take turns without verbal reminders from teacher
S-21 to share materials, activities

her messing up. I can't wait to get in that pool."

Reflecting his feelings, the lead teacher says, *"Victor really wants to go swimming."*

Brad quickly adds, *"If we can't go, I'm going by myself on Saturday."*

"Sounds like you are afraid that we will not be able to go, just like John Kennedy's brothers were afraid they couldn't go on the boat ride because they had 'messed around.' "

Lewis says threateningly, *"When someone messes up my swimming, I'm gonna get them on the bus. I'm gonna get them."*

Reflecting again, the lead teacher says *"Lewis doesn't want anyone messing up."* She shakes her head slowly, looking at the group, *"It makes him . . ."* She pauses. The group is watching her.

Brad quickly interjects the missing word, *"mad!"*

Victor adds, *"Makes me mad when things get messed up . . . so mad I could cut someone. I'm mad at that girl!"*

The lead teacher responds, *"It's really good when kids can say they are mad. Kendra, do you get mad when people mess around?"*

"Yeah, it ruins things."

"Right. Sometimes it does." During the conversation the lead teacher has been watching Maria with concern. Maria has been listening intently to the discussion. No feelings of anger are now apparent. The lead teacher decides to approach Maria in a more neutral manner. *"Maria, what would you do if you were John Kennedy's brother and you wanted to go on the boat ride? Remember, he's mad."*

Maria responds slowly, *"I'd tell him I wanted to go; that we wouldn't fight no more."*

"Good idea, Maria! That's exactly what they did; and they went on the boat ride." The lead teacher then asks the group emphatically, *"Is anyone excited about going swimming?"*

Victor responds with a grin, *"Yeah, we're excited, but we ain't mad. It's easy to get excited about swimming."*

Now eagerly involved Maria says, *"Yeah, I'm gonna jump in that pool so fast."*

The lead teacher senses that the group is ready to finalize this discussion. There is a certain amount of cohesion among group members. She closes the discussion by telling them that part of work time tomorrow will be reviewing rules for the swimming trip and talking about what they can do at the pool. She is already planning ahead. She plans to individually recognize each child's participation in today's discussion of feelings, including their fear of not being able to participate in the activity. She also makes a mental note to bring out in the open their ability to express their feelings of excitement and pleasure.

At this point, the lead teacher senses that an appropriate point has been made and that no further gains can be accomplished by extending the discussion. She advises the group that work time is next. With this cue from the teacher the class relaxes knowing what to expect. Each child gets his individual work folder from the shelf. Only Lewis holds back, and the teacher stimulates his interest by saying, "Wait till you see what's in that folder for you today." During work time the teachers move quietly around the table as is necessary. With a teacher on each side of the table, group and individual support can be given easily, as well as academic help and intervention when needed to remotivate. Redirection is the first choice among techniques during work time. The goal is to motivate the individual for the work activity and to stay with the group.

Lewis is frustrated again today trying to write the date from memory. He swears and slams the table. When he asks appropriately for help, one of the teachers moves to him, providing minimal cues for writing the sounds he hears. Maria, aware of her own higher academic skills, observes the others. She finds security in success. She tries to help Kendra with her assignment, reflecting her desire to be friends. The support teacher smiles supportively at Maria, "It's good you want to help. That's what friends do for each other. When she finishes you girls can get together."

Victor needs constant verbal intervention, remotivating, and signals from the teacher to lower his voice or refrain from storytelling. Brad's work is deliberate and slow. He enjoys Victor's clowning.

As the majority of the group nears completion of academic assignments, the lead teacher signals the approaching end of work time: "Work time is nearly over." Several quiet activities are available in another area of the room for those who complete their work early.

A final cue for those lagging behind comes, "We are almost ready for recreation. I hope everyone will be able to go out with us."

The recreation therapist enters the room and gathers those together who have finished work time. He takes on the lead teacher's role during the time he works with the group.

The class goes as a group downstairs to the outside playground. They gather in a preplanned area for talk about the rules and expectations. Contributions from the children are essential if discussion of rules is to have any lasting impact.

Today the game is kickball. Each child, in turn, gets three kicks. There is no competition. The recreation leader is the pitcher. The other players field from the bases, rotating as their turn comes. A score will be added for each ball caught by a fielder. The group cooperates well, enjoying the security of the often-repeated game rules. Lewis, who had remained behind with the support teacher to complete his work, rejoins the class. He is greeted by the recreation leader. Lewis moves nonchalantly through the activity, but the smile at the corners of his mouth cues the teachers that he is invested in the game more than he wants to admit.

Rules are maintained during the game and the consequences of breaking rules have been discussed. Brad misses a turn for leaving the group. He does not return when Kendra and Lewis remind him to come. The teacher reflects to the group, *"It sure is tough without a first baseman. We have the other bases covered and are ready to go. Kids who are in their positions are ready for their own turn."* Brad accepts the consequences and races back to first base.

But when these same consequences are applied to Maria, her wrath is evident. She storms away from the group to save face or to avoid coping with the consequence of missing a turn. She cries, *"You're not fair! I was on my way back to base."* And her body posture says, *"I hate you and your rules."*

As Maria's controls seem to wane, the recreation therapist says, *"Trouble on second base. Maria's having a hard time. She needs to go to the outfield and talk with one of the coaches."*

The support teacher takes the cue and

Tomorrow the group's work time will include use of the following Stage Three behavioral goals:
B-15 to verbalize consequences if group rules are broken
B-16 to give simple reasons for rules
B-17 to verbalize other ways to behave in a given situation

The teacher's comment to Lewis implies many things: sharing a secret, personal interest, implied recognition that he will be interested, and confidence in him.

For work time the group is physically close but interaction is not necessary. Individual academic tasks are prepared especially for each child's developmental objectives. The difficulty level and amount of work is often adjusted downward to allow for a child's tolerance level and need for success.

Transitions from work time to the next activity may be the most difficult part of a Stage Three schedule. Chapter 4 offers suggestions for ways to bridge this period.

The planning phase provides opportunities for work on behavior objectives B-13 through B-16 and socialization objectives S-21 and S-22.

Both lead and support teachers remain with the group during recreation, participating as support teachers for the recreation therapist.

The children understand the teachers' cues to each other. The teachers' interactions serve as models for children's interaction.

moves to help Maria. She approaches her calmly, respecting Maria's need for some physical distance between them. They walk toward the street in front of the center and then back into the building.

As soon as Maria is inside, away from the group view, she begins throwing magazines around the building lobby.

She proclaims loudly and clearly that she could care less about the group or anyone's concern for her. With considerable physical intervention, the support teacher helps her leave the lobby area. Maria is half resisting now walking to the quiet room. She and the support teacher have had a number of Life Space Interviews resulting from similar situations.

Maria resists interacting at first, *"Leave me alone, you — I want to get out."* Physical restraint is necessary to keep her, in her anger, from hurting herself or the teacher. While Maria is calming down, the teacher reflects her apparent feelings of anger and frustration. She also sets a specific expectation, *"When you stop trying to bite me, we can sit down and talk."* Maria is able to calm down rapidly. Within five minutes she is snuggled beside the teacher who no longer needs to touch or restrain her. As the Life Space Interview progresses, they talk about what happened, why Maria had to leave the group, how she feels, and how the incident could have ended differently. Before returning to class, they talk about how hard it will be to walk in at snack time and rejoin the group.

Snack time is filled with spontaneous conversation: some meaningful; some indicative of constructive interaction between children; some revealing pride in individual success in the game; and some imaginative storytelling which is identified as such, accepted, and redirected.

Victor: *"I used to play on a baseball team, and one day I hit a home run that went 500 miles. No one ever found the ball it went so far. I hit a couple of other home runs in that game too."*

Maria: *"You can't hit a ball 500 miles."*

Teacher: *"Victor, it looked like you made a couple of good catches today at recreation."*

Victor: *"Yeah, I caught three fly balls."*

Brad: *"Wow, you really got that one Maria kicked. I can't catch those high ones."*

Victor: *"Well you have to keep your eye on the ball. My father told me that. I'll show you how to do it tomorrow."*

Brad: *"Okay."*

Lewis: *"He can't catch it if it's right to him."*

Teacher: *"Maybe with some coaching he can. Everyone made some good catches today and we had a very high score. Does anyone remember the score?"*

Lewis: *"It was 17."*

Teacher: *"Right. What was yesterday's score, Kendra?"*

Kendra: *"Eleven."*

In this activity as in others, the support and lead teachers are aware of Kendra's hesitations. They speak directly to her or touch her to interrupt staring episodes. Her verbal participation is minimal, a reflection of her lack of communication skill. Attempts to ask questions and to draw her into the group interaction are not consistently successful because she fears rejection from the group. Often Kendra looks to Maria for approval and help. Lewis as usual tests the limits, requires verbal redirection, and devours verbal and nonverbal support as if never receiving enough.

As the group finishes eating, the lead teacher moves to conclude snack time, *"Two minutes left. You know what that means."* She scans the group. The support teacher picks up this cue and begins talking about the next activity. She asks Maria to remove the remaining graham crackers from the table. Brad flicks his milk carton across the room. The lead teacher responds to Brad by reflecting his progress. *"Brad, for three of the four days this week you put this carton in the waste basket. Four out of four would be a perfect record."* Brad runs up and gets the milk carton and puts it in the correct place. The teacher openly enjoys his pleasure in completing this task and moves near his chair while she begins to help the group organize the next activity.

Setting a quiet tone by speaking softly, the lead teacher again becomes the focal point for the children's attention. Special time is the next activity. For several days, the group has been planning a creative drama based on the *Wizard of Oz.* Yesterday they painted the yellow brick

A child in crisis is removed from the group to lessen the anxiety of peer pressure and the need to save face. Physical restraint to be effective requires that the teacher be firm, consistent, and supportive. The child who acts out aggressively needs the assurance that someone can intervene and help him regain control. The small quiet room's restricted space provides the privacy and seclusion necessary for minimal physical intervention.

Staying tuned into all the children and reading their faces for the unverbalized feelings requires teamwork. The support teacher can reflect to the lead, "Kendra feels good about finishing her work today;" or the lead teacher might comment "Lewis, you had a hard time today at recreation but those were good ideas you had for the story."

Snack time requires considerable sensitivity and teamwork from the teachers to keep the conversation on a positive note and involving every child.

Each change of activity in the daily schedule can mean a new start for a child. Although he may have faltered at one task, he can be successful in the next.

road and made scenery murals. Today they dramatize the first part of the story. The story is a familiar one for this group, and each child has selected the character he will be.

Everyone finds his place near the scenery. Kendra needs to be encouraged to leave the table for her part in the story. Brad, too, is reluctant to get involved but joins the group. Maria begins walking down the yellow brick road. She enjoys this type of expressive activity and seems totally engrossed in the story, narrated by the lead teacher. She meets Victor, the Tin Man, and asks him to come along to Oz with her. They exchange comments and walk along together. Then they meet Lewis as the Scarecrow. The support teacher has given considerable attention to Lewis to help him maintain self control until his time to get into the drama. The characters converse in a friendly tone and go off together on the journey.

Brad is restless. He's feeling neglected. As the Wizard he has not entered the play yet and is tired of waiting. The team has not sufficiently supported him or has misplanned the activity. The smooth, cooperative effort dissolves as Brad makes fun of Kendra's effort at being the lion. *"That old fat girl can't say the words."* Kendra flies into him, swinging and mumbling. The support teacher physically intervenes within seconds moving Brad away from Kendra, and enduring some blows herself. She and Kendra leave for the quiet room. There they explore her feelings about Brad's comments. The monitor enters the classroom, as previously arranged, and is given cues from the lead teacher that Brad had a hard time waiting. Brad is still excited and runs out of the room, down the stairs. The monitor follows him.

The lead teacher then brings the children together, praising them for staying in control, reminding them that Kendra will return as soon as she feels better and talks with the support teacher.

With that interlude behind them, the drama continues with the children having a picnic in the field of daisies. There the witch puts them to sleep. Kendra returns and the three characters want her to wake them up. She shakes them, smiling and involved again. Maria says, *"Say where you are going."*

And Kendra with Maria's prompting says, *"I want to go to Oz."* The lead teacher reflects that the characters are glad to have the lion along on the trip to Oz and the drama continues. Soon it is time to stop. The lead teacher tells the group that night is coming and the characters must find a forest to sleep. The group table is designated as the "friendly forest" and they all return as the story stops.

Brad returns just as the group settles down at the table. Sensing Brad's alienation from the others, the lead teacher talks a moment about Brad's part and how tomorrow all the characters will make it to Oz to see the Wizard and how happy they'll be to get his help. Brad smiles slightly. As the group makes positive, individual comments toward his role tomorrow he brightens considerably. This class often shows feelings of empathy toward each other. Each one knows what it's like to have a hard time and to feel alone because of it.

They shake hands across the table, a practice used for a daily closing activity. The group is commended for the cooperation shown in certain activities. *"We had a few hard times today, but it's good to have the group ready for tomorrow's episode on the trip to Oz!"*

THERE MUST BE CARRYOVER INTO HOME AND SCHOOL

Victor

His Parents At the time Victor enrolled, the staff recommended marital counseling for his parents. A private source seemed appropriate, but his parents did not follow through on the recommendation even though they had indicated their desire for assistance. In addition, their participation in Victor's Developmental Therapy program was minimal. The team monitor telephoned them frequently, requesting that at least one of the parents attend conferences. They failed to keep any appointments for 10 weeks. It was not until Victor had been

The successful outcome for this activity depends upon flexible structure. Consequences for breaking rules (B-15), reasons for group rules (B-16), and finding other ways to behave (B-17) will be worked out only as situations arise. A strong focus initially on rules could serve to inhibit practice of socialization and communication skills.

Restructuring might have allowed Brad and Kendra to continue the drama. Noticing Brad's restlessness the teacher might have used the following to intervene: "Let's all stop now and see if the Wizard is ready. You rest and I'll see if he is at the castle." This approach gives direct group recognition to Brad plus brief interaction with the teacher.

The support teacher could assist Brad in preparing his castle while he waits. For example helping him to get the castle ready, should he have visitors.

The group might be told that the Wizard is tired and old and has a hard time waiting. They might plan a way for one or all of them to reach the castle soon.

The support teacher might officially be designated as the palace guard to keep the Wizard informed as to where the group of characters is on its trip to Oz, and therefore keep Brad involved.

The class ends with the group seated around the table just as they were at the beginning. The group is brought together and individuals are each given support and recognition for contribution to the group effort.

Often, parents, like the children, must establish trust in the center program before they can willingly cooperate with the needed effort it takes for lasting changes.

in the program for three months that his mother indicated by telephone that he had made some improvement in his behavior at home. At this point, his mother began to keep appointments.

The monitor then switched her efforts from helping the parents seek services elsewhere to observations of Victor's Developmental Therapy class with an emphasis on management techniques. This approach seemed to be successful until his mother became ill during her pregnancy. However, she continued to be involved in transporting him from school to the center. The monitor met her in the parking lot at least once a week. Although she usually said she was in too much pain to pay attention, his mother did involve herself in discussions about Victor's needs. And since there was danger of her losing the baby, the monitor suggested that someone else transport Victor to the center. But she continued to bring him even on those days when her husband was at home.

After the birth of the baby, more telephone calls were made requesting a conference with the parents. The appointments were arranged only to be broken. This failure to keep the appointments was not in keeping with the interest Victor's mother expressed during the many telephone and parking lot conversations. The monitor suspected that the parents probably had some fear of a private session so an invitation was sent inviting them to the evening Parents' Group meeting. Victor's mother responded to the invitation and attended the meeting. The monitor was careful to telephone her the day of the meeting, reminding her of the time.

Some of the anxiety about coming to the center must have been dispelled by the meeting because she came in for the next scheduled appointment. The

purpose of this conference was to observe the demonstration of management techniques hopefully to be used at home. The monitor also discussed ways to help Victor reduce his anxiety about separating from his mother, a problem which had intensified since the birth of the baby. Later, his mother was able to assure Victor that he would not be left alone. She encouraged him to hold his new infant brother. As a result of his mother's constant assurance, Victor's anxiety seemed to decrease in school and at home.

Unfortunately, his parents continue to be in need of marital counseling, but it is doubtful whether they will participate in any activity of this nature.

Intermittent contact with his mother will continue, centered around Victor's successful participation in the regular school setting. Eventually, the monitor hopes to discuss Victor's feelings in regard to his stepfather legally adopting him.

His School Victor needed consistency between home, school, and center. Conferences with his school teachers revolved around setting limits constructively, using positive rather than negative statements, and structuring activities for Victor to successfully participate. Victor's fourth grade teacher called to ask if she could come to the center to observe him in class. The team monitor observed with the teacher, explaining the techniques used by the center staff for managing disruptive behavior. Soon Victor's participation at the center was reduced from four afternoons a week to three afternoons as the teachers reported he was getting attention in more appropriate ways at school.

When Victor's stepfather adamantly demanded that he not attend the center anymore, a joint parent-teacher confer-

To avoid anxiety, make sure that the purpose, goals, or expectations for the parents are clearly communicated.

Many times parents find it difficult to understand a child's behavior and real reasons for some of his difficulties. Look for hidden feelings and unspoken words in your effort to help decrease a parent's anxiety.

Careful, detailed planning with the school is usually necessary to insure consistency of expectations and to avoid misunderstandings that often arise.

ence was arranged by the treatment team. The conference was held at his regular school and all concerned aired their feelings. The team felt that Victor was showing progress, but it would be too much to expect him to continue doing well without continued assistance for another five-week period. His school teachers agreed and his stepfather reluctantly concurred. Close weekly contact with Victor's school was important as he began his last month of treatment. About mid-month he became extremely anxious about coming. He seemed to be fearful of some of the more aggressive children. Again, close work with his regular teachers helped pinpoint the feelings he was expressing both at school and at the center. It seemed Victor's rebellious attitude toward treatment may have been reflecting his growth and independence. The frustration he displayed was therefore appropriate to his need to be on his own at school. His teachers wanted to give him the chance. He was given more responsibility and handled it well. Before the end of the treatment period, he was provisionally terminated on the basis that his regular teachers could provide the needed direction for his continued maturation.

Lewis

His Parent It was not until Lewis had been in the program for over a year that his mother began to become somewhat involved in the treatment program. The monitor wrote letters and made home visits at least once a week in attempts to get her involved. Usually, the oldest daughter would greet the monitor at the door with the message that her mother was upstairs asleep or not at home. The monitor was aware of the mother's depressions and realized that the mother could not be expected to understand

Lewis' problems, when she was not able to function adequately herself.

Finally, the monitor requested the help of the school principal to encourage Lewis' mother to present herself at the center. He responded, pointing up the need of the center staff to conduct periodic testing, which could not be done without her permission.

Unexpectedly, she appeared at the center one afternoon. It was clear that she was emerging from her depression. She explained that she had begun to organize her life, including marrying the man that she has lived with for some time. She also had a job.

She reported that Lewis was not a behavior problem at home. The monitor emphasized Lewis' needs for his mother to listen to her son, especially about his feelings. They also explored the expectations she set for him. For instance, Lewis told his mother that he was going to finish school and buy the family a house. She communicated her pleasure and expectation. This was a typical example of the expectations she placed on him. Of course, in his current situation Lewis also saw this as an impossible task, and so his failure set continued.

The mother's uplifted spirits lasted for about two months, and the depression began to set in again. She telephoned the monitor, requesting that a home visit be made. At that time the mother informed the monitor that she was committing herself to the state mental hospital for treatment. She asked that the monitor check on Lewis regularly to see if he was attending school and his group at the center. Shortly after the mother's hospitalization, the monitor did visit with Lewis at home. No adult person had assumed any responsibility for him during her absence. The monitor arranged for Lewis and his sister to move to their grandmother's home. The grand-

It is important for a monitor not to mistake a parent's inability to function as a lack of love or concern for a child.

Children often act out frustrations without awareness of the underlying causes. The treatment team working with school personnel was able to identify these feelings and make necessary revisions in procedures to bring out the real issues for more constructive results.

There are times in treatment when the monitor is called upon to demonstrate unlimited concern. This will cement the trust that is essential to implementation of a therapy program with parents.

mother was responsive to Lewis' needs and was able to help him cope with the idea of his mother's hospitalization. Lewis would get up late at night to ask questions about the hospital and when his mother would return.

She remained hospitalized for two weeks. After her return home, she no longer attempted to evade the monitor when home visits were made but seemed to welcome the opportunity to become involved again in her role as a parent. She tried many times to follow up on the suggestions made by the monitor to ease Lewis' anxiety about school and his inability to cope with school expectations. However, her efforts were so inconsistent that they produced more harm than good. At this time also, she began to feel pressure from the school and a passive attitude began to prevail. The monitor's focus then changed from what could be done to help Lewis, to providing emotional support for his mother.

In the meantime, with a few weeks remaining in the school year, Lewis was suspended. The monitor was able to help his mother see that his suspension was probably a therapeutic event after all. At that point he was not at all able to manage himself in the school environment. He continued in his Stage Three class at the center where the focus was upon ways to meet the expectations at regular school. Before the end of the school year, he reentered school with no further trouble.

For the summer, the center's recommendation was that he attend the day camp program at the local Boys' Club. One of the center staff members was there during the afternoons to provide help to children referred there by the center. Lewis' mother seemed pleased at the idea of Lewis attending camp. How-

ever she did not fully encourage him to participate. Lewis protested against going and she gave in to his wishes.

The monitor again visited the mother to remind her that Lewis would need some type of group experience or he would need to return to the center for the summer session. After this conference, the monitor attempted to contact her for a few days but with no success. Lewis and his mother were missing and no one could, or would, tell of their whereabouts. Finally, she did return home and a conference was held. She related that she had gone away a few days for rest. Before her departure she had given serious consideration to the center's recommendations and decided to look for a day camp program for Lewis. She pointed out that the monitor had done many things to help her; now it was time to do some things for herself. She had enrolled Lewis in a camp operated by the local Community Relations Police. After he returned from that camp she made arrangements for him to attend a sports day camp held at one of the local high schools. It was clear that Lewis' mother was really showing that she felt better about herself and her role as a parent.

His School Frequent teacher and principal conferences were made to help plan how to keep Lewis functioning in the school setting. These conferences focused on structure and consistency to provide outer controls. Lewis needed to know the limits and the consequences imposed for classroom behavior. Teachers were encouraged to use praise and to find specific, helpful tasks at which he could succeed. Recommendations were also made for intensive academic remediation. Teachers were supported in their efforts to give Lewis school work he could do successfully in order to prevent

What seems like a traumatic turn of events sometimes can be utilized to plan for future successes.

It was the responsibility of the monitor in this situation to avoid taking sides and, instead, to interpret the events so that feelings of hostility and resentment would not close lines of communication between school and home.

inappropriate behavior. The teachers asked for suggestions about how to handle problem behavior, in particular, his disruptive acting out. Redirection and the use of conduct points were suggested. Lewis' strengths and progress were emphasized to him by both his classroom teachers and the treatment team. One of Lewis' teachers could not handle him and had very negative feelings. A center teacher, at the school's request, participated in the class as the teacher's aide. This procedure did much to stabilize the school situation because Lewis could see the connection between center and school. From September until May the school was able to maintain Lewis with this sort of back-up from the center.

Kendra

Her Parents Extensive contact was recommended for Kendra's parents. Her mother attempted to keep all of her scheduled weekly appointments. Her father promised to come to the center but was not able to arrange his work schedule to do so. The monitor contacted him several times at home during the first eight weeks of Kendra's program. The program focus with her father centered around helping him to accept and interact with Kendra more supportively. He seemed to relate to his sons in a positive manner and Kendra received any attention that was left over.

On occasions when the monitor visited their home, the parents seemed to be happy with each other. The father sat very close to his wife and discussed Kendra's difficulties, volunteering that he did some things to help her. He said that on many occasions he attempted to talk with Kendra, but she usually shied away from him. He could not under-

stand why she was so quiet, often sitting doing nothing. The monitor suggested that both parents talk with Kendra at least ten minutes each day about her interests, rather than waiting for problems to arise as the topic of conversation.

The center's psychiatrist recommended to the family that Kendra's doctor consider medication for curbing the petit mal seizures. The monitors also discussed the possibilities of a dieting plan for Kendra, to be supervised by the family doctor. The parents followed both recommendations.

The monitor continues to help Kendra's mother follow up on the medication schedule and the dieting plan. They also continue to work on ways for the mother to assume more responsibility for the household needs. Presently, Kendra is responsible for most of the cooking and cleaning, even though her mother is not regularly employed. The entire family still responds to the mother as the "queen bee," catering to her desires.

Attempts will continue to involve her father in Kendra's treatment program on a regular basis. Home visits are scheduled at times when he is there. A major emphasis is to get him to the center, not only to provide a neutral ground for him to discuss his perceptions of relations within the family but also to observe ways to elicit responses from his daughter.

Her School In second grade Kendra was referred to the school's special services program. She was tested at that time by a school psychologist, who recommended placement in a special class. Her need for remedial training and basic concept learning was reported, but no follow-up had resulted. By sixth grade, the school counselor had sought help from the center.

It is difficult for some parents to recognize hostile feelings they may have toward other members of the family. It is even more difficult to direct this insight, if it comes, into constructive results. The monitor in this situation felt that a focus on effective parenting skills would bring about positive family changes.

Efforts were directed toward building the self-confidence of the parent in his ability to communicate with his child and to understand her emotional needs.

The center staff recommended remedial academic services for Kendra. Her aggressive behavior was seen as a reaction to academic failure and classroom pressures.

A highly individualized remedial reading program was imperative. Results of the test data were summarized in an educational planning conference, and recommendations were made to school personnel. A referral was made to the school's learning disability program. In addition, enrollment in a Stage Three Developmental Therapy class was suggested for 10 weeks only in order to assist her school with unmanageable aspects of her behavior. Concurrently, it seemed important to help Kendra develop a relationship with one person at school who could be available during crisis.

Look for other significant persons that can contribute to the treatment program in the regular school setting.

The school counselor seemed ideal for this responsibility as she had a particular interest in Kendra's progress and was sensitive to the frustrations which arise when an older child cannot do academic work.

Being able to lend emotional strength to another in crisis requires a good deal of empathy, compassion and personal stability on the part of the monitor.

Developing the ability to "step into another's shoes and out again" may be somewhat difficult for a beginning monitor for too often there is a tendency to over-identify with the persons experiencing the difficulty and linger too long in the relationship phase of treatment.

This counselor, along with Kendra's homeroom teacher, became an important member of the treatment team. Jointly they were able to bring consistency in expectations and procedures into most aspects of Kendra's day. More importantly, however, this combined effort promoted a feeling in Kendra of being cared for and valued.

Brad

His Mother At the time of Brad's entry into the program, marital counseling was recommended for his parents. This recommendation was not carried out and divorce followed. The father subsequently remarried. Extensive contact was then necessary to support Brad's mother through the crisis.

She did not feel that she had sufficient strength to carry on with her life. Many hours were spent helping sort through her strengths and weaknesses, her hopes and despairs. The monitor hoped that some self confidence would emerge. Together they drew up a weekly plan of what she needed to do in order to mobilize herself. The monitor enlisted the help of a friend of Brad's mother who was a professional mental health person and very sensitive to needs. Through considerable support and an emphasis on reality, Brad's mother gradually pulled herself together and assumed the role of head of the household.

During the latter stage of counseling, attention was directed toward her interaction with Brad and what she could do to help him overcome some of his difficulties. To help him gain self confidence, she assigned chores to him, hoping that he would take more responsibility for meeting the expectations of others. Brad also was discouraged from calling her at work three or four times a day. At first this was difficult for his mother. She felt that she would not be meeting the boy's emotional needs. However, with the monitor's reassurance, she was able to set a limit on the phone calls.

While Brad's mother needed considerable help in separating her role as a parent from her own emotional needs, she also needed help in learning new management techniques. With the monitor she observed Brad's group at a scheduled time each week. The focus was on learning the techniques the teacher used to help children in the group control themselves.

Another difficult area for Brad's mother was in not allowing her feelings about her former husband to have an effect on her dealings with Brad. It was hard for her to listen to Brad talk about his father, expressing his wish for him to come home. However, she was able to call upon a strength she had no idea that she possessed. Eventually she even allowed Brad to visit his father.

It required almost a year before his mother was able to completely mobilize herself and to feel somewhat comfortable with the idea of being mother and father to two boys. Center contact was then reduced to an on-call basis. As Brad's termination from the program became imminent, his mother also seemed ready to assume the responsibilities for Brad's continuing progress.

His School Brad's school was in a rural area. The treatment team teacher stayed in contact each week with his regular school teacher, either by telephone or by a visit to the school. Also another teacher from the center made regularly scheduled visits to Brad's school. These visits provided ongoing contact with the principal and teachers. Brad's teacher would call the center on days when he seemed to be seriously upset. Throughout the family crisis and a hostile divorce, this close communication between school and center enabled both classes to meet Brad's needs. Eventually, he was able to talk to his school teacher instead of having crying spells or becoming violently ill.

Maria

Her Parent When Maria was enrolled in the program, the center staff recommended that her mother participate in an evening parent education group conducted at the center once a week. Unfortunately, the heavy demands of her employment made this impossible.

Contact with Maria's mother was intermittent. Occasionally, she came to the center to observe the teacher demonstrating management techniques. Home visits were more effective and focused on

helping her plan a program for Maria at home. Maria's mother realized that her closeness and interest would influence Maria's behavior. With the monitor's encouragement she planned to spend at least 15 minutes a day with Maria, listening to her thoughts and giving the needed nurturance. Eventually she decided to give Maria a birthday party, the first she had ever had. The monitor participated in the planning, and Maria's smile told the story of the party's success.

During these home visits, the monitor explored with the mother her role as parent. They talked about ways to make changes in how she handled behavior problems. It was suggested that instead of losing patience and yelling, she make an attempt to be firm and consistent when enforcing rules. Also, she was advised to stop doing chores for Maria after the child ignored her mother's request. Maria's mother worked very hard for these changes. She also tried ways to rid herself of the "I'd rather do it myself" attitude. Many general discussions on child development were held and specific management techniques were planned. Gradually the mother began to reduce her expectations. It was difficult for her to understand Maria's need to act like a young girl, but gradually she began to exhibit a new awareness of the girl's development and needs. She began to allow Maria to accompany her on shopping trips, and also to participate in the selection of her clothing.

As Maria continued to progress in the program, so did her mother. She often needed someone to supply the words to say to Maria, but she recognized the child's need for nurturance and guidance, and she continued to seek simple, concrete management techniques for helping Maria learn self regulation.

Her School Maria's teacher in fourth grade was a meek, mild man-

Sometimes parents are ineffectual in child rearing practices because they lack sufficient knowledge to implement change. The task is to provide opportunity for learning adequate parenting techniques suited to their lifestyles, without lowering their self concepts.

nered, insecure man. She could easily frustrate and try his patience. The treatment team provided consultation to him in how to handle her erratic behavior and inability to control herself.

Maria was academically superior to her fourth grade classmates. She worked quickly and became restless, demanding more things to do. The teacher was encouraged to try to be prepared with extra work. Through the teacher the treatment team kept informed of Maria's relationship with her peers. She seemed to control a group of children who "respected her out of fear." The team and the school staff planned many strategies to develop Maria's attitudes and values for group participation. The team also worked with the school to lessen Maria's excitement during the transition from the center back to school. As Maria's teacher became firm and specific with her, as well as giving her praise for appropriate behavior, the team was able to work with Maria on her problems in accepting authority. The importance of consistency and a positive attitude in

working with Maria was emphasized to the school.

Toward the end of the year, the principal, teacher, and treatment team discussed promoting Maria to sixth grade instead of fifth. Her size, age, and academic ability supported this move. This promotion was interpreted to Maria as recognition of her efforts at controlling herself. She was also assigned to the school safety patrol. Since there was no summer school program, it was recommended that Maria continue in the summer program at the center and attend a day camp. The treatment team for the summer class worked to prepare her for a good start in sixth grade. The success of this move depends upon Maria's ability to see her teachers not only as authority figures but as concerned adults working together with her interests and feelings in mind.

EPILOGUE

These Stage Three children were working on mastery of developmental objectives

Table 1. Length of Treatment and Subsequent School Placement

	No. of weeks in Stage III	Present school placement
Lewis	109	Regular school (provisionally)
Brad	27	Regular school
Kendra	10	Regular school
Victor	16	Regular school
Maria	30	Regular school

that would help them to be successful members of a group. When the basic skills had been mastered at the center, they were applied to their interpersonal relationships at home, at school, and in the community. It is in these settings that these children now can have a try at using the skills independently. All of the children were terminated (see Table 1) with confidence that they could enter the full-time schedule of the public school with some degree of success. However, setbacks may occur because of unexpected changes at home or school. For this reason follow-up by the treatment team is essential.

Victor was terminated before the end of his second 10-week treatment period. He began to yield his will to the group and frequently encouraged other children to exchange some of their ideas with him. He demonstrated an awareness and understanding of the consequences for inappropriate behavior, for he no longer felt a need to break rules just to test the limits. While continuing to have some difficulty maintaining himself during the crises of other children, there was a conscious effort on his part to master this objective. Perhaps most important, his parents and regular school teachers felt competent to help him continue his progress.

The school administration and center staff planned that Lewis would be allowed to reenter school in the fall. It was agreed that his situation at school would continue to be closely monitored by his treatment team. For the time being, his situation is classified as "provisionally terminated."

At the end of the school year, Lewis' mother reported that he was beginning to respond to the limits set by her at home and that healthy lines of communication were being established. He also began developing friendships with a few peers.

Kendra developed a greater feeling of self worth during the treatment period. She began verbalizing a few consequences if rules were broken and could talk about other ways to maintain self control. She was not able to spontaneously verbalize her feelings unless given an enormous amount of positive reinforcement and time to do so. Many times others in the group would attempt to help her by providing the words for her to repeat. Incidents of aggression were reduced although it was apparent that she still had aggressive feelings. At her termination, the staff recommended that she continue in the girls' group conducted in her school by the school counselor and one of the center teachers. In addition, the remedial academic program continued. Because of this support Kendra adjusted well to a regular seventh grade program.

Brad was able to make steady progress during his treatment period. Aggressive behavior at school was reduced and feelings of anxiety were controlled. As he felt more comfortable discussing feelings, rather than acting them out, he frequently would ask to talk with the center teacher who provided consultation services in his school. He was able to discuss individual feelings and to participate in problem-solving sessions, indicating that he had reached Stage Four in many respects. At termination, an intensive remedial reading program was suggested for him, and his school was able to provide one. He was also encouraged to participate in Little League baseball and the local YMCA activities. His mother responded to these recommendations. Brad was able to maintain a successful adjustment throughout the next year. Periodically, his mother called the center for encouragement, but no sustained program was needed for her.

When Maria was terminated, physical intervention was no longer necessary.

The significant contribution made by the regular teachers of these children to their post-termination success cannot be overemphasized. For this reason, the time a treatment team spends with the teachers can be a most important part of the treatment effort.

She was able to maintain control and proceed with the routine of the group, even when other children were in crisis. She made many requests for opportunities to discuss other ways to behave. She was also able to relate her concerns appropriately. Among the group members, and also in her neighborhood, she had made beginning friendships. At times, Maria was able to describe some of the characteristics of her new friends and showed a great sensitivity to their needs. Although there were times when she was impatient with children who had fewer skills, she was able to maintain self control. With improved verbal skills, she began to find gratification from her part in group activities, especially writing and telling experience stories. As a result of Maria's improved attitude toward school, the center's recommendation for her promotion to sixth grade was accepted. After termination, she received intermittent contact from center staff in school and at home. Having developed a number of Stage Four skills, Maria would telephone certain teachers at the center when she felt a need to talk about problems with someone outside her family or school.

chapter 10

THE STAGE FOUR CLASS BRINGS SATISFACTION IN GROUP PROCESSES

Anthony Beardsley, Lead Teacher, and
Barbara Geter, Monitor-Parent Worker

Identity

Insight

Interaction

Values

Communication

Investment

Tolerance

Flexibility

Expectations

Foresight

INTRODUCTION

Unlike the other stages of Developmental Therapy, a Stage Four class looks very much like a group of neighborhood youngsters. You will see them planning, preparing, and carrying out constructive and exciting activities. In a neighborhood group, children learn to get along with others. In a Stage Four class the same process is at work. The only difference between these two settings is the need in a Stage Four class for a skilled adult to keep the experiences productive ones.

Children at Stage Four are generally a pleasure to work with. They come into the Stage Four class as participating group members with a background of success from their experiences in prior stages. These children are willing to abide by the rules of the group because they know the rationale for rules and the consequences when rules are broken.

Stage Four classes are interesting and exciting for the children and teachers. Having fun is beneficial in a treatment program when children are growing from the experience. It is easy, however, for a teacher to be so involved in the many, complex incidents occurring in a Stage Four class that goals are obscured. Only close attention to the objectives will keep the program on target.

In this chapter you will notice that few special techniques have been included. The major emphasis should be upon nonsimulated childhood experiences and increased involvement with the child's regular school and his family.

JERRY

Jerry is a tall, attractive 12-year-old, enrolled in the seventh grade. His parents have been divorced for five years. He lives with his mother and three sisters in a small rural community. His mother sought help at the center because of her inability to control his behavior at home and because of her concern for his poor academic performance. Information gathered from the school, however, conflicted with the situation as reported by Jerry's mother. The school saw Jerry as a good student with average abilities. Behaviorally, his teachers felt he was no more of a problem than any other child in his class.

When Jerry's situation was reviewed by the staff it seemed that he was in a difficult situation. It was difficult for him to reconcile religious teachings at home (particularly pacifism) with the aggressive day-to-day demands made by peers at school. As a result of this conflict, he seemed to have taken a fatalistic attitude toward these school occurrences and saw himself as being a victim in fights, where he subjugated himself to his peers.

Clearly his mother was communicating much more than her concern about Jerry's behavior. Her perceptions regarding the severity of his difficulties were interpreted as a plea for herself. She was eager to participate in weekly meetings with the monitor from Jerry's treatment team. Together they discussed interpretations of Jerry's behavior and she developed greater awareness of appropriate expectations for a boy his age. Perhaps the greatest gain was through emotional support for herself in dealing with the situation of being a single parent. Additionally, she benefited from discussions concerning effective child management techniques that could be implemented at home.

School liaison efforts were particularly difficult because Jerry did, in fact, perform within the expectations of the school. But because of his home situation, Jerry's chances of continuing normal development were threatened and he was accepted for Developmental Therapy as a preventive move.

Jerry's mother identified 24 high priority problems:

demands excessive attention
short attention span

overactive
resists discipline
aggressive toward children
lacks comprehension
does not follow directions
crying spells
easily frustrated
lacks confidence
fails for attention
temper tantrums
immature
speech problems
untruthful
moody
regressive
complains
repeats
echoes
unaware
manipulative
suspicious
jealous
reading difficulties

In comparison, his teacher only identified two high priority problems: excessive talking and reading difficulties.

The clinical diagnosis at time of entry was a mild reactive disorder.

Jerry was enrolled at the center in a Stage Four class. Beginning treatment at Stage Four is very unusual, but in Jerry's situation it seemed to be necessary in order to effectively intervene in his home environment. Jerry was enrolled in center classes for only one treatment period (10 weeks). The developmental objectives for Jerry were:

Behavior

B-23   to verbally express cause and effect relationship between feelings and behavior

Communication

C-20   to use appropriate words or gestures to show feeling responses to

environment, materials, people, or animals

C-23   to recognize and acknowledge feelings in self

Socialization

S-24   to recognize and describe characteristics of others

S-28   to verbally indicate preferences among members of the group by differentiating personal characteristics

Academics

A-40   to recognize and write numerals to represent groupings

A-45   to read basic primary vocabulary words spontaneously in sentences

A-51   to read and write quantitative words for measurement of distance, time, money, fractions

ROY

Roy is a 10-year-old enrolled in the fourth grade. He is overweight, has a low self concept, and feels that other children in his school do not want his friendship. To compensate for his weight problem, Roy takes money from his mother and shows it to his classmates to gain their friendship and esteem. Roy's parents are divorced; his two brothers live with his father while Roy and his mother live alone. He visits his father periodically.

Roy's mother works on a night shift and although Roy is cared for by a neighbor, he is essentially alone. His mother's concern about Roy's stealing activities prompted her to seek help from the center.

Although her request for help was interpreted as genuine concern, her relationship to Roy raised serious questions as to the effectiveness of the parent-child interactions. It seemed clear that: (a) Roy's mother was inadvertently reinforcing his compulsive eating habit through the use of food as a reward; (b) she was setting up situations in which Roy found it very easy to steal from her; (c) she was reinforcing the dependency ties that seemed to exist between herself and her son; and (d) Roy seemed to be modeling many of his mother's eating habits. Additionally, Roy's mother, herself an isolate, encouraged Roy's isolationism. This was done by failing to encourage peer interaction and encouraging his general inactivity and overeating. Because of her obesity, marital status, and lack of social acceptance in the community, she had a very low self concept. Roy interacted with his peers in much the same way as she did. Negative feelings about himself were rampant.

Roy's problems at school were aggravated by the fact that his attempts at buying friends simply were not working. Although he attempted to satisfy increased demands for money and candy, his peers were continuing to exclude him from social situations and further antagonized him by teasing. As the amounts of money Roy brought to school increased, his teachers became more and more concerned.

At the time of his referral, high priority problems identified by both home and school were:

stealing
apathetic
careless and unorganized
lacks confidence

The clinical diagnosis was a moderately severe reactive disorder.

Roy was initially enrolled at the center in a Stage Three class. He mastered Stage Three objectives in 10 weeks. Because of the inability of his mother to provide a climate for continuing matura-

tion, termination was not recommended at that time. He was then enrolled in the Stage Four class where successful experiences with peers were particularly emphasized.

Intervention in the home situation involved supportive therapy for Roy's mother, allaying her anxiety about his stealing, developing some insight regarding her motivations for keeping Roy isolated from others, interpreting Roy's motives for stealing, and encouraging her to allow Roy's emerging independence and separation from her. It was felt that with movement toward these parent objectives, the compulsive eating habits of both Roy and his mother would decrease.

The following objectives were used during his first 10-week treatment period in Stage Four:

Behavior

B-17 to verbalize other ways to behave
B-22 to implement alternative behavior
B-23 to verbally relate behavior to situations and incidents

Communication

C-22 to verbally recognize feelings in others
C-23 to verbally recognize feelings in self
C-24 to verbally praise other children

Socialization

S-21 to suggest activity or preference to teacher
S-23 to indicate preference for another child or children
S-24 to recognize differentiating personal characteristics of others

Academics

A-47 to write basic vocabulary words from memory and dictation

A-48 to participate in group activity, i.e., writing and/or telling an experience story

JIM

Jim, an unattractive young boy of 11 years, was unable to maintain acceptable behavior in school. He refused to do his work, was self abusive and self derogatory, and became violently aggressive when teachers placed demands on him. His physical appearance, unusual mannerisms, and violent outbursts made him a prime target for teasing from peers and served as the basis for his low self concept. His aggressive behavior in the group setting was baffling to his teachers since they knew that Jim was conforming and tractable when working alone with a teacher.

Jim is the third child in a family of four children. In early childhood Jim ran a very high fever for which he was hospitalized. He was subsequently given an EEG in which minimal damage to the motor area of the brain was noted.

Jim's mother is an extremely tense and defensive woman who suffers from congenital palsy. Because she is emotionally in need herself, she is unable to provide Jim and the other children with adequate emotional nurturance and feels "put upon" by her responsibilities in the family. His father, although passive in other areas of family life, serves as disciplinarian for the children.

Jim was referred to the center when his behavior at school degenerated to the point of suspension. Attendance was the single problem identified by the parents as a high priority problem. In comparison the school reported 10 high priority problems.

demands excessive attention
short attention span
distractible
perseverative
immature
aggressive toward children
aggressive toward property
lacks confidence
speech problems
unable to express feelings

The psychiatric diagnosis was schizophrenia, adult type, with neurological impairment.

Jim desperately needed skills in relating to others, as well as behavioral controls. His parents needed help in providing a stable, consistent, nurturing home environment. The school needed to be aware of the reasons for Jim's inappropriate behavior and more effective techniques in dealing with his behavior.

He was initially enrolled in a Stage Three class and accomplished the objectives in 16 weeks. He has now been in a Stage Four class for 20 weeks. Jim's current Stage Four objectives are:

Behavior

B-21 to spontaneously participate in activities previously avoided
B-24 to respond to provocation with verbal and body control
B-25 to respond appropriately to suggestions made by another child

Communication

C-20 to express feelings appropriately
C-27 to express awareness of feelings in others

Socialization

S-25 to suggest an activity to the group
S-29 to assist another child in conflict

Academics

A-45 to express himself through rhythm

A-54 to write for communication of information to others

A-56 to write of feelings and attitudes

BILL

An attractive, intelligent, 10-year-old, Bill was enrolled in fifth grade when his school adjustment seemed to deteriorate. He comes from an upper middle class family and is the youngest of three children. Although Bill is of high intellectual ability, he has a history of poor academic performance. His verbal fluency served as an obstacle to meaningful peer interaction. He reportedly got along poorly with his brother, with whom he shared a room, was enuretic, and generally quite fearful. Additionally, at times he chose to involve himself in fantasy to the extent that both his parents and teachers became concerned.

The number of high priority problems reported by his parents and teachers clearly indicated an acute situation:

demands excessive attention
short attention span
distractible
apathetic
forgetful
overactive
careless and unorganized
easily frustrated
lacks confidence
talks excessively
listening difficulties
moody
avoids participation
unaware
avoids new situations
manipulative
academic problems in:
    reading
    arithmetic
    spelling
    written communication

The clinical diagnosis was initially reported as acute reactive disorder with suspected learning disability.

Clearly, there was a need to create awareness in Bill of his potential for successful academic performance. Recognition and support were essential on the part of his teachers to counteract the insecurity he felt in school. The center's efforts in school involved consultation with his teachers to the end that more therapeutic teacher/student interaction would transpire. It was hoped that such interactions would promote heightened self esteem.

Bill's parents were in need of counseling with regard to: (a) interpretation of Bill's increased reliance on fantasy, (b) Bill's confused feelings regarding adolescence, (c) the parents' interaction with Bill, and (d) more effective child management techniques for them to use.

Bill was enrolled in a Stage Three class for 23 weeks. When he began the last five weeks of his Stage Four class the objectives were:

Behavior

B-18 to refrain from inappropriate behavior when others are losing control

B-19 to maintain self control and comply with group procedures

B-22 to implement alternative behaviors

Communication

C-22 to verbally recognize feelings in others

C-23 to recognize feelings in self

Socialization

S-22 to participate without inappropriate response to activity suggested by another child

S-23   to indicate friendship by preference for a particular child

S-24   to recognize and describe characteristics of others

Academics

A-53   to write individual experience stories

A-54   to write for communication of information to others

A-56   to write of feelings and attitudes

MARY

Mary, an attractive 10-year-old, proved to be a very disruptive force in her fourth grade classroom. During particularly aggressive episodes, her teachers found it hard to bring her under control. Mary would go to any length to get the attention of teachers and peers. She frequently resorted to stealing from her teacher and others. She seemed to be able to learn but at times flatly refused to participate in academic work. Mary's functioning was two to four years below grade level in school and according to the WISC she scored in the borderline range of intelligence. The Bender placed her at the six-and-a-half-year level.

Her background was fraught with extreme deprivation and poverty. Her mother was reported to be mentally deficient and to be incapable of using adequate judgment in everyday situations. Mary's two brothers were receiving aid to the disabled, and her older sister was in the adolescent unit at a state mental hospital. The family situation was so disorganized that Mary was removed from the home by court order and placed with an elderly, decrepit great-aunt. Although this was not an ideal home situation, it was an improvement over her prior environment.

As Mary's disruptive behavior became more and more frequent in the school, her teachers contacted the center for help. At the time of this referral many high priority problems were noted in the area of behavior and academics. Mary's great-aunt, with much assistance from the intake social worker, also identified several high priority problems.

Clinical classification of Mary's case presented considerable problems to the center staff. Finally, severe socioeconomic deprivation was agreed upon as most representative of her primary problems. Initially Mary was enrolled in a Stage Two class. She remained in Stage Two for 23 weeks of treatment. Then she moved up to Stage Three for 18 weeks. Progress was extremely slow but steady. Upon her mastery of most of the Stage Three objectives, it was determined to be in Mary's best interest to continue with Stage Four. She obviously needed greater skill in relating to peers in appropriate ways and in gaining their acceptance.

Stage Four objectives used for Mary were:

Behavior

B-17   to tell other, more appropriate ways to behave

B-19   to maintain self control and comply with group procedures

B-20   to respond appropriately to choices for leadership

B-22   to implement alternative behaviors toward others

Communication

C-22   to verbally recognize feelings in others

C-23   to recognize and acknowledge feelings in self

C-24   to use words to praise others

Socialization

S-23 to indicate developing friendship by preference for a particular child

S-24 to recognize and describe characteristics of others

S-25 to suggest group activity directly to peer group

S-26 to respond appropriately to choices for leadership in the group

Academics

A-48 to participate in writing experience stories

A-49 to write full name, address, and date from memory

A-50 to read and write basic vocabulary spontaneously

A-51 to read and write quantitative words

The treatment team's intervention in the home situation was largely for support of Mary's aunt in maintaining as consistent an environment as possible. The team monitor spent many hours reviewing realistic limit setting and establishing feasible consequences for inappropriate behavior. The monitor also spent considerable time helping the aunt with problems of transportation and obtaining needed social services through other community resources.

During the beginning phases of Mary's treatment, crisis intervention in the school was considerable. It was not unusual for the lead teacher to make four or more visits a week to assist the school with Mary's disruptive behavior. Extensive consultation with Mary's teachers at school was essential to develop more therapeutic approaches for dealing with her problem behavior. In time, the center facilitated a more suitable academic placement, to provide remedial assistance.

By the time Mary entered Stage Four, contacts with the school were only necessary on a weekly basis to exchange information on Mary's progress and to plan strategies.

LEARNING COMES FROM EACH OTHER

Let's look in on a Stage Four class. This class seems to be a rather small group: four boys, one girl, and two teachers. The room is small and brightly decorated with art work the children have done. A group mural stretches across one wall showing a scene of a fire engine being washed and waxed. The idea for the mural was generated by the children after a recent trip to a fire station. Several fire engines carved by the children from balsa wood are displayed on the window ledge. The children and teachers are sitting around a table at the far end of the room. On the wall directly behind the lead teacher is a poster made by the children, indicating activities chosen by the group for the class.

Right now they are just starting SPECIAL TIME. Let's listen.

Teacher: *"Who remembers what we talked about right before we went home on Friday?"*

Jim: *"I know . . . we talked about how it was raining out and what we should do when walking in the rain."*

Teacher: *"You're right, we did talk some about the rain before we left. What else did we talk about . . . something that we decided to do this week?"*

Jerry: *"I remember! We decided to have our own carnival; kinda like the one we went to at the high school where they had all kinds of games and stuff."*

Bill: *"Yeah. And we were going to make our own money to buy tickets with—oh yeah, and a ticket booth."*

Mary: *"Oh, that's a stupid idea. I don't . . ."*

Teacher: *"Mary, do you remember that sign you made for the play we put on a few weeks ago? You know the title sign with the . . ."*

Mary: *"Oh that one . . . sure!"*

Jerry: *"Hey, I remember too; that was a*

Field trips can be used to work on many Stage Four objectives, for example, making suggestions for trips (S-25); selecting "buddies" (S-28), choosing a leader (B-20).

Beginning this activity by having children recall what they had decided previously provides carry-over from their last class meeting. This also is the first step toward objective S-30 in socialization.

The teacher interrupts Mary in order to keep the conversation moving in a positive direction.

Jerry is praising Mary for her art ability (C-24) and the teacher is not reacting. At this stage it is no longer necessary for the teacher to constantly support children. Their rewards should come from the group.

really good sign! Maybe you could paint some signs of the games we're gonna play!"

Bill: "Yeah . . . and how much they cost."

Teacher: "Sounds like we're really going to need someone who can do a good job with painting signs!"

Mary: "I guess I could do it . . ."

Teacher: "It feels good to know that people like the way you do things. Right, Mary?"

Roy: "I got it. Mary, if we taped butcher paper on that big old refrigerator box, could you paint some signs and things right on that?"

Mary: "Guess I could."

Here the teacher felt it necessary to intervene in order to provide direction to the group.

Teacher: "Okay, we have about 20 minutes left for today so let's get organized and decide who will do what."

Roy: "Jerry and I could go down to the storage room and get that old refrigerator box and start to cut up butcher paper."

Jerry: "Yeah!"

Both Jerry and Roy are working on S-28. By mentioning how they feel, the teacher encourages their friendship with each other.

Teacher: "You two fellows really like to do things together. It's nice to have friends! Remember how to go down to the storage room?"

Jerry: "Yeah, we know. Quiet enough so we won't disturb the other classes."

Teacher: "Right! What else needs to be done?"

Jim: "Don't we need to make some money and tickets?"

Mary: "I could draw some faces on the money if you and Jim would cut it out."

Bill: "I'm not cutting anything out with Jim or anybody else. The money was my idea and I'm doing it myself! I can put pictures on the money myself."

Children at Stage Four regress at times to lower stages of behavior. This happens to individual children in the group rather than the group as a whole.

Jim: "I suppose you think you're gonna be the only one to have money, stupid?"

Bill: "Watch who you call 'stupid'!"

Teacher: "Just a minute, now. It doesn't make anyone feel good to be called names. Bill, how does it make you feel when people don't want to do things with you?"

Bill: "Just fine, I like to do things by myself. Anyway he called me 'stupid'!"

For the teacher to go into any further detail about Bill's behavior would be counterproductive. Bill is now aware of what his behavior was producing. Now he needs to get back into the group activity (B-21).

By saying "Good idea" to Bill, the teacher encourages socialization objective S-25 and also helps Bill feel better about his contribution.

Teacher: "Well, if you make the money all by yourself and it's all your money, and you won't let anyone else help make the money, what might happen when you go to buy a ticket?"

Bill: "I don't know!"

Reviewing the group's successes is a good way to give added meaning to the day's activities.

Teacher: "How would you feel about sel-

Finally, the teacher is establishing an attitude of anticipation for another good day on Wednesday.

ling a ticket to someone who would not let you help make the money?"

Bill: "Guess I wouldn't sell him any tickets!"

Teacher: "I see. You know, you sure have some good ideas for the carnival. You want to help set it up and play the games, right?"

Bill: "I sure do!"

Teacher: "Well, Jim and Mary have started cutting out the money! Do you want to help?"

Bill: "Yes!"

Teacher: "Sometimes when people say things that make us mad we like to call them names! What happens when we do that? Does it help?"

Jim: "No, it just makes things worse . . . guess I forgot about that! Hey Bill, here's a pair of scissors."

(ten minutes pass)

Teacher: "It's just about time to leave for the day. We had better clean up. Wow! Just look at the ticket booth Roy and Jerry have been working on . . . hard to believe it once was an old box!"

Support teacher: "That really does look nice! They have it all ready for Mary to paint on some fancy signs."

Teacher: "They sure do. And look at all this money . . ."

Bill: "We've made 5's, 10's, and 20's. Lots of money! Let's put it all in this box so it will be safe."

Teacher: "Good idea! Now before we leave, what needs to be done when we come in Wednesday?"

Mary: "Paint the ticket booth."

Roy: "Make some tickets!"

Jerry: "Yeah. And we'll have to decide what games we're going to play."

Jim: "I think one of the games should be marbles."

Teacher: "Jim can hardly wait till Wednesday to decide on games. Think about what you want and we'll have a lot of ideas to choose from. Do you think we'll be able to have the carnival by Friday?"

Group: "Yeah!!!"

Teacher: "Okay! We had a good day today . . . got a lot done, and we have our special time all planned for Wednesday. Let's go home."

A CHALLENGE TO CHILDREN

A visitor might legitimately ask, "Why do these kids need a special class at all?" To answer this question, let's go back 10 weeks, to the beginning of the class.

It is the first day. The teachers and children are planning classroom procedures and rules. The group decides to write these rules on a large piece of construction paper and post it in their room. Here are the procedures and rules they came up with.

1. No fighting, kicking, or spitting on the bus.
2. Don't run or talk in the hallways.
3. No fighting, kicking, or spitting in class.
4. Don't talk back to the teacher.
5. Don't call anybody bad names.

During their school years these children have heard rules, procedures, and requests stated over and over again, in negative terms: "Don't run in the halls!" "No, you can't go outside now!" "Don't sass your teacher." Through the years they have internalized these negative concepts and now consider them as the only basis for group process and classroom organization. They view school as a place where they *have to go* and where they *can't* do things. School and group activity represent constraints, defining what they cannot do.

Being aware of such attitudes, the teacher asked the children during the next class meeting to review the rules to see if they wanted to make any changes. At first they said they could find nothing wrong with their rules and felt they were very appropriate. A discussion ensued concerning their group goal for the 10-week period and how rules should help them accomplish their goal. In their own words, the goal had real meaning, "Learning to work and play together."

The teacher then asked if they could make another list of rules stating the same thing but making the rules say "yes" instead of "no". The children thought it was a challenge to write rules without using the words "don't" and "no", and they responded with enthusiasm. Their second list contained these rules.

1. Stay in your seat.
2. Listen while others talk.
3. Be polite.
4. Ignore trouble.
5. Stick to the point.
6. Talk when its your turn.
7. Do something friendly every day.

Both lists were posted on the wall and for the next few weeks the teacher and the class referred to both lists when planning an activity or solving a problem. When situations arose in which the group needed to refer to the rules both lists were read and the group would decide which rule sounded most appropriate. In situations where there had been a fight or if the class activity fell apart because of disagreements in the group the children usually agreed upon the first list as the most appropriate for the situation. However, when the group discussed plans for special time, game time, or art time, or planned for field trips, they would always decide on the second list of rules. The teacher pointed this out to the class and, as time passed, the group chose the second list more and more often.

At the end of two weeks the group decided to take down the first, negative list of rules and leave up the second, positive list. They felt it was better to have rules that reminded them of what they could do than to have rules about what they could not do. The children also recognized that if they followed the list of positive rules there really would

Rules should be stated in positive ways, suggesting productive outcomes.

Notice that the first rules are stated negatively and have to do with problem situations. It is obvious that the children have a negative set toward school and, more importantly, toward the group process itself.

At Stage Four the objectives go beyond making rules for the group and knowing their consequences. They deal much more with the child's feelings and the feelings of others, for example, talking about one's own feelings (C-23).

This Stage Four group learned to see procedures and rules as something that could benefit them. They also learned that positive rules can guide them toward successful group participation.

be no trouble in the room, whereas with the first list of rules it was almost inevitable that trouble of some kind would occur. The teacher asked the group to come up with a title for their list of rules. They called it, "Things to Remember For a Good Day."

A CHALLENGE TO TEACHERS

Teachers at Stage Four must have a thorough working knowledge of Stage Three and Stage Four Objectives. It is not unusual for a Stage Four child at times to regress to Stage Three characteristics.

As a teacher of a Stage Four class, you must keep in mind that these children will not constantly act as ideal group members. It is important to remember that they still have problems, and it is not unusual for a child to be a perfect angel one day and a little devil the next. This is most often the reason that children need a Stage Four class. They have the skills to be successful in life but do not consistently put them to use. Your job, then, is to help them realize how much more they can enjoy life using the controls and skills they have at hand.

The teacher of Stage Four children has a greater challenge to be an "accepted" adult than at any other stage of Developmental Therapy.

The manner in which you attempt to get the message across is of utmost importance. They need an individual whose opinion of them is of crucial and significant importance. Ideally, you become the model whose behavior they will emulate. You also must be ready to provide another basic emotional need, nurturance, while allowing for as much independence as a child can manage. The Stage Four child has acquired skills; now he needs to feel good about these skills, and he needs for these skills to be recognized by significant people in his life. Concomitantly, recognition of his skills by others should be perceived by himself as honest and real.

Because these children cannot be fooled by empty praise and condescending encouragement, you need to be completely honest in your interaction with them in class. If you are a person in

whom they can believe, then it means something when you say, "You know, I really liked that story you wrote about your trip to the mountains. It was very interesting!"

Also, situations will arise where they must talk things out. They need to know you will give them straight answers. "You may be right that the bus driver was grouchy this morning, but do you think it helped matters when you started making all that noise? Have you ever felt grouchy?"

As a group leader there are times when you may have to set limits. "There is just no way we can use the art room this week. Other classes have already reserved it. Shall we reserve it for early next week?"

Be a real person in class. Remember that you are part of the group too. And as a real person you may be wrong at times. "I guess you're right. This game isn't as much fun as I thought it would be; do you have any suggestions?"

Being an authentic person to a Stage Four group culminates in the relationship you establish with the support teacher. With heightened sensitivity toward others, the Stage Four child looks closely at the relationships between adults. More comfortable than ever before with himself, he is able to see the actions and reactions of adults to each other as clues to the relationship between them. His experience with adult relationships outside the center frequently have been poor and limited; and he wants to know how other adults treat each other.

To show that adults can be caring and considerate, the teachers of a Stage Four class have a great responsibility as models. The children watch closely to see how the teachers respond to each other, and because they are Stage Four children they are capable of seeing a lot.

They can perceive genuine respect of one adult for another. They sense attitudes, no matter how veiled or covert. They also can recognize subordination of one adult to another, if it occurs. So, the adult-adult relationships in a Stage Four class become as significant to progress as the child-group and child-adult relationships.

It is especially desirable to have a male and a female teacher in the Stage Four class. In this way the children are exposed to a cooperative, mutually supportive relationship between sexes. When this relationship impresses a child, modeling and identification will occur. A new dimension is thereby added to a child's potential repertoire of responses, extending his own capabilities as the adult he will become.

Regular classroom teachers are crucial to the total treatment program too. Because of the increased amount of time a child is spending in the regular classroom, much of your time as a Stage Four teacher will be spent working with classroom teachers. Your first task with the classroom teacher is to convince her that this child really can fit in and make progress in her class. It should be pointed out to the teacher that in the near future the child will no longer need special help at all. Stage Four children possess adequate skills to make good progress in school; however, they do not put these skills to use consistently. The type of environment the teacher creates in the classroom will determine the extent to which the child uses the skills he has at hand.

Initial planning meetings should revolve around the child's skills and qualities which need to be brought out in the classroom setting. Plans and strategies to accomplish this goal in the classroom should be a joint effort between you and the classroom teacher. Together, the strategies you come up with should help facilitate generalization of Developmental Therapy objectives from the treatment class to the regular classroom. One example might be a child's need for more opportunities to exhibit leadership in a group. A plan may be devised in which the child is selected more often to be first during certain periods, and he might be assigned to be the "director" during part of music time. The selection of the activity is very important. It should be an activity that the child has first experienced in the treatment class and in which he has had a significant measure of success.

The importance of the exchange of information about the child's progress between you and the classroom teacher cannot be overemphasized. In your planning of activities for the treatment class, an up-to-date account of regular school activities which are presenting problems for the child is essential. Also, by coordinating your treatment class activities with regular school and community programs, Stage Four becomes a viable experience where the child can practice his group skills and then carry over what he learns into the regular classroom and neighborhood.

During weekly conferences with the classroom teacher, along with exchanging information about the child's behavior and planning appropriate activities, you should begin to prepare the teacher for the center's eventual withdrawal from the case. Reviewing the successes the child has in school and in treatment, comparing the skills the child is exhibiting with his earlier skill levels, and noting the reduced need for individual attention are topics which should be discussed when considering termination.

When termination is imminent, the teacher should be prepared for some temporary regression. She should be as-

Remember that the regular classroom teacher should be considered a part of the treatment team who eventually will be handling situations without your help.

When terminating a child, you must be reasonably convinced that the child will be able to continue to progress with his regular teacher.

sured that this will not be severe and will not last long. It is important also to remind her that if any serious problems come up you will be available to assist. Convey confidence to the teacher that the child can make the necessary adjustment for termination. Make it a point to indicate that much of the success the child has shown is attributable to the classroom setting the teacher has provided.

A CHALLENGE TO PARENTS

There are many similarities and parallels between the roles of teachers and parents of Stage Four children. Being an effective parent of a Stage Four child depends to a great extent on the quality of communication between the parents and the child. As the child learns to reach out appropriately to others, it is essential that the parents similarly reach out in new ways to the child. Active listening is a basic step for doing this, and parents of Stage Four children are encouraged to listen with a new ear. Often this can communicate "caring" more effectively than any other response. Parents are also encouraged to use reflection with their Stage Four child in the same way that the technique is used at Stage Three. These two responses on the part of parents will bring on a new phase of relations in which the child is able to use a few of his newly acquired skills for interpersonal relations with his family. At first the child's moves are tentative. The parents must be prepared to attend to body language and to actively decode messages. They often need assistance in learning these processes and in recognizing their own ambivalent feelings about their child's emerging independence and erratic behavior.

Parents are sometimes threatened by

Working with parents of Stage Four children is largely a matter of helping parents establish the kind of relationship which permits a degree of independence and a climate for reciprocal support in problem solving.

their child's insistence on assuming adult mannerisms. Typically they react by strong disapproval or by unconsciously encouraging dependency. When the Stage Four child balks at either of these parental responses, parents frequently enter into a power struggle with the child. When this occurs, the monitor must guide the parents toward greater insight into the Stage Four child's development and his equally strong needs for independence and dependence. To do this, the monitor helps parents learn more about the developmental milestones all children face at this stage. With such information parents are more able to set *realistic* expectations for their child as he vacillates between adult-like and child-like behavior.

Relationships between parents and children at Stage Four can be rich and rewarding. Monitors have found that when this occurs, treatment seldom needs to continue. With this in mind, seven suggestions for Stage Four monitors are offered.

1. Be sure that parents understand what to realistically expect, and not expect, of a Stage Four child.
2. Interpret the dynamics of the Stage Four child's developmental needs, using specific incidents for illustration.
3. Encourage parents to actively change their own responses to their child's newly acquired skills as rapidly as they occur.
4. Assist parents in identifying conditions prone to produce power struggles, and plan ways to allow for independence to the extent that the child is capable.
5. Clarify for the parents situations in which the child may be vulnerable, and develop strategies which help the parents assist the child in problem-solving efforts.
6. Encourage parents to be effective lis-

teners and communicators, emphasizing the reciprocal aspects of communication. 7. Support parents in their role of responsibility, and help them to see that this can be accomplished without tyranny.

Parents will vary as widely as children do in their capacities to respond. If you have parents who fail to respond significantly, settle for less than the full range of cooperation. If you find only one way to improve parent-child relationship, you may have accomplished a considerable amount. Keep in mind that a Stage Four child has much working for him, and he may be able to keep the momentum going with only marginal support from parents. This was the case with several of the children introduced earlier in the chapter. Yet each was able to continue to progress, making a satisfactory adjustment to school.

EPILOGUE

All of these children are currently making good progress in regular public schools without the support of a Stage Four class.

Jim and Mary meet with their school counselor once a week for help in developing more positive attitudes toward school. The other children are not currently in need of any type of special help.

To say that these children no longer have any problems would be inaccurate. But to observe how they handle their problems now is to realize that they have the skills to meet the challenges of growing up.

Table 1. Length of Treatment and Subsequent School Placement

	No. of weeks in			
	Stage II	Stage III	Stage IV	Present school placement
Jerry	—	—	7	Public school, eighth grade
Jim	—	16	28	Public school, eighth grade
Roy	—	10	10	Public school, seventh grade
Bill	—	23	9	Public school, eighth grade
Mary	23	18	17	Public school, seventh grade, remedial program

chapter 11

SCHOOL LIAISON AND AND FIELD SERVICES

Bonnie Lee Mailey

Observing

Organizing

Responding to Crisis

Listening

Sharing

Supporting

Planning

Specifying

Communicating

Defining

The major goal of the school follow-through program is to strengthen relationships between the child's regular school teacher and his center team, by improving communication so that both environments can reinforce the progress of the child.

Specific objectives for accomplishing this general goal are:

1. To make weekly contact with the child's regular school to exchange information about the child's current adjustment in both places, center and school.
2. To provide an emergency or crisis resource to the child's regular school by being available for consultation, by telephone or by contact, on an emergency basis.
3. To establish linkage for the child between his center program and his regular school program by having his center teacher visit him in his regular program.
4. To provide assistance to the child's regular teacher by encouraging observations of the child's program at the center and by sharing Developmental Therapy treatment objectives (DTORF ratings) and techniques.
5. To provide intermittent support to the child and his regular school during the period of "provisional termination" (also called "tracking").

With close linkage, the center program should not be isolated from the child's daily school life, and carryover should be greatly enhanced from the center class to the regular classroom.

The major effort should be that of sharing. Each agency should view the other as a component of the total life style of the child. If approached in this way, good working relationships can be established, communication facilitated, and the sharing of progress and problems becomes a team effort. The treatment team needs school information to in-corporate into the therapy program. At the same time, the school profits by getting consultation and guidelines for assisting the child at school, as well as support in managing problem behavior. Both teachers benefit from the insights, viewpoints, and experiences of the other. Only in this way can two differing environments link and become cohesive and meaningful to the child.

CONDUCTING AN EDUCATIONAL PLANNING CONFERENCE

School followthrough for children enrolled at the center begins with an educational planning conference. The purpose of this conference is to present the results of testing and the recommendations made by the center staff and to help the school plan a supportive program for the child. The staff should be available to help the school in implementing the child's school program.

The following steps provide guidelines for conducting an educational planning conference.

1. Review diagnostic folder and staffing treatment sheet prior to meeting.
2. Introduce participants and discuss reason for the planning conference.
3. Review presenting problems as identified by the teacher.
4. Summarize testing results (family interview report is not reviewed ordinarily).
5. Outline staffing recommendations focusing upon Developmental Therapy stage and major treatment objectives.
6. Discuss problems the school is having and explore ways problems can be tackled in light of staff recommendations.
7. Discuss recommended date and time for child to start at the center. The time

By the end of the third week all teachers of school age and preschool children should be contacted. Subsequent contacts depend upon many factors, but a visit to the school once a week is recommended.

should be acceptable to the teacher; if she feels the proposed time will impair her program and progress, alternatives should be considered. Transportation arrangements should be discussed in detail. It is important that these details are completed for children about to enter and that a contact person at school is identified.

8. In closing the educational planning conference, review the following: the date the child is to start, when and where he will be picked up and returned, and the name of the team member who will be doing school liaison work; encourage the participants to return for an observation of the child's program; and mention both weekly school contacts and the 10th-week conference.

9. Always walk the participants to the door. Offer to show them the building if this is their first visit.

School followthrough ordinarily is the responsibility of the lead teacher in the treatment team. In rural areas served by the center, a school person with responsibility for special services may be needed to maintain the liaison between center and school. Often this person arranges the initial meeting between the child's regular teacher and the treatment team. In other instances this school person serves as an intermediary for all school contacts. Ideally, this person should be available to help the school carry out specific aspects of the child's school program. When such a person is experienced and well respected in a particular school, it is possible for school followthrough procedures to be worked out to suit each particular child's needs.

After the educational planning conference, which should be the first visit, the treatment team member assigned to

The educational planning conference may be conducted at the school or center. However, if the teacher has not visited the center, it may be helpful to have her see the child's therapy classroom.

school liaison, in planning with the child's teacher and other school personnel, determines whether the next visit would be more useful as an observation of the child while in his regular class or as a conference with the teacher. Occasionally, the visit may include a contact with the child. In any instance, the next visit is always arranged with the child's teacher and the school principal. It is desirable to meet with the principal so that he can be informed of the nature of the school followthrough and can be included to the extent of his availability and willingness. A supportive, involved principal can contribute immeasurably to the success of the school followthrough program. Each principal will have a particular procedure for visitors to his building.

Sensitivity to the regular classroom teacher's situation and awareness of her general views of the center are major factors in ultimately meeting center objectives for school followthrough. In particular, awareness of the following situations is helpful.

1. The regular classroom teacher has a large number of children, with a large number of demands for her attention, leadership, and support. The center's small treatment groups look insignificant to a teacher with "30 problem children" in her room for six continuous hours each day.

2. The regular classroom teacher has limited special services and resources to back up the teacher, particularly when a disturbed child is in crisis, out of control, or demanding her entire attention.

3. Some teachers have expectations that the center should serve all children identified and referred. Often they expect immediate and dramatic improvement, and are highly critical of center

services which they perceive as inefficient and slow. Transportation schedules are most often criticized.

4. Some teachers are hostile toward outside, professional practices and look for errors and contradictions to support their views. In particular, such teachers often criticize the child's schedule at the center as interfering with their classroom program. They also tend to be critical of a recommendation for provisional termination.

5. Many teachers are very effective in dealing with disturbed children in their classes and only need the assurance and support that they are handling problems in the best way for the given situation. Providing support and a means to ventilate frustrations may be all that is needed.

6. School staff may view the center staff in a way different from the way they actually are working. It is important that the school staff understand responsibilities and roles of various center staff with whom they may come in contact and view the center program as a supplement to their own school program for a child.

7. Awareness by the center staff of the influence teachers' characteristics have on the problems and subsequent adjustment of a child is particularly important to effective school followthrough. Among significant characteristics are the following.

Positive teacher characteristics
Creative, adaptive
Energetic, vivacious (but not overwhelming)
Flexible
Perceptive of child's needs, interests
Accepting of child apart from behavior or problem
Consistent in approach
Open to suggestions, new ideas, change

Ability to implement suggestions
Child oriented
Ability to use positive reinforcement appropriately
Faith in child's ability to grow
Recognizes own strengths and weaknesses
Ability to separate own needs from those of child
Ability to objectively assess the ongoing program
Ability to change as child grows

Negative teacher characteristics
Combative
Personal
Inconsistent
Seductive
Provocative
Defensive
Threatened
Over reacting
Intolerant
Defeatist attitude; guilty
Rationalization of mistakes
Compulsive
Projecting
Autocratic
High strung
Over control of self
Lethargic

CONDUCTING A SCHOOL FOLLOW-THROUGH CONFERENCE

Be sensitive to the tone of the conference and the manner of approach. Comments made to the child's regular teacher are not just pleasant conversation but come from a preplanned structure of ideas and principles to be communicated. The manner in which these messages are relayed, the timing of these comments during the conference, any repeated comments for emphasis, and the entire *direction* of the conversation should be meaningful and purposeful. Some messages originally planned for inclusion may be omitted, whereas some unexpected incidents or changes might produce a new emphasis.

Have specific major focus objectives noted from the four curriculum areas. It is important that these goals are clear to the classroom teacher; however, you may be working with some goals in the center that would be premature as major focus goals in the classroom. Even if working on the same goals, the procedures used in school (worked out between you and regular teacher) may vary from procedures used in the center. In any event, these differences should be discussed and made clear: Is the management different? Should it be? Is the goal realistic for the regular teacher? The number of specific objectives worked on in the school generally is less than the number worked on at the center. New goals to be worked on at school should be related to problems arising in the school, but developed around developmental objectives.

Remember the treatment program discussions at staffings and the stages of development for the child. Know thoroughly: a) observable behavior; b) possible underlying meanings behind behavior; c) child's stages of behavior, socialization, communication, and academic skills; d) the child's perception of his problem, of his school life, center life, and home life; and e) what changes his teacher may expect as he moves through each stage of therapy and each objective. Children often operate at different developmental stages in different settings. Be sure to explore this possibility with the teacher. Be ready with detailed information about the child in the center program, but don't consider yourself as the advisor to the teacher or major source of advice. Try to understand how the teacher perceives you (this varies from teacher to teacher and school to school).

Even when teachers make you feel comfortable and are eagerly asking questions, *be cautious*. First get *their* ideas. From what they discuss, try to determine what they did that worked and what are still problems to them. Work together on a procedure they can be comfortable using.

Map out the road ahead in a realistic way, but be positive. With many disturbed and behavior problem children, regression should be expected. Encourage a teacher to see progress even during periods when the child slips back. When carryover is slow, don't doubt the classroom teacher's technique or ask, "What went wrong?". Let teachers know that we can't expect miracles overnight and every small step forward is significant toward a long range goal. Be positive and confident of procedures you suggest. Often teachers get discouraged and say a technique won't work. Explore with them reasons why it might not have worked. Your confidence should be realistic. Also explore examples of improvement as they happen in the group.

Be cautious in giving out clinical information from staffing (home details, etc.). This is confidential information. Learn to phrase main needs, concerns, and recommendations in appropriate terms. For example, rather than say, "Charles has strong repressed hostility toward his teacher," you may say, "It means a great deal to Charles to feel accepted by adults—for instance, to know he is liked by you. His teacher is important to him." Another example: rather than say, "Tests indicate Sam really hates his father because his parents are divorced," a more positive remark, "Sam feels the loss of his father. A male recreation director could serve a very meaningful role in his school program." When caught off guard regarding some detail of home or school, it is better to say nothing than say too much.

You may hear things about other center staff members or other teachers. Don't over react. Even if you personally feel that the reported situation is not appropriate, use tact in your response so that things don't grow out of proportion. If you hear criticism about a co-worker, relay it only when you feel it is something that person would like to know and would grow from. None of us are beyond constructive criticism. However, relay of trite or petty information can easily sound one sided, accusative, or ridiculing, while constructive criticism can be of benefit to all.

Get to know your principals and how they would like each visit conducted. Sometimes a principal may wish to have conferences with you regarding a child and the child's classroom teacher. Take cues from him. Get to know the school secretary; be friendly. Always let her know when you enter and leave the school. When leaving, try to arrange for the next visit. This reduces the amount of phone calling and gives a continuity to school followthrough.

WHEN YOU MEET WITH ANGER, NEGATIVISM, COOLNESS

When a teacher first realizes you are not there to take away her problem, she may be hostile or perplexed. She then learns that she not only is expected to keep the child in her class but that she must work along with the center during the period of treatment. The manner in which you relay this information will make the difference as to whether or not she will cooperate. If she begins to try out suggested procedures, she will need frequent reinforcement. You must "hang in there" with her and support the school effort with frequent contacts.

A defensive teacher may feel you are observing her critically even though your words are "flowery." When observing (if you do), pick out *specific* realistic things to support her with, even if the rest of the session seems chaotic.

Some teachers may continue to make negative remarks regarding what the child reports that he does at the center, such as, "All we do is play." Communication is essential so that the teacher understands, in detail, the child's program at the center.

If negative management techniques come out in the initial contact, don't react while you are establishing relationships. On the other hand, don't indicate it is great! The best response is to indicate that you are accumulating information. Respond, ". . . and how does he react to that?". Don't be too quick to begin getting things straightened out. Let the teacher talk it out. Sometimes this is all that she really wants. Use your intuition from there. It may be best to wait until another time to develop a detailed plan of change. Take your cues from her. After initial blow off, some teachers are eager for a plan of action. Other teachers just have a loud bark anyway. Be careful not to pull back or be defensive. There is often a predictable response pattern with teachers and, usually after initial testing, your accepting and consistent response is what they really hope to see in you as a professional consultant. If they see you as "solid," they really want to join the team, although some can't afford to show it. When the time comes to try to change ineffective techniques, you should be in a stage in the relationship where the teacher has talked out the problem and is waiting and/or asking for reaction, advice, or response. Never move in to begin this until you feel this coming from the teacher.

At times, one teacher will become critical of another teacher of the same child. This may be done openly or with smooth indirectness. Focus back on the child. How does he respond? Does his behavior vary under different conditions? What conditions elicit the most desirable behavior? What could be done to create more of these conditions? Look for positive elements which tie in to the child's developmental objectives. With two or more teachers, you may be in a situation where teachers try to get at each other by asking you direct questions as to management. For example, "Is it good to make Johnny miss creative art when the entire class is participating?" or, "Is it good that Helen has to take notes home to her mother? She always gets a spanking." or, "Should you jerk a child bodily into line?" A teacher may be telling you techniques used by another teacher sitting next to you! Be cautious steering your way through these situations until you are familiar with the teachers and staff.

Remember that a negative, defensive teacher is a perplexed teacher who is usually involved emotionally with the problem and has usually tried everything, but no one thing long enough. Let her talk (but take mental notes; you can use her words later). Reflect her feelings. Cut through all the verbal intanglement of frustration with a beginning suggestion; give her *one* thing to try tomorrow, then follow up the next day. Don't let her get carried away with too many problems she is trying to change at once; it is best if you work on *one* until progress is made. Encourage her to "hang in

there"; no harm (*in some cases*) to admit there are days you would give up too.

Also, let the teacher know a miracle won't happen and certainly not overnight; but with home, school, and center working together improvement will come.

Questions to Consider During and After A Teacher Contact

1. What is the teacher's general attitude toward this child? Are any positive comments made spontaneously as problems are related?

2. Do you have to *ask* this teacher to tell you what the child's strengths are? If so, what is her response?

3. Does the teacher seem uneasy about being questioned or asked to discuss the child? If she seems reluctant, why?

4. Does the teacher seem overly eager to blame the child for classroom problems?

5. What seems to be her purpose in talking? Would she respond to consultation and follow-up, or does she seem anxious to be rid of the child?

6. Is this teacher too personally caught up in the child's problems? Does she mention all the things she has "done for" this child? Does she dwell at length on heart-breaking incidents in the child's background or does she relate information matter-of-factly and leave interpretations to you?

7. Does she seem consistent? Does she indicate that she has "tried everything and nothing works"? Does she indicate that at times she gives in to manipulation?

8. Is the classroom atmosphere warm accepting but structured; or rigid and demanding; or is structure absent altogether?

9. How might the child view this teacher: Warm, responsive, but "workable"? Nervous and highstrung? Cool, detached and autocratic? Would he have to *work* for approval and acceptance?

10. How flexible is the teacher: Does she seem sensitive and responsive to individual differences in a group? If so, is she able to respond to these needs comfortably, or would she tend to resent the child or see any adaptation on her part as an inconvenience? Does she seem "set" on one method or approach only?

11. How does this teacher respond to aggression? Does she over react, or get emotional and trigger more emotional reactions from the child and the group? Does she imply that the child does these things to get *at her?*

12. Is the teacher able to see cause and consequences in problem situations? Can she give you precipitating incidents that caused the child's reaction, or does she seem unsure about why and explains that he always causes disturbances.

13. Are the teacher's interactions with the child almost always concerned with a behavior problem so that the group, as well as she, come to view the child as negative, or even rejects him? Does she relate that others come and tell her about this child's behavior?

14. Does the teacher indicate that she ever talks with the child to get his perception and feelings about any situation? Or does she seem to automatically blame him?

15. Would this teacher be able to constructively handle the group in any crisis situation with any one child?

16. Would the teacher be able to turn the negative into a positive experience for the child and group, or does she accentuate the negative? Can she use praise effectively?

17. Does this teacher seem aware that preventive measures are often helpful?

18. Is the teacher spontaneous? Can she use humor constructively?

19. How verbal is this teacher with feelings and group tone? Would comments and conversations always be focused on academics and instruction? Would behavioral issues always be viewed as right or wrong?

20. Would children in her class be motivated to come to school each day? Are they interested in their class and group?

MAINTAINING THE SCHOOL LIAISON

The Crisis Call

On a crisis call, however strongly a child is reported to be "out of control" or in distress, respond supportively to the school that they did well to call you; that they helped by staying calm throughout; and that planning with them for management strategies (after the initial blow in the school) is what you are there for. Provide interim suggestions for managing the crisis, if indicated. Often, after an initial release of anxiety, the teacher will begin to see at least temporary solutions herself. It is usually desirable for the teacher and principal to manage the crisis if the outcome is to be generally beneficial to the child. In a few instances, where a center team member has had ongoing contact with the child and the school, it may be advisable to make an emergency visit to the school. This would be particularly true when the school staff feels unable to cope with the child. Another alternative would be to call the county consultant for a crisis visit to the school. In a few instances, when the school liaison team member has a conflicting schedule, another treatment team member might make the crisis visit. All crisis calls and visits should be followed up within the week by a conference with the teacher to plan constructive strategies to help the child and school reduce the likelihood of a repeat crisis.

Encourage an open line between you and the teacher of the child. Relay information as frequently as the teacher indicates she wants it. *Do not make calls to the school and relay information to any other person in the school* (unless it is to have the teacher call you). When you and the teacher have a good working relationship in the school and she is beginning to implement a followthrough program, work toward having her visit the center for observation with you.

When Returning From A School Contact

The success of the school followthrough aspect of the treatment program depends upon the effectiveness of the communication between school and center. Report the results of each school contact to the treatment team at the daily debriefing. Obtain from the team information or new program directions to be conveyed to the school; and convey to the team ways that the child can be helped at the center to be more successful at school.

chapter 12

SERVICES TO PARENTS

Mary Margaret Wood

Empathy

Cooperation

Relationship

Communication

Respect

Encouragement

Recognition

Demonstration

The overall goals of services to parents are to provide information to parents about the needs of referred children and to assist parents in meeting these needs through their involvement in various center programs and services. These two goals are broken down into four specific outcome objectives.

1. To encourage parents and staff to share information concerning the child's needs and developmental progress in behavior, communication, socialization, and academics during the period of the child's treatment, at home and center.

2. To encourage parents' involvement with the center to the extent recommended at staffing and at 10-week intervals during the period of the child's treatment.

3. To stimulate parents' interest in the child's growth and development so that during the second and subsequent 10-week treatment periods they will develop various appropriate activities and procedures to use with their children at home.

4. To provide crisis help and assistance to parents at their request, obtaining supportive help for family and personal needs from other community resources.

The key words in the statement of overall goals, "provide information about . . . needs" and "assist . . . in meeting these needs," imply the essential commitment of the center to parent involvement. Children can be taught to behave successfully in numerous controlled clinical settings; however, the test of the effectiveness of a child's program comes when that child is at home or at school. In order to attain lasting results for the child, then the people he lives with, parents or parent figures, must assist the child in generalizing the successful behavior he experiences in the center setting to his real world. This implies involvement of parents in understanding the needs of the child and assisting the center staff by implementing appropriate activities to meet the child's needs at home. To this end, parents are seen as a vital part of the center treatment program.

BASIS FOR PARENT PROGRAMS

The present model for parent programs and services is the product of two years of staff planning, trial implementation, evaluation, and program readjustments at the Rutland Center. Certain concerns have influenced the program. In particular, clear parameters had to be established regarding the scope of the parent service. The decision was made early in program development that parent services would center primarily around the developmental needs of the children. The intent of the parent service, then, primarily became one of keeping parents and staff informed about the child's continuing development at home and center.

Rationale for limiting the scope of parents' services came from three main observations. First, the cost for a full, extensive program involving enhancement of parents' personal development, parent counseling, and training would reduce considerably the resources available for the children's services. Second, not all parents need extensive services in order to help the center help their child; their own interests, needs, and personal resources vary greatly. Third, limited parent services were successful during the first two years of center operation as measured by the successful termination of a majority of children served with little or no parent service.

Several assumptions about parents underlie the present form of the parent services.

The staff is indebted to the thoughtful review of the Service-to-Parents program by Dr. Samuel E. Rubin and Dr. Robert Lange. At the request of Rutland Center, these consultants reviewed the numerous options and procedures developed during the two years and have made a considerable contribution in support of a limited but effective effort.

1. Parents' understanding and involvement with their child tends to enhance the child's growth and development.

2. Parents' lack of understanding or involvement may not significantly work against the child's growth and development, particularly with parents of older children.

3. Parents' unique assets and problems determine the amount and type of program or service they need and are able to use.

4. Parents' ability to participate depends upon how comfortable they are with the staff and how confident they are with the program for their child.

5. Parents can develop increased effectiveness with their children when they progress in positive feelings about themselves as parents, seeing for themselves positive changes in their child which they can attribute to specific parental skills they have developed.

Implicit in all of these assumptions is the need for the center staff to inform, to support, and to be accessible to parents. What is happening to the child and how it is affecting others in his family is the essential focus. Using a developmental reference from Developmental Therapy, parents and staff prepare, together, to respond to new patterns of behavior as they emerge in the child. When parents reach the point of involvement with the center where they can plan and implement appropriate and successful experiences for their children at home, the primary goal of the center's service to parents has been reached.

TYPES OF PARENT PROGRAMS

Providing for parent services is an integral part of center planning for each child and his family. The treatment team working directly with a child is also responsible for developing a program with the parents that best helps the parents become involved with the center to the extent recommended at staffing or, later, at the 10th-week conferences.

There are five specific programs for parents: 1) parent conferences, 2) Parent's Auxillary Association, 3) observation, 4) home, and 5) parent training. These programs are chosen by the parents according to needs, interests, and the availability of their time. Often programs are combined. For instance, parent conferences and observations often are used jointly.

Parent Conferences

At weekly appointments, parents and the treatment team discuss the child's progress at school, home, and center. These conferences can serve to facilitate the partnership aspect of the treatment program. Both the treatment team and the parents share information so that the child's development will be enhanced in both settings.

Parents' Auxiliary Association

This is an organization of parents who meet in the evening once a month at the center. All parents are welcomed. This program offers the parents an opportunity to meet and get to know other parents whose children are enrolled in the center program. Information may be shared, programs to help the center may be planned and implemented, and the feeling of isolation that may be felt by the parents of an emotionally disturbed child may be reduced at these meetings. The group also is involved in a number of helping activities. Parents report that this is a significant way that they can reciprocate and "do something for the center."

Observation

Parents can learn about the center program by observing the class through a two-way mirror with staff members who are also working with the child. For many parents, observing may be their first opportunity to actually see their child interacting successfully in a group situation. Observation may be helpful to a parent who wants to see a particular objective being implemented. Also, observation gives parents the opportunity to really know what is going on with their child at the center.

Home

The monitor and parents plan new management routines for parents to use at home. Often these planning sessions are conducted in the home. It is difficult for a staff person to understand the home situation of which parents speak until he actually sees the family members on their own ground. Parents may feel that the home contact is the best way to explain themselves. In this case, the home program may be chosen.

Parent Training

Parents learn the skills used by the center staff by working as a support teacher with a treatment team at the center. The amount of time required depends upon the parents' time and interest. This program carries the observation program a step farther. It can be very useful to the parent who feels the need to actually use Developmental Therapy techniques and wants to learn them in a monitored situation. The feedback on the parents' progress is then immediate.

IMPLEMENTING THE PARENT PROGRAM

Parent Planning Conference

When a child is accepted into the center, a parent planning conference is held with the child's parents, the intake personnel, and the treatment team monitor who will work with the parents. The intake supervisor is responsible for making the appointment, and the intake social worker usually conducts the conference.

The parent planning conference has four major goals:

1. To communicate to the parents the test results and recommendations made by the center staff
2. To discuss the meaning of these results and recommendations with the parents for clarification
3. To establish a communication link between the monitor and the parent
4. To plan cooperatively the programs to be conducted at the center and at home

At the conference, time should be devoted to each of these four goals.

First, report test results and recommendations: a) summarize psychological, educational, and psychiatric testing results; b) review recommended major treatment objectives as related to the four curriculum areas and stages of Developmental Therapy; and c) summarize recommendations for school, the center, and home. Discuss with parents the meaning of the test results and their long term implications for home and school. This discussion is of great importance to parents. All parents are concerned with the future of their children; perhaps this is especially true of parents of emotionally disturbed children. During this discussion, the center staff hopes to begin to build a bond of trust between the staff and the parents because the staff, too, is concerned about the future of each child.

Discuss projected treatment time and progress. The projected treatment time is presented to parents as a tentative reference point. The center program consists of 10-week treatment periods, and at the end of each 10-week period, each child is reevaluated on the Developmental Therapy Objectives Rating Form as to the progress he has made while in the treatment program. Inform the parents that a special 10th-week conference with parents will be held.

A decision should be reached by the parents as to whether or not they want their child to participate in the recommended center program. This decision rests entirely with the parents, and staff should never make the assumption that parents automatically agree. If parents do not agree to participation, the door should be left open to future contacts and the school should be appraised of the parents' decision. If parents agree, the conference should continue into a discussion of the parents' own involvement.

The extent of home involvement should be discussed. It is hoped that the parents will make a commitment at this point as to the type of program they would like. However, some parents need time to discuss and plan their involvement at home. If this is the case, then a date and time for the next meeting is planned, and a specific program can be discussed at that time.

During this latter part of the discussion, the monitor usually assumes leadership for the conference. This is the person the parents will be working with from this point on, and at this time the transfer should be made from the intake personnel to the monitor. This is the last contact that the parents will have with the intake personnel, who convey that the transfer to the monitor will be rewarding for the center and the parents in the sense of getting into the actual process of helping the child.

At the end of the parent planning conference, the monitor should remind the parents of the time and place of their next appointment. The monitor's name is written down for the parents along with the center's phone number.

Types of Participation

Planning for parent participation begins with information gathered at the first intake conference and culminates at the time of staffing. At staffing the staff considers the parents' strengths, resources, problems, and limitations. The parents' readiness to participate, the amount of involvement that can be reasonably expected, and explicit information about the parents' contributions to the child's development are also considered. From all available information, the staff recommends one of three levels of participation.

1. *Minimal participation*, requiring:
   a) signed request for service,
   b) participation in the intake conference
   c) participation in the parent planning conference
   d) participation in the 10th-week conferences
2. *Intermittent participation,* requiring:
   a) all of the activities cited in minimal participation
   b) occasional contact at center or home during a 10-week treatment period (not including the 10th-week conference); these contacts are initiated by the monitor but may be of a crisis, "walk-in" nature

3. *Extensive participation,* requiring:
   a) all of the activities cited in minimal participation
   b) once-a-week contact at center or home, either individually or in a group; these contacts are planned and scheduled in advance by the parents and monitor; four or more broken appointments during a 10-week treatment period would constitute intermittent participation even though weekly contacts had been agreed upon

From this recommendation for an amount of participation, the monitor has a particular objective established to work toward.

Parent programs begin the second week of each quarter. Monitors in each treatment team make personal contact with each of the parents of children in the group, usually by telephone. To maintain close, personal touch, secretaries do not arrange for these appointments, and letters are not used. It is important also to be sure parents know whom they are to meet, for what length of time, and the exact location. Often a previous monitor will be on hand to greet parents and introduce them to the new monitor if this had not occurred at the previous 10th-week conference.

Some parents will only be able to participate in minimal ways, particularly during the first 10-week treatment period. Some parents will be having such problems at home that home planning and visiting will be essential. Other parents are ready for observation and others for learning Developmental Therapy skills by working in the support teacher role much as the volunteers do, learning while working. When parents elect to do this, the support teacher comes out of the classroom and the parent works in that position for a specified part of the day.

Parents do not always need to be seen individually. For example, a monitor may notice that several parents are confronted with similar problems and similar "major focus objectives." It might be very useful to schedule these parents for a 30-minute group session for a discussion of those particular problems shared in common and techniques parents have used for solving them. These parents also might observe the class for 30 minutes as a group. During that observation period, the lead teacher might meet with the parents while the monitor takes her place in class. This gives parents opportunity to ask questions of the lead teacher and also to observe the monitor with their children.

Exchanging Information During A Parent Session

Whatever type of session is used by parents and monitor, it is essential that an exchange of information occur and that parents and monitors establish specific objectives.

In the course of an appointment, several questions should be kept in mind to provide a direction for the exchange of information.

1. What are the objectives? (Reasons for the conference, observation, home visits, etc.) If the objectives can be stated clearly, parents can be helped to see a purpose more clearly.
2. What are the child's current DTORF major treatment objectives?
3. How are objectives being met in the center classroom?
4. How have the techniques changed since last time?
5. How has the child's behavior changed since last time?

6. Have these changes been noted at home?

7. What level of parent participation was recommended at staffing, and what directions should center services take with the parents?

8. Which objectives are parents working on at home?

9. What activities are the parents using to meet these objectives?

10. Why are teachers using certain techniques (to accomplish specific objectives)?

11. How comfortable do the parents seem?

12. What elements in the program do they respond to?

13. What tends to cause parents to withdraw from open exchange?

14. What were the high priority problems originally identified by the parents?

15. To what extent are these increasing or decreasing with each visit?

16. What techniques do the parents see as reasonable for them to use at home to solve specific problems?

A session with parents and the treatment team monitor is viewed as an exchange of information between persons concerned with the child's well being. It is as important to obtain parents' perceptions of problems, goals, growth, and change in their child, as it is to present to them the center's report of progress, problems, and change. Some parents may freely offer information about their child, but in some cases the monitor may have to ask questions or otherwise draw the parent into the conversation. In order to facilitate this type of dialogue, the general tone of the conference should be congenial, friendly, and concerned. In other words, parents should be made to feel comfortable enough to talk about their child.

One of the first things conveyed in a parent-monitor session is a general orientation to the child's center classroom and daily treatment program. This is especially important for parents of children who are new or for parents of children who are moving from one stage of therapy to another. This orientation might include a short explanation of the general goals for that stage of therapy in the four curriculum areas, a discussion of daily class activities using the class schedule, and a brief discussion of how this differs from the child's previous class. It is important to make this orientation as specific as possible, in order that the parents understand what their child does when he attends class at the center.

Generally, conferences should focus on information exchange. In reporting progress to parents, it is important to keep in mind two factors. First, obvious success is important in conveying a sense of confidence that the child is progressing. Second, specific examples help to clarify success. To make communication as clear as possible, actual classroom instances and materials may be described.

Various evaluation data such as test results and DTORF are used to report progress to parents. Pertinent data can be summarized from these records for the monitor's use during the conference.

The DTORF can be used to show movement from one goal to the next in each curriculum area. Although it is suggested that the DTORF be used as a framework for reporting progress, the report should be limited to discussing only goals which were or will be major focuses for the child. When using the DTORF, the following steps might be taken to define progress.

1. Define a specific DTORF objective to be mastered
2. Describe behavior which constitutes mastery

3. Describe child's past behavior
4. Define child's progress in relation to mastery of the specific objectives

At this point (discussion of child's progress toward mastery), it is imperative to obtain the parents' perception of where the child is in relation to the objective. It is also important to help parents to relate these current objectives to objectives at home and to original referral problems. By obtaining the perceptions of parents concerning "what has made the difference" in eliminating a problem, and by supporting them in their attempts toward reaching their objectives, more effective home management will be a natural outcome.

Any session also should identify factors that are impeding or fostering change at the school, home, or center. It is the responsibility of the treatment team to recognize parents' techniques which have fostered change and to encourage parents to develop adaptations when necessary for use at home.

Although change usually produces positive behaviors, it is important to help parents understand that acting-out behavior also can be a natural outcome of positive growth and that such behavior can be rechanneled and result in further growth for the child. By reporting on such possible behavioral changes, the feeling that all persons involved with the child are working together is reinforced, and no one is surprised by a sudden, drastic change in a child's behavior.

After a child has been in treatment for some time, future plans for him should be discussed with both the parents and the school. These plans may consider either continuation or termination of services. In either case, the decision should be presented in terms of progress in mastering Developmental Therapy objectives and in reduction of

problems originally identified. If the decision is made that a child should continue at the center, some indication should be given to the parents as to what goals should be accomplished before their child can be terminated. Any change in center classrooms for the next quarter also should be discussed. This is especially applicable if a child is to change from one stage of therapy to another.

Each session ends with a summary of what has been discussed, observed, and planned for that week at home. Parents are given a specific time for the next appointment. Finally, it is important to walk to the front door of the center with parents. It is essential also that parents feel that they will be recognized and welcomed the next time they come to the center and that their participation and involvement are significant.

Immediately after each session, a record should be completed by the monitor and returned to the evaluation team. After data are recorded, this card is filed with previous cards, thereby recording, sequentially, the type of parent involvement and the outcomes.

The 10th-Week Conference

The 10th-week conference provides an opportunity for parents, the monitor, and the lead teacher to exchange and review information concerning the child's progress during a 10-week treatment period at the center and at home.

The main purposes of the conference are to mutually exchange information about the child's progress at the center and at home during the 10-week period, and to mutually plan modifications in objectives, program, and procedures for the next 10-week treatment period.

For parents participating in a minimal way, the 10th-week conference is the only opportunity for them to become acquainted with techniques and materials used at the center and to inform the treatment team about management of the child at home, his behavior, and other changing circumstances which may affect his behavior. In either situation, the 10th-week conference is a vital factor in the treatment team's work with the parents and the child.

The monitor arranges for the 10th-week conference with the parents and the lead teacher. Usually the support teacher does not participate, but the regular classroom teacher may be asked to attend. Before the conference, the lead teacher and the monitor should consider the following.

1. Who will attend the conference?
2. Who will open and close the conference?
3. What would make the parents comfortable?
4. Review the current center, home, and regular school situations.
5. Review results of past contacts.
6. Summarize the broad, general messages needed to relate to parents.
7. Consider implications for home management.
8. Consider relevance of discussing future plans for child (continue at the center, consider termination or services elsewhere).
9. Prepare site of conference and room arrangement to make parents comfortable.

At the 10th-week conference, first discuss, using concrete examples, specific progress in the four curriculum areas. The DTORF may be used when appropriate. Discuss the progress in terms of the referral problems and the therapeutic goals. Ask the parents what changes they have noted at home and what they perceive as problems, growth, and changes.

Discuss behavior that can be expected at home and in the classroom, so that the parents are prepared for new behavior in the child and new alternative responses for themselves. Discuss factors that impede or foster change, including the techniques used at the center, at home, and at school.

Ask the parents to summarize their responses to the overall progress of the child during the 10-week period. The DTORF summary and parents' views may be used to help parents develop home objectives and activities to meet these objectives. At this time, implications for home management also can be discussed.

Toward the end of the conference, discuss plans for the future. If the child is close to being terminated, this can be discussed. If the child is being moved to another level of therapy, provide a new classroom and program orientation. This is especially important for new parents and includes explaining the class schedule, telling about activities, etc. For the parents whose child has been in the program, explain program changes, show the parents the child's work folder, and discuss particular changes over the 10 weeks. Give parents information about the new schedule, new class assignments, transportation, and new objectives to be used. Whenever possible, introduce parents to the monitor of their child's new treatment team, and advise them that the new monitor will call them for an appointment during the second week of the program.

Finally, encourage the parents to extend their commitment to participate further in child-parent programs. Their role is a vital one in the success of the center treatment program.

appendix

DEVELOPMENTAL THERAPY CURRICULUM OBJECTIVES

To be used with Developmental Therapy Objectives Rating Form

Behavior Objectives

STAGE I:
Responding to the Environment with Pleasure

STAGE I BEHAVIOR GOAL: *TO TRUST OWN BODY AND SKILLS*

■ 1. to respond to sensory stimulus by *attending* to source of stimulus by body response or by looking directly at object or person (in situations using tactile, kinesthetic, visual, auditory, gustatory, and olfactory modalities). (Same as academic objective A-1.)
Examples:
    a. After a stimulus has occurred, child indicates some awareness by looking or responding with body language.
    b. When teacher starts to play guitar, child indicates awareness by turning head to source of sound, looking at guitar or teacher, or smiling.
    c. When teacher places child's hand in water, child indicates awareness by splashing or clapping hands together, withdrawing hands, or looking briefly at water.

■ 2. to respond to stimulus by *sustained attending* to source of stimulus (continued looking at object or person after initial stimulus-response has occurred). (Same as academic objective A-2.)
Examples:
    a. After initial stimulus, child continues to watch teacher strum guitar during a song or continues to smile or move body to music.
    b. Child continues to look at or play in water.

■ 3. to respond with motor behavior to *single* environmental stimulus: object, person, sound. (Child gives appropriate motor or verbal response to the command "Give me ——". No choices offered.) (Same as academic objective A-3.)
Examples:
    a. Teacher says, "Give me the ball." Child picks up ball and gives it to teacher.
    b. Teacher says, "Do you want a turn?" Child then strums guitar. No verbal response needed.
    c. Teacher says, "Do you want scissors?" Child nods head or says "yes" or "no." Child reaches for scissors.

■ 4. to respond with motor and body responses to *complex* environmental and verbal stimuli (through imitation "Do this"; through completion of verbal direction; minimal participation in the routine; *given physical intervention* and *verbal cues*). (Same as academic objective A-4.)
Examples:
    a. Teacher says, "It's time to play in the water." Teacher puts her hands in the water and splashes (to show child what to do). Then child puts hands in the water and splashes.
    b. Teacher says, "This is a boat. Let's push it." Teacher pushes boat as example. Child does not respond, so teacher places child's hand on boat. Then child begins to play with boat. Teacher says, "Good, you're playing with the boat" and pats child on the back.
    c. Teacher announces, "It's play time." Child gets up but is not sure in what direction to move. Teacher steers child (with hand on back) to play area. Child sits down in play area but doesn't initiate play, so teacher hands child a toy. Child takes toy.

■ 5. to actively *assist* in learning *self help* skills (toileting, washing hands, dressing, putting arms in coat when held [should be based upon chronological age expectations in combination with developmental expectations; mastery not essential]).
Examples:
    a. Child indicates need to use bathroom (verbal or nonverbal); tries to pull down pants.
    b. Child tries to turn on water; puts hands under water; tries to use soap.
    c. Child pulls up pants or tries to button pants.

■ 6. to respond *independently* to play material. (Verbal cues may be used; age-appropriate play is not necessary.)
Example:
    Child spontaneously picks up a doll, holds it, rubs hair, moves doll's limbs (but does not rock baby, try to take off doll clothes, or put baby in bed as would be expected of a child that age).

■ 7. to respond with *recall* to the routine *spontaneously*. (Child moves to next planned activity without physical stimulus; verbal cues or touch may be used.)
This objective is intended to help organize a child to the extent that when the activity is announced, the child is aware enough of the routine to move to the next activity.
Example:
    When teacher says, "It's play time," child moves to play area without having to be physically moved by teacher.

STAGE II:
Responding to the Environment with Success

STAGE II BEHAVIOR GOAL: *TO SUCCESSFULLY PARTICIPATE IN ROUTINES AND ACTIVITIES*

■ 8. to use play materials *appropriately*, simulating normal play experience.
  Example:
  > *Child plays with toys with awareness of their function, both as representative, real-life objects (play stove for cooking), as well as objects for pretending (play stove turned over makes a castle wall). He does not see toys as objects to be destroyed but as objects which he uses to facilitate his fantasy or to play out real-life situations. For a child who has difficulty discriminating reality from fantasy, it would not be appropriate for the child to continually pretend.*

■ 9. to *wait* without physical intervention by teachers. (Verbal support or touch may be used.) (Same as socialization objective S-14.)
  Examples:
  > a. *Child races up to roll on the mats but is out of turn. Teacher says, "Wow, you are really happy about having mat time! I can't wait to see how well you do your cartwheel after Ricky finishes." Child goes in turn.*
  > b. *Mike wants the cookies, and he wants them NOW. Teacher says, "Do all of you remember how we shook Mike's hand yesterday because he could wait to have his cookie?" Mike is able to wait.*
  > c. *Child wants his turn first at kickball. Teacher says, "I remember that fly ball you caught yesterday. You were standing right here" or "Everyone gets a chance to kick and catch. It's your turn to catch now." Child moves to field.*

■ 10. to *participate* in *activities such as work time,* story time, talking time, juice and cookie time without physical intervention by teacher. (Verbal support or touch may be used.)
  Examples:
  > a. *Child moves away from story circle. Teacher exclaims and points to the book, "Wow, look at that huge wolf's teeth!" Child moves back into circle.*
  > b. *Child moves in and out of chair during work time. Teacher says, "This work is easy when you're sitting in your chair." (Important then to support child during completion of work.) Child continues work to completion.*
  > c. *Child begins to pour milk on the table. Teacher says, "Kids drink their milk here." Child stops pouring milk.*

■ 11. to *participate* in *activities such as play time,* mat time, games, music, art time without physical intervention by teacher. (Verbal support or touch may be used.)
  Examples:
  > a. *Child is reluctant to go through transition and, instead of going to play time, remains apart from group. Teacher says, "When you come to the play area, you'll get to play with the doll." Child moves to play area.*
  > b. *Child loses control and threatens another child physically. Teacher moves between two children and says, "I know you want that truck, but I hear a big red fire engine trying to get out of the toy cabinet." Child ceases fight and goes to toy cabinet.*
  > c. *Child yells out words of a song very loudly, instead of singing, during music time. Teacher turns to other child who is singing appropriately and says, "Your soft voice sounds so pretty." Child stops yelling.*

■ 12. to *spontaneously participate* in routines without physical intervention. (Verbal support or touch may be used, but child indicates some personal initiative to comply with routine.)
  Examples:
  > a. *Teacher says, "It's work time." Child picks up work folder (if that is the routine previously set up).*
  > b. *During snack time and before play time, children begin discussing what they will play during play time, indicating that they know routine. Child subsequently moves to play.*
  > c. *Teacher says that play time is almost over. Child begins to bring his play to closure and realizes that it is time to put toys away. Child begins putting toys away.*

STAGE III:
Learning Skills for Successful Group Participation

STAGE III BEHAVIOR GOAL: *TO APPLY INDIVIDUAL SKILLS IN GROUP PROCESSES*

■13. to verbally *recall group rules* and procedure. (Same as communication objective C-15.)
Examples:
   a. *Before going outside to play the teacher questions the group about the rules of a game they have played previously.*
   b. *After taking 10 cookies at once during snack time, the teacher asks the child about the rule for taking cookies. The child responds, "Oh ya, only one at a time."*
   c. *During a talk, the child is able to verbally recall the rule he or she has broken. (May continue to break the same rule.)*
   d. *Before leaving the classroom, the group may review the rules for riding the bus or walking through the building.*

■14. to contribute to *making group expectations* of conduct and procedures. (Same as communication objective C-17.)
Example:
   During a group discussion on rules for the class, children might respond in the following ways:
   "We should walk down the stairs."
   "Children should stay in their seats while riding on the bus."
   "Work is done at the table, so we should stay in our chairs."

■15. to *verbalize consequences* if group's expectations are not reached. (Same as communication objective C-18.)
Examples:
   a. *When questioned about what is going to happen if a child continues to fight on the bus, child may say, "I won't be able to ride it anymore" or "The bus driver is going to kick me off and get mad."*
   b. *During a crisis situation, the teacher may ask the child, "Why are we in the quiet room?" The child responds, "Because I was kicking John, and I had to leave the room."*
   c. *When a child misses snack time because he was having problems during the activity, he can say, "I did not get my snack because I caused trouble in class, and I had to leave the room."*
   d. *Teacher asks the child, "What would happen if. . . ." and the child can tell the consequences.*

■16. to give *simple reasons* for group's expectations. (Verbal cues from teacher may be used.) (Same as communication objective C-21.)
Examples:
   a. *A teacher may ask the question, "Why should we have a rule about hitting?" The child may respond in these ways:*
   "Hitting hurts."
   "When children are hitting it causes trouble."
   "Children don't like to get hit."
   b. *Teacher asks a question about the classroom rule on talking. The child may say, "One person should talk at a time, because if everyone talked it would be hard to hear."*
   c. *Teacher asks a question about the rule on walking down the stairs. Child answers, "After class we should walk down the stairs, because if everyone ran someone could fall and get hurt."*

■17. to tell other, *more appropriate ways* to behave in a given situation; individual focus. (May not be able to implement alternatives.)
Examples:
   a. *The teacher might ask, "What else could you do other than hit John?" Child responds, "I guess I could tell the teacher that he is making me mad."*
   b. *After shouting in class to get attention, a child might say, "I can raise my hand instead of shouting." (This may come after a question by the teacher.)*
   c. *A group of kids has been having a hard time coming up the stairs after recreation class; kids have been running around the building instead of going to the classroom. In group discussion about this problem, kids are able to say, "When we walk right up the stairs, instead of running around the building, we can get started sooner on our project."*

■18. to *refrain* from inappropriate behavior or breaking group rules *when others* in the group *are losing control* (given verbal support by teacher.)
Examples:
   a. *A child does not join two other children in name calling.*
   b. *A child remains in his seat when others are out of their seats fighting, running around, etc.*
   c. *A child remains involved in a recreational activity when others in the group are not participating.*

■19. to maintain *self control* and *comply* with group procedures (given classroom structure and verbal support by teacher).
Example:
   Child participates in all classroom group activities appropriately and according to structure established by the teacher (work, art, recreation, group games, snack, etc.).

STAGE IV:
Investing in Group Processes

STAGE IV BEHAVIOR GOAL: *TO CONTRIBUTE INDIVIDUAL EFFORT TO GROUP SUCCESS*

■20. to respond *appropriately* to choices for leadership in the group (either not being selected or being selected leader). (Same as socialization objective S-26.)

Example:
> The group decides to role play a voyage on a ship. One child is selected to be the captain, and the rest of the children are to be the crew. The child chosen as the captain responds appropriately to his role as leader, and the other children respond appropriately to his leadership and assume their roles as the crew members.

■21. to *spontaneously participate* in activities *previously avoided* (without teacher structure). (Same as socialization objective S-27.)

Example:
> Child has previously avoided taking part in group activity involving making up a story and talking into a tape recorder. Child spontaneously offers to take part in the activity.

■22. to *implement* appropriate alternative behavior toward others (minimal interpersonal interaction needed).

Examples:
> a. When one child is verbally or physically annoying another child, the child with mastery of this objective will be able to select and implement an appropriate behavior, such as informing the teacher, asking the other child to leave him alone, or removing himself from the situation.
> b. Child is able to select and implement a positive approach to interaction with others. A child wishes to join an ongoing activity and is able to verbally request or otherwise signal his desire to be included in the activity, rather than resort to inappropriate behavior, such as withdrawing or causing a disruption.

■23. to *verbally express cause and effect* relationship *between feelings and behavior*, between group members, and between individuals (group problem solving). (Same as communication objective C-29.)

Example:
> Group is engaged in a project, such as painting the club house, and one member of the group is not participating. Child is able to express his own feelings and those of the group that result from the other child's failure to help in the activity by stating, "I'm mad, and we're all mad because he won't help us paint." Group is then able to arrive at a solution to the problem and continue with the activity.

■24. to respond to *provocation* with verbal and body control (with verbal support from teacher).

Examples:
> a. A child is being verbally and/or physically provoked by another child and is given verbal support by the teacher, such as, "Tom is just trying to make you mad." Child is then able to maintain control.
> b. During work time, a child is called "stupid" because he is having difficulty with his work. The teacher says, "Everybody has different kinds of work, and some children are better at some things than others." Child who was provoked continues with his work.

■25. to respond to suggestions of a *new, real-life* experience, or change with appropriate verbal and body control (can come either from teacher or another child).

Examples:
> a. The teacher suggests to child that he join the Boys' Club and helps him to do so. Child attends and participates in Boys' Club activities.
> b. Public school teacher suggests that child begin taking physical education class at school instead of another class; child complies.
> c. Child conforms to rule established by parents (cleaning his room once weekly; being at home at a certain hour for dinner daily).
> d. Child has begun to refrain from teasing with peers at Center. He exhibits the same restraint toward siblings at home upon suggestion of teacher.
> e. During conference between child and teacher, it is suggested that child's time spent at Center be reduced from three to two days. Decision is jointly reached, and child is able to maintain appropriate behavior at school, functioning with reduced support from Center.

STAGE V:
Applying Individual/Group Skills in New Situations

STAGE V BEHAVIOR GOAL: *TO RESPOND TO CRITICAL LIFE EXPERIENCES WITH ADAPTIVE AND CONSTRUCTIVE BEHAVIOR*

■26. to *respond* to a critical interpersonal or situational experience *with constructive suggestions* for change, as with constructive problem-solving behavior.

Communication Objectives

STAGE I:
Responding to the Environment with Pleasure

STAGE I COMMUNICATION GOAL: *TO USE WORDS TO GAIN NEEDS*

■ 1. to *attend* to person speaking. (Child looks directly at adult when adult initiates verbal stimulus; eye contact not necessary.)

Example:

> *Teacher greets children as they arrive. "Here is Johnny." Johnny directs his body or eyes toward teacher, or he may smile without looking directly at teacher.*

■ 2. to *respond* to verbal stimulus with a *motor behavior*. (Following a command, child points to answer or makes a choice.)

Examples:

> a. *Teacher says, "Sit here by me." Child sits down near teacher.*
> b. *Teacher says, "Pick up the one you want." Child picks up a chocolate cookie.*

■ 3. to *respond* to verbal stimulus and single object with a *recognizable approximation of the appropriate verbal response.* (Child gives approximation, by word or gesture, to indicate use or correct answer to question, "What is this?"; object present; function or name acceptable). (Same as academic objective A-8.)

Examples:

> a. *Teacher says, "What is this?" (ball) Child attempts a "b" sound.*
> b. *Teacher says, "What is this?" (milk) Child says, "milk."*
> *(Teacher may have to repeat the word for the child before the child makes the approximation.)*
> c. *Teacher says, "What is this?" (hair brush) Child gestures brushing hair.*

■ 4. to *voluntarily initiate* a recognizable verbal approximation *to obtain a specific object* or activity. (Child produces recognizable approximation spontaneously, e.g., "wa-wa" for water.) (Same as academic objective A-9.)

Examples:

> a. *Teacher puts milk on the table, and child spontaneously says, "Nilk, nilk."*
> b. *Child tries to say teacher's name.*

■ 5. to produce a *recognizable word* to obtain a *desired response from adult* (e.g., "water" instead of "wa-wa" for water. (Verbal cues may be used.) (Same as socialization objective S-8.)

Examples:

> a. *Teacher puts milk on the table, and child says, "Milk."*
> b. *At art time, teacher is holding art materials. Child says, "Paper, paper." Teacher gives child paper.*

■ 6. to produce a *recognizable word* to obtain a *desired response from another child.* (Verbal cues may be used.) (Same as socialization objective S-9.)

Examples:

> a. *At play time, child sees another child with his favorite truck. He walks up and says, "Truck."*
> b. *Child starts to take toy away from another child. Teacher says, "Say, 'give me the truck.' " Child repeats.*

■ 7. to produce a *meaningful*, recognizable *sequence of words* to obtain a desired response from adults or children in the classroom. (Bizarre language not acceptable; socially inappropriate word sequences acceptable).

Examples:

> a. *Child says, "I want glue."*
> b. *Child says to another child, "I'm going to hit you."*
> c. *Child says to teacher, "Go away."*

STAGE II:
Responding to the Environment with Success

STAGE II COMMUNICATION GOAL: *TO USE WORDS TO AFFECT OTHERS IN CONSTRUCTIVE WAYS*

■ 8. to *answer* a child's or adult's request with *recognizable,* meaningful *words.* (Response does not have to be accurate, correct, or constructive.)
Self explanatory

■ 9. to exhibit a *receptive vocabulary* no more than two years behind chronological age expectations (as indicated by the PPVT or other means).
Example:
The child comprehends what others are saying even if he does not talk (gesture or words accepted).

■10. to *label simple feelings* in pictures, dramatic play, art, or music: sad, happy, angry, afraid (by gesture or word).
Examples:
a. *Teacher shows picture of child crying and asks, "Is he sad or happy?" Child says, "Sad."*
b. *Teacher shows two pictures and asks, "Which is sad?" Child points to correct choice.*
c. *Child paints picture and says, "This is a mean picture."*

■11. to use simple word *sequences* to command or request of another child or adult in ways *acceptable to classroom procedures.* (Bizarre language content or socially inappropriate word sequences are not acceptable; behavior is not a consideration.)
Example:
Child can say to teacher or another child, "I want your red color" or "Give me milk." If child uses loud or whiney voice, teacher can repeat more appropriately, and child will say it again modeling teacher.

■12. to *use* words to *exchange minimal information with an adult.* (Child initiates conversation; requests or questions not applicable.)
Examples:
a. *During milk and cookie time, child says, "My Mommie makes cookies."*
b. *Child says to teacher, "This is a red crayon."*
c. *Child says, "I want to go home."*

■13. to *use* words spontaneously to *exchange minimal information with another child.* (Minimal verbal spontaneity with information content; requests or questions are not applicable.)
Self explanatory

STAGE III:
Learning Skills for Successful Group Participation

STAGE III COMMUNICATION GOAL: *TO USE WORDS TO EXPRESS ONESELF IN THE GROUP*

■14. to *accept praise* or *success* without inappropriate behavior or loss of control.
Examples:
   a. *Child accepts a pat on the back as praise. (A child does well on a task; teacher touches shoulder or pats back to reinforce, and the child does not pull back or act inappropriately.)*
   b. *Teacher says, "John you did a good job on your work today." The child accepts the praise.*
   c. *After telling a story in class, the child looks to the teacher for support. The teacher smiles at the child, and this reinforcement is accepted positively.*

■15. to verbally *recall group rules* and procedure. (Same as behavior objective B-13.)

■16. to use words spontaneously to *describe own* ideas, activity, work, or self to another adult or child.
Examples:
   a. *When asked by the teacher to walk on stilts the child says, "I can't walk on stilts. I am too short."*
   b. *When questioned about a watercoloring, a child explains what it represents and why he painted it. He says, "This is the house that I used to live in, and I am making all the trees the same way they used to be."*
   c. *When discussing a role playing activity, a child might say, "I had to walk around a lot and check everybody to make sure that they were being good."*

■17. to contribute to *making group expectations* of conduct and procedure. (Same as behavior objective B-14.)

■18. to *verbalize consequences* if group's expectations are not reached. (Same as behavior objective B-15.)

■19. to use words or nonverbal gestures to *show pride* in own work, activity, or to make positive statements about self.
Examples:
   a. *During work time a child says, "Hey, look at my work. I'm all finished."*
   b. *During recreation a child says, "Boy, today I kicked the ball really well, farther than anyone else!"*
   c. *During art a child may simply hold up his picture, without any comment, to show someone.*

■20. to use *appropriate words* or gestures to *show feeling responses* to environment, materials, people, or animals. (Teacher uses classroom activity to elicit response.)
Examples:
   a. *A child may suggest that they (the group) hang some pictures on the wall because the wall looks so blank.*
   b. *A child reports to the teacher or class, "Last night the thunder storm was really loud, and I could not sleep."*
   c. *A small puppy is brought into the classroom, and the child is aware that one must handle the animal gently. He displays this behavior both physically and verbally, or is able to express his feelings and say, "I am afraid of dogs."*

■21. to give *simple reasons* for group expectations. (Verbal cues from teacher may be used.) (Same as behavior objective B-16.)

STAGE IV:
Investing in Group Processes

STAGE IV COMMUNICATION GOAL: *TO USE WORDS TO EXPRESS AWARENESS OF RELATIONSHIP BETWEEN FEELINGS AND BEHAVIOR IN SELF AND OTHERS*

■22. to *verbally recognize* feelings in others: sad, happy, angry, afraid (either spontaneously or in response to questions).
Examples:
    a.   *Child enters the room and slams the door. Another child comments, "Johnny must be really mad."*
    b.   *Teacher asks, "How did that make Tom feel?" Child responds, "I guess he didn't like it."*

■23. to *recognize* and *acknowledge* feelings *in self:* sad, happy, angry, afraid.
Example:
    Child enters the classroom smiling and states that he made an A on his spelling test at school. The teacher, or another child, replies that he must be happy about doing so well on his test. The child is able to nonverbally shake his head to affirm; smiles; verbally responds to acknowledge that he is happy; or does not deny the statement.

■24. to use words *to praise* or personally support *others.*
Examples:
    a.   *Child praises another child for a good catch in softball.*
    b.   *Child supports another child by providing assistance on a math worksheet.*
    c.   *Child stands up for a child being criticized by others.*

■25. to *express experiences and feelings* through art, music, dance, or drama. (Child does not need to give verbal explanation.)
Examples:
    a.   *Child has been on a fishing trip with his family over the weekend. At art time, he draws a picture of himself and members of his family in a boat fishing.*
    b.   *For music, each child contributes his interpretation of a thunder storm using various percussion instruments.*
    c.   *After a difficult time completing his work at work time, a child aggressively pounds clay on the table.*

■26. to *use words* to express *own feelings* spontaneously and appropriately.
Examples:
    a.   *During game time, child verbally expresses happiness over having hit a home run in softball.*
    b.   *Child says, "When I use red paint, it makes me feel bad."*
    c.   *Child tells another child, "I don't like you to say that."*

■27. to *use words* appropriately to express awareness of feelings *in others* (peers, adults).
Examples:
    a.   *Child is able to express awareness of another child's feelings by stating, "Johnny really feels bad about losing his new watch."*
    b.   *Child is able to determine teacher's feelings and verbally comments, "Mr. Jones thinks that Joe is acting silly."*

■28. to relate *real-life* experiences and feelings through stories, art, drama, or music with accompanying verbal expressions.
Examples:
    a.   *During the planning of a child drama about a circus, a child expresses the fear he experienced when he first encountered a lion at the circus (with accompanying facial expression).*
    b.   *Following a story read by the teacher about a runaway child, a child responded, "Oh well, I ran away from home once, but when it started to get dark I was afraid and ran home."*
    c.   *During art, a child says, "I'm going to make a clay boat just like the one we used for fishing at summer camp. Boy, you should have seen the fish I caught! It was this big." (Child uses hands in expressing the size of the fish.)*

■29. to *verbally express cause and effect* relationship *between feelings and behavior,* between group members, and between individuals (group problem solving). (Same as behavior objective B-23.)
Example:
    Group is engaged in a project, such as painting the club house. One member of the group is not participating. Child is able to express his own feelings and those of the group that resulted from the other child's failure to help in the activity by stating, "I'm mad, and we're all mad because he won't help us paint." Group is then able to arrive at a solution to the problem and continue with the activity.

STAGE V:
Applying Individual/Group Skills in New Situations

STAGE V COMMUNICATION GOAL: *TO USE WORDS TO ESTABLISH AND ENRICH RELATIONSHIPS*

■30. to use words to initiate and maintain *positive relationships* (peer and adult).

Socialization Objectives

STAGE I:
Responding to the Environment with Pleasure

STAGE I SOCIALIZATION GOAL: *TO TRUST AN ADULT SUFFICIENTLY TO RESPOND TO HIM*

■ 1. to be *aware* of others. (Child looks at adult or another child when adult or another child speaks directly to child or touches him.)

Examples:

    a. *Child is sitting at the table staring at the wall. Teacher calls child by name and touches child on the back. Then child turns head toward adult. (Child may not be responding to his name as much as to the physical contact from the teacher.)*

    b. *Child is aimlessly wandering around the room. Teacher puts her arm around the child and says child's name. Child turns head away from adult. (Child is obviously aware of the contact from the adult but resists looking at the adult.)*

■ 2. to *attend* to other's behavior. (Child looks at adult or another child spontaneously.)

Example:

    Teacher is giving help to child. Second child watches the teacher and child together.

■ 3. to *respond* to adult when child's name is called. (Child looks at adult or away; appropriate or inappropriate response acceptable.)

Example:

    Teacher calls child's name. Child looks up or around to teacher. (In this objective, child does not need to be physically aroused, as in socialization objective S-1. Child differentiates his own name from other children's names. He may look away, instead of toward teacher, when name is called.)

■ 4. to *imitate* simple, familiar acts of adults (gesture, words, or activities).

Examples:

    a. *After adult washes hands, child tries to wash hands.*

    b. *Teacher rests head on hand at table; child does it too.*

    c. *During play time, teacher sits by child, stacks up blocks, and knocks them down. Then teacher pushes blocks to child. Child begins to stack blocks, then knocks them down modeling adult.*

    d. *Child mimics teacher's speech inflections.*

■ 5. to engage in *organized solitary play* (with direction from teacher if necessary; age-appropriate play not necessary).

Examples:

    a. *Child purposefully piles blocks together or builds a house. Teacher may initiate activity by stacking blocks as example and saying, "Let's stack the blocks."*

    b. *Child puts on cowboy hat and climbs on jungle gym to ride his "horse." (Teacher may talk about what the child is playing in order to sustain the experiences.)*

    c. *Child feeds and dresses a doll.*

    d. *Child climbs up and down the slide.*

■ 6. to respond to adult's verbal and nonverbal *requests to come* to him. (Child moves next to adult and looks at him, and child accepts adult's touch.)

Examples:

    a. *Teacher says, "Come over here by me." Child moves next to teacher and allows teacher to put arm around him.*

    b. *During story time on floor, teacher holds arm out to child to get him to move next to her. Child moves over by teacher and looks at her.*

■ 7. to respond to *single verbal request* or command given directly to child. (Child follows adult's verbal direction with appropriate physical movement.)

Example:

    Teacher says, "Sit down." Child sits down. Teacher says, "Hang up your coat." Child hangs up coat without physical intervention.

■ 8. to produce a *recognizable word* to obtain a *desired response from adult* (e.g., "water" instead of "wa-wa" for water; verbal cues may be used.) (Same as communication objective C-5.)

■ 9. to produce a *recognizable word* to obtain a *desired response from another child*. (Verbal cues may be used.) (Same as communication objective C-6.)

■10. to produce a *meaningful*, recognizable *sequence of words* to obtain a desired response from adults or children in the classroom. (Bizarre language not acceptable; socially inappropriate word sequences acceptable.) (Same as communication objective C-7.)

■11. to exhibit a *beginning* emergence *of self* (indicated by any one of these: age-approximate human figure drawing; gesturing pleasure at one's work; use of personal pronoun (I, me, my); or looking at self in mirror).

Examples:

    a. *Child looks at self in mirror; child does not avoid it.*

    b. *Child uses personal pronoun but may not be gramatically correct ("me going" or "me toy").*

    c. *Child takes his drawing up to teacher with smile and conveys pride in work.*

■12. to *seek* contact with adult *spontaneously*. (Child moves next to adult, touches him, or seeks his attention by word or gesture.)

Examples:

    a. *Child walks into room at beginning of class and comes to teacher for a hug.*

    b. *During play time, child moves next to teacher and strokes her hair.*

STAGE II:
Responding to the Environment with Success

STAGE II SOCIALIZATION GOAL: *TO PARTICIPATE IN ACTIVITIES WITH OTHERS*

■13. to *participate spontaneously* in specific parallel activities with another child using similar materials but not interacting.
Example:
>   *Child plays with toy truck while another child is using a car. They are organized individually, i.e., each runs on his own highway, and "traffic" of other child serves as no impetus for interaction.*

■14. to *wait* without physical intervention by teachers. (Verbal support or touch may be used.) (Same as behavior objective B-9.)

15. to *initiate* appropriate minimal movement toward another child within the classroom routine. (Child, through gesture and action, begins minimal appropriate social interaction with another child.)
Examples:
>   *a. Child remembers that another child missed his turn.*
>   *b. Child wants to sit by a certain child.*
>   *c. Child goes over to join another child already engaged in play.*

■16. to *participate* in a verbally directed sharing activity. (Child passes materials or gives toy to another.)
Examples:
>   *a. Child passes cookies within the classroom structure.*
>   *b. Child gives toy to another. (Verbal cues may be used.)*
>   *c. Child can use same paint, water, or box of crayons that another child is using.*

■17. to *participate* in cooperative activities or projects with another child during play time, indoor or outdoor. (Child is involved actively with another child; verbal support or touch may be used.)
Examples:
>   *(Involvement in a free play situation or organized game where a child is able to organize his play and allow for successful interaction with another child in the group.)*
>   *a. Child attends a "tea party" with other children.*
>   *b. Child puts out "fire" at another child's "home."*
>   *c. Child stays in circle and plays "drop the hankie" following structure of group's game.*

■18. to *participate* in cooperative activities or projects with another child during organized class activities. (Child is involved actively with others; verbal support or touch may be used.)
Examples:
>   *(The child engages in activities which the teacher directs by determining the procedure which will guide the children toward desired outcomes, products, etc.)*
>   *a. Child has a defined place on a large piece of paper for a group mural where each child has a specific area to complete.*
>   *b. Child role plays a story book character as other children serve as audience.*
>   *c. Child makes Kool-Aid with another child.*

STAGE III:
Learning Skills for Successful Group Participation

STAGE III SOCIALIZATION GOAL: *TO FIND SATISFACTION IN GROUP ACTIVITIES*

■19. to *take turns* without verbal reminders from teacher.
Examples:
  a. *During game time, a child waits in his chair until time for him to take his turn.*
  b. *During recreation, a child plays his correct position while waiting for his turn to bat.*
  c. *Child accepts the appointment of another child as leader after teacher explains that he will have a turn at being leader.*
■20. to *share* materials, activities (minimal verbal reminders from teacher).
Examples:
  a. *During a group discussion about where materials should be placed in the room, a child is able to offer his ideas or feeling about the way that it should be done. "Let's keep all work materials on that shelf and keep our art stuff on this one."*
  b. *A child may have all the red paint during art time, but when another child asks for some of the red paint, he does share.*
■21. to *suggest* activities or preference for play materials to the teacher for group activity.
Examples:
  a. *A child says to the teacher, "We have played kick ball a lot, so let's play softball today."*
  b. *A child says, "I like to play with the stilts, so during game time today, can we use them?"*
  c. *Child says, "Let us play with the instruments today instead of singing."*
■22. to participate *without inappropriate response* to activity suggested by *another child.*
Example:
  When a suggestion is made, such as in socialization objective S-21, and the teacher decides to follow the suggestion, a child is able to participate in these activities without inappropriate response such as, getting mad, running away, disrupting the activity, or using abusive language.
■23. to indicate *developing friendship* by preference for a particular child or children.
Examples:
  a. *A child puts his arm around another child or asks him to be on his side during a recreational activity.*
  b. *A child makes a peanut butter sandwich at snack time for another child and passes it to him spontaneously.*
  c. *A child helps another child appropriately, and usually spontaneously, with his work.*
■24. to *recognize* and describe characteristics of others.
Examples:
  a. *A black child notices a white child's hair is different and talks about the differences.*
  b. *A child might say, "John is really fat, so he cannot run very fast."*
  c. *"John is taller than me, so he can reach higher."*
  d. *"I do not like John; he talks all the time and always gets the rest of us in trouble."*

STAGE IV:
Investing in Group Processes

STAGE IV SOCIALIZATION GOAL: *TO PARTICIPATE SPONTANEOUSLY AND SUCCESSFULLY AS A GROUP MEMBER*

■25. to *suggest* appropriate group activity directly to peer group (without teacher participation).
  Examples:
   a. *Child suggests to group, "Let's ask Mr. Jones if we can play football today at recreation."*
   b. *Child suggests to group, "Let's make a TV show for the teachers and the other kids."*
■26. to respond appropriately to choices for *leadership* in the group (either not being selected or being selected leader). (Same as behavior objective B-20.)
■27. to *spontaneously participate* in activities *previously avoided* (without teacher structure). (Same as behavior objective B-21.)
■28. to verbally indicate preferences among members of the group by *differentiating personal characteristics.*
  Examples:
   a. *Child states that he wants to go sit next to Tom because Tom is good in math and has offered to help him with his work.*
   b. *Child states that he wants Johnny to be on his team in softball because Johnny is a good player and never strikes out.*
■29. to *physically* or *verbally assist* another child in difficult situation; to come to support of another.
  Examples:
   a. *One child has become upset during art time because he didn't get the model car that he wanted. Another child is able to assist him by offering to trade models with him.*
   b. *One child is having difficulty learning to walk on stilts. Another child supports him verbally by stating, "You stayed up longer that time. You'll get it."*
■30. to participate in *group planning* and constructive problem solving (with or without minimal teacher participation).
  Examples:
   a. *A field trip is being discussed in the group, and several different suggestions are made as to where the group should go. The teacher says to the group, "Now, how can we decide where we are going to go?" A child in the group suggests taking a vote in order to decide.*
   b. *Child is faced with a group activity, such as softball, where he doesn't feel that he can be successful. Teacher asks group, "How can we assign positions so that everyone will be successful?" Group discusses alternatives and concludes that child will be a good catcher.*

STAGE V:
Applying Individual/Group Skills in New Situations

STAGE V SOCIALIZATION GOAL: *TO INITIATE AND MAINTAIN EFFECTIVE PEER GROUP RELATIONSHIPS INDEPENDENTLY*

■31. to *initiate* and *maintain* effective interpersonal and group relationships.

Academic Objectives

STAGE I:
Responding to the Environment with Pleasure

STAGE I ACADEMIC GOAL: *TO RESPOND TO THE ENVIRONMENT WITH PROCESSES OF CLASSIFICATION, DISCRIMINATION, BASIC RECEPTIVE LANGUAGE, AND BODY COORDINATION*

■ 1. to *respond* to sensory stimulus by *attending* to source of stimulus by body response or by looking directly at object or person (in situations using tactile, kinesthetic, visual, auditory, gustatory, and olfactory modalities). (Same as behavior objective B-1.)

■ 2. to *respond* to stimulus by *sustained attending* to source of stimulus (continued looking at object, or person after initial stimulus-response has occurred). (Same as behavior objective B-2.)

■ 3. to *respond* with motor behavior to *single* environmental stimulus: object, person, sound. (Child gives appropriate motor or verbal response to the command, "Give me ——." No choices offered.) (Same as behavior objective B-3.)

■ 4. to respond with motor and body responses to *complex* environmental and verbal stimuli (through imitation "Do this"; through completion of verbal direction; minimal participation in the routine; *given physical intervention* and *verbal cues*). (Same as behavior objective B-4.)

■ 5. to respond with rudimentary *fine motor skill* to simple manipulative tasks associated with two-year level.
Examples:
  a. *Can build tower of six to seven blocks.*
  b. *Can align two or more blocks together to make train.*
  c. *Imitates circular stroke and vertical stroke.*
  d. *Can maintain spoon in upright position.*
  e. *Can pull on a simple garment.*

■ 6. to *imitate words* or *action of adult* upon request. (Adult gives *word and object* and says, "This is ——. Say ——." Child imitates with approximation.)
Examples:
  a. *Teacher says "bye bye" and waves. Child approximates "bye bye" and waves.*
  b. *Teacher holds ball out to child and says, "Ball". or "This is a ball." Child reaches for ball.*
  c. *Teacher says, "Say, 'ball'" Child says, "Ba" or "Ball" and is given ball.*

■ 7. to respond by *simple discrimination* of objects. (Child gives correct *motor or verbal* response to the command, "Give me ——." [two different objects presented].)
Example:
  Teacher puts crayons and scissors on table and says to child, "Give me the crayons." Child can discriminate between the two objects and hands the correct item to teacher.

■ 8. to *respond* to verbal stimulus and single object with a *recognizable approximation* of the *appropriate verbal response*. (Child gives approximation, by word or gesture, to indicate use or correct answer to question, "What is this?" [object present; function or name acceptable]). (Same as communication objective C-3.)

■ 9. to *voluntarily initiate* a recognizable verbal approximation *to obtain* a *specific object* or activity. (Child produces recognizable approximation spontaneously, e.g., "wa-wa" for water.) (Same as communication objective C-4.)

■10. to indicate short term *memory* for objects and people. (Child identifies missing objects and missing members of group.)
Examples:
  a. *During play time, David goes to bathroom with support teacher. Carolyn, who has been playing with David, turns around and says, "Where's David?"*
  b. *Teacher has a doll and a truck, puts one behind her back and says, "What did I hide?" The child says, "Truck."*
  c. *Right after milk and cookie time, teacher says, "What did you eat?" Child says, "Milk and cookies."*

■11. to *respond with classification of similar objects* with *different attributes*.
Examples:
  a. *Child fits geometric blocks into puzzle box opening without using trial and error method.*
  b. *Child can do simple (single pieces) puzzle, fitting shapes into matching spaces.*
  c. *Child can match picture to real object.*

■12. to indicate short term *memory* for *verbal expressions*. (Child repeats appropriate three-word phrases spontaneously. Teacher questions or cues may be used; bizarre repetition of TV commercials or echolalia is not appropriate.)
Examples:
  a. *During milk and cookie time child reaches for milk and says, "I wa-milk."*
  b. *After play time, child anticipates story time and says, "Now it's story time," repeating expression teacher has used often.*
  c. *Child is taken to bathroom and says, "Wash with soap," repeating expression teacher has used often.*

■13. to perform *body coordination* activities at the three/four-year level.
  Examples:
    a.   Child can ride a tricycle.
    b.   Child can alternate feet going up stairs.
    c.   Child can stand balanced on one foot.
    d.   Child can catch bounced ball.
    e.   Child can throw ball, two hands overhead.

■14. to match *similar pictures* (when presented with both identical and different pictures).
  Examples:
    a.   Teacher presents picture cards and tells child, "Find all the pictures like this" or "Find all the pictures that are the same as this one." Child completes task correctly by sorting or pointing.
    b.   Teacher gives child work sheet and says, "Draw a circle around all the pictures that look like this one." Child completes task correctly.

■15. to indicate recognition of *color names* with the correct response. (Child responds correctly to the command, "Give me ___." [red, blue, and yellow] by picking out correct color from three choices).
  Self explanatory

■16. to *perform eye-hand coordination* activities at the four-year level.
  Examples:
    a.   Builds a bridge from cubes.
    b.   Copies a circle.
    c.   Draws man with two parts.
    d.   Buttons and unbuttons.
    e.   Strings beads.

■17. to recognize *own body parts* (eye, hand, foot, nose, leg, arm, knee). (Any response appropriate; gesture, word, etc.)
  Self explanatory

STAGE II:
Responding to the Environment with Success

STAGE II ACADEMIC GOAL: *TO PARTICIPATE IN CLASSROOM ACTIVITIES WITH LANGUAGE CONCEPTS OF SIMILARITIES AND DIFFERENCES, LABELS, USE, COLOR; NUMERICAL PROCESSES OF ORDERING AND CLASSIFYING; AND BODY COORDINATION*

■18. to recognize *uses* of objects, toys, etc.
Examples:
  a. *Teacher has object or picture of object like a shovel. Child knows what it is used for and can tell or act it out.*
  b. *Teacher hands ball and says, "What can you do with this?" Child says or acts it out by throwing, kicking, bouncing, or rolling it.*

■19. to recognize *detail in pictures* by gesture or word.
Example:
  Teacher says, "Where's the girl in the picture?" "Where's her nose?" Child points or describes correctly.

■20. to *rote* count to *ten.*
Example:
  Child can count to 10 (saying words not counting objects).

■21. to *count* with *one-to-one* correspondence to *five.*
Example:
  Child can count five objects.

■22. to *name* colors (black, purple, orange, green). (Child is able to choose color if given the word; child is able to give approximation of word when presented with color.)
Examples:
  a. *Teacher says, "Show me something purple." Child points.*
  b. *Teacher presents object and says, "What color is this?" Child names color of object.*

■23. to *count* with *one-to-one* correspondence to *ten.*
Example:
  Child can count 10 objects.

■24. to perform *eye-hand coordination* activities at the *five-year level.*
Examples:
  a. *Draws a recognizable person with body.*
  b. *Copies triangle, rectangle.*
  c. *Prints a few letters from memory.*
  d. *Copies first name from model.*
  e. *Draws simple house representation.*

■25. to recognize *differences* among shapes, symbols, numerals, and words. (All forms must be mastered; child need not know how to read words in order to recognize differences among them.)
Examples:
  a. *Teacher shows child a card with several similar and one different geometric shapes and asks, "Which one is different?" or "Which one is not the same?"*
  b. *Teacher gives child work sheet with one word repeated numerous times and one different word says, "Mark the one that is not like the others."*

■26. to *categorize* items which are *different but have* generally *similar characteristics* or associations.
Examples:
  a. *Teacher gives child a stack of picture cards and says, "Put all the people in this pile and put all the animals in this pile."*
  b. *Teacher prepares worksheet for child and says, "Draw a line to the pictures that belong together." (Sheet contains pictures of chicken and egg, dog and bone, pencil and paper, paint and brush.)*

■27. to write a recognizable *approximation of first name,* without assistance. (Adult may initiate request; no model used.)
  Self explanatory

■28. to *discriminate* concepts of opposition (*up, down; under, over; big, little; tall, small; hot, cold; first, last*). (Child is able to demonstrate or point, given opposites in pictures.)
  Self explanatory

■29. to perform *body coordination* activities at the *five-year level.*
Examples:
  a. *Skips using alternate feet.*
  b. *Walks on walking board.*

■30. to *recognize groups* of objects to *five* (How many?).
  Example:
    Teacher holds up card with dots for brief viewing. Child identifies number without counting.
■31. to *listen* to story telling.
  Example:
    Child can direct and maintain attention to the story being told or read by the teacher. (Verbal support or touch may be used.)

STAGE III:
Learning Skills for Successful Group Participation

STAGE III ACADEMIC GOAL: *TO PARTICIPATE IN THE GROUP WITH BASIC EXPRESSIVE LANGUAGE CONCEPTS; SYMBOLIC REPRESENTATION OF EXPERIENCES AND CONCEPTS; FUNCTIONAL, SEMICONCRETE CONCEPTS OF CONSERVATION; AND BODY COORDINATION*

■32. to recognize *groups* of objects *to ten.*
Examples:
    a. *Teacher holds up card with dots for brief viewing. Child identifies number in groups without counting.*
    b. *When playing with dominoes, child recognizes number groups without counting.*

■33. to demonstrate *left to right orientation* for visual motor tasks.
Examples:
    a. *Child looks at left page before right page of picture book.*
    b. *Child puts sequence pictures together so that story is shown as happening from left to right.*
    c. *Child completes work sheet with left to right movement.*

■34. to recognize *written names* for *color words* (red, blue, yellow). (Child selects appropriate color word.)
    Self explanatory

■35. to recognize *written labels* (own name, chair, table, part of written schedules).
    Self explanatory

■36. to *recognize* and *write numerals* to represent groupings (1 to 10). (For mastering this objective, child must be able to accomplish both activities, recognizing numerals and writing numerals to represent groups from 1 to 10.)
Examples:
    a. *Child can recognize numeral (e.g., 1 = "one") and can show teacher corresponding numbers of objects.*
    b. *Child can look at a group of objects and write the correct numeral.*

■37. to *write first* and *last name* and date with written *example to copy.*
    Self explanatory

■38. to perform *eye-hand coordination* activities at the *six-year level.*
Examples:
    a. *Drawing a person with arms, legs, clothes, etc.*
    b. *Writing first name legibly from memory.*
    c. *Tying shoes.*

■39. to perform *body coordination* activities at the *six-year level.*
Examples:
    a. *Throwing and catching a ball with control.*
    b. *Recognizing right and left.*
    c. *Walking backwards.*
    d. *Clapping in rhythm.*
    e. *Roller skating.*

■40. to *recognize* and *write numerals* to represent groupings (11 to 20).
Examples:
    a. *Child recognizes numeral 15 ("fifteen") and shows teacher corresponding number of objects (one-to-one counting not used).*
    b. *Child looks at group of objects drawn on work sheet and can write correct numeral without one-to-one counting.*

■41. to *write alphabet* or simple words (with or without model).
    Self explanatory

■42. to *do* numerical operations of *addition* and *subtraction* through ten.
Example:
    For mastering of this objective, child should be able to write the correct answer to all numerical operations of addition and subtraction through 10 with 90-percent accuracy.

■43. to use *ordinal concepts* verbally (first, fifth, last).
Examples:
    a. *A child is able to find the fourth drawer in a treasure hunt.*
    b. *Child says, "I do not want to be second; I want to be first."*
    c. *"I was the first (second, last) to get to class today."*

■44. to *listen to a story and respond* with appropriate answers to questions; by comments or gestures.
   Examples:
      a. *Teacher reads a story; child laughs at appropriate incidents.*
      b. *Teacher begins to tell a story; child contributes what comes next.*
■45. to *read* basic primary vocabulary words *spontaneously* in sentences.
   Example:
    To master this objective child should have 90% reading accuracy for 100 first grade reading words.
■46. to *do* simple numerical operations of *addition* and *subtraction* above 10.
   Example:
    To master this objective child should be able to add and subtract with 90-percent accuracy (no regrouping—borrowing or carrying).
■47. to *write* basic words *from memory* or dictation.
   Example:
    To master this objective child should be able to write 30 basic words from memory or dictation with 90-percent accuracy.
■48. to *participate* in group activity for *writing experience story,* dictating to teacher, or working on murals.
   Examples:
      a. *After an experience story, a child is able to work with other children doing a group watercolor about the story on a large single piece of paper.*
      b. *While dictating a group story for the teacher to write, the child can verbally give ideas or information that contributes to the story.*

STAGE IV:
Investing in Group Processes

STAGE IV ACADEMIC GOAL: *TO SUCCESSFULLY USE SIGNS AND SYMBOLS IN FORMALIZED SCHOOL WORK AND IN GROUP EXPERIENCES*

■49. to *write* full name, address, date, *from memory*.
   Self explanatory
■50. to *read* and *write* basic vocabulary spontaneously *in complete sentences*.
   Self explanatory
■51. to *read* and *write* quantitative words for measurement of distance, time, money, fractions.
   Self explanatory
■52. to *contribute* to *group projects* requiring expressive skills.
   Examples:
   a. *The group is using the tape recorder to record a story that they are making up for special time. Child is able to take his turn and contribute to the group story.*
   b. *Child is able to work with other members of the group in writing a script for a play.*
   c. *Child is able to role play a situation developed by the group.*
■53. to *write* individual *experience stories*. (Child writes own experience story with teacher assistance on difficult words.)
   Example:
   Child is able to write an individual story based on a topic, such as, my class's field trip, my favorite sport, etc.

STAGE V:
Applying Individual/Group Skills
in New Situations

STAGE V ACADEMIC GOAL: *TO SUCCESSFULLY USE SIGNS AND SYMBOLS FOR FORMALIZED SCHOOL EXPERIENCES AND PERSONAL ENRICHMENT*

■54. to *write for communication* of information to others.
Self explanatory
■55. to *read for pleasure* and for personal information.
Self explanatory
■56. to *write of feelings* and attitudes in prose or poetry.
Self explanatory
■57. to *read to obtain information* on the feelings and behaviors of others.
Self explanatory

Index